Migrating to Android for iOS Developers

Sean Liao

Apress

Migrating to Android for iOS Developers

Copyright © 2014 by Sean Liao

ISBN-13 (pbk): 978-1-4842-0011-7

ISBN-13 (electronic): 978-1-4842-0010-0

Publisher: Heinz Weinheimer
Lead Editor: Steve Anglin
Development Editor: Lori Bring
Technical Reviewer: Alex Decker
Editorial Board: Steve Anglin, Mark Beckner, Ewan Buckingham, Gary Cornell, Louise Corrigan, Jim DeWolf,
    Jonathan Gennick, Jonathan Hassell, Robert Hutchinson, Michelle Lowman, James Markham,
    Matthew Moodie, Jeff Olson, Jeffrey Pepper, Douglas Pundick, Ben Renow-Clarke, Dominic Shakeshaft,
    Gwenan Spearing, Matt Wade, Steve Weiss
Coordinating Editors: Anamika Panchoo, Melissa Maldonado
Copy Editor: Kim Burton-Weismann
Compositor: SPi Global
Indexer: SPi Global
Artist: SPi Global
Cover Designer: Anna Ishchenko

Distributed to the book trade worldwide by Springer Science+Business Media New York, 233 Spring Street, 6th Floor, New York, NY 10013. Phone 1-800-SPRINGER, fax (201) 348-4505, e-mail orders-ny@springer-sbm.com, or visit www.springeronline.com. Apress Media, LLC is a California LLC and the sole member (owner) is Springer Science + Business Media Finance Inc (SSBM Finance Inc). SSBM Finance Inc is a Delaware corporation.

For information on translations, please e-mail rights@apress.com, or visit www.apress.com.

Apress and friends of ED books may be purchased in bulk for academic, corporate, or promotional use. eBook versions and licenses are also available for most titles. For more information, reference our Special Bulk Sales–eBook Licensing web page at www.apress.com/bulk-sales.

Any source code or other supplementary material referenced by the author in this text is available to readers at www.apress.com. For detailed information about how to locate your book's source code, go to www.apress.com/source-code/.

Contents at a Glance

Contents

About the Author

Ever since working on a PalmOS PDA app in 2000, **Sean Liao** (PMP®) hasn't missed any major mobile evolutions. He has written mobile code for PalmOS, JavaME, Microsoft .NETCF, and BlackBerry, and he also has some Nokia Symbian experience. He has been a seasoned Java solution architect since 1998.

In 2009, Sean started iOS programming, and then began Android programming the same year by following the same porting strategy, based on years of hands-on mobile programming experience. Currently, Sean is primarily engaged in creating iOS apps and porting them to Android as a bonus.

About the Technical Reviewer

Alex Decker is a mobile application developer specializing in enterprise applications. He graduated from the University of Illinois and is currently living with his wife in California.

Acknowledgments

Looking back on the journey of my first book-writing experience, clearly, I realize now that I would have never started it without the encouragement from my lovely wife, Lily. I would never have completed the book without her support. I also got really motivated by my two little princesses, Megan and Melanie. As I was writing the book they would come by to ask me silly questions repeatedly, like: Can I help you, Daddy? Daddy, will the book be this thick? Daddy, can your book be my bedtime story? Will you play with me more after you finish it?

I knew I would never give up.

Special thanks to my publisher, who has faith in this topic, and the editors who never stopped making it better. Their professional services and guidance are unparalleled. I am really grateful to have had the publisher and the editorial team with me at all times.

Introduction

In 2000, I started my first PalmOS mobile app for an inventory-tracking project. The initial project was a full-staffed team effort that consisted of mobile developers, SAP consultants, supply-chain SME, J2EE middleware developers, QA testers, solution architects, business sponsors, and so forth. JavaME came up strong in 2002, followed by Pocket/Windows Mobile. I did several mobile projects converting the mobile apps to the PocketPC platform by blindly translating JavaME mobile code to C# .NETCF mobile code. The "translation" efforts prolonged the whole product life cycle. The project achieved higher ROI as the product life extended, because the extra cost of translating mobile code was surprisingly low. Ever since then, I have been translating front-end mobile apps among JavaME, BlackBerry, and Windows Mobile platforms.

In 2009, by repeating the same porting process, I created my first simple iOS app by translating a Windows mobile app. That started my iOS programming journey and which eventually led me to becoming a fulltime iOS developer. It was a no-brainer for me to try porting to Android later.

When you have the whole solution completed for your iOS app, all the issues have been verified and the other deliverables and project artifacts are already reusable. Knowing the Android market share, I always clone my iOS apps to Android. The return on investment (ROI) immediately gets improved because the level of efforts for the Android porting proves to be only a fraction of the entire project's effort—again and again. It would be just a waste to not do it.

The primary objective of this book is to help experienced iOS developers leap into native Android mobile development. It is easier than you think, and this book will make it even easier with iOS analogies (and mapping guidelines) so you can immediately translate common mobile use cases to Android.

Who Is This Book For?

This book is specifically written for iOS developers who want to take advantage of their mobile knowledge and make the mobile applications available on the Android mobile platform. The book will show you that you already have the fundamentals for the Android platform. Let me show you that you are very close to becoming an Android developer. Let me show you the common programming subjects and frameworks using your familiar iOS vocabulary so that you immediately understand, without lengthy explanations, because you already know the mobile subjects from being an iOS developer.

You don't need experience in the Java language, although it does help a lot. The most important qualities of Android developers do not include Java programming language experience. It is the mobile SDK and framework knowledge that distinguishes you from other Java programmers. You know one programming language already since you are an iOS developer, so you should be comfortable reading Java code. I also made the sample code extra-readable, so you will have no problem following through the programming subjects and the Java sample code.

There are tons of Java language references out there; you should find them handy sooner or later when you are ready to get serious.

How This Book Is Organized

In Part I, you will get the Android development toolkit up and running in no time. With the Android IDE, you will be guided in creating tutorial projects that will become your porting sample projects. I believe this is the best way for you to get hands-on experience while learning programming topics.

Part II of this book shows you how to plan and structure your Android apps by following the same iOS thinking process: create a storyboard and break the app into model-view-controller (MVC) classes. You will be able to reuse most of the existing software artifacts and design from the iOS counterparts. The common mobile topics are followed, including user interface, managing data, and networking with remote services. After you finish Part II, you will be able to create simple but meaningful Android apps with rich UI components, and to handle common CRUD (create, read, update, delete) operations locally and remotely. There are still more Android goodies to come.

In Part III, this book recaps the Android framework fundamentals with code instead of just descriptions. You will discover the uniqueness of the Android framework and appreciate many features that you normally don't have in iOS. Several powerful and repeatable mobile UX patterns are also introduced. Once you get here, you should be fully convinced that you can do everything in Android just like you do in iOS. The last chapter walks you through a case study that ports a complete iOS app to Android. It recaps how to use the iOS analogies and mapping guidelines from the topics in previous chapters. You can also use the book's table of contents to help find the porting guidelines as needed.

When you complete the journey, you will be able to use the right tools to effectively port your existing iOS apps to Android.

Part 1

Prepare Your Tools

A handy tool makes a handy man. This is very true for creating software, too. You use Xcode to write, compile, debug, and build code; it is an Integrated Development Environment (IDE) for iOS programming. ADT in Eclipse is an IDE for Android programming, which offers comparable tools and features as Xcode. The first part of the chapter walks you through the installation options and steps for getting it up and running. All the topics in this book come with sample code. You will need to use the IDE to learn from these sample projects and you will use the IDE to create world-class Android apps, too.

For native Android programming, Java is the designated programming language. The chapters in this part will give you enough knowledge to read the sample code, in case you are not exposed to the Java language yet. You will feel comfortable using the code from this book as your own code, without assuming you already know Java.

Setting Up the Development Environment

It is more fun to see apps run than to read the source code, and you cannot get hands-on programming experience by just reading books. Let's get the development environment up and running first so that we can use it—and learn Android programming along the way.

The Android Developer Tools Plugin for Eclipse

IOS ANALOGY

Just as Xcode is an IDE for creating iOS apps, the ADT plugin for Eclipse is an IDE for creating Android apps.

The *Android Developer Tools (ADT) plugin for Eclipse* is the Android-programming integrated development environment (IDE) that we will go over in detail. It is a full Java IDE that includes the Android SDK to help you build, test, debug, and package your Android apps. It is free, open source, and runs on most major operating system (OS) platforms, including the Mac OS. The ADT plugin is not a developer's only choice, but probably the one most commonly used. We will use it throughout this book.

Installing the All-in-One Bundled Package

The all-in-one bundled package is the best option for most Android developers. It is similar to Xcode installation: there is no need to sort out the dependencies and no need for manual configurations. It actually wasn't available when I started Android programming a couple years ago.

With a single download, the ADT Bundle includes everything you need, including the following:

- Eclipse

- The ADT plugin for Eclipse

- Android SDK Tools

- Android Platform-tools

- The latest Android platform

- The device emulator image for the latest Android platform

Get the single download for your Mac at `http://developer.android.com/sdk/index.html#mac-bundle`.

It is a ZIP file. Unzip it and put the contents of the ZIP file anywhere you want; for example, if you put it in `/Applications/adt-bundle-mac`, it should look like Figure 1-1.

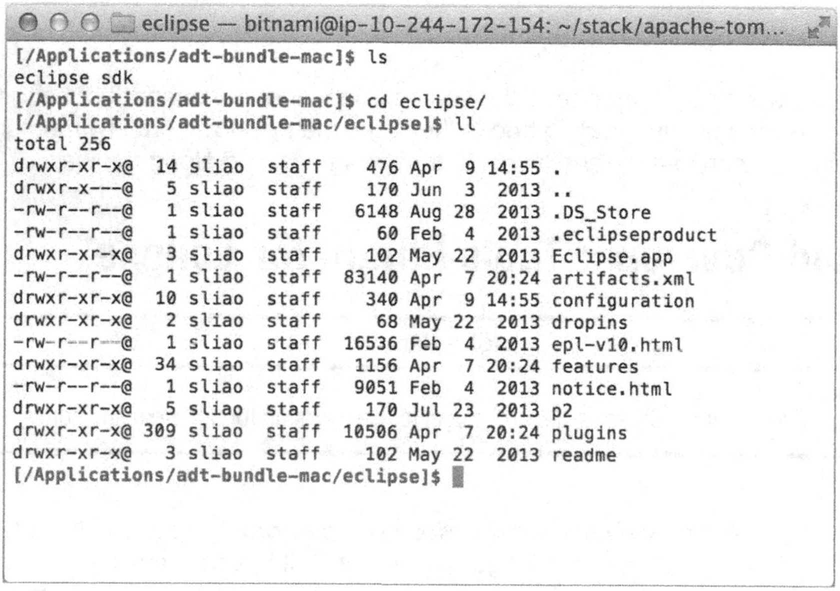

```
⊝ ○ ○  📁 eclipse — bitnami@ip-10-244-172-154: ~/stack/apache-tom...
[/Applications/adt-bundle-mac]$ ls
eclipse sdk
[/Applications/adt-bundle-mac]$ cd eclipse/
[/Applications/adt-bundle-mac/eclipse]$ ll
total 256
drwxr-xr-x@  14 sliao    staff      476 Apr  9 14:55 .
drwxr-x---@   5 sliao    staff      170 Jun  3  2013 ..
-rw-r--r--@   1 sliao    staff     6148 Aug 28  2013 .DS_Store
-rw-r--r--@   1 sliao    staff       60 Feb  4  2013 .eclipseproduct
drwxr-xr-x@   3 sliao    staff      102 May 22  2013 Eclipse.app
-rw-r--r--@   1 sliao    staff    83140 Apr  7 20:24 artifacts.xml
drwxr-xr-x@  10 sliao    staff      340 Apr  9 14:55 configuration
drwxr-xr-x@   2 sliao    staff       68 May 22  2013 dropins
-rw-r--r--@   1 sliao    staff    16536 Feb  4  2013 epl-v10.html
drwxr-xr-x@  34 sliao    staff     1156 Apr  7 20:24 features
-rw-r--r--@   1 sliao    staff     9051 Feb  4  2013 notice.html
drwxr-xr-x@   5 sliao    staff      170 Jul 23  2013 p2
drwxr-xr-x@ 309 sliao    staff    10506 Apr  7 20:24 plugins
drwxr-xr-x@   3 sliao    staff      102 May 22  2013 readme
[/Applications/adt-bundle-mac/eclipse]$ ▊
```

Figure 1-1. The adt-bundle-mac folder structure

All you need to do is download it and unzip it. Please allow me to repeat: you won't need to configure it after you install it. Go ahead and launch the Eclipse.app. Let's keep it in the Mac OS Dock so that you can launch it at any time.

If you don't want to mess with the ADT plugin, you may choose to skip the next section and go straight to the "MacBook Retina Display" section.

Installing the Eclipse ADT Plugin

You may choose to manually install the components in the ADT Bundle and go through the configuration steps. The ADT plugin for Eclipse is a custom plugin for the Eclipse IDE that provides an integrated environment to develop Android apps. It extends the capabilities of Eclipse to let you quickly set up new Android projects, build an app user interface (UI), debug your app, and create app packages (APKs) for distribution.

I installed and configured the ADT plugin manually because I also use Eclipse for JavaEE programming, and I want to share common Java classes between JavaEE server code and Android client code. If you choose to install the plugin to your existing Eclipse instance, chances are you already have experience with the Eclipse IDE.

If you are not a JavaEE developer or just want to keep things simple for now, you should skip the following instructions and do the all-in-one bundled package installation.

> **Note**   Even if you already have Eclipse installed, you still can have multiple Eclipse instances. You should only need to go through this plugin option if you need to share Java classes between Android projects and J2EE projects.

If you decide to go with the manual ADT plugin option for your existing Eclipse app, please visit the Android official site (`http://developer.android.com/sdk/installing/installing-adt.html`) for detailed instruction.

For the Mac OS, you can also follow the "Installing the ADT Plugin Cheat Sheet," which is modified from the preceding URL for your convenience.

INSTALLING THE ADT PLUGIN CHEAT SHEET

Do the following to download the ADT plugin:

1. Open the Install wizard from the Eclipse top menu bar by selecting **Help ➤ Install New Software** (see Figure 1-2). Click **Add** to add a new site.

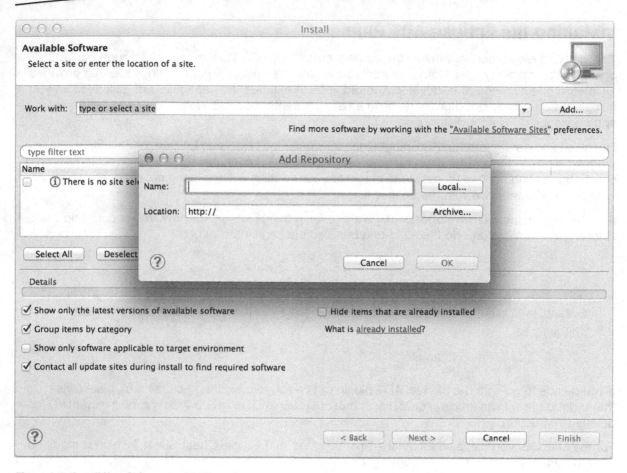

Figure 1-2. Install New Software ➤ Add Repository

2. In the **Add Repository** dialog, enter the following and then click **OK**.

    a. Enter **ADT Plugin** in the **Name** field.

    b. Enter **https://dl-ssl.google.com/android/eclipse/** in the **Location URL**.

    Note   If you have trouble acquiring the plugin, try using "http" in the Location URL instead of "https".

3. In the **Work with** drop-down, make sure the ADT Plugin repository is selected (see Figure 1-3).

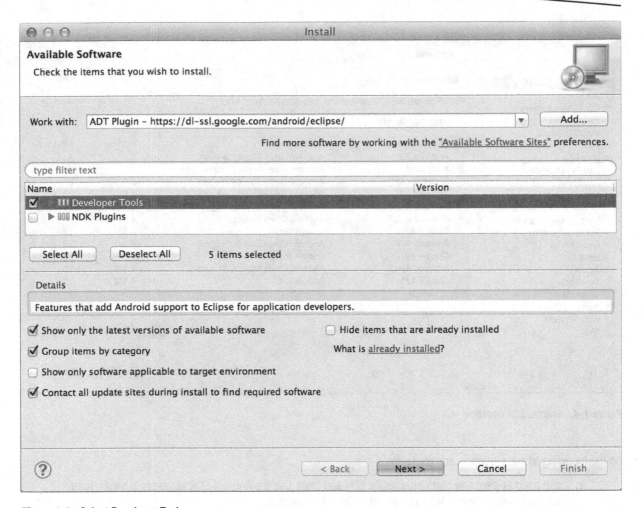

Figure 1-3. Select Developer Tools

  a. Select the **Developer Tools** check box and then click **Next**.

 4. You should see a list of the tools to be downloaded. Click **Next** and follow the onscreen instructions to complete the installation. When the installation completes, restart Eclipse.

Do the following to specify the Android SDK location:

 1. Get the Android SDK, which contains the framework libraries and the development toolkit.

  a. Download the ZIP file from http://developer.android.com/sdk/index.html#download.

  b. Unzip the file to your **SDK Location** folder, which is /Applications/adt-bundle-mac/sdk.

 2. From the Eclipse top menu bar, select **Eclipse ➤ Preferences…** to open the Eclipse Preferences screen (see Figure 1-4). Select **Android** from the left panel and enter your SDK Location: **/Applications/adt-bundle-mac/sdk**.

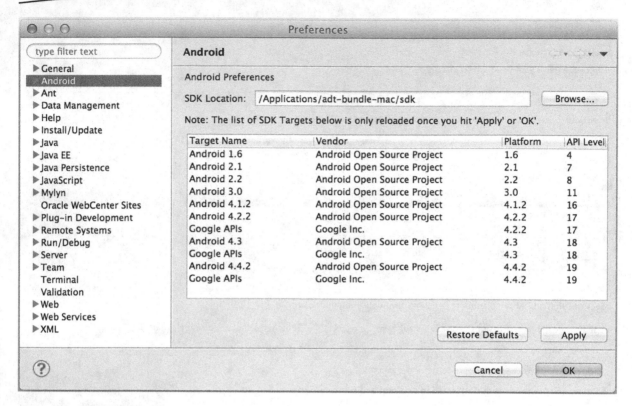

Figure 1-4. Android SDK Location

Do the following to add platforms and packages:

1. You need at least one platform-specific SDK and tools. Use the Android SDK Manager to obtain them for the latest platform (API 19 is the latest as of this writing).

2. From the Eclipse top menu bar, select **Window ➤ Android SDK Manager** to launch the Android SDK Manager. Figure 1-5 shows the platform API and tool packages that I have installed.

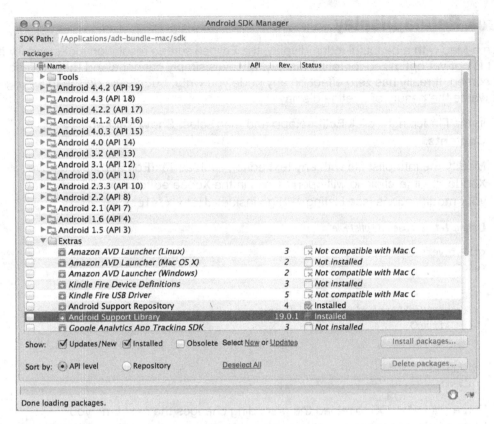

Figure 1-5. Android SDK Manager

3. You want to install at least the following three packages (actually the first two, but you will need the last one later):

    a.   Tools

    b.   The latest Android API: Android 4.4.2 (API 19) as of this writing

    c.   Extra: The Android Support Library

Follow the onscreen instructions to complete the installation.

MacBook Retina Display

If you have a Mac with a beautiful retina display, the Eclipse screen resolution looks awfully bad because it is not yet optimized for retina display. My eyes simply cannot stand the low resolution on my retina screen. It really has zero effect on any code you write, but please do the following so that you don't waste the beauty of a retina display:

1. In the Finder, right-click **Eclipse.app** and then select **Show Package Contents**.

2. Modify the Info.plist file with any text editor, such as TextEdit.app. If you have Xcode, double-clicking will open the file in the Xcode editor as well. Note that your modifications (see Listing 1-1) go inside <dict> </dict>.

    Listing 1-1. *Eclipse Info.plist File*

    ```
    <plist version="1.0">
    <dict>

        ...
      <key>NSHighResolutionCapable</key>
        <true/>
        ...

    </dict>
    </plist>
    ```

3. Force your Mac OS to reload the preceding changes the next time you launch Eclipse.app. This can be easily achieved using the shell touch command.

4. Open the Terminal program and issue the touch command, as shown in Listing 1-2.

    Listing 1-2. *The Touch Command*

    ```
    [/Applications/adt-bundle-mac/eclipse]$ cd /Applications/adt-bundle-mac/eclipse
    [/Applications/adt-bundle-mac/eclipse]$ ls
    Eclipse.app        configuration      epl-v10.html      notice.html      plugins
    artifacts.xml      dropins            features          p2               readme
    [/Applications/adt-bundle-mac/eclipse]$ touch Eclipse.app/
    ```

Bingo! Eclipse should have a retina display now.

The Eclipse Workbench

You just got the right tool, but you need to know how to use it. Let's spend some time with Eclipse first because it appears quite different from Xcode. I think it is actually more sophisticated than Xcode because it has a broader goal: it provides a plugin platform so that you can extend the IDE by creating a plugin for your unique development tasks. For example, the ADT plugin for Android that you just installed is a plugin toolkit for Android development. In the Java world, you can use Eclipse for almost any Java solutions, including JavaEE, JavaME, the Blackberry SDK, various third-party vendor solutions, or SDKs. There is also a C/C++ plugin called Eclipse CDT for the C/C++ toolchain and make utility. There is an Eclipse plugin for the Symbian mobile development toolkit as well.

The Eclipse Workspace

Enough of the motivational talk, let's start using Eclipse and create a workspace.

IOS ANALOGY

Same as the Xcode workspace idea, the Eclipse workspace is a logical grouping of related projects; however, the Eclipse workspace needs to be a physical folder.

Please complete the following steps to create an Eclipse workspace:

1. Launch Eclipse and enter a folder name for the **Workspace** (see Figure 1-6), such as /Users/sliao/Documents/adtWs.

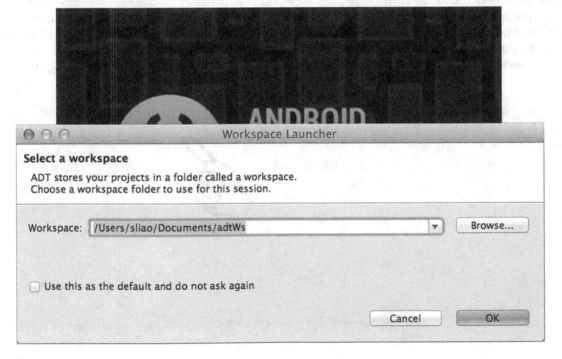

Figure 1-6. The Eclipse Workspace Launcher

2. Click **OK**. You will get the Welcome! screen (see Figure 1-7) the first time you create a new workspace. Let's close it for now. You can always get back to this screen from the top menu bar by selecting **Help ➤ Android IDE**.

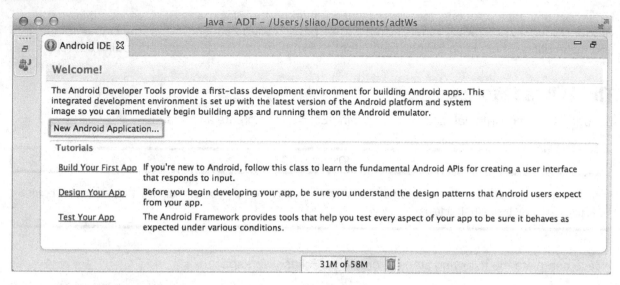

Figure 1-7. *The ADT Welcome! screen*

A single Workbench window is displayed, as shown in Figure 1-8. A Workbench window offers one or more perspectives. A *perspective* contains editors and views, such as the Package Explorer. Upon the Workbench window launching for the first time, the Java perspective is displayed. Good, we need a Java perspective because Java is the language for Android programming. You can always click the Java button in the perspectives toolbar to switch to the Java perspective (see Figure 1-8).

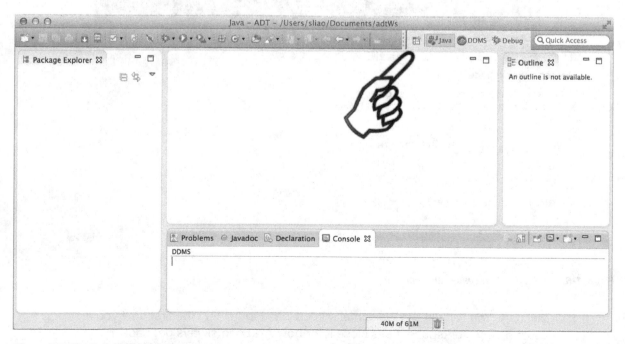

Figure 1-8. *The Eclipse Workbench*

3. Go ahead and play with this window to satisfy your curiosity if you wish.
    Don't be afraid of messing up anything. For example, there are many options
    in the menu bar and a few buttons on the toolbar. The context menu always
    contains hidden gems. You can get back any time by going to the menu bar
    and selecting **Windows ➤ Reset Perspective...**.

Learning Eclipse has been one of my best investments of time. It is the only tool that I am still using since Y2K. I did not get many chances to reuse the same tool for other technologies. If you have been in IT for a long time, you know what I am talking about.

Eclipse can do a lot, more than the Android IDE. But you don't need to know everything today. After all, it is a tool, and you naturally get better at it when you use it often. We will focus on using it for Android programming.

Create an Android Project Using the Template

You just got the right tool, and it is up and running. Wouldn't you like to see some real action—like creating an Android app and see it running? I'd like that, too! You can make sure your IDE is working properly as well.

My very first Xcode app was actually created using the **Create a new Xcode project** template (see Figure 1-9) when I had no idea what Objective-C looked like. All I wanted was to see something running in no time. Yep, Xcode did it for me nicely. I was very happy with myself when I felt I created an iOS app without knowing anything! Hey, there is nothing wrong with making yourself happy right?

The Eclipse with ADT plugin offers the same thing.

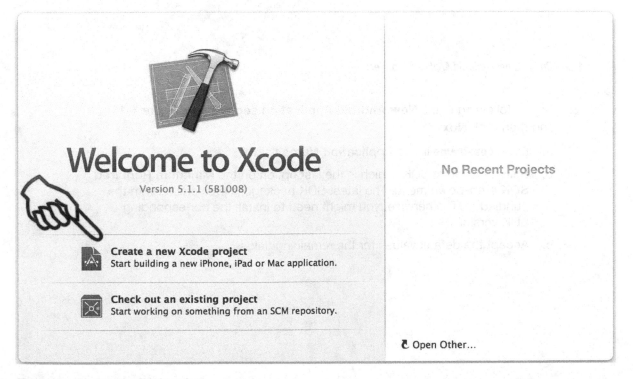

Figure 1-9. Create a new Xcode project

The objective of this lesson is to create an Android app as quickly as possible. Let's hold any programming questions for now to finish the project as fast as you can. Please complete the following steps:

1. Launch the **Eclipse.app** if it is not launched yet.

2. Open the **Android Application wizard** from the Eclipse top menu bar and select **File ➤ New ➤ Android Application Project** (see Figure 1-10).

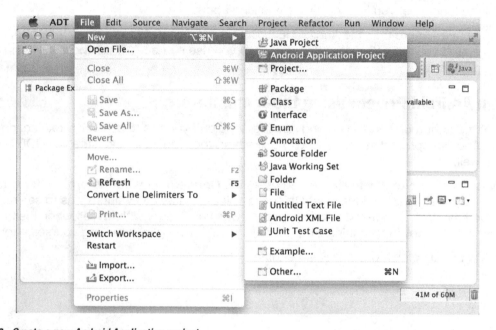

Figure 1-10. Create a new Android Application project

3. Do the following in the **New Android Application section** (see Figure 1-11), and then click **Next**.

   a. Enter **LessonOne** in the **Application Name** field.

   b. Select the latest SDK, which is the last option on the **Minimum Required SDK** drop-down menu. The latest SDK package is preinstalled with the bundled ADT; otherwise, you might need to install the corresponding SDK version.

   c. Accept the default values for the remaining fields.

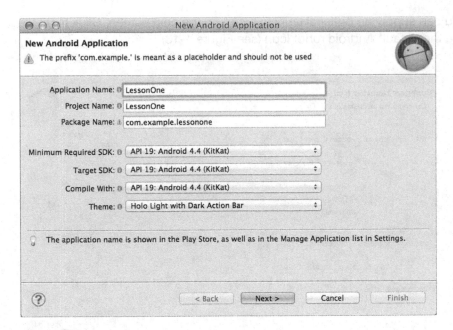

Figure 1-11. New Android Application section

4. On the next screen, keep all the default values in the Configure Project section (see Figure 1-12). Click **Next**.

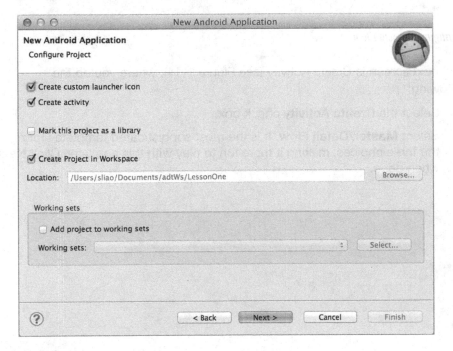

Figure 1-12. Configure Project

5. You can supply an optional launcher icon on the next screen. Click **Next** to use the default Android robot icon (see Figure 1-13).

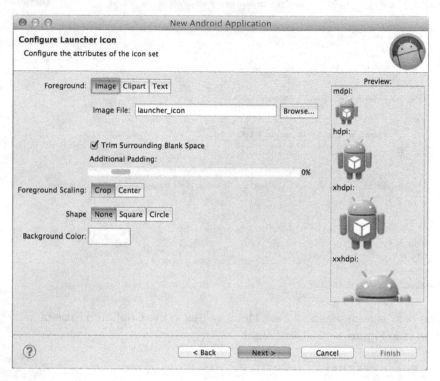

Figure 1-13. Configure Launcher Icon

6. The next screen is Create Activity (see Figure 1-14), where you do the following:

   a. Select the **Create Activity** check box.

   b. Select **Master/Detail Flow**. It is the most sophisticated template among the three choices, making it more fun to play with this app later. Click **Next** when done.

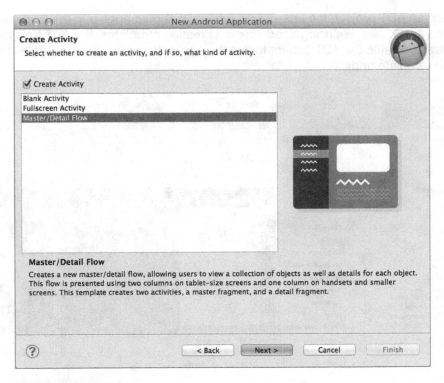

Figure 1-14. Create Activity with templates

7. Keep the prefilled values on the following screen (see Figure 1-15). They will not be used because you are not going to write any Java code yet. Click **Finish**.

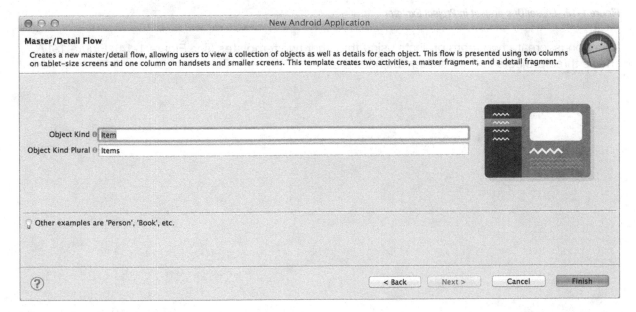

Figure 1-15. Java class for list items

You just created an ADT project, the LessonOne project. It should appear in the Package Explorer view (see Figure 1-16). Just like using Xcode project creation templates, the ADT New Android Application wizard creates the ADT project folder, the application source code, and all the resources for building the template apps.

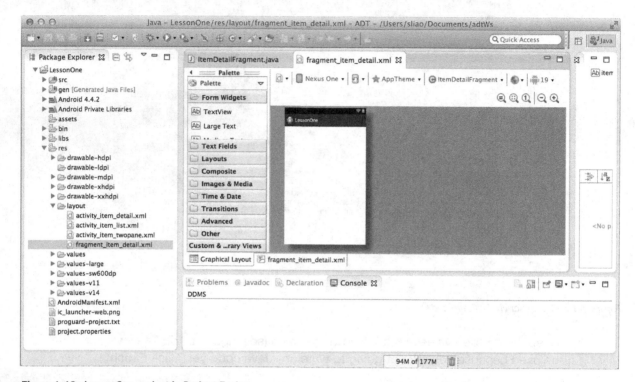

Figure 1-16. *LessonOne project in Project Explorer*

As a bonus, create two more projects using the other two templates (see Figure 1-14). Figure 1-17 shows three projects in the Package Explorer view.

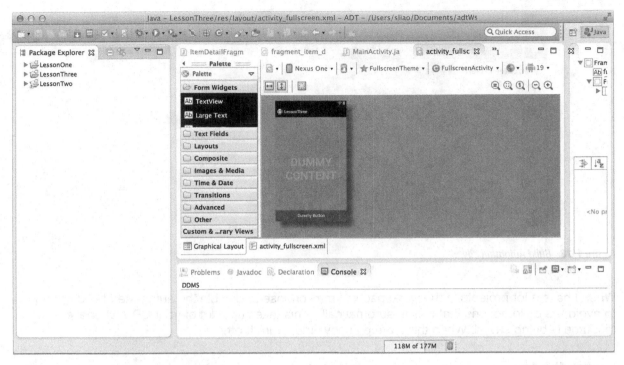

Figure 1-17. Three projects in Project Explorer

Build the Project

IOS ANALOGY

The Xcode Build action keyboard shortcut on the Mac is Command-B (⌘B).

The Eclipse workbench is set to *Build Automatically* by default (see Figure 1-18); you don't need to build ADT projects explicitly. Let's keep this option; I just wanted to point out that you can disable this option and do a manual build (⌘B) if you wish to.

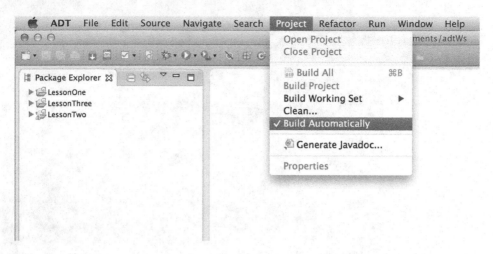

Figure 1-18. Build Automatically

When I have a lot projects in the workspaces, I may choose to disable the automated build option to avoid the build actions that kick in automatically. This takes up a lot of your CPU whenever any resource is being saved. When this feature annoys me, I turn it off.

Launch the App

IOS ANALOGY

The Xcode Run action keyboard shortcut on the Mac is Command-R (⌘R).

The LessonOne project should have no errors. You can launch the app and see it run on device emulators or on Android-powered devices. The emulator is a very important piece of any IDE. In the following steps, you will prepare an Android Virtual Device (AVD) and launch the LessonOne project onto a device emulator.

1. From the LessonOne project context menu, select **Debug As ➤ Android Application** (see Figure 1-19).

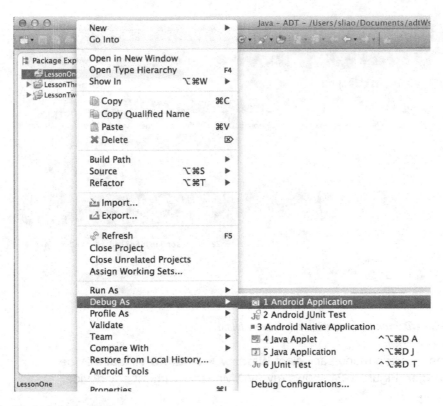

Figure 1-19. Debug As Android Application

2. You most likely will get to the following screen, Android AVD Error (see Figure 1-20), since you haven't created any Android Virtual Device (AVD) yet. You can click the **Yes** button to get to the Android Virtual Device Manager tool. However, I want to show you another path so that you can create an AVD any time you want to. Click **No** to close the error dialog.

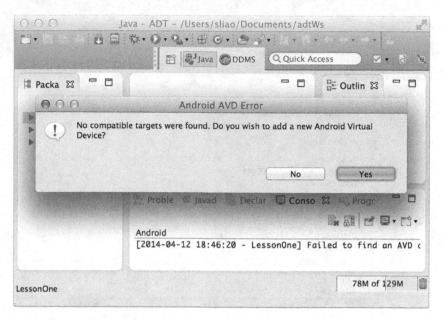

Figure 1-20. Android AVD Error: No compatible targets were found

3. In the ADT top menu bar, select **Window ➤ Android Virtual Device Manager**. Figure 1-21 shows my AVD Manager without any device.

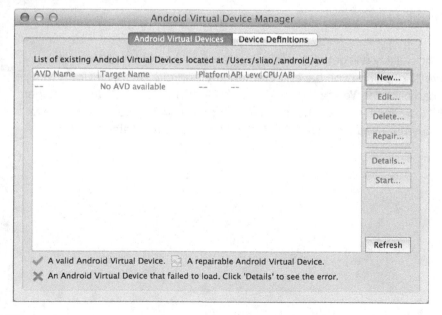

Figure 1-21. AVD Manager

Note   You can select New, Edit, or Delete for any existing AVD. Repair does not seem to work for me. I simply delete and create a new one instead. The Device Definitions button shows the preset AVD definitions; you will find this useful when you want to test your app and know the specs.

4.   Click the **New. . .** button to continue creating your first AVD (see Figure 1-22). Leave everything as the default, except the following:

    a.   Enter any name, such as **nexus7**, in the **AVD Name** field.

    b.   Select **Nexus 7** from the **Device** drop-down menu.

    c.   Select the highest API level from the **Target** drop-down menu. This is the most significant attribute. The Target needs to be compatible with the Minimum Required SDK specified for your app in Figure 1-11, which should be what you entered when creating the LessonOne project.

    d.   Optionally, enter information for any other fields with your app's required specific hardware. For example, if your app saves data on external storage, you will experience an error if information in the SD Card section is not specified.

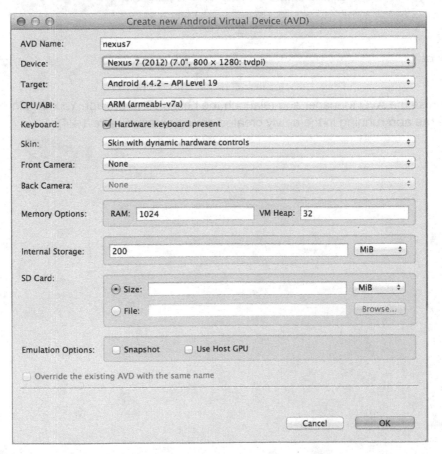

Figure 1-22. Create AVD

5. Figure 1-23 shows the newly created AVD, which is compatible with the LessonOne project.

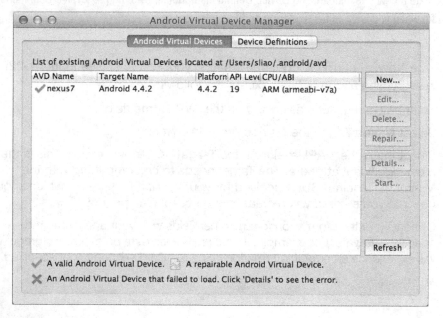

Figure 1-23. AVD list

6. Dismiss the AVD Manager and relaunch the LessonOne project. You should see the app running in the newly created emulator (see Figure 1-24).

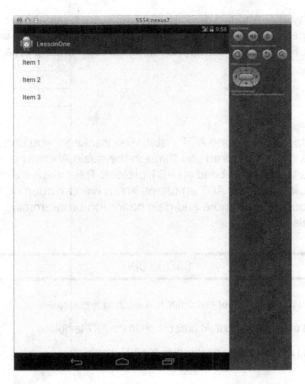

Figure 1-24. LessonOne app in emulator

Note   I always experience a timeout error on the first try. You might experience the same error if your machine is not fast enough. The newly created AVD seems to take too long to start up. If you get an error message, relaunch again *after* the emulator has started.

Play with the app and the emulator. A mouse-click event on an emulator is equivalent to a touch event on a real Android device. If you don't have a device yet, definitely play with the emulator to get familiar with the emulated Android device.

Tip   Rotate the emulator (fn+Ctrl+F12) in landscape mode to see how the LessonOne app does. Check http://developer.android.com/tools/help/emulator.html#KeyMapping for the emulator keyboard mappings.

To launch the app onto physical Android devices, the steps are basically the same. However, it might not work immediately, depending on your device model. We will talk about on-device debugging in detail in a later chapter. For now, if your app is launched and running on an AVD, your mission is completed!

Summary

By downloading the Xcode-like all-in-one ADT installation package, you can get your Android IDE ready without hassle. This chapter walked you through the basic Android programming tasks in the Eclipse workspace, with a template to build an ADT project. This chapter also showed you how to debug and run your Android app in an ADT emulator. You haven't written any code yet, but your tool is working and verified. You will learn more and gain hands-on programming experience from the guided exercises along this journey.

CHECKPOINT

- You have installed the ADT on your computer. It is working and verified.

- You have created one to three Android projects using the ADT template.

- You have built and run an Android project onto the ADT emulator.

Great start!

Chapter 2

Android Programming Basics

Creating mobile apps for both iOS and Android is fun and rewarding. With the right tools in place, you are ready to write code, build, and run Android apps now. Java is the programming language for writing Android apps. Also, the Java programming model is different from other Java platforms. Your next steps should be learning the fundamentals of the following:

- The Java programming language
- The Android framework

If you are able to read Java code, go ahead and skip the Java programming subchapter if you want. The programming language is more of a tool than a technology for creating meaningful apps. For this book, I will not dive too deeply into Java techniques. The best way to learn new tools and languages is with practical experience and practice. However, the whole book uses code to explain Android concepts and technologies. The purpose of the first part of this chapter is to ensure that you can read the Java code in this book. To achieve this goal, you will be creating a HelloJava project. You will be able to read the Java code in this book when you are able to write the code.

Regarding the second part of the chapter, I actually don't think you can be a good Android developer without a good understanding of the fundamentals of the *Android Application Framework*. There are shortcuts to getting into Android programming. You definitely can take advantage of your existing mobile knowledge to shorten the learning curve. In the long run, however, I believe you will be limited and will still need to come back to the fundamentals when you want to fly freely with any creative ideas. You may not need to understand everything about the Android framework in the beginning, but I believe knowing "just enough" to feel the different programming paradigm will allow you to march into Chapters 3 and 4. Later, the materials are heavily step-by-step instructions based; while you follow these mapping instructions, I also want you to have the right thinking process so that the ideas stick better with you.

In the second part of this chapter, you are going to create a HelloAndroid ADT project so that you can visually relate the fundamental concepts in a simple but typical Android project. No specific programming technique will be introduced in this chapter. Lengthy descriptions are also simplified because I don't think they will stick in your head now if you don't have Android programming experience yet. After this chapter, if you understand the roles of the software artifacts in the HelloAndroid project, you can be certain you are on the right track for next steps.

The Java Language in a Nutshell

Java, which is used to create Android apps, is one of the easiest object-oriented programming (OOP) languages. Java has simpler syntactical rules than Objective-C. I am very confident that learning the Java language won't be the highest hurdle for you. You will start writing Java code soon. If you have been in software programming since before the iPhone evolution, you probably already know C/C++/C#, or JavaScript—or maybe you know Java already. Java is just another natural programming language for the C++/C# developer.

You can choose to skip this chapter if you have no problem reading Java code. If you are totally new to it and you only know Objective-C, please go over this chapter to quickly get familiar with Java programming tasks in the Eclipse environment. You will create the HelloJava program in Eclipse. It will help you read the Java code and build your Android projects throughout the book.

IOS ANALOGY

Language Syntax Comparison in an Absolute Nutshell

Objective-C	Java
#import "Xyz.h"	import packagename.Xyz;
@interface Xyz : NSObject	public class Xyz extends Object
@protocol Abc	public interface Abc
@interface Xyz : NSObject <Abc>	class Xyz extends Object implements Abc
@property int mProperty;	private int mProperty;
-(id)init	public Xyz() // no return value
Xyz* obj = [[Xyz alloc] init];	Xyz obj = new Xyz();
-(void) doWork: (NSString*) arg;	public void doWork(String arg)
[obj doWork: arg];	obj.doWork(arg);
// comments ...	// comments ...

Note   Full Java programming rules are beyond the scope of this book. This chapter is only intended to show basic Java syntax and usages through examples so that you can read the Java code in this book.

HelloJava with Eclipse

Instead of my describing the usages and syntax rules in a formal way, you are going to create a HelloJava project and write the code list from the iOS analogy table yourself. You really don't need to remember exact Java syntax rules because the compiler will tell you if you are doing something wrong. Eclipse actually gives you suggestions on how to fix it, too. Not only will you learn Java in a nutshell from writing the code yourself, you will also do the following common programming tasks in Eclipse: create a class, build and compile a project, and use the debugger.

Create a Java Project

Eclipse.app is used to create Java programs for various Java platforms, including Android, JavaEE, JavaSE, and so forth. To demonstrate basic Java and to highlight the syntactical differences between Java and Objective-C, you are going to create a stand-alone JavaSE program, because it is really simple and you can focus on the subject without being sidetracked by other questions.

To create a Java project in Eclipse, follow these instructions:

1. Launch the **Eclipse.app** if it is not launched yet.

2. Start the **New Java Project** wizard (see Figure 2-1) from the top menu bar by selecting **File ➤ New ➤ Java Project**. Then do the following:

    a. Enter **HelloJava** in the **Project name** field.

    b. Accept the default values for the other fields. Click **Finish** to complete this task.

    c. Optionally, click **Next** to view other default project settings before you click Finish.

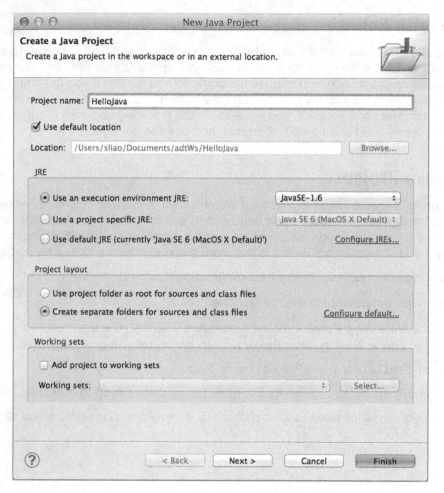

Figure 2-1. Create a new Java project

The HelloJava project appears in the Eclipse Package Explorer view, just like the LessonOne Android project in Chapter 1.

Create a Java Class

IOS ANALOGY

Objective-C @interface

You are going to create two classes. The first one demonstrates how to instantiate an object instance and invoke methods by sending messages to the other Java object. This class also contains the Java app entry method. The second class demonstrates very fundamental Java declarations, including class, fields, and methods.

To create the first class, complete the following steps:

1. Expand the newly created HelloJava project, right-click the $PROJ/src folder to bring up the folder context menu (see Figure 2-2), and select **New ➤ Class**.

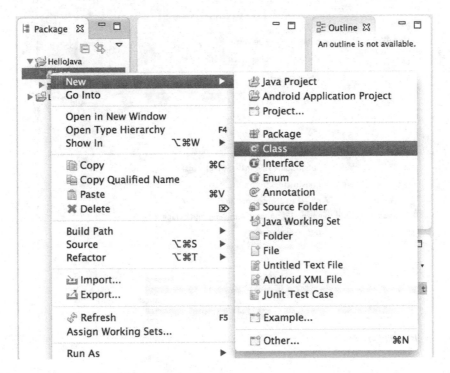

Figure 2-2. Create a new class from the folder context menu

2. Complete the following requirements in the **New Java Class** dialog (see Figure 2-3):

    a. Enter **com.pdachoice.hellojava** in the **Package** (a.k.a. namespace) field.

    b. Enter **Main** in the **Name** (class name) field.

    c. Select the **public static void main(...)** check box.

    d. Accept the default values for the remaining fields.

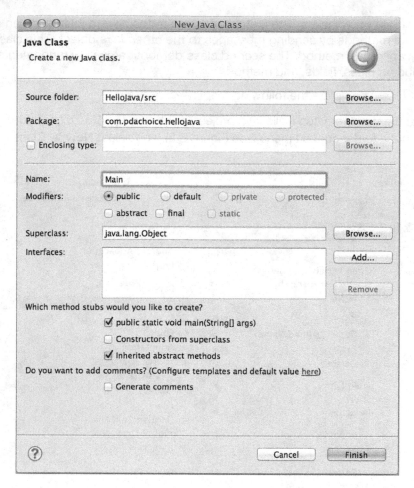

Figure 2-3. New Java class dialog

Note   To avoid namespace collision, a prefix is commonly used in Objective-C. In Java, every class needs to be declared in a package (a.k.a. namespace).

3.   Click **Finish** to complete the wizard. The barebones Main class with the Java app entry method is created in the src/com.pdachoice.hellojava/Main.java file, as shown in Figure 2-4.

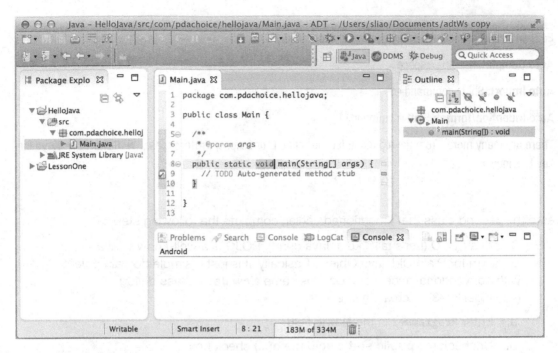

Figure 2-4. HelloJava Main.java

This Main class has one method, the Java program entry method. Just for fun, let's add one line of code to print out some string; for example, "Hello, Java!" (see Listing 2-1).

Listing 2-1. Java Program Entrance Method

```
public static void main(String[] args) {
    // print out "Hello Java" in Console
    String message = "Hello, Java!";
    System.out.println(message); // same as NSLog(@"...") in iOS
}
```

IOS ANALOGY

- **iOS app main.m:** int main(int argc, char *argv[ ])
- **iOS app log output:** NSLog(@"Hello, Java")
- **Xcode Type Ahead with autocompletion feature:** Ctrl+<space> (same as the Eclipse Java editor)

> **Eclipse Tip**   Eclipse Java editor command shortcut keys:
>
> **Auto Completion:** Ctrl+<space>
>
> **Auto Import:** Shift+command+o
>
> **Auto Indention/format:** Shift+command+f
>
> There are many more. From the top menu bar, select ADT (or Eclipse) **Preferences...** ➤ **General** ➤ **Keys** for key bindings.

To create the second class that I mentioned earlier, complete the following steps:

1. Create a *POJO* (Let's talk like a Java guru!). POJO is a well-known Java acronym for Plain Old Java Object. Basically, it is just a simple domain object with conventional accessors. Use the same **New Java Class** dialog (see Figure 2-3) to create a one.

   a. Enter **Programmer** in the **Name** field.

   b. Uncheck the **public static void main(...)** check box.

   c. Click **Finish**. The Programmer.java file should be created and displayed in the Eclipse Java editor, as shown in Listing 2-2.

   Listing 2-2. A Simple POJO Class

   ```
   package com.pdachoice.hellojava;

   public class Programmer {

       public Programmer() {
           // TODO Auto-generated constructor stub
       }

   }
   ```

2. Create a Programmer property (a.k.a. Java field): name. Manually create the conventional getter and setter: getName() and setName(...) as shown in Listing 2-3.

   Listing 2-3. Java Property

   ```
   public class Programmer {

       ...
       // Java field
       private String name;
   ```

```
    public String getName() {
        return name;
    }

    public void setName(String name) {
        this.name = name;
    }
    ...

}
```

Note   There are no header files in Java. Unlike Objective-C header files that define the public methods or properties, Java uses an access modifier to control the accessibility, that is, *public*, *protected*, *private*, and so forth. Whereas the private method can only be used inside the Java class implementation, public methods are like the Objective-C defined in the header files, which are accessible by other classes outside of the implementation class.

In Java, a *property* is implemented as a private Java field with public accessors, very similar to the Objective-C @property.

Eclipse Tip   There are lots of goodies everywhere in the context menu. For example, the Java class **Context Menu ➤ Source ➤ Generated Getters and Setters...** Eclipse IDE generates the conventional getters and setters, as you did in Listing 2-3.

Create a Java Interface

IOS ANALOGY

The Objective-C @protocol defines object obligations.

In object-oriented programming, it is important to define a set of behaviors that are expected of certain objects. In Objective-C, you use the @protocol. In Java, you declare interface.

These terminologies seem a little bit confusing here because the @interface is a keyword in Objective-C that defines class, whereas *interface* is a keyword in Java for object obligation, a.k.a. contract, or @protocol in Objective-C.

Other than the different terminologies, the Java interface is just like the Objective-C @protocol that defines method signatures without implementation bodies.

Create a Java interface called MobileDeveloper by doing the following:

1. Similar to creating a new class, right-click the $PROJ/src/com.pdachoice. hellojava folder. From the context menu, select **New ➤ Interface**. Complete the following requirements as shown in Figure 2-5:

    a. Enter a namespace such as **com.pdachoice.hellojava** in the **Package** field.

    b. Enter an interface name such as **MobileDeveloper** in the **Name** field.

    c. Select **public** as the Modifier.

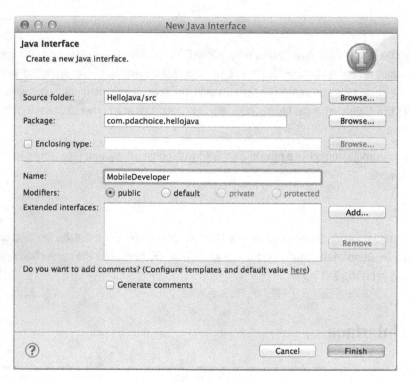

Figure 2-5. The create Java interface dialog

2. From the Java editor, add a method, writeCode. Listing 2-4 shows the entire MobileDeveloper interface.

Listing 2-4. MobileDeveloper Java Interface

```
package com.pdachoice.hellojava;

public interface MobileDeveloper {
    public void writeCode(String arg);
}
```

Implement the Interface

For a Java class to confront to the expected behavior, we make the class implement the Java interface that defines the expected behavior. To make the `Programmer` class implement the `MobileDeveloper` interface, do the following:

1. From the Java editor, modify `src/com.pdachoice.hellojava/Programmer.java` and declare the `Programmer` class to implement the `MobileDeveloper` interface as shown in Listing 2-5.

   Listing 2-5. Declare Java Interface Implementation

   ```java
   public class Programmer implements MobileDeveloper {
       ...
   }
   ```

   > **Note** Until you complete the next step, the Eclipse compiler complains that the class must implement the required method.

2. Provide the `writeCode` method implementation body, as shown in Listing 2-6.

   Listing 2-6. Java Method Body

   ```java
   package com.pdachoice.hellojava;

   public class Programmer implements MobileDeveloper {

       ...
       @Override
       public void writeCode(String arg) {
           // some dummy implementation
           String str = String.format("%s wrote: Hello, %s!", this.name, arg);
           System.out.println(str);
       }
       ...

   }
   ```

   > **Note** System.out.println(str) sends the string to the output console.

Use the Java Class and Method

You have created a Java Programmer class and implemented the MobileDeveloper obligations, pretty much the same way you normally do in Xcode except with different syntax. Next, you will use the class you just created. No surprise, it is the same in principle but in a different syntax, sending a message to the receiver from the sender.

IOS ANALOGY

Programmer* you = [[Programmer alloc] init];

[you setName:@"You"];

[you doWork:@"Java"];

Do the following to see how the Eclipse debugger works:

1. Modify the Java app entry method in `src/com.pdachoice.hellojava/Main.java` to use the `Programmer` class, as shown in Listing 2-7.

    Listing 2-7. Java Entry Method: main(...)

    ```java
    package com.pdachoice.hellojava;

    public class Main {
        public static void main(String[] args) {
            // print out "You wrote: Hello, Java!" in Console
            Programmer you = new Programmer();
            you.setName("You");
            you.writeCode("Java");
        }
    }
    ```

The Eclipse Java Debugger

Debugging and fixing code is one of the most fun and most common programming tasks. To be productive, knowing how to use the debugger in an integrated development environment (IDE) makes a big difference. You normally would set a *breakpoint* in the right line of code to see the programming flow by *step thru code* and/or *inspect variables*. Do the following to see how the Eclipse debugger works:

1. To set a breakpoint, double-click the gray vertical bar in the Java Editor view. Open `src/com.pdachoice.hellojava/Main.java` and double-click line 6, as shown in Figure 2-6.

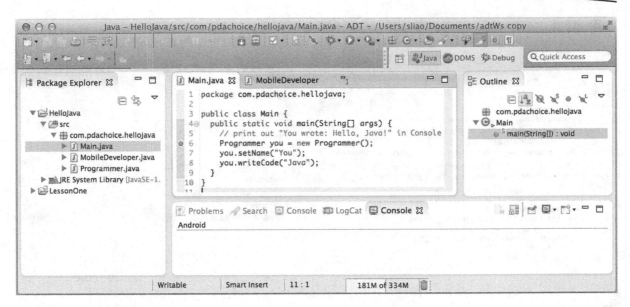

Figure 2-6. Breakpoint

> **Note**   To turn on line numbers in Eclipse editors, go to the ADT top menu bar and select **Preferences...** ➤
> **General** ➤ **Editors** ➤ **Text Editors** ➤ **Show Line Numbers**.

2. To run the HelloJava project in the debugger, from the HelloJava project
    context menu, select **Debug as** ➤ **Java Application**. If the Confirm
    Perspective Switch dialog appears, click **Yes**.

3. The Java program will start and stop at line 6, where the breakpoint was set
    in **Debug Perspective** (see Figure 2-7).

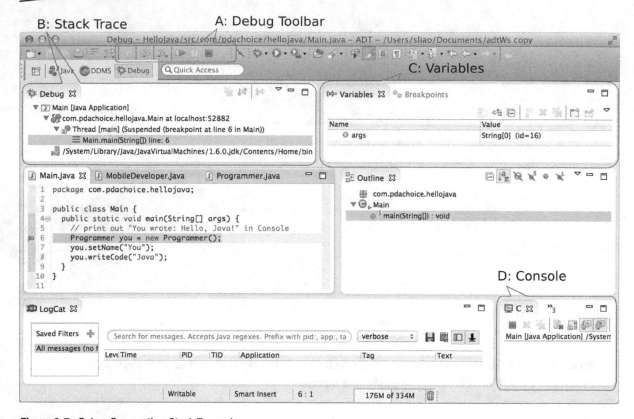

Figure 2-7. *Debug Perspective, Stack Trace view*

> **Note** I have highlighted four views in the Debug Perspective for your attention: **Debug Toolbar (A)**, **Stack Trace (B)**, **Variables (C)**, and **Console (D)**.

4. The **Debug Toolbar (A)** contains those common debugger action buttons—Resume, Suspend, Step Into, Step Out, Step Over, and so forth. The icons actually look similar to those in Xcode. Let's step to line 7 using the **Step Over** button in the **Debug Toolbar**.

> **Eclipse Tip** Move the mouse over the buttons in the **Debug Toolbar (A)** to see the hover text.

5. You should see that the Programmer variable appears in the Variables view. Expand the variable to see its internal Java field, name (see Figure 2-8). Step Over one more line to line 8. It highlights the variables that have a new value.

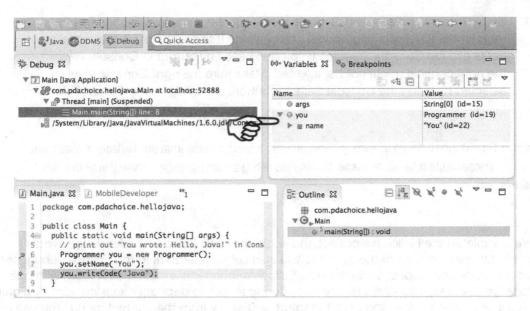

Figure 2-8. Debug Perspective, Variables view

6. Keep an eye on the **Output Console** (see region D in Figure 2-7). Step Over one more line to execute the last line of code. The screenshot in Figure 2-9 shows the program output in the Output Console.

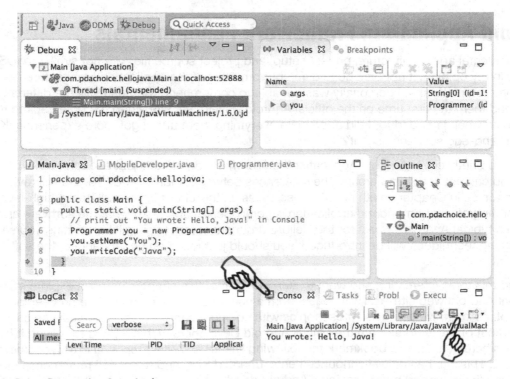

Figure 2-9. Debug Perspective, Console view

7. Stack Trace, Variables, and Console views all have a similar look and feel in most of the IDE, including Xcode. The only one that might not be that trivial in Eclipse is the Console Selector. If you don't see any output in Console view, the right console might not be selected. Make sure the right Console view is selected by using the Console Selector button, as highlighted in Figure 2-9.

Eclipse Tip   During a debug session, you can bring up a context menu from any variable or statement. You can choose **Context Menu ➤ Inspect** during the debug session to inspect a variable or evaluate a statement.

You have completed the HelloJava project and wrote the code listed in the language syntax comparison table at the start of this chapter. You also set a breakpoint in the Eclipse debugger to step through code and inspect variables. The Eclipse debugger is as good as Xcode, with one more advantage: you actually can evaluate any code during an active debugger session. Simply highlight any variable or an expression, and select **Inspect** or **Display** from the context menu. You can get the results immediately, without restarting the Java program. I think that this is very handy and saves a lot of debugging time.

As you follow through Android projects in this book, you will discover more tips and get more productive in the Eclipse IDE environment.

Android Application Framework Fundamentals

The fundamental app architecture, project setup, and project source files are not similar to iOS projects. In my opinion, it appears quite different from most of the application architectures in most of the common platforms. I personally was not able to comprehend the beauty of the differences when I read them the first time on the official Android Developers site. I had to come back to revisit these topics when I needed to. I did appreciate everything more after I got more experience. Kind of a chicken-and-egg scenario, isn't it?

I decided to briefly cover Android Application framework fundamentals just enough for now so that you can get your head around the differences between Android and iOS. We will revisit the same topics in Chapter 5 with practical use cases. In this chapter, you will gain a high-level understanding of what an Android application is composed of and learn what the software artifacts are for in a typical Android project for the HelloAndroid project that you will be creating yourself. No programming techniques will be introduced; you should just focus on understanding the software components.

If you find this topic interesting and want to learn more after this chapter, you can explore more at the official Android web site. You will benefit from a deeper understanding before proceeding to the next chapter. Again, we will revisit these topics with coding techniques and practical use cases later. I borrow most of the lectures from the official Android Developers web site, and simplified it for iOS developers here. It is time to bookmark the following link: `http://developer.android.com/develop/index.html`. This site has official announcements, updated SDK and tools, API references, and almost everything needed by professional Android developers.

Android Applications

```
┌─────────────────────────────────────────────────────────────────────────────┐
│                              QUICK OVERVIEW                                    │
└─────────────────────────────────────────────────────────────────────────────┘
```

1. Android applications are composed of one or more application components (activities, services, content providers, and broadcast receivers).

2. Each component performs a different role in the overall application behavior and each one can be activated individually (even by other applications).

3. Each project contains a manifest file that declares all components in the application and also declares the application requirements, such as the minimum API version and any hardware configurations required.

4. Noncode application resources (images, strings, layout files, etc.) should include alternatives for different device configurations (such as different strings for different languages and different layouts for different screen sizes).

Android applications are written in the Java programming language along with resource files and any software artifacts required by the SDK tools. You use Android SDK tools to compile all the software artifacts and bundle them into an archive file with an .apk file extension, called an *Android package file*. A single Android package (.apk) file normally contains one application that can be loaded onto Android devices.

Each Android application is assigned a unique user ID. Only the same user ID has access to any of the files in the application. Also, when the application runs, it runs in its own Linux process that has its own Java virtual machine (JVM). This ensures that the application code and the runtime memory are used in isolation from other applications. This way, each app can only access the files and memory belonging to itself by default. In other words, unless you explicitly share data using allowed techniques, you can assure your users that your application and user data are protected in a secure environment.

> **Note** *The Principle of Least Privilege*: Each Android application, by default, has access only to the components that it requires to do its work, and no more.

```
┌─────────────────────────────────────────────────────────────────────────────┐
│                               IOS ANALOGY                                     │
└─────────────────────────────────────────────────────────────────────────────┘
```

Both iOS and Android are Unix-like BSD-compliant operating systems. The iOS apps are archived with an .app suffix and each lives in its own security sandbox, too.

Security and sharing data are generally advanced topics. You will be introduced to a common data-sharing method among different apps in Chapter 5, but not in this chapter.

Application Components

There are four application components defined in Android system:

- Activity
- Service
- Content provider
- Broadcast receiver

Each Android application contains one or more Android application components. *Activity* is the component that most straightforwardly compares to an iOS app; it is the Android component that presents the user interface to users and normally is executed in the foreground to interact with users, just like iOS apps do. There are also three other types of application components. Each type serves a distinct purpose.

When it comes to creating Android apps, the application components are the essential building blocks. As a developer, you write code to create application components that define how the system or other apps activate your component. When the application component is activated, the component lifecycle methods that perform the intended application behaviors are executed.

All Android developers should know the four Android application components, but I think it could be fairly dry for a beginner to just read the definitions and rules of the application components. Let's go over this topic in simplified terms first. In this chapter, I am going to put a little more weight on the activity component. You will create a HelloAndroid project that contains only an activity, so that you can visualize it. Although the other three application components are intended for different usages, the Android framework treats them the same in many regards (of course, there are some differences as well). We will revisit these topics with sample code in Chapter 5.

Activity

Although an activity is not a must-have application component in every Android application, it is likely the most-used component among the four. Every Android app with a user interface must have an activity component, because an activity is the only application component that provides a user interface with which users can interact with, such as dialing the phone, taking a photo, sending an e-mail, viewing a map, or anything else your application wants to convey to users via the user interface.

Prior to fragment being introduced in API 11 in 2011, you had to create multiple activity application components for multiple screens in an Android app, which always seemed like overkill to me. Fragment is similar to activity from user interface perspectives, but it is not an application component. It is bounded with a layout file just like activity.

In simple terms, you can think of fragment as a subactivity and the activity as a parent container.

I like to use the iOS UIViewController as an analogy to an Android fragment, and the iOS container view controller as an analogy to an Android activity:

- One fragment manages one content view: for example, an iOS storyboard scene or XIB file vs. Android layout file.

- An activity coordinates child fragment(s) just like iOS container view controller coordniates child UIViewController(s).

- Both Android and iOS have lifecycle callback methods: for example, an iOS viewDidAppear vs. an Android onResume, and so forth.

To port an iOS app to Android, you will certainly use fragment with activity. Details are coming up in Chapters 3 and 4.

Service

In contrast to activity, the service application component doesn't have a user interface. Since it doesn't need to interact with users directly, the service component is a good choice for computing tasks that don't require users to attend to the app. Users can be away from or switch to other apps while the service code continues to run in the background. Playing music or downloading large files while the user is away are good examples of using service components.

Content Provider

As the name implies, the content provider manages shared application data. Recall from earlier in the chapter (see the note about the Principle of Least Privilege) that an application cannot share its data by default. For applications to provide data service, you can create a content provider to manage shared data and provide information services. For example, Android system apps like Calendar and Contacts contain a content provider to allow other apps to retrieve or insert data.

Broadcast Receiver

You can think of Android broadcast receiver usage as similar to the iOS NSNotificationCenter mechanism, but it can live on its own. It is designated to respond to any broadcast announcements, such as system shutdown or low-battery broadcasts. You can also send your own broadcast intents and use broadcast receiver components to receive data from other apps for implementing certain interprocess communication (IPC) use cases.

Intents and Intent Filters

IOS ANALOGY

UIActivity/UIActivityViewController is the closest comparison in iOS. Definitely, you get more freedom in the Android platform. Also, UIApplication.openURL may achieve similar use cases in iOS, but for sure not as seamlessly as Android does.

A unique aspect of the Android system design is that any application can start another application's component. This makes integrating any existing app fairly easy. If some apps already contain certain screens or certain features, you can incorporate them into your apps by simply activating the particular application components from your code, including those preloaded system apps. For example, if you want the user to be able to make a phone call from within your app, instead of writing your phone call features and creating the dial-pad UI, and so forth, you can simply use the preloaded system phone app. To your users, it seems as if the phone dialer is a part of your application.

These are fairly unique aspects not presented in iOS; there is very limited interprocess communication support in the iOS SDK. You will write code for reusing the preloaded system apps, as well as your own application components, after you become more familiar with basic Android development tasks.

Application Resources

Most of the apps are composed of more than programming code; for example, a typical iOS project contains Object-C source code, libraries, one or more storyboard files, images or multimedia files, property archive files, an info.plist, and so forth. Xcode compiles and builds the whole project and bundles all the artifacts required for an app. Similarly, an Android application is composed of more than just Java code—it requires other resources, *application resources*, such as images, audio files, and anything relating to the visual presentation of the application; for example, you need to define animations, menus, styles, colors, and the screens with XML files.

For every application resource that you include in your Android project, the SDK build tools define a unique integer ID, which you can use to reference the resource from your Java code or from other resources defined in XML. For example, if your application contains an image file named logo.png (saved in the res/drawable/directory), the SDK tools generate a resource ID named R.drawable.logo, which you can use to reference the image and to insert it in your user interface.

Your Android application normally runs on a wide range of Android devices with different device configurations, such as screen sizes and resolutions, language and locales, and so forth. The Android framework recognizes many types of device configurations and loads the appropriate application resources if applications provide different sets of application resources for any particular device configuration. This is called an *alternative resource*. When providing a specific type of alternative resource, you append the appropriate *configuration qualifier* to the resource folder so that the Android system can clearly load the right set based on this identifier. You will revisit this topic in Chapter 5.

Let's take a break from the preceding lectures and create the HelloAndroid project next. You are going to use the live project to visualize how the concepts are translated into software artifacts in the Android project.

The HelloAndroid Project

Let's create a HelloAndroid project so we can see the project files that comprise Android fundamentals in a typical Android app. I remembered a tutorial doc from Apple called "About Creating Your First iOS App." I think it is perfect for our objectives. You will port this iOS app to the Android platform. The screenshot shown in Figure 2-10 is what you want to achieve in Android.

Figure 2-10. *A beginner's first iOS app*

As an iOS developer, you know this iOS project can be created in three minutes. The same Android project can be created with the same effort as well. However, let's do it more slowly and cross-reference the lectures mentioned earlier.

Create an ADT Project

To create a new Android Development Tools (ADT) project, use the **New Android Application** dialog (see Figure 2-11) to start. The following steps are repeated from an exercise in Chapter 1.

1. In Eclipse, start the **Android Application Project** wizard from the top menu bar and select **File ➤ New** (or start from the Package Explorer context menu):

   a. For the **Application Name**, select **HelloAndroid**. This is the app name that appears to users.

   b. For the **Project Name**, enter **HelloAndroid**. This is the name of your project directory and the project name in Eclipse.

c. For the **Package Name**, enter `com.pdachoice.helloandroid`. Each Android app has a package name attribute that must be unique across all applications installed on the Android system. It's generally best if you use a name that begins with the reverse domain name of your organization or publisher entity.

d. For the **Minimum Required SDK**, select **API 19**. This setting lets you select the lowest version of Android platforms that your app will support. Older devices run on a lower API. The lower you can declare here, the more devices you can support. However, you might lose the new API features in your apps. You need to choose between supporting older devices and newer API features.

e. For the **Target SDK**, select **API 19**, which is the latest version (default), of this writing. The Target SDK indicates the highest version of Android with which you have tested your application.

f. For **Compile With**, select **API 19** (the latest version as of this writing). By default, this setting is set to the latest version of Android available in your ADT so that you can take advantage of the latest framework API. The devices supported are limited to the minimum required SDK specified earlier.

g. Select a **Theme**. This specifies the Android UI style to apply for your app. SDK provides many system themes; you can choose one to start with before customizations.

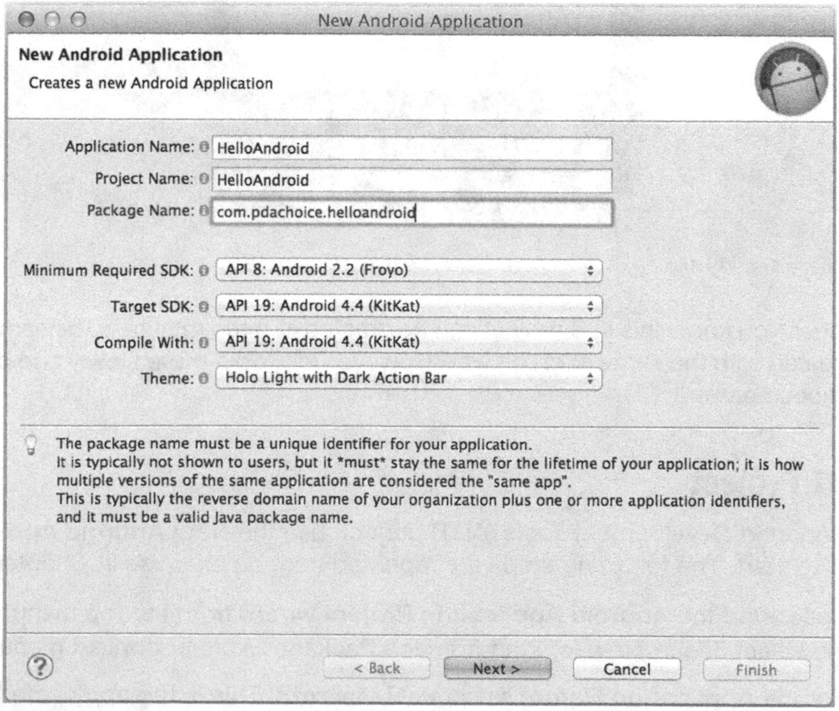

Figure 2-11. New Android app dialog

2. On the next screen, which configures the project, make sure that **Create Activity** is checked and that **Mark this project as a library** is *not* checked. Activity is one of the most frequently used Android app components with a user interface. This app will contain one activity. Leave the rest at the default settings and click **Next** (see Figure 1-12).

3. The next screen will help you create a launcher icon for your app. You can play with it if you like; whatever you do here will probably not break anything. Or, you can just click **Next** (see Figure 1-13).

4. For a barebones Android app, select **Blank Activity** and click **Next**.

5. To keep the project simple, make sure the **Navigation Type** is **none**. The default **Activity Name**, the **Layout Name** and **Fragment Layout Name** are just fine. Leave them as is and click **Finish**.

Note   The layout files are the screen associated with the activity. Similar to an XIB file or a storyboard scene in an iOS app, you call it *layout* in Android.

The barebones project is created and it now appears in the Eclipse workbench. Figure 2-12 depicts a typical Android project directory structure.

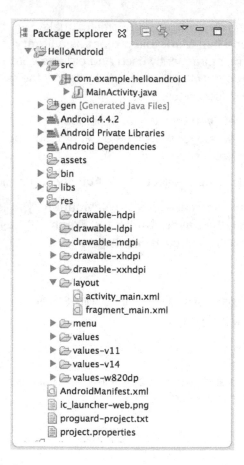

Figure 2-12. *Android project folder structure*

All the project files need to be in the correct folder (as shown in Figure 2-12) as follows:

- $PROJ/src: Java source files. This is where you will find the Java source files, including the implementation of Android application components. For example, you have created an activity called MainActivity.

- $PROJ/libs: Java libraries, or JAR files, go in the folder. Java libraries are just like static libraries used in your Xcode project.

- $PROJ/res: This is where you find all the application resource files, including layout files, strings, image files, and so forth. The folder and subfolder names have significant meanings that cannot be changed; different types of resources are organized in appropriate subfolders.

There is an important file named AndroidManifest.xml. It has to be located in the project root folder. I am going to explain it first because it explicitly discusses many of the Android app basics introduced earlier.

The Application Manifest File

IOS ANALOGY

Information property list file, Info.plist.

The Android system needs to know all the concepts you have read about regarding Android app fundamentals. The Android system gets the information from a file in the application bundle package called the *Android manifest file*. It is a human-readable file in XML format that the developer creates. Each Android app must name this file AndroidManifest.xml and be located in the project root folder. This file explicitly tells the Android system what the app is all about; for example, the application components in it and the attributes of these components, and so forth. Recall that I mentioned you can activate any component in any app by sending the appropriate intent message to the Android system (not to the app directly). This is how the Android system knows how to forward the intent message to the right target: by reading the application manifest file that describes the application's components and the intent matching rules.

AndroidManifest.xml also describes the following important information to the Android system:

- Certain sensitive or security-related API that requires a user's explicit permission; for example, using the Internet or any communication adapters, reading the user's contacts or current location, and so forth.

- A minimal Android API level. This is to avoid your app getting installed on Android devices that cannot execute any of the API used in your app.

- The hardware required by the app, such as a camera, GPS, NFC, SD card, or any other hardware, or the minimum screen resolution you chose for your app, and so forth.

There are many more.

Let's take a close look at the HelloAndroid AndroidManifest.xml, as shown in Listing 2-8.

Listing 2-8. HelloAndroid AndroidManifest.xml

```xml
<?xml version="1.0" encoding="utf-8"?>
<manifest xmlns:android="http://schemas.android.com/apk/res/android"
    package="com.pdachoice.helloandroid"
    android:versionCode="1"
    android:versionName="1.0" >

    <uses-sdk
        android:minSdkVersion="8"
        android:targetSdkVersion="19" />
    <application
        android:allowBackup="true"
        android:icon="@drawable/ic_launcher"
        android:label="@string/app_name"
        android:theme="@style/AppTheme" >
```

```
        <activity
            android:name="com.pdachoice.helloandroid.MainActivity"
            android:label="@string/app_name" >
            <intent-filter>
                <action android:name="android.intent.action.MAIN" />

                <category android:name="android.intent.category.LAUNCHER" />
            </intent-filter>
        </activity>
    </application>

</manifest>
```

The Android manifest file content is written in XML format. Those XML tags and attributes define the intended purposes to the Android system. Pay attention to the following tags, which clearly describe the concepts you have read earlier in this chapter.

- package="com.pdachoice.helloandroid": Earlier I mentioned that each app must have a unique name (see the "Android Application" section). Use this attribute of manifest to define a unique name for your app.

- android:minSdkVersion="8": This attribute of <uses-sdk> defines the minimal Android SDK level required to install the app.

- <activity> ... </activity>: This is how you declare any application component in your app. In the HelloAndroid app, you created one activity and you declared the activity here to let the system know.

- <intent-filter>: Earlier I mentioned that a developer needs to define how application components can be activated by appropriated intent. This tag tells the system how intent can be used to activate this component. For this activity in the HelloAndroid app, the combination of the action and category attributes actually tells the system that this Activity can be launched from the system launch app. More details in Chapter 5.

I can define more in-depth attributes, but you probably don't need to know them all at once. You can look up the syntax and official definitions for the complete XML attributes online from: http://developer.android.com/guide/topics/manifest/manifest-element.html.

Device Debugging

Now I'll demonstrate one of the most important attributes: android:minSdkVersion. You always need to answer an important question in the Android manifest file for almost all Android projects. Recall the Android Virtual Device (AVD) emulator from Chapter 1. How do you feel about the emulator? It's not bad, right? But do you run out of patience waiting for the emulator to come up? AVDs are free and have practical values in Android development because not many developers can buy all the different types of devices needed to certify their apps. Device fragmentation is for sure a bigger problem on Android platforms. (Watch out, iOS is catching up on this issue, too.)

Still, the emulator is a lot slower than using most of the real devices. I highly recommend getting at least one Android device. It is also more convenient and more fun!

To run the HelloAndroid project on your Android device, do the following:

1.   Enable USB debugging on your device (a one-time setup).

    a.   On most devices running Android 3.2 or older, you can find the option under **Settings ➤ Applications ➤ Development**.

    b.   On Android 4.0 and newer, it's in **Settings ➤ Developer options**.

Note   On Android 4.2 and newer, the **Developer options** feature is hidden by default. To make it available, go to **Settings ➤ About phone** and tap **Build number** seven times. Return to the previous screen and you will be able to find **Developer options**.

---

2.   Set up your computer to detect your device. Most of you are developing on Mac OS X since you are already iOS developers, so this should work and you can skip this step.

Note   If you are not developing on Mac OS, please use the online instructions to install the USB driver with appropriate configurations: http://developer.android.com/tools/device.html.

---

3.   Connect your device to your computer's USB port.

4.   The rest of the steps are the same as those in the "Launch the App" section in Chapter 1, except you need to select the run target from the **Android Device Chooser** screen (see Figure 2-13).

    a.   If you see your device on the list, you are lucky to have one of the latest and greatest devices on the market. Choose it to run the app on your device. The screenshot shown in Figure 2-13 shows that I have a *Nexus 4* Android phone connected to my computer.

    b.   I am actually hoping you don't see your device on the list, so I can show you one of the manifest elements, <uses-sdk>, that I mentioned earlier.

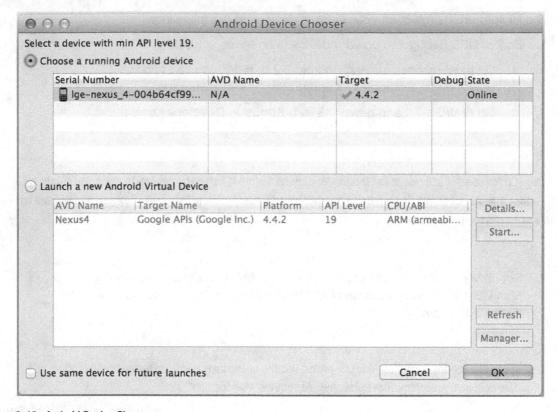

Figure 2-13. Android Device Chooser

5. If your device doesn't meet the required application requirements declared by
    the HelloAndroid project, your device won't appear on the **Android Device
    Chooser**. Only eligible AVDs or devices will appear on the list. Check the
    minSdkVersion attribute in the ADT HelloAndroid manifest file. Same as with the
    Google Play Store, your phone can only see the apps that your device is eligible
    to use. The Android system avoids the apps that cannot run on your device.

> **Note**   Just like an iOS app, you can limit you app runtime target at a certain iOS version. You want to make
> sure that only qualified devices can install your app, rather than letting your apps just crash from runtime on
> nonsupported devices.

6. Check the Android version of your phone. On the device, launch the **Settings**
    app, scroll to the end of the list, and select **About phone**. Figure 2-14 shows an
    Android phone with OS *2.3.6*, which maps to *API Level 10* (see online reference:
    http://developer.android.com/about/dashboards/index.html.

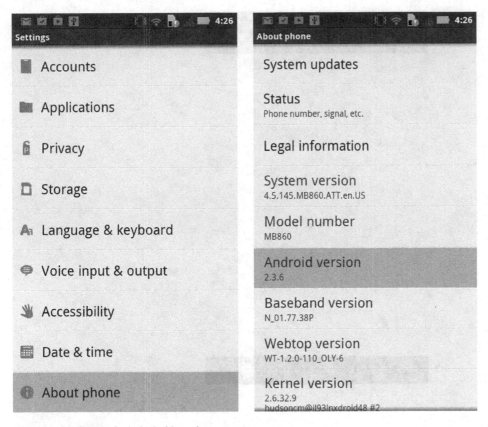

Figure 2-14. The device's Android version

ADT is smart enough to recognize that it is not a legible device for this Android project. One quick fix is to lower the HelloAndroid app requirement by changing it to 8 or below; for example, by changing it to 4 (`android:minSdkVersion="4"`).

Build and relaunch the HelloAndroid project. Android 2.3.6 version supports API 8 or below, and this device will now appear in in the Android Device Chooser. You should see the barebones HelloAndroid app running on the device (see Figure 2-15).

Figure 2-15. HelloAndroid

> **Note**   It doesn't look like the iOS app yet (see Figure 2-10). We will complete the app in Chapter 3.

If you were not able to run the HelloAndroid project on your device, you will not be able to run the LessonOne project for the same reason. Can we do the same thing by changing the following in the LessonOne manifest file?

```
android:minSdkVersion="4"
```

It doesn't even compile!

Remember that the most sophisticated template was chosen for the LessonOne project. That template uses newer APIs that were not available until *API Level 11* was introduced on Honeycomb devices. This is really not a simple issue: either you decide not to use the new features from higher API levels or you choose not to support older platforms. There are constant debates between the number of Android devices you want to support and the features you want for your apps. This is also true for your iOS apps.

You don't use an iOS 7–specific API in your project and expect the app to run on older versions of iOS; for example:

- **Auto Layout** was introduced in iOS 6. Do you want to use this feature for the ease of development? Or do you *not* use it so that you can reach iOS 5 devices?

- **Social Framework** was also introduced in iOS 6. Do you want to use this feature for your app? Or do you not use it, considering there are users still using iOS 5? Or do you write additional code for iOS 5 and below to achieve what essentially the new iOS 6 APIs do?

I have no clear answers for your project because it requires business justifications. You should follow a similar thinking process to make intelligent decisions for your mobile apps, just as you and your business sponsors normally do. Most likely, you have done that for your iOS apps. More or less, similar business and mobile factors apply to your Android apps as well. After you make the business decision, you declare this decision in the application manifest file.

Android publishes and updates device distribution statistics charts frequently, that you can find it on the official Android Developers site: `http://developer.android.com/about/dashboards/index.html`.

Summary

We actually talked about a lot of things on the surface, starting with Java language comparisons to Objective-C. The purpose of these comparisons is not to emphasize the differences, it is just a way to quickly show you that the object-oriented programming concepts actually are very similar — except the syntactical differences that you can clearly identify in side-by-side listings. You still create classes, and send and receive messages to objects by calling the receiver's methods.

The second part of this chapter, Android Application Framework Fundamentals, was actually hard for me to write because these are new concepts to iOS and not easy to comprehend without prior experience. I could have chosen to defer these topics to the end of the book, but I feel it is very important to prepare you for accepting the Android programming mind-set from the beginning. If you don't have questions now, great, you are ready for next step. If you do have questions, this is truly better because that is what every learning journey is all about: find the questions first and find the answers to the questions next.

In Chapter 5 and Chapter 6, we will go over Android application components in more detail, and you will create sample projects yourself. All I wanted to do now is put some general ideas in your head so that when you revisit them, or they come to you, something might ring a bell. For now, as long as you know there is "the Android" way of thinking, you are ready for next chapter.

CHECKPOINT

Does the following sound familiar to you now?

- Java syntax looks different from Objective-C. But many object-oriented programming tasks are similar: create classes and methods, then send messages to the receiver by calling the receiver's methods.

- The Eclipse editor and debugger aren't bad, right? The context menu contains gems everywhere.

- There are four application components. How many can you name?

- The activity component is the application component with a user interface to interact to users, just like iOS apps.

- Android apps contain various application resources, such as strings, images, screens, and so forth.

- Does *alternative resource* ring a bell?

- The Android manifest file tells an Android system what the app is in XML format.

There are more, but I do not expect you to remember them all ☺. We will revisit them.

Part 2

Come Sail Away: A Roadmap for Porting

In Part II, you will receive the porting guidelines and the matching techniques from the start to the end of the Android project. You will plan and structure your Android apps following the same thinking process you normally use with iOS apps. After you finish Part II, you will be able to create simple but meaningful Android apps with rich UI components, and to handle common CRUD operations locally and remotely.

Your migrating-to-Android roadmap is similar to the iOS Getting Started roadmap at a high level, with translation guidelines in lower-level implementation. This Android "getting started" roadmap is customized for iOS developers, which fits with your comfortable iOS thinking process:

1. Create an iOS-like simplified Android storyboard using the counterpart iOS app and storyboard as your Android app wireframe.

2. Detail the Android content views using the counterpart iOS storyboard scenes as your user interface (UI) mockups.

3. For each Android class, continue with the top-down approach to port the Objective-C properties and the signatures of every method from the counterpart Objective-C class. Focus on preserving the method signatures with an empty method body.

4. Fill in the blanks one method at a time. Most of the time, the caller and receivers and "dots" will just connect to each other without any glitch by blindly translating the iOS implementation to Android at the method level.

Part II shows you the common screen navigation patterns that you normally encounter in your iOS apps, and how to carry out the same tasks in Android apps. This is really the key step of the porting process. Not only do you get a draft iOS-like storyboard, it also results in iOS-like MVC structured classes that are mapped to the counterpart Objective-C classes. The rest of the chapters in Part II provide instructions on how to convert the common mobile implementation tasks from iOS SDK to Android SDK—including user interface, saving data, networking, and so forth—that are widely used in almost any iOS app. Again, after completing Part II, you will be capable of creating Android apps that are simple but meaningful.

Chapter 3

Structure Your App

Recall the roadmap for porting iOS apps to Android, which we just talked about in the introduction of Part II. It is the first step in setting the foundation and structure of your Android app. In this software implementation phase, you naturally need to make design decisions on how you'd like to structure your app in terms of organizing your code into classes. In iOS, you naturally break down your iOS GUI app into MVC classes, starting with creating a storyboard prototype using the Xcode storyboard feature. For your porting purposes, you want to follow your iOS thinking process using the same top-down approach: create the iOS-like storyboard first.

In this key step, you are aiming at class-level mappings from iOS counterparts. We will discuss the well-known *model-view-controller* (MVC) concept in Android first, followed by how to create the iOS-like storyboard deliverable in Android. With the guided *screen navigation patterns*, the iOS-like storyboard naturally breaks your Android apps into MVC components that can be mapped to iOS counterparts.

Model-View-Controller in Android

IOS ANALOGY

- **Content view**: A scene in a storyboard file or in an XIB file using Interface Builder. There is no storyboard-like feature in ADT.

- **Content view controller**: UIViewController.

- **Event listener**: In Java, this is much like the delegate object in Objective-C in the well-known event-delegation design pattern, or in the publisher-subscriber design pattern described in the Gang of Four's (GoF) design pattern book.

- **Container view controller**: UINavigationController, UITabbarController, UIPagerController, and so forth.

The iOS model-view-controller (MVC) design pattern specifies that a GUI application consists of a data model, a presentation, and control layers, as shown in Figure 3-1.

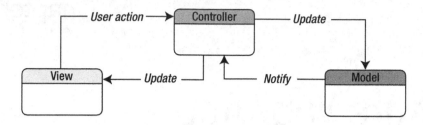

Figure 3-1. MVC

In this discussion, we refer to the view participant as the *content view*, and the controller participants as the *content view controller*. These terminologies are used in iOS documents. However, MVC is a well-known design pattern in many platforms and has been around for a long time. It should also be applicable to Android GUI apps, and you definitely can model your Android apps the same way. And if you do, the effort to translate your iOS app to Android becomes more systematic and straightforward—all the way from higher-level class coding blocks to low-level method coding.

For content view in iOS, you use a storyboard or Interface Builder to create the user interface and to edit properties of UI components. In Android, you use the Eclipse graphical layout editor. When porting iOS apps to Android, I simply use the iOS storyboard as the UI mock-up document for my Android project.

For the content view controller in iOS, you define and instantiate subclasses of the `UIViewController` class to manage the content view, which makes up a portion of your app's user interface. Together with the visual composition editor and framework API, you connect UI components with `IBOutlets` and delegate component events to the `IBAction` implemented in your controller class.

Unless your iOS app only has one screen, you normally deal with another type of controller, called a *container view controller*. You choose a specific container view controller from the iOS SDK to implement the screen navigation patterns for presenting the screens, such as `UINavigationController` and `UITabbarController`, and so forth.

There seems to be no explicit MVC vocabularies defined in the Android MVC framework. However, the Android application architecture and tools implicitly enforce separating content view from content view controller. You can definitely design your Android app using the same MVC design pattern. This is actually a prerequisite for using the iOS-to-Android porting strategy, because we want to get a class-level mapping in place first.

Let's start with content view and content view controller. We will talk about the container view controller next.

In April 2014, the new ADT version 22.6 modified the Create Android Project Blank Activity template, and the template project gives you the preferred iOS-like MVC structure. Your HelloAndroid project is actually mapped to the iOS app fairly well—right out of the box. I used to manually create the structure myself. Now, we only need to go over the HelloAndroid project files to understand the purpose.

Content View

```
                    IOS ANALOGY
```

A scene in a storyboard or an XIB file created using Interface Builder.

A content view provides a visible area in an application so that users can interact with the app. The content view defines how to render itself with contents and can interact with user actions. You use storyboards or Interface Builder to create a content view in iOS.

To create a content view in Android, you need to create an Android layout file by using the *ADT graphical layout editor* or any text editor.

ADT Graphical Layout Editor

```
                    IOS ANALOGY
```

Interface Builder, which creates individual screens in XIB files. Since iOS 5, you can use storyboards in Xcode to create scenes for all the screens and the connections among them. (There is no storyboard-like feature in ADT.)

Android projects maintain each screen in an individual XML file called a *layout file*. All the layout files are located in the `res/layout/` folder or any `res/layout-<qualifier>` folders. The layout file is in a human-readable XML format. You can use any text editor to edit it directly. Similar to Xcode storyboards or Interface Builder, ADT provides the graphical layout editor to facilitate the content view creation visually, without the user memorizing the XML tag/attributes definitions.

Recall the HelloAndroid project created in Chapter 2 (see Figure 2-18); it doesn't look exactly like the counterpart iOS app yet. It only has one content view defined in the `res/layout/fragment_main.xml` file. We still need a button and a text input field. The text label is not at the right location yet. Also, the app needs to do something when users interact with the user interface. Your mission is to modify the existing HelloAndroid app to make it look and behave like the counterpart iOS app (see Figure 2-11).

Let's use the ADT graphical layout editor to finish the user interface in the HelloAndroid project.

> **Note**   The ADT template also creates an activity_main.xml layout file. This file is for the container view controller, the MainActivity. Please ignore it for now.

To modify the content view, `res/layout/fragment_main.xml`, do the following:

1. Double-click the layout file, `HelloAndroid/res/layout/fragment_main.xml`, to open it in the layout editor, which contains the following labeled elements, as shown in Figure 3-2:

    a. **Palette view (A)**: Android UI widgets categorized by type.

    b. **Layout editor (B)**: Graphical layout editor or XML text editor.

    c. **Outline view (C)**: A component containing hierarchy.

    d. **Properties editor (D)**: Allows quick edits for attributes of the UI widget.

    e. **Bottom tabs (E)**: Toggles between graphical layout and XML text-editing modes.

Figure 3-2. Graphical layout editor

2. In iOS, you probably use either springs and struts or AutoLayout. In Android, you choose the appropriate *layout manager*. The layout manager definitely can do more than iOS counterparts, and deserves its own coverage (see Chapter 4). For now, let's keep the RelativeLayout for a quick transition from iOS to Android. It is actually the closest match to iOS AutoLayout.

3. Reposition the existing "Hello World!" label by dragging it to the desired location.

Tip In Eclipse, observe the hover hints and alignment line indicator while you drag widgets over the layout. Each Eclipse view or editor has a tab on top. Double-click the tab title to get a full view.

---

4. Click to expand the **Text Fields** category in **Palette** view (see Figure 3-3), which reveals the available text fields. For our HelloAndroid requirement, let's drag the **Text Field** of the **Plain Text** type (the first one) and position it in the desired location.

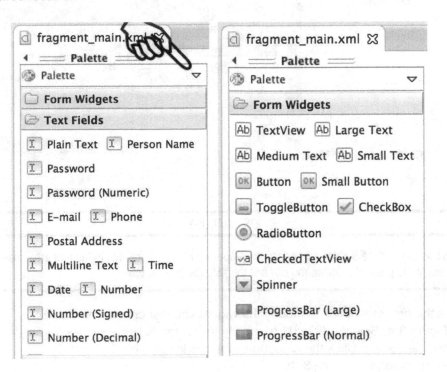

Figure 3-3. Pallet view

Tip In Eclipse, you can switch the style of the palette view using the upper-right upside-down triangle selector.

---

5. To create a button, expand the **Form Widgets** category, and then drag **Button** and drop it onto the desired location on the form.

6. You can rearrange the widgets as many times as you like. The positions of three widgets should look like they do in Figure 3-4, which shows the layout editor and the outline view.

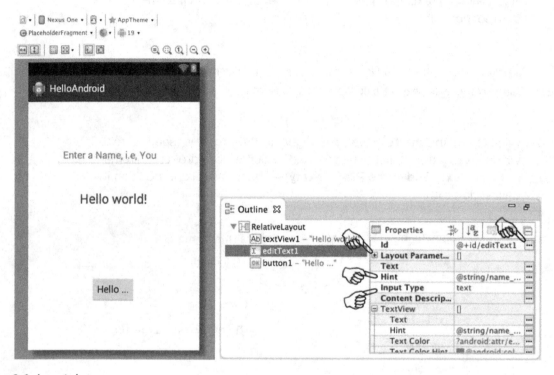

Figure 3-4. *Layout views*

7. Use the property editor to modify the widget you just created as shown in Figure 3-4. Select **editText1** to modify the widget's Id properties in the properties editor. Click the **...** button, which is located on the right (see the pointer in Figure 3-4).

   a. In the **Rename Resource** screen, enter `editTextName` in the **New Name** field (see Figure 3-5).

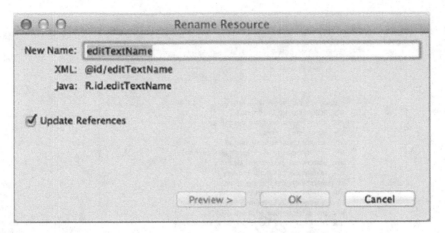

Figure 3-5. Rename Resource

> **Note**   The user interface is stored in XML files, which is an important Android resource. Hard-coded values in any source file are discouraged. In this case, the widget names should really be constant. The preceding editor converts the literal to a constant value in the gen/packagename/R.java file. From Java code, you can make references to any UI widget using constant defines instead of the string literal.

8. Continue to modify Layout Parameters of the EditText. Click the + (plus) icon to the left (see the pointer in Figure 3-4) to expand the Layout Parameters group. You don't need to change anything now. I just wanted you to glance through the attributes related to how the widgets are positioned.

9. Continue to modify the Hint property. Click the **...** button, which is located on the right. The Resource Chooser screen appears, as shown in Figure 3-6.

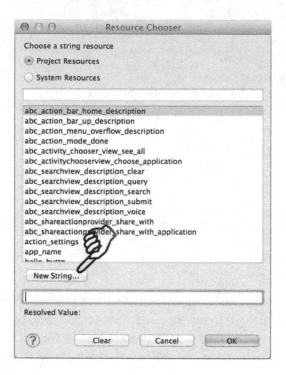

Figure 3-6. Resource Chooser

IOS ANALOGY

It is called a *placeholder* in the UITextField.

---

a. Select **Project Resources**. Click the **New String...** button.

b. Enter the following values in the **Create New Android String** screen (see Figure 3-7):

- Enter **Enter a Name, i.e., You** in the **String** field.

- Enter **name_hint** in the **New R.string.** field.

- Click **OK** when done. This creates an Android string resource: "Enter a Name, i.e., You".

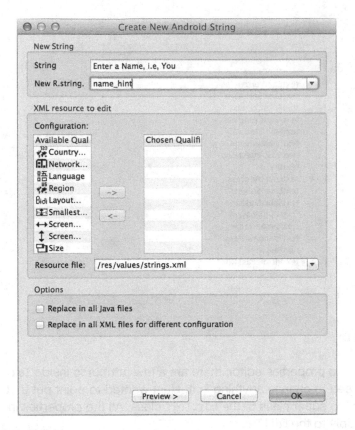

Figure 3-7. Create a New Android String

> **Note**   A string is an application resource. It should not be hard-coded in any source files. The string resources are placed in the res/values/strings.xml file. It is a text file and you can edit it directly, or use an editor. In your Java code, you use the Android framework API to retrieve string resources.

IOS ANALOGY

iOS strings are localized in localizable.strings files.

10. Continue to modify the Input Type property of the EditText. Click the ... button.

   a. The Select Flag Values screen appears, as shown in Figure 3-8. Select **text** and click OK.

Figure 3-8. Select Flag Values

11. Continue in the properties editor, there are a few attributes inside TextView; you don't need to change anything in it. I just wanted to point out that TextView is the super class of the EditText class. All the properties in TextView apply to the EditText.

12. Further down the properties editor, take a look at the **View** group. You don't need to change anything in it. I just wanted to point out that View is the super class of all user-interface widget classes, including the EditText widget. EditText inherits the properties in the View class.

Tip In Eclipse, observe how the mouse hovers on any of the properties.

---

13. To modify the textView1 TextView widget, select **textView1** first and modify its properties in the property editor as you did above:

   a. To modify the Id, click the **...** button. Use Rename Resource (see Figure 3-5) to assign a New Name: **textViewHelloName**.

14. Update the Text Size of the TextView. Go to **TextView ➤ Text Size**. Click the **...** button to use the Resource Chooser (see Figure 3-9) to create and assign a New Dimension, as follows:

   a. Click the **New Dimension...** button.

   b. Enter **hello_name_textsize** in the **Name** field.

c. Enter **24sp** in the **Value** field.

d. Click **OK** when you are done.

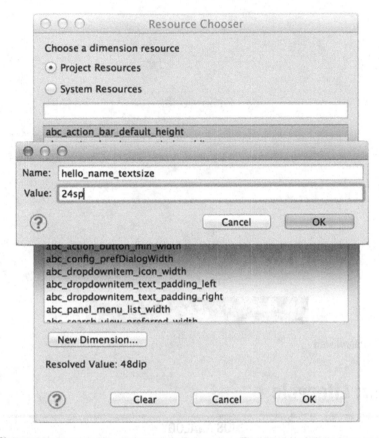

Figure 3-9. Resource Chooser

15. Similarly, select **button1** to modify the **Id** property in the property editor. Click the **...** button to use Rename Resource dialog (see Figure 3-6) to assign a New Name: **buttonHello**.

16. To modify the button text, go to **TextView ➤ Text**. Click the **...** button to use the Resource Chooser dialog to assign a New String, as follows:

a. Click the **New String...** button.

b. Enter **Hello ...** in the **String** field.

c. Enter **hello_button** in the **New R.string.** field.

d. Click **OK** when you are done.

You have completed the content view in an Android layout for your HelloAndroid project. You may build and launch the HelloAndroid app. The app should look similar to the layout file, as shown in Figure 3-10.

Figure 3-10. HelloAndroid content view

View Controller: Lifecycle

IOS ANALOGY

- UIViewController
- viewDidLoad:
- viewWillAppear:
- viewDidAppear:
- viewWillDisappear:
- viewDidDisappear:
- viewDidUnload:

Similar to the iOS `UIViewController` class, lifecycle callbacks notify the states of the view controller when content view is being rendered. There are certain tasks that need to be performed in certain states to make sure the content view is rendered smoothly. This applies to both iOS and Android. In my opinion, the Android lifecycle concept is not a beginner topic but is easy for iOS developers to pick up because the purpose is the same: you want to perform certain computing tasks at the right lifecycle.

Activity Lifecycle

Both iOS and Android go through a series of lifecycle events when content view is being rendered. When an Android activity is activated, it potentially goes through an *activity lifecycle* and the activity is notified of this change in state through the activity's *lifecycle callback methods*. In iOS, these lifecycle events are directly related to the controller's content view states. In Android, the lifecycle events are described as the states of the activity (view controller) itself. More specifically, the activity lifecycle events are triggered when the Android system is creating it, stopping it, resuming it, or destroying it, and so forth. These callbacks provide developers the right timing to perform specific tasks that are appropriate to the state changes.

There is no need to try to match these events directly from Android to iOS. The concept appears the same: view controller or content view goes through a series of lifecycle events, and you want your code to be executed at the right time to ensure a smooth GUI-rendering process.

I find that the diagram shown in Figure 3-11, which is from the official Android Developers site (`http://developer.android.com/training/basics/activity-lifecycle/starting.html`), is very useful. I have it stuck on my wall so that I can reference it without having to memorize it.

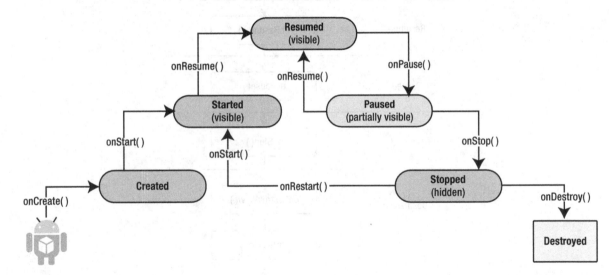

Figure 3-11. Activity lifecycle

Implementing these activity lifecycle events is essentially the same as writing your iOS `UIViewController` lifecycle callback methods: you create the subclasses of activity and choose to override these system methods to receive timely callbacks. You don't have to provide implementations for all of these lifecycle events, but you do need to implement certain common user interface tasks in the right callback to ensure that the user interface is rendered smoothly.

Fragment Lifecycle

Similar to an activity, a fragment has its own lifecycle states and callbacks during the state transitions. Managing the lifecycle of a fragment is a lot like managing the lifecycle of an activity. You can think of a fragment just like the subactivities of its parent activity. Figure 3-12 depicts the lifecycle of a fragment, and the callbacks to the active fragment in its parent activity.

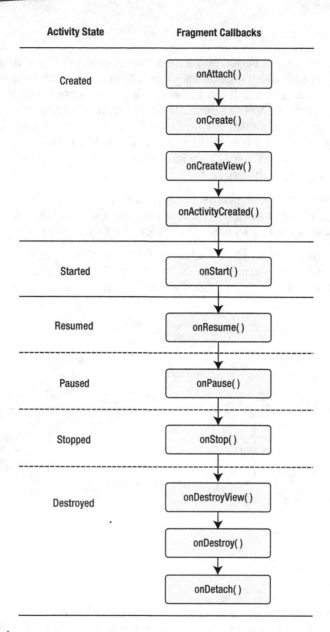

Figure 3-12. Fragment lifecycle

You choose to provide implementation when you want to receive the lifecycle callbacks. However, more likely, you will implement the following lifecycle methods for its intended purpose.

onCreate()

The system calls the onCreate() method when creating the fragment. Normally, you should initialize essential components of the fragment that you want to retain when the fragment is paused or stopped, and then resumed.

onCreateView()

```
                              IOS ANALOGY
```

I normally translate the code in viewDidLoad() onto Fragment.onCreateView(…).

The system calls the onCreateView() method when it's time for the fragment to draw its user interface for the first time. To draw a UI for your fragment, you must return a layout, or content view, of this fragment.

onResume()

```
                              IOS ANALOGY
```

viewDidAppear()

The system calls the onResume() method every time the layout becomes visible. Generally, you can safely translate the iOS code in viewDidAppear() into this method.

onPause()

```
                              IOS ANALOGY
```

viewWillDisappear()

The system calls the onPause() method when the content view is about to become not visible, for example, leaving for another layout. This is usually where you should commit any changes that should be persisted beyond the current user session (because the user might not come back).

onStop()

```
                              IOS ANALOGY
```

viewDidDisappear()

The system calls the onStop() method when the content view is not visible.

Again, just like iOS UIViewController, you don't have to provide all the lifecycle callbacks. When you do, make sure you call super() to inherit the implementation from the super class.

The XML layout file introduced in the "ADT Graphical Layout Editor" section of this chapter is essentially the content view participant in the MVC design pattern. The view controller in MVC needs to know its own content view and has a practical need to keep references to the UI widgets in content view in order to update or respond to them. We will talk about the linkage next.

Content View Controller: Fragment

IOS ANALOGY

UIViewController

Recall that in the MVC design pattern, the view controller manages the content view that makes up the user interface. The view controller also responds to component events triggered by user actions.

In earlier Android years, before API 10, you needed to create one activity for each screen. I always felt that this became too heavy for multiple screen apps, because an activity is also an Android application component that is more than the UIViewController in iOS. If we follow this pattern, we end up having a lot of application components in one app. I did not like it. I must not have been the only person who disliked this because a new Fragment class became available in the API Level 11 platform.

A fragment represents a behavior or a portion of user interface in an activity. Just like an activity, a fragment manages its own content view (a layout file), which users can interact with to perform a task. You can combine multiple fragments in a single activity to build a GUI application with a multipane/multiscreen user interface.

I heavily use Fragment as my view controller in my Android mobile apps. Ever since it became available, it has been my first choice for translating an iOS UIViewController. I have also changed my design style by using fewer activities. In most cases, my Activity simply serves as a top-level coordinator/container controller that glues my Fragment view controller and everything else together.

My design decision was probably more of a way in which I could apply my iOS-thinking process to the Android platform for porting purposes. It did not originate from pure Android programming principles during my early Android programming years. However, the most recent ADT version (April 2014 as of this writing) actually updated the Create Android Project Blank Activity template to use the Fragment class—even for a single-screen app like your HelloAndroid project! This makes me really confident that my iOS-to-Android porting strategy is really not only for my porting purposes. Using Fragment as the content view controller is also now a good Android thinking process.

The Fragment class comes with the Create Android Project Blank Activity template inside MainActivity.java; it is called PlaceholderFragment. It is a Java *inner class*, but it is still a Java class.

> **Note**   A Java inner class is a class-defined inside another Java class. We will talk about it later.

Let's exam the PlaceholderFragment class and step through the essential fragment tasks.

Pair with Content View

IOS ANALOGY

For scenes in a storyboard, you use the identity inspector to assign the custom UIViewController class.

One of the most important fragment tasks is to pair it with its content view, the layout file. In the HelloAndroid app, to pair the content view (res/layout/fragment_main.xml) with the content view controller (PlaceholderFragment), Listing 3-1 depicts how to establish the content view–to–content view controller relationship in the PlaceholderFragment.onCreateView(...) lifecycle callback:

> **Note** The code comes with the Blank Activity template; you don't need to modify it. I just wanted to show it to you.

1. Almost always implement the onCreateView(...) fragment lifecycle callback method to establish the linkage to the content view layout file, with the exception of the subclass of ListFragment that already pairs with a ListView in the super class ListFragment.onCreateView(...) under the hood.

2. To reference the content view—the fragment_main.xml layout file—use the R.layout.fragment_main constant to define it.

> **Note** ADT generates an R.id.fragment_main Java constant by the file name of the layout file.

3. Use an inflater to create a content view object from the layout file and return the view object.

> **Note** LayoutInflater is a system utility class that converts an XML layout file to a Java object.

Listing 3-1. Fragment.onCreateView(...)

```java
public class MainActivity extends ActionBarActivity {
  ...
  /**
   * A placeholder fragment containing a simple view.
   */
  public static class PlaceholderFragment extends Fragment implements {

    public PlaceholderFragment() {
    }
```

```
    @Override
    public View onCreateView(LayoutInflater inflater, ViewGroup container,
                            Bundle savedInstanceState) {
      View rootView = inflater.inflate(R.layout.fragment_main, container, false);
      return rootView;
    }
  }
}
```

> **Note**   A fragment lives inside an activity. Please ignore the activity-fragment linkage code for now. We will detail the relationship between an activity container view controller and a fragment content view controller when I discuss screen navigation patterns. For now, let's just focus on how to establish the linkage between a layout content view and a fragment view controller.

Interact with Widgets in Content View

To interact with users or convey information to your users, you normally write code, as follows:

1. Frequently, you need to create Java fields to keep object references to the UI widgets so that you can update the widget attributes, like the look and feel or rendering the information.

IOS ANALOGY

IBOutlet

---

a. In the res/layout/fragment_main.xml, you have assigned an id to all three widgets, such as android:id="@+id/textViewHelloName". To obtain the Java object references to these UI widgets, use R.id.textViewHelloName.

> **Note**   ADT automatically creates Java static constants that reference to @+id/xxx in layout files. In Java code, use R.id.xxx to reference the UI widget.

b. Use View.findViewById(...) to find the child view element and keep the object references as Java fields, as shown in Listing 3-2.

Listing 3-2. Reference to View Widgets

```
/**
 * A placeholder fragment containing a simple view.
 */
public static class PlaceholderFragment extends Fragment {
// Java fields
private Button buttonHello;
private EditText editTextName;
private TextView textViewHelloName;

public PlaceholderFragment() {
}

@Override
public View onCreateView(LayoutInflater inflater, ViewGroup container,
                         Bundle savedInstanceState) {
  View rootView = inflater.inflate(R.layout.fragment_main, container, false);

  buttonHello = (Button) rootView.findViewById(R.id.buttonHello);
  editTextName = (EditText) rootView.findViewById(R.id.editTextName);
  textViewHelloName =
      (TextView) rootView.findViewById(R.id.textViewHelloName);

  return rootView;
 }
}
...
```

2. To interact with widget controls, implement the traditional event-delegation pattern, or the so-called *event listener* in Java vocabulary.

IOS ANALOGY

```
UIControl addTarget:self
action:@selector(onClick:)forControlEvents:UIControlEventTouchUpInside];
```

Or use IBAction in a storyboard scene.

---

3. Declare the Fragment class to implement OnClickListener. A target object must implement the component event listener interface—a.k.a. *delegate protocol* in Objective-C. Listing 3-3 simply gets the user input from the editTextName widget and assigns it to the textViewHelloName widget.

IOS ANALOGY

Many iOS widgets use a delegate property that handles the delegate protocol, such as UIAlertView, UIWebView, UITableViewController, and so forth.

Listing 3-3. Declare and Implement onClickListener

```java
public static class PlaceholderFragment extends Fragment implements OnClickListener {
  ...
  @Override
  public void onClick(View v) {
    String name = editTextName.getText().toString();
    textViewHelloName.setText("Hello, " + name);
  }
}
...
```

Note   You will need to add import statements; just do autoimport: Shift+command+o.

4. Designate the component action delegate. You normally say *set* or *register* the event listener in Java vocabulary, as shown in Listing 3-4.

Listing 3-4. set onClickListener

```java
public static class PlaceholderFragment extends Fragment implements OnClickListener {
  ...
  @Override
  public View onCreateView(LayoutInflater inflater, ViewGroup container,
                           Bundle savedInstanceState) {
    ...
    buttonHello.setOnClickListener(this);
    ...
  }
  ...
```

5. I rarely experience zero compilation errors on the first try. Chances are, you have some compilation errors and you will need to fix them. But, in case you have had no problems so far, let's seed a problem on purpose so that you can see how ADT shows errors. A typo will do it. You will see errors noted with red marks, and warnings with yellow marks. They are listed in the **Problems** view, as shown in Figure 3-13.

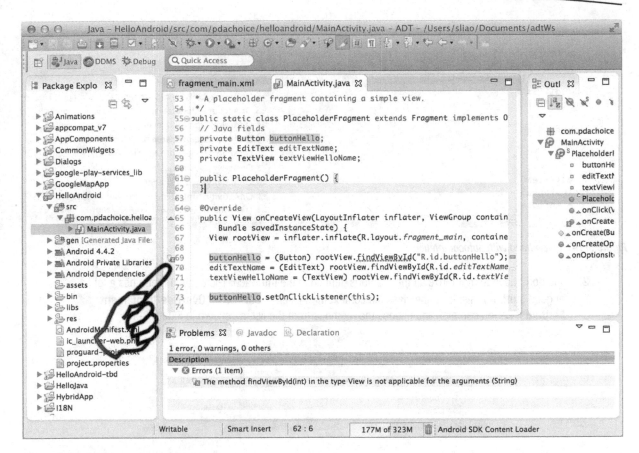

Figure 3-13. Problems view

> **Tip**   In Eclipse, if you cannot find the Problems view, you can always open any view from the menubar by selecting **Window ➤ Show View ➤ Other…**. Double-clicking the line item in the Problems view will bring you to the exact error. There is also a Quick Fix option in the problem item context menu.

ECLIPSE EXERCISES

1. Most of the widgets listeners are inner interfaces in the View class and are named as OnXxx conventionally. Try this: type **View.On** followed by Ctrl+<space>. The Eclipse autocompletion feature shows a list of interfaces that you can choose from (see Figure 3-14).

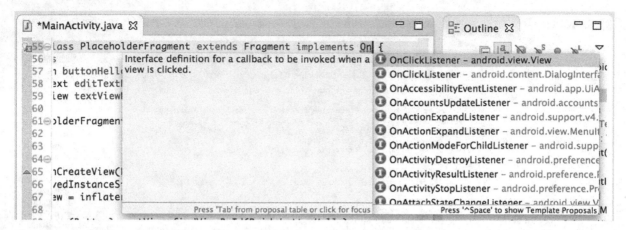

Figure 3-14. Type-ahead with autocompletion

2. You don't have to memorize all the methods defined in the interface. The context menu has a lot of good stuff. Try this: from the class file context menu, select **Source ➤ Override/Implement Methods…**. You can pick and choose the methods from the list, as shown in Figure 3-15.

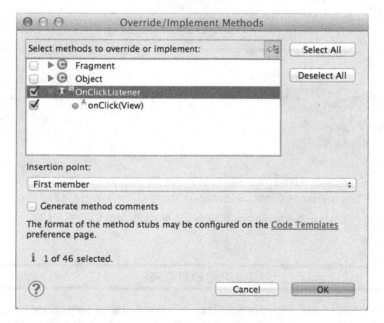

Figure 3-15. Override/Implement Methods

3. An error can actually be your friend: instead of remembering the interface method, or doing the previous step, you can choose not to do anything and get an error first. By clicking the red mark, the Java editor might give you suggestions. In this case, simply select **Add unimplemented methods** and let the IDE supply the method skeletons (see Figure 3-16).

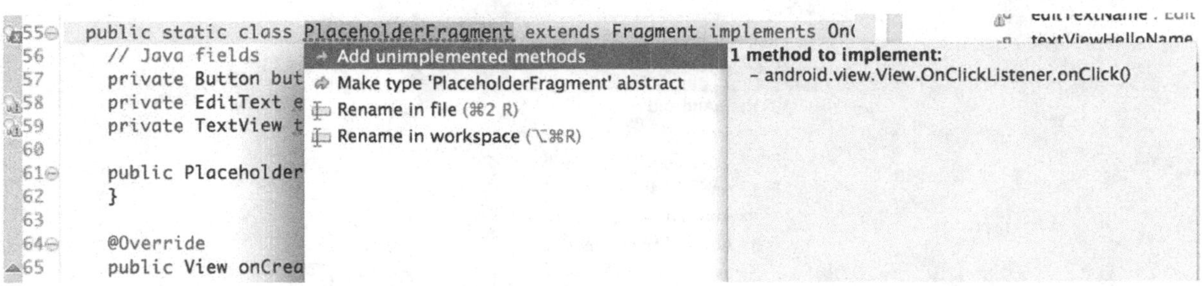

```
 55⊖    public static class PlaceholderFragment extends Fragment implements On(
 56         // Java fields      → Add unimplemented methods          1 method to implement:
 57         private Button but  ⟳ Make type 'PlaceholderFragment' abstract   – android.view.View.OnClickListener.onClick()
 58         private EditText e   ⫴⬚ Rename in file (⌘2 R)
 59         private TextView t   ⫴⬚ Rename in workspace (⌥⌘R)
 60
 61⊖       public Placeholder
 62       }
 63
 64⊖       @Override
 65        public View onCrea
```

Figure 3-16. Add unimplemented methods

Backward-Compatibility Using the Android Support Library

Fragment and many new framework classes were introduced in Android 3.0, API Level 11. The problem is there are still older devices prior to API Level 11 that do not get the system OS upgrade. In other words, if you create Android apps using these new classes, the app won't be available for older devices with an API prior to Level 11, including the Gingerbread devices, which are still in the majority as of this writing.

The *Android Support Library* comes to the rescue. It allows you to use some of the recent Android APIs in your app while running on earlier versions of Android. For instance, the Support Library provides a version of the Fragment APIs that you can use on Android 1.6 (API Level 4) and higher. Practically speaking, you can probably just ignore Android 1.5 and older. They currently account for only 0.1% of the total market. And this 0.1% of devices probably just consists of people's spare backup phones anyway. ☺

This used to be an important programming task that developers would need to manually import, and then they would manually configure the project. If you have the new ADT installed from the all-in-one bundle, or you have updated your old ADT plugin since April 2014, your Android projects created from ADT templates are all set for using the Support Libraries, including your HelloAndroid project. If you see appcompat_v7 in your workspace and you are wondering how it got there, it is because the ADT Create Android Project templates automatically imports the Support Library project and configures your project to use it—and you are all set to use the Support Library (see Figure 3-17).

Figure 3-17. Support Libraries

Still, it is a very important concept that I wanted to show you. You may choose to come back later, or at least glance through it just to put a seed in your head for now.

Currently, there are three versions of Support Libraries—v4, v7, and v13—that are designed for compatibility support for API levels 4, 7 and 13, respectfully.

The v4 Support Library is simply a static JAR file. In my opinion, Fragment is the most important class in v4 library. Without it, you can only use fragments for devices with API Level 11 or greater. To use the fragment from the v4 Support Library, all you need to do is put the android-support-v4.jar in your PROJ/libs/ folder and simply use it in your code. This backported Fragment class can run on older devices as low as API Level 4.

```
import android.support.v4.app.Fragment;
```

v7 is more than a JAR file, it is an Android Library project that can be used by other Android projects. It is more than just Java classes—it is the whole Android project, including the Java classes and the application resources that allow you to have the new widgets running on older devices as low as API 7.

> **Note** This detailed ADT project setup and the configuration steps are primarily for those who are using an older ADT, because you may need to set it up yourself using the Support Library. Since April 2014, the newer Create Android Project template automatically sets up the Support Library for you.

Let's say that you have an Android project and you want to port it for older devices using the v4 Support Library (for example, to take advantage of the fragment usage). The easiest way to do this is to update your current ADT plugin. You may need to manually download the v4 Support Library and set up the build path for your ADT project, as follows:

> **Note** Perhaps you should just install the new ADT bundled package, just as you do when you get a new Xcode update (see Chapter 1). It is a very rare reason why you would still want to use an outdated ADT.

1. Download the Android Support package using the **Android SDK Manager**. From the top menubar, select **Windows ➤ Android SDK Manager** (see Figure 3-18).

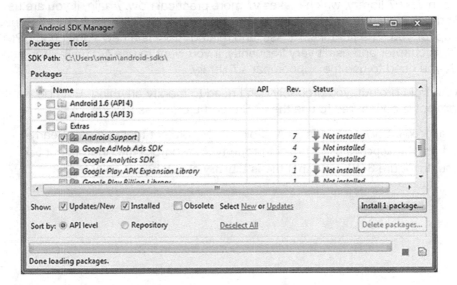

Figure 3-18. Download the Android Support Library

2. The Android Support package is installed in the `<sdk>/extras/android/support/` folder that contains v4, v7, and v13 in the v4, v7, and v13 subfolders, respectfully.

3. In ADT, create the `$PROJ/libs/` folder from the project context menu and select **New ➤ Folder**.

4. Select the parent folder. You want to select the project root folder, such as HelloAndroid.

5. Enter **libs** as the **Folder** name.

6. Drag and drop `<sdk>/extras/android/support/v4/android-support-v4.jar` from the Finder into the previous Eclipse project folder, `$PROJ/libs/`.

7. Add the `android-support-v4.jar` JAR file to the project build path. From the JAR file context menu, select **Build Path ➤ Add to Build Path**.

8. To use classes from the Support Library, import the classes from the Support Library namespace: `android.support.v4`. For example: `import android.support.v4.app.Fragment;`.

9. The preceding `Fragment` class is backward-compatible up to the Android API Level 4 platform. Otherwise, if your app doesn't need to run on older platforms, import the `Fragment` class from `import android.app.Fragment;`.

The v7 Support Library is more useful, but it is only backward-compatible with API Level 7. However, because the number of v4 devices in the market is decreasing dramatically, consider the richer features ported in the v7 library, which makes v7 more practical now. Again, if you are using the new ADT Create Android Project template, such as with the HelloAndroid project, the v7 Support Library is already set up for you. The `ActionBar` class (and related APIs) is a new addition in API 11; you will see it soon in this chapter and use it very frequently. If you want to use `ActionBar` for devices as low as API Level 7, you need to use the appcompat_v7 library.

For your HelloAndroid project, you probably don't need to modify anything. But I do want to show you how the project is configured to use the v7 Support Library, as follows:

1. The `appcompat_v7` project is an Android Library project that you can clearly see from the `appcompat_v7` project property screen from the Android context menu. In Figure 3-19, note that the **Is Library** check box is selected.

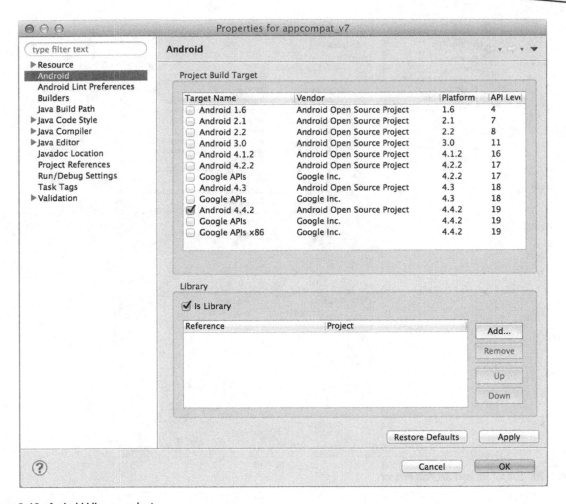

Figure 3-19. *Android Library project*

2. The HelloAndroid project is using the appcompat_v7 android project that you can see from the HelloAndroid project property screen (see Figure 3-20) at context menu ➤ Android. The appcompat_v7 Android library project is in the Library list.

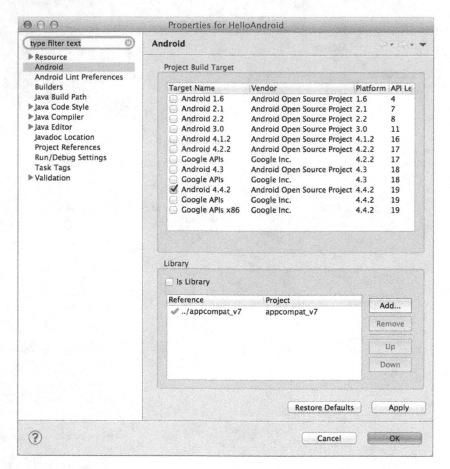

Figure 3-20. Use v7 Support Android Project

By the way, you can make your ADT project an Android Library—just select **Is Library**. The layout, images, and any application resources, as well as the Java classes, in your Android project become reusable to other Android projects.

Container View Controller: Activity

IOS ANALOGY

Container view controller, i.e., UINavigation Controller

Previously, you have seen the `PlaceholderFragment` class that pairs with its own content view. From a user interface perspective, a fragment is considered to be a child of the activity that presents a content view. Just like the iOS container view controller, the parent activity is responsible for managing its child fragment. Take a look at Listing 3-5, which comes with the Create Android Project template.

Listing 3-5. MainActivity Manages Child Fragment

```java
public class MainActivity extends ActionBarActivity {

  @Override
  protected void onCreate(Bundle savedInstanceState) {
    super.onCreate(savedInstanceState);
    setContentView(R.layout.activity_main);

    if (savedInstanceState == null) {
      getSupportFragmentManager().beginTransaction().
        add(R.id.container, new PlaceholderFragment()).commit();
    }
  }
}
...
```

Listing 3-5 does the following:

1. In the onCreate(...) lifecycle callback, the MainActivity pairs with its content view, activity_main.xml (see Listing 3-6). The activity layout is an empty screen; its root element, FrameLayout, has no widget in it. This is on purpose because the content of the FrameLayout will come from the child fragment's content view in the runtime.

   Listing 3-6. An Empty FrameLayout

   ```xml
   <FrameLayoutxmlns:android="http://schemas.android.com/apk/res/android"
     xmlns:tools="http://schemas.android.com/tools"
     android:id="@+id/container"
     android:layout_width="match_parent"
     android:layout_height="match_parent"
     tools:context="com.pdachoice.helloandroid.MainActivity"
     tools:ignore="MergeRootFrame" />
   ```

2. The rest of the code in onCreate(...) simply uses FragmentManager to push the fragment transaction to a stack called the *back stack*, and the content view of the fragment is placed into the preceding FrameLayout, referenced by R.id.container.

Without getting into the FragmentManager API definition right now, the concept is actually very easy to understand. It is just like iOS UINavigationController, which has a UIView that you probably rarely need to use directly. If you want to display a content view from a specific child UIViewController, you push the child UIViewController to the navigation stack. To go back to the previous screen, just do a pop, or the Back button in the navigation bar will do the pop for you. This is exactly what the onCreate(...) method does.

The code from the ADT template gives us all the MVC elements we need, which is good enough for you to see the container view controller concept right now. We are going to refactor it to make the iOS-to-Android mapping more trivial. The container view controller is a key to the success of the porting journey: screen navigation patterns. Later, we will resume the topics of practical usages and detailed mapping guidelines.

ADT LOGGING

Previously, the code in the HelloAndroid project mostly came from the ADT template. You will need to write more code, and it is time to learn logging in ADT because logging is a very important task for any programmer. I always want to set up the logging environment and have my logging code in place in the very early stages of the coding phase. Proper logging eases the pain of troubleshooting. It is actually part of the programming fun. ☺

ADT and Eclipse make logging fairly easy. Crash data and exceptions are collected by an ADT utility called, **LogCat**. Logs from various Android apps and systems can be viewed together or be filtered. You can use shell commands to view the log output, or in the Eclipse workbench, you can simply use LogCat view to view or filter the logs.

Let's go over the LogCat view in Eclipse.

1. Launch the HelloAndroid project. From the context menu, select **Run As ➤ Android Application**.

2. The HelloWorld app should be running on the Android emulator or your physical device.

3. Select **DDMS** on the perspective toolbar to switch to the DDMS perspective that contains the LogCat view by default, as shown in Figure 3-21.

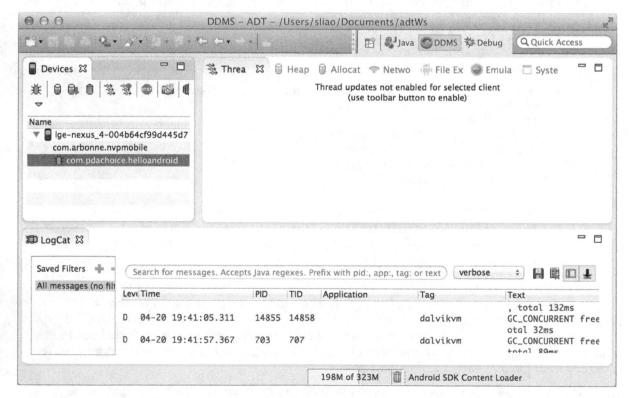

Figure 3-21. DDMS perspective

> **Tip**   In Eclipse, use Show the View dialog whenever you want to open any view manually; for example, if you don't see the LogCat view, from the top menubar, select **Window ➤ Show View ➤ Other** . . . .

4. For easier viewing, you may double-click the **LogCat** tab to enable a full screen view in the workbench (see Figure 3-22). The LogCat view contains the following:

   - **Command toolbar**: Features Save Log, Clear Log, Toggle Saved Filters view, and the Toggle Scroll Lock (from left to right).

   - **Live-search filter**: This is in the Text column.

   - **Log level**: **V**erbose, **D**ebug, **I**nfo, **W**arn, **E**rror, and **A**ssert.

   - **Saved Filters view**: You can create or delete saved filters. There are two default filters—**All** and **Attached process**.

   - **Primary view**: Shows the Log records.

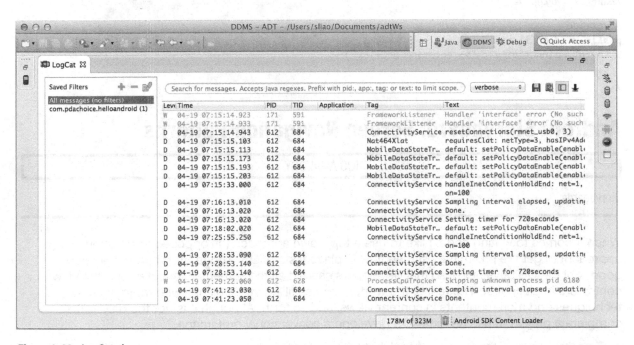

Figure 3-22. LogCat view

5. Select the **Clear Log** button to clear log records from view so you can easily see the ongoing logs without scrolling up and down. Crash data or uncaught exceptions are automatically sent to LogCat view.

6. To write code to generate logs, simply use the android.util.Log class, which has the following methods:

    - Log.v(…) // verbose

    - Log.d(…) // debug

    - Log.w(…) // warning

    - Log.e(…) // error

IOS ANALOGY

NSLog(…)

Try Listing 3-7 to see the simple log entry shown in LogCat view.

Listing 3-7. log.d(…)

```
@Override
public void onClick(View v) {
  Log.d("MainActivity", ">> entering onClick");
  ...
}
```

Android Storyboard: Screen Navigation Patterns

IOS ANALOGY

Storyboards.

When it comes to writing code, I like to use a top-down approach (as opposed to a bottom-up approach) to get the preliminary screen flow in place first. In iOS, Xcode Storyboard is a really good tool for iOS developers so that developers can get all the screens connected and the view controllers in place first. The rest of the work becomes filling in the blanks with more detailed techniques and more contents in content views, and so forth. Although it is not the only way to complete a project, it has become iOS developers conventional preference.

ADT doesn't have a storyboard-like tool, but I still do the top-down approach using repeatable patterns and conventions that I have developed over the years. Considering the smaller screen size relative to desktop or web apps, it is even more crucial to use well-known navigation patterns to make mobile apps more predictable. A consistent and predictable navigation pattern guides users to complete a task with multiple screens. Efficient navigation is one of the cornerstones of a well-designed app.

We will focus on the most common screen navigation patterns supported in both iOS and Android. All the content views used in these projects are intended to be simple, because they are not the primary objectives. To create more beautiful and meaningful content views, we definitely need to look into view and layout topics (see Chapter 4). For now, simply use the layout editor as much as possible and temporarily hold your questions about the layout file's XML syntax rules.

Navigation Stack

```
IOS ANALOGY
```

UINavigationController

The *navigation stack* is widely used to manage screen transitions, and particularly for displaying information hierarchy, such as a master drilldown list. To show the next screen, you push the next view controller into the navigation stack. To go back to the previous screen, you pop out the previous view controller in the navigation stack.

In iOS, you use `UINavigationController` to push and pop the child `UIViewController`. A Back button is provided on the navigation bar.

Let's create an Android version of the following simple iOS app with the default navigation bar, as shown in Figure 3-23.

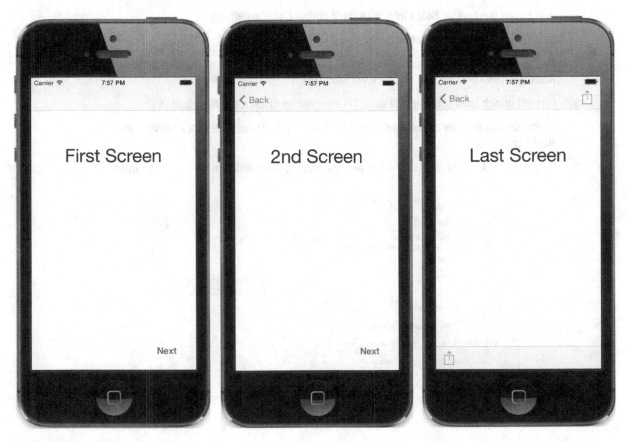

Figure 3-23. iOS navigation stack

ADT PROJECT PREPARATION

To create a new ADT project using the New Android Application Blank Activity template (for more information about this template see the "Create an Android Project Using the Template" section in Chapter 1), do the following:

1. Open **New Android Application** from the top menubar and select **File ➤ New ➤ Android Application Project** (see Figure 1-10). Enter the following values:

    a. Enter the Application Name: **NavigationStack**.

    b. Enter the Project Name: **NavigationStack**.

    c. Enter the Package Name: **com.pdachoice.navigationstack**.

    d. Select Minimum Required SDK: **API 8** (the default).

    e. Select Target SDK: **API 19** (the default).

    f. Select Compile With: **API 19** (default to the latest).

    g. Select the Theme: **Holo Light with Dark Action Bar** (the default).

    h. Click the **Next** button when done.

2. On the **Configure Project** screen (see Figure 1-12 in Chapter 1), accept all the default values (**Create Activity** should be selected) and click the **Next** button.

3. On the **Launch Icon** screen (see Figure 1-13 in Chapter 1), click the **Next** button.

4. On the **Create Activity** screen (see Figure 1-14 in Chapter 1), select **Blank Activity** and click the **Next** button.

5. On the **Blank Activity** screen (see Figure 3-24), accept the default values and click **Finish**.

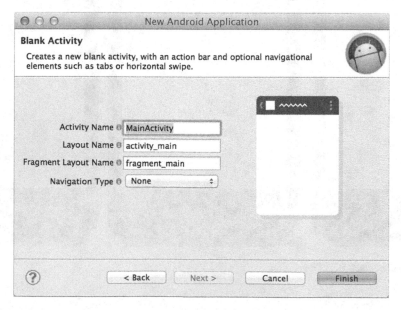

Figure 3-24. Blank Activity

The newly created NavigationStack project should have no errors. Nothing is new: it contains a very simple MainActivity.java file, one activity_main.xml file, and a fragment_main.xml layout file. We are going to implement the navigation stack pattern in this project.

Content View Controller: Fragment

IOS ANALOGY

UIViewController

The iOS app must have three content views and three UIViewControllers that you can clearly see from the iOS app (see Figure 3-23) or the iOS storyboard scene. At the end of this section, you will have three Fragment classes and three layout files that map to the counterpart UIViewControllers and storyboard scenes in the iOS Xcode project.

Use the iOS app as the UI mock-up for your Android app. You need three Fragment classes to manage three content views. Continue with the following in the newly created NavigationStack ADT project:

1. Create the screenone_fragment.xml layout file for the first content view. From the res/layout/ folder context menu, select **New ➤ Android XML File**. Use the **New Android XML File** wizard (see Figure 3-25) to create the initial layout file, as follows:

   a. Select **Layout** as the Resource Type.

   b. Enter **screenone_fragment.xml** as the File.

   c. Select **RelativeLayout** as the Root Element.

Figure 3-25. New Android XML File

2. Open the newly created `screenone_fragment.xml` in the ADT graphical layout editor. Add a `TextView` from the Form Widget category and use the properties editor to enter the following `TextView` attributes:

   a. Enter **textViewLabel** as the Id.

   b. To update the Text, click the **...** button and use **Create New Android String** dialog to assign a String resource:

      i. Enter **First Screen** in the **String** field.

      ii. Enter **label_screenone** in the **New R.string.** field.

   c. To update the Text Size, click the **...** button to use the Resource Chooser to create and assign a New Dimension:

      i. Enter **label_textsize** in the **Name** field.

      ii. Enter **36sp** in the **Value** field.

3. Add a **Button** from the **Form Widget** category:

    a. Enter **buttonNext** as the **Id**.

    b. To enter Text, click the … button and use the **Create New Android String** dialog to assign a string resource:

        i. Enter **Next** in the **String** field.

        ii. Enter **button_next** in the **New R.string.** field.

XML EDITOR

For modifying the layout, it may be quicker to just modify the XML file directly. Listing 3-8 shows the screenone_fragment.xml file in text edit mode.

Listing 3-8. *screenone_fragment.xml*

```xml
<?xml version="1.0" encoding="utf-8"?>
<RelativeLayout
  xmlns:android="http://schemas.android.com/apk/res/android"
  android:layout_width="match_parent"
  android:layout_height="match_parent">

  <TextView
    android:id="@+id/textViewLabel"
    android:layout_width="wrap_content"
    android:layout_height="wrap_content"
    android:layout_alignParentTop="true"
    android:layout_centerHorizontal="true"
    android:layout_marginTop="90dp"
    android:text="@string/label_screenone"
    android:textSize="@dimen/label_textsize"/>

  <Button
    android:id="@+id/buttonNext"
    android:layout_width="wrap_content"
    android:layout_height="wrap_content"
    android:layout_alignParentBottom="true"
    android:layout_alignParentRight="true"
    android:layout_marginBottom="20dp"
    android:layout_marginRight="20dp "
    android:text="@string/button_next"/>

</RelativeLayout>
```

The layout file is a human-readable text file in XML format.

4. Create the ScreenOneFragment.java content view controller for the
    screenone_fragment.xml content view. From the src folder context menu,
    select **New ➤ Class**. Use the **Create Java Class** wizard to create a Java
    class, as follows:

    a. Enter **NavigationStack/src** as the Source folder.

    b. Enter **com.pdachoice.navigationstack** as the Package.

    c. Enter **ScreenOneFragment** as the Name.

    d. Enter **android.support.v4.app.Fragment** as the Superclass (or browse).

Note   The android.support.v4 namespace is from the v4 Support Library.

---

5. To pair the ScreenOneFragment with its content view, create the content
    view object from the layout file and return the contentView from the
    Fragment.onCreateView(...) lifecycle callback (see Listing 3-9).

    Listing 3-9. Pair with Layout File

```
public class ScreenOneFragment extends Fragment {
  private View contentView;

  @Override
  public View onCreateView(LayoutInflater inflater, ViewGroup
                           container,Bundle savedInstanceState) {
    contentView = inflater.inflate(R.layout.screenone_fragment, container,false);

    return contentView;
  }
}
```

Note   To reference the screenone_fragment.xml layout resource from Java code, use the R.layout.
screenone_fragment.

---

6. To create a Screen Two layout file, you can repeat the preceding steps. Or,
    since it is very similar to Screen One, using **Copy**, **Paste**, and **Edit** in the
    layout file is quicker. From the screenone_fragment.xml file context menu,
    select **Copy**, and then select **Paste** to the same folder.

7. Enter **screentwo_fragment.xml** as the new file name (see Figure 3-26).

Figure 3-26. Enter new file name

8. String resources are stored in the `res/values/strings.xml` file. Modify `res/values/strings.xml` to create two new strings (see Listing 3-10). You will need them later.

    Listing 3-10. *Create String Resource*

    ```
    <?xml version="1.0" encoding="utf-8"?>
    <resources>
       ...
       <string name="label_screentwo">2nd Screen</string>
       <string name="label_screenthree">Last Screen</string>
       ...
    </resources>
    ```

9. Modify `screentwo_fragment.xml` to use the preceding new string resource (see Listing 3-11).

    Listing 3-11. *Use String Resource in Layout File*

    ```
    <RelativeLayout ... >

    ...
    <TextView
        ...
        android:text="@string/label_screentwo"
        ...
    />
    ...

    </RelativeLayout>
    ```

10. To create the Screen Three layout, `screenthree_fragment.xml`, do the following:

    a. Copy `screenone_fragment.xml` and paste it into a new file named `res/layout/screenthree_fragment.xml`. Edit it in the layout editor.

    b. Modify the `TextView` `android:text` attribute to use the new string resource, `label_screenthree`.

   c.   There is no Next button on the last screen, so delete the entire Button XML element. Listing 3-12 shows the completed `screenthree_fragment.xml` file.

Listing 3-12. screenthree_fragment.xml

```
<RelativeLayout ...>

<TextView
  android:id="@+id/textViewLabel"
  android:layout_width="wrap_content"
  android:layout_height="wrap_content"
  android:layout_alignParentTop="true"
  android:layout_centerHorizontal="true"
  android:layout_marginTop="90dp"
  android:text="@string/label_screenthree"/>

</RelativeLayout>
```

11.   To create the ScreenTwoFragment content view controller, copy-and-paste works pretty well on Java classes, too:

   a.   Copy ScreenOneFragment.java and paste it into a new file named ScreenTwoFragment.java.

   b.   Modify the newly created ScreenTwoFragment class to pair with the screentwo_fragment.xml layout file (see Listing 3-13).

Listing 3-13. ScreenTwoFragment.onCreateView(...)

```java
public class ScreenTwoFragment extends Fragment {
  private View contentView;

  @Override
  public View onCreateView(LayoutInflater inflater,
                           ViewGroup container,Bundle savedInstanceState) {
    contentView = inflater.inflate(R.layout.screentwo_fragment,
    container, false);

    return contentView;
  }
}
```

12.   Repeat the previous step to create the third Fragment class, ScreenThreeFragment.java (see Listing 3-14), and then update the onViewCreate(...).

Listing 3-14. ScreenThreeFragment.onCreateView(...)

```java
public class ScreenThreeFragment extends Fragment {
    private View contentView;

    @Override
    public View onCreateView(LayoutInflater inflater,
                        ViewGroup container, Bundle savedInstanceState) {
        contentView = inflater.inflate(R.layout.screenthree_fragment, container, false);

        return contentView;
    }
}
```

There should be no compilation errors, and you can build and run the current NavigationStack project. It still shows the layout view from the PlaceholderFragment layout file. You created the three fragments and each manages its own layout content view. But they are still stand-alone and are not being used yet. We still need to connect the dots: load the fragment view controller's content view from the PlaceholderFragment.

Container View Controller: Activity

IOS ANALOGY

Container view controller, i.e., Navigation Controller, UITabbarController, UIPageViewController from iOS SDK.

The only missing piece in this project is a way to manage the child fragments to show the right fragment layout content view at the right time. In iOS terms, we need a *container view controller* to manage the child view controllers, such as UINavigationController. There is no such UINavigationController in Android. You need to create the custom Android container controller yourself, and this is what we are going to do next.

A fragment is designed to represent the user interface and it should always be embedded in an activity. The MainActivity naturally is the best candidate for being the container view controller that manages the screen navigations.

The code from the Blank Activity template works just fine for a single fragment. Let's modify it to make it more capable of pushing and popping the content view controller.

FragmentManager

Android doesn't have the iOS-like UINavigationController container controller, but it does provide framework API to do the same thing: the FragmentManager and FragmentTransaction classes provide API to add, remove, or replace a fragment and manage the last-in, first-out screen navigation stack behavior.

Continue with the ADT NavigationStack project by doing the following:

1. In the `MainActivity` class, implement the following method (see Listing 3-15) that mimics the iOS navigation stack behavior.

IOS ANALOGY

- (void) pushViewController: (UIViewController *) *viewController* animated: (BOOL) *animated*.

---

  a. To show the new fragment in the activity, use the `FragmentTransaction.replace(...)` method.

  b. To implement the screen navigation stack behaviors, use the back stack managed by the `FragmentManager`. If you want to pop it out later, add it to the back stack.

  c. Commit the transaction.

Listing 3-15. Push to Navigation Stack

```
// to be called when you want to show the viewController in Activity
void pushViewController(Fragment viewController, boolean addToStack) {
    // 1: Create a FragmentTransaction from FragmentManager via activity
    FragmentManager manager = getSupportFragmentManager();
    FragmentTransaction transaction = manager.beginTransaction();

    // 2: tug in this toFragment into Activity ViewGroup
    transaction.replace(R.id.container, viewController,
                        viewController .getClass().getSimpleName());

    if (addToStack) {
        // 3: add the transaction to the back stack so we can pop it out later
        transaction.addToBackStack(null);
    }

    // 4: commit the transaction.
    transaction.commit();
}
```

2. To show a fragment, such as `ScreenOneFragment`, when `MainActivity` launches (see Listing 3-16) do the following:

  a. Call `pushViewController(...)` in `Activity.onCreate(..)` and pass `false` to avoid adding an initially empty view to the back stack.

  b. Delete the code that displays the `PlaceholderFragment`.

Listing 3-16. Call pushViewController(...)

```
public class MainActivity extends ActionBarActivity {

  @Override
  protected void onCreate(Bundle savedInstanceState) {
    super.onCreate(savedInstanceState);
    setContentView(R.layout.activity_main);

    this.pushViewController(new ScreenOneFragment(), false);
    // if (savedInstanceState == null) {
    // getSupportFragmentManager().beginTransaction()
    // .add(R.id.container, new PlaceholderFragment()).commit();
    // }
  }
  ...
```

3. To go back to the previous screen, use FragmentManager.
    popViewController(), as shown in Listing 3-17.

```
┌──────────────────────────────────────────────────────────────────────┐
│                           IOS ANALOGY                                  │
└──────────────────────────────────────────────────────────────────────┘
```

- (UIViewController *) popViewController Animated: (BOOL) *animated*.

Listing 3-17. popViewController

```
// go back to prev screen
void popViewController() {
  FragmentManager manager = getSupportFragmentManager();
  manager.popBackStack();
}
```

4. To show Screen Two when clicking the **Next** button, in the
    ScreenOneFragment, register the button onClick handler, this, which
    implements the Button widget OnClick event (see Listing 3-18).

```
┌──────────────────────────────────────────────────────────────────────┐
│                           IOS ANALOGY                                  │
└──────────────────────────────────────────────────────────────────────┘
```

Many iOS widgets have a delegate property that handles the delegate protocol, such as UIAlertView, UIWebView, UITableViewController, and so forth. In Java, you said register the event listener. This is different terminology, but we are essentially talking about the same thing.

a. Declare the ScreenOneFragment class to implement the
    View.OnClickListener (see Listing 3-18).

b. Delegate button onClick events to the listener:
    nextButton.setOnClickListener(this).

c. Provide View.OnClickListener implementation.

Listing 3-18. *Handle Button.onClick action*

```
// Declare Button OnClickListener interface
public class ScreenOneFragment extends Fragment implements OnClickListener {
  ...
  private View nextButton;

  @Override
  public View onCreateView(LayoutInflater inflater, ViewGroup container, Bundle savedInstanceState) {
    ...
    nextButton = contentView.findViewById(R.id.buttonNext);
    // Delegate button onClick events
    nextButton.setOnClickListener(this);
    ...
  }

  // Provide interface implementation
  @Override
  public void onClick(View v) {
    // Step E: delegate to MainActivity
    ScreenTwoFragment frag = new ScreenTwoFragment();
    ((MainActivity) getActivity()).pushViewController(frag, true);
  }
}
```

> **Tip** In Eclipse, you don't have to memorize all the methods defined in the interface. The context menu has a lot of good stuff (see Figure 3-15).

5. To show Screen Three when the Next button is selected on Screen Two, add the button event delegation code in the ScreenTwoFragment (see Listing 3-19).

Listing 3-19. *Handle Screen Two Button.onClick Action*

```
public class ScreenTwoFragment extends Fragment implements OnClickListener{
  ...
  private View nextButton;

  @Override
  public View onCreateView(LayoutInflater inflater, ViewGroup container, Bundle savedInstanceState) {
    ...
    nextButton = contentView.findViewById(R.id.buttonNext);
    nextButton.setOnClickListener(this); // Delegate button OnClick events
    ...
    return contentView;
  }
```

```
@Override
public void onClick(View v) {
  ScreenThreeFragment frag = new ScreenThreeFragment ();
  ((MainActivity) getActivity()).pushViewController(frag, true);
}
}
```

6. Screen Three is the last screen. There is no action button and no need for any event-handling code.

7. In `MainActivity.java`, the Blank Activity template automatically loads the activity options menu and handles the options menu selection in the `MainActivity`, the container view controller. We prefer delegate the UI widgets events and interact with the UI widgets to the view controller, the Fragment. Remove the code related to the options menu in `MainActivity.java`, as follows:

   a. Comment out `onCreateOptionsMenu(...)`.

   b. Comment out `onOptionsItemSelected(...)`.

8. Build and run the app. You should get something that looks similar to Figure 3-27.

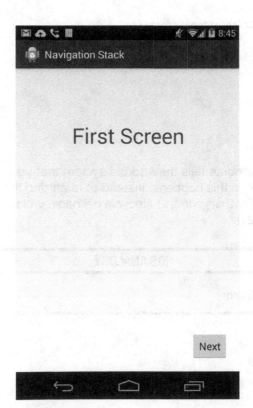

Figure 3-27. The first screen in the NavigationStack app

You're almost done with the project—just a couple more side topics that I think are good for you to know.

Device Orientation

By default, the Android system restarts the running activity when the device's configuration changes, such as device orientation, a change of locale or language, and so forth. This default behavior may not be what iOS developers normally expect. For example, change the device orientation when the current NavigationStack app is running. This app always goes back to Screen One when the device orientation changes. In fact, everything is reinitialized because the activity and fragments are destroyed and re-created. The new ones need to go through all the lifecycle callbacks—even content views are reinflated from the layout files. This behavior is definitely not the same as iOS apps.

To prevent the default behavior of restarting the activity, add the `android:configChanges= "orientation|screenSize"` attribute to the activity XML element in the `AndroidManifest.xml` file (see Listing 3-20).

Listing 3-20. android:configChanges

```
<?xml version="1.0" encoding="utf-8"?>
<manifest...>
  ...
  <application ... >
    <activity
      android:configChanges="orientation|screenSize"
      ...>

      ...

    </activity>
  </application>

</manifest>
```

This `android:configChanges` attribute tells the Android system that your app wants to handle the configuration change itself. When this happens, instead of restarting the running activity, the system simply calls the `onConfigurationChanged(...)` lifecycle callback, which you can override in the Activity class (see Listing 3-21).

IOS ANALOGY

- (void)didRotateFromInterfaceOrientation:

Listing 3-21. Device Orientation Callback

```
@Override
public void onConfigurationChanged(Configuration newConfig) {
  super.onConfigurationChanged(newConfig);
```

```
// do the needful, for example:
if (newConfig.orientation == Configuration.ORIENTATION_LANDSCAPE) {
  Toast.makeText(this, "landscape", Toast.LENGTH_SHORT).show();
} else if (newConfig.orientation == Configuration.ORIENTATION_PORTRAIT) {
  Toast.makeText(this, "portrait", Toast.LENGTH_SHORT).show();
}
}
```

For our own purpose of preventing the activity from restarting, we don't need to provide the override because we only want to prevent the system default behavior.

> **Note**   There is a trade-off for preventing the activity restart: the system automatically loads the alternative application resource based on the new device configuration. For example, you may have different layout files for different orientations. In this case, preventing an activity restart and reloading the appropriate layout file may have you lose more than what you gained. We will talk about alternative resources in Chapter 6.

FINAL TOUCH

You have completed the main topics in this ADT project, comparing the Android app with the iOS app look and feel (see Figure 3-23). Optionally, you can now tighten some minor cosmetic loose ends, as follows:

1. The activity title bar displays the app title specified by the activity android:label="@string/app_name". String resources are stored in the res/values/strings.xml file. Let's change it to **Navigation Stack**, as shown in Listing 3-22.

    Listing 3-22. app_name String Resource in strings.xml

    ```
    <?xml version="1.0" encoding="utf-8"?>
    <resources>
        ...
        <string name="app_name">Navigation Stack</string>
        ...
    </resources>
    ```

2. Examine the layout files. I have hard-coded values in several XML measurement attributes. Just like string resource, these values should be externalized as a *dimension resource*. Add new measurements in res/values/dimens.xml, as shown in Listing 3-23.

    Listing 3-23. Dimension Resources

    ```
    <resources>
        ...
        <dimen name="label_marginTop">90dp</dimen>
        <dimen name="button_marginEnd">20dp</dimen>
        ...
    </resources>
    ```

3. Replace the hard-coded measurements with the preceding dimension resources; for example, in screenone_fragment.xml, as shown in Listing 3-24.

Listing 3-24. Using Android Resources

```
<RelativeLayout ... >
  <TextView
    ...
    android:layout_marginTop="@dimen/label_marginTop"
    ... />
  <Button
    ...
    android:layout_marginBottom="@dimen/button_marginEnd"
    android:layout_marginRight="@dimen/button_marginEnd "
    ... />
</RelativeLayout>
```

You don't want to create a custom Back button to match the one in the iOS navigation bar because Android platforms have a system Back button on the bottom of the screen that offers the Go Back behavior. To follow Android user experience (UX) conventions, you should just use the system Back button in your app. The final NavigationStack Android app should look similar to Figure 3-28.

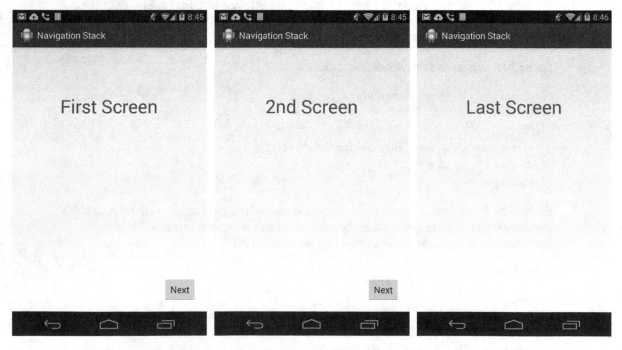

Figure 3-28. NavigationStack final touch

MVC Project Template

ADT built-in project templates (see Chapter 1) are very valuable. They demonstrate several common and important UX patterns. However, unlike iOS project templates, I normally don't use them directly to start my ADT projects. The main reason is because they seem less MVC-oriented compared to the iOS MVC pattern, which is very important for iOS-to-Android porting topics.

We need to implement Android apps with the MVC design pattern using the fragment view controller and the activity container view controller. We can create our template project for this purpose. Let's make an MvcTemplate project from the previous NavigationStack project.

> **Note**   In a nutshell, the ways that iOS and Android facilitate screen transitions are fundamentally different. In iOS, you normally choose the appropriate container view controller from the SDK to transition the content views among view controller children. In Android, you often use the back stack introduced in the NavigationStack app (except with some specialized layouts). This makes the NavigationStack a perfect candidate for our purpose.

ADT PROJECT PREPARATIONS

Copy the NavigationStack ADT project and paste it into a new project (⌘c, ⌘v), as follows:

1. The project name is **MvcTemplate**.

2. Rename the ADT Application package. From the MvcTemplate project context menu, select **Android Tools ➤ Rename Application Package**. Enter a new package name: **com.pdachoice.renameme**.

3. Rename the src/com.pdachoice.masterdetail Java package. From the package context menu, select **Refactor ➤ Rename...** (Alt+⌘r) and do the following:

   a. Enter a new name: **com.pdachoice.renameme**.

   b. Select **Update references**.

4. Modify the app_name in res/values/strings.xml, as shown in Listing 3-25.

   Listing 3-25. strings.xml

   ```
   <resources>

     <string name="app_name">Rename Me</string>
     ...

   </resources>
   ```

5.   Build and run this MvcTemplate project to make sure everything is done correctly. It should look just like the NavigationStack app (see Figure 3-28) except the title, "Rename Me".

With this template project, each content view is managed by a fragment view controller just like each content view is associated with a UIViewController in iOS. We will use MvcTemplate project to create new ADT project whenever possible. I use this project to jumpstart my Android apps a lot.

Master List with Details Drilldown

IOS ANALOGY

UITableViewController

If your app needs to display a list of items from which users can tap to view more detailed information, this is very common style to use. You present a master list of items on the screen, and the user selects one item and drills in. This master list can display as much information as you want for each item. It may be everything from a simple text list to a list of images, or a combination of both.

This is probably one of the most common mobile navigation UX navigation patterns used by system apps and third-party apps in any major mobile platforms. Both Android and iOS provide usage guidelines and offer system API to promote consistency by making the implementation easy for developers. In fact, both Xcode and ADT supply project templates for creating apps with a master list with the details drilled down. Recall that we already use this template in the LessonOne app.

Using the Xcode template, you can get the following iOS master-detail template app running within a minute. Initially, it presents the master list with no items. The Add button adds a timestamp to the list. By selecting an item on the list, the app shows the detailed screen with the selected item content. You will port this iOS app (see Figure 3-29) to the Android platform.

Figure 3-29. Master List Detailed Drilldown

ADT PROJECT PREPARATIONS

There are two screens. You need two fragments: one for the master list and the other for the detailed item content view. However, for the list view fragment, the Android SDK provides a very good one that you will use instead of creating it yourself. Let's use the MvcTemplate project to start this new Android project.

1. Copy the MvcTemplate ADT project and paste it into a new project (⌘c, ⌘v).

2. The project name is **MasterDetail**.

3. Rename the ADT Application package. From the MasterDetail project context menu, select **Android Tools ➤ Rename Application Package**. Enter a new package name: **com.pdachoice.masterdetail**.

4. Rename the src/com.pdachoice.renameme Java package. From the package context menu, select **Refactor ➤ Rename…** (Alt+⌘r) and do the following:

   a. Enter a new name: **com.pdachoice.masterdetail**.

   b. Select **Update references**.

5.   Modify res/values/strings.xml, as shown in Listing 3-26.

Listing 3-26. app_name String Resource

```
<?xml version="1.0" encoding="utf-8"?>
<resources>

  <string name="app_name">Master Detail</string>
  ...
</resources>
```

6.   You only need to create one fragment, as follows:

a.   Delete the src/ScreenTwoFragment.java and src/ScreenThreeFragment.java classes (multiselect and fn+Delete).

b.   Delete the res/layout/screentwo_fragment.xml and res/layout/screenthree_fragment.xml files (fn+Delete).

c.   Rename the ScreenOneFragment.java class (Alt+⌘r) as **DetailFragment**.

d.   Rename the res/layout/screenone_fragment.xml resource (Alt+⌘r) as **detail_fragment**.

e.   detail_fragment.xml only needs one TextView and nothing else. Modify it as shown in Listing 3-27.

Listing 3-27. detail_fragment.xml

```
<?xml version="1.0" encoding="utf-8"?>
<RelativeLayout
  xmlns:android="http://schemas.android.com/apk/res/android"
  android:layout_width="match_parent"
  android:layout_height="match_parent">

  <TextView
    android:id="@+id/textViewTimestamp"
    android:layout_width="wrap_content"
    android:layout_height="wrap_content"
    android:layout_centerHorizontal="true"
    android:layout_centerVertical="true"
    android:text=""
    android:textAppearance="?android:attr/textAppearanceLarge" />

</RelativeLayout>
```

7.   You may build and run this prep project to make sure it works.

ListFragment

Previously, we only created one fragment for the detail view. For the master list fragment and the content view, the Android SDK provides a framework class and layout file to simplify this common task: ListFragment.

Continue with the MasterDetail project by doing the following:

1. Create the view controller for the list view screen using ListFragment. From the src folder context menu, select **New ➤ Class**, and then do the following:

   a. Enter **MasterDetail/src** as the Source folder.

   b. Enter **com.pdachoice.masterdetail** as the Package.

   c. Enter **MasterListFragment** as the Name.

   d. Enter **android.support.v4.app.ListFragment** as the Superclass (or browse).

2. You *don't* need to create a layout file for your MasterListFragment. The super class ListFragment already pairs with a system layout file that contains a ListView widget.

> **Note**   Make sure to call super(…) in these lifecycle callback methods.

3. To populate the list view items, implement an adapter for ListFragment. The adapter is responsible for making a view for each item in the underlying data set. ListAdapter is a specialized adapter for each item in the ListView widget. To supply the views for each row with items in the list, you can implement a custom class that conforms to the ListAdapter interface. The Android framework also provides convenient adapters that are suitable for many common situations. In this case, each row in the list view is simply a one-line text TextView widget. You can choose to use the framework ArrayAdapter class instead of implementing your own adapter as shown in Listing 3-28. The ArrayAdapter constructor takes the following arguments:

   a. The current context: getActivity()

   b. The layout containing a TextView: android.R.layout.simple_list_item_1

   c. The data to represent in the ListView: new ArrayList<String>()

```
                              IOS ANALOGY
```

Similar to the *data source* concept in iOS, such as UITableViewDataSource.

Listing 3-28. Set Up the List Adapter

```java
import java.util.Date; // don't choose java.sql.Date
...
public class MasterListFragment extends ListFragment {
  ArrayAdapter<Date> mListAdapter;

  @Override
  public void onCreate(Bundle savedInstanceState) {
    super.onCreate(savedInstanceState); // must call super
    ...
    // setup adapter, aka data source in iOS
    mListAdapter = new ArrayAdapter<Date>(getActivity(),
      android.R.layout.simple_list_item_1, new ArrayList<Date>());
    this.setListAdapter(mListAdapter);
    ...
  }
  ...
}
```

> **Note** The Android Application Framework comes with many application resources or public uses. To use them, use the appropriate system namespace, android, to reference them. For example, android.R.layout. simple_list_item_1.
>
> This layout only contains a one-liner TextView widget, which is commonly used for list view items with one TextView in it.

4. Enable the **options menu**. The Android options menu is very similar to desktop app menus on the menubar. On older Android devices with four system buttons, it is the menu button at the bottom of the screen. On devices with API Level 11+, the options menu is located in the action bar presented in the top-right corner.

5. By default, the options menu is set in an activity and inherits all of its fragment children. To append action items to the options menu in the fragment, you need to enable it (see Listing 3-29).

Listing 3-29. Enable the Options Menu

```
public class MasterListFragment extends ListFragment {
  ...
  @Override
  public void onCreate(Bundle savedInstanceState) {
    super.onCreate(savedInstanceState); // must call super
    ...
    setHasOptionsMenu(true);
    ...
  }
  ...
}
```

6. The options menu is rendered from the menu resource file (similar to content view in the layout resource file). Modify the existing default menu layout, res/menu/main.xml, as shown in Listing 3-30.

Listing 3-30. Menu Layout

```
<menu
xmlns:android="http://schemas.android.com/apk/res/android"
xmlns:app="http://schemas.android.com/apk/res-auto">
  <item
    android:id="@+id/action_add"
    android:icon="@android:drawable/ic_input_add"
    app:showAsAction="always"
    android:title=""/>
</menu>
```

7. Similar to inflate, the content view layout file in onCreateView(...), you need to specify the menu resource in the onCreateOptionsMenu(...) lifecycle method, as shown in Listing 3-31.

Listing 3-31. onCreateOptionsMenu

```
public class MasterListFragment extends ListFragment {
  ...
  @Override
  public void onCreateOptionsMenu(Menu menu, MenuInflater inflater) {
    inflater.inflate(R.menu.main, menu);
  }
  ...
```

8. Upon selecting the **Add** menu item in the **options menu**, add a timestamp to the ListView (see Listing 3-32):

   a. The system invokes the onOptionsItemSelected(MenuItem item) lifecycle callback.

   b. To add an item to ListView, add the data to the ListAdapter: mListAdapter.

   c. To refresh the ListView widget, call notifyDataSetChanged().

```
┌─────────────────────────────────────────────────────────────────┐
│                          IOS ANALOGY                             │
└─────────────────────────────────────────────────────────────────┘
```

[UITableViewDataSource reloadData]

Listing 3-32. onOptionsItemSelected

```java
public class MasterListFragment extends ListFragment {
  ...
  // callback method when menu items are selected.
  @Override
  public boolean onOptionsItemSelected(MenuItem item) {
    if (item.getItemId() == R.id.action_add) {
      mListAdapter.add(Calendar.getInstance().getTime());
      mListAdapter.notifyDataSetChanged();
    } else {
      // other menu item
    }
    return true;
  }
  ...
```

9. When the list item on the ListView is selected, you want to show
    DetailFragment (see Listing 3-33).

Listing 3-33. onListItemClick(...) Callback

```java
public class MasterListFragment extends ListFragment {
  ...
  // callback method when list item is selected.
  @Override
  public void onListItemClick(ListView l, View v, int position, long id) {
    Fragment detailFragment = new DetailFragment();

    Bundle parms = new Bundle();
    Date timestamp = mListAdapter.getItem(position);
    parms.putString("ts", timestamp.toString());
    detailFragment.setArguments(parms); // pass data to other Fragment

    ((MainActivity) getActivity()).pushViewController(detailFragment, true);
  }
  ...
```

a. The system invokes the ListFragment.onListItemClick(...) callback.

b. To pass data to other fragments, use Fragment.setArguments(parms).

> **Note** To pass data to another fragment or activity, you need to create a serializable Bundle object, as shown here. Generally, you don't want to use setters to set data into fragment properties, because the Fragment or Activity object could be destroyed or reinitialized when the activity or fragment restarts and goes through the lifecycle events.

10. `DetailFragment` should display the selected list item passed from `MasterListFragment`, as shown in Listing 3-34.

Listing 3-34. DetailFragment Inflate Layout

```java
public class DetailFragment extends Fragment {
  private View contentView;
  private TextView textViewTimestamp;

  @Override
  public View onCreateView(LayoutInflater inflater, ViewGroup container,
                           Bundle savedInstanceState) {
    contentView =
      inflater.inflate(R.layout.detail_fragment, container, false);

    Bundle args = this.getArguments();
    String ts = args.getString("ts");
    textViewTimestamp =
      (TextView)contentView.findViewById(R.id.textViewTimestamp);
    textViewTimestamp.setText(ts);

    return contentView;
  }
}
```

11. Now you have completed the `MasterListFragment` class. You can show its content view upon app launches, as shown in Listing 3-35.

Listing 3-35. Push MasterListFragment to Back Stack

```java
public class MainActivity extends FragmentActivity {

  @Override
  protected void onCreate(Bundle savedInstanceState) {
    ...
    // adding the first fragment to the navigation stack.
    pushViewController(new MasterListFragment(), false);
  }
  ...
```

12. Build and run the app. You should get something similar to Figure 3-30.

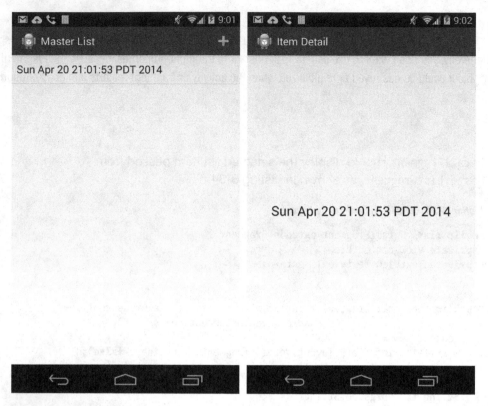

Figure 3-30. Master List and Detail views

FINAL TOUCH

You have completed the main topics in this ADT project, comparing the Android app with the iOS app look and feel. Optionally, you can tighten some minor cosmetic loose ends, as follows:

1. Change the title text when pushing and popping the navigation stack. You want to update the title when the screen appears, onResume(), as shown in Listing 3-36.

    Listing 3-36. Update Activity Title

    ```
    @Override
    public void onResume() {
      super.onResume();
      getActivity().setTitle("Item Detail"); // or Master List
    }
    ```

The Fragment.onCreateView(…) method is only called once when the fragment content view is inflated from the layout resource. Fragment.onResume(…) is called whenever the view becomes visible.

Build and run the Android app to see the app you just created.

GridView

```
                        IOS ANALOGY

```

UICollectionViewController

GridView is just a variant of the master-detail drilldown pattern using a different UI widget to show the master list. However, on tablets or large-screen devices, GridView is widely used due to greater space efficiencies that use multiple columns to organize the master list items, rather than a one-dimensional simple list. On iOS platforms, it was actually much harder to achieve this UX until UICollectionViewControllerbecame available, beginning with iOS 6.

It would be a waste if you don't try this variant right now, because it is a really useful widget that takes very little extra effort. The key word is GridView widget.

```
                 ADT PROJECT PREPARATIONS

```

Let's cut to the chase and create another ADT project.

1. Copy the MasterDetail ADT project and paste it into a new project named **MasterGridDetail**.

> **Tip** ⌘c and ⌘v work on folders and the whole project in Eclipse, too.

2. Rename the ADT project package name declared in AndroidManifest.xml. Enter a new package name: **com.pdachoice.mastergriddetail** (see Listing 3-37).

    Listing 3-37. Manifest Package

    ```
    <manifest
      ...
      package="com.pdachoice.mastergriddetail"
      ... >

      ...
    </manifest>
    ```

3. Rename the src/com.pdachoice.masterdetail Java package name. From the package context menu, select **Refactor ➤ Rename...** (Alt+⌘r) and do the following:

    a. Enter a new name: **com.pdachoice.mastergriddetail**.

    b. Select **Update references**.

4. Modify the app_name in res/values/srings.xml, as shown in Listing 3-38.

Listing 3-38. app_name in res/values/srings.xml

```
<resources>

  <string name="app_name">MasterGrid Detail</string>
  ...

</resources>
```

5. Build and run the new MasterGridDetail ADT project; it should work the same as the MasterDetail app, except for the app_name.

Continue with the newly created MasterGridDetail project to replace the ListView with the GridView widget:

1. There is no ListFragment-like framework class for GridView. You need to create your layout file with the GridView widget. Create the res/layout/mastergrid_fragment.xml, file as shown in Listing 3-39.

Listing 3-39. mastergrid_fragment.xml

```
<?xml version="1.0" encoding="utf-8"?>
<GridView xmlns:android="http://schemas.android.com/apk/res/android"
  android:id="@+id/gridViewMaster"
  android:layout_width="fill_parent"
  android:layout_height="fill_parent"
  android:numColumns="3">
</GridView>
```

2. Create a fragment view controller that pairs with the previous layout. Most of the code in the previous MasterListFragment class can be reused. There is no practical difference except using your own custom layout that contains the GridView instead of the ListView widget (see Listing 3-40):

   a. Rename (Alt+⌘r) MasterListFragment.java to MasterGridFragment.java. Java programmers are normally very picky about class name.

   b. Make the MasterGridFragment class extend Fragment instead of ListFragment.

   c. For now, use the same ArrayAdapter and the android.R.layout.simple_list_item_1 system layout to show a timestamp in a simple TextView widget.

   d. We are *not* extending ListFragment anymore. Comment out or remove the lines with a trivial compilation error.

   e. Please rename mListAdapter as **mGridAdapter**. Java developers normally are picky on naming.

> **Tip**   Select any variable and do Alt+⌘r to rename the variables and update the references.

Listing 3-40. MasterGridFragment.onCreate

```java
public class MasterGridFragment extends Fragment {

  ArrayAdapter<String>mGridAdapter;

  @Override
  public void onCreate(Bundle savedInstanceState) {
    ...
    // setup ListView data source
    mGridAdapter = new ArrayAdapter<String>(getActivity(),
      android.R.layout.simple_list_item_1, new ArrayList<String>());
    //  this.setListAdapter(mGridAdapter);
    ...
  }
  ...
```

3. As usual, implement onCreateView(...) to pair with the content view layout and keep object references to the UI widgets, and so forth (see Listing 3-41). Set the GridView adapter, a.k.a. the *data source* in iOS.

Listing 3-41. gridview.setAdapter

```java
public class MasterGridFragment extends Fragment {

  private GridView gridview;

  ...
  @Override
  public View onCreateView(LayoutInflater inflater, ViewGroup container,
                           Bundle savedInstanceState) {
    gridview = (GridView)inflater.inflate(
      R.layout.mastergrid_fragment, container, false);

    // set data source and item click listener
    gridview.setAdapter(mGridAdapter);
    ...
  }
  ...
```

4. To handle the GridView item clicked, register the handler, this, which implements the AdapterViewItemClick event (see Listing 3-42):

    a. Declare the MasterGridFragment class to implement the OnItemClickListener.

    b. Delegate component events to the this listener.

    c. Provide listener implementation: onItemClick.

Listing 3-42. GridView itemClicked Action Delegate

```java
public class MasterGridFragment extends Fragment implements OnItemClickListener {
  private GridView gridview;
  ...
  @Override
  public View onCreateView(LayoutInflater inflater, ViewGroup
                            container,Bundle savedInstanceState) {
    ...
    // set GridView item click listener
    gridview.setOnItemClickListener(this);
    ...
  }

  // OnItemClickListener implementation
  @Override
  public void onItemClick(AdapterView<?> l, View v, int position, long id) {
    Fragment detailFragment = new DetailFragment();

    Bundle parms = new Bundle();
    String timestamp = mGridAdapter.getItem(position);
    parms.putString("ts", timestamp);
    detailFragment.setArguments(parms); // pass data to other Fragment

    ((MainActivity) getActivity()).pushViewController(detailFragment, true);
  }
  ...
```

5. Build and run the `MasterGridDetail` ADT project. Everything should behave the same, except the items are rendered in a three-column GridView instead of a one-column `ListView` (see Figure 3-31).

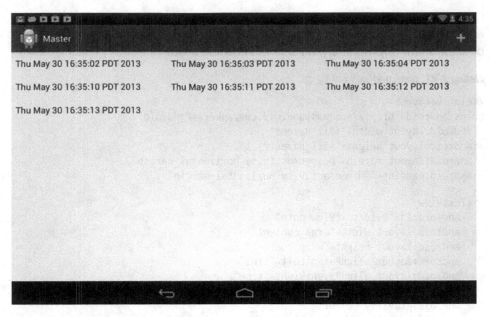

Figure 3-31. Android GridView

Adapter

In the previous MasterGridDetail project, we use the simple ArrayAdapter class to bind arrays of timestamps with a simple system layout, android.R.layout.simple_list_item_1, to show a simple TextView widget for each grid cell. This is very easy and provides a clean look and feel on smaller devices. However, it might be too simple for tablets or certain use cases when you actually have the space to show more than a one-liner TextView (see Figure 3-31). Frequently, you will want to implement your own Adapter class that binds more sophisticated data with a grid cell, or list item views from more sophisticated custom layout file(s).

Let's create your own custom Adapter class and the custom layout for each grid cell.

1. Instead of using the system layout, android.R.layout.simple_list_item_1, create your own layout file for the grid cell. From the res/layout/ folder context menu, select **New ➤ Android XML File** to create the initial layout file, as follows:

    a. Select **Layout** as the Resource Type.

    b. Enter **date_grid_cell.xml** as the File.

    c. Select **RelativeLayout** as the Root Element.

2. Open the newly created date_grid_cell.xml file in the ADT graphical layout
    editor. Add three **TextView** widgets from the **Form Widget** category and
    position them appropriately, as shown in Listing 3-43.

    Listing 3-43. date_grid_cell.xml

```
<RelativeLayout
xmlns:android="http://schemas.android.com/apk/res/android"
  android:layout_width="fill_parent"
  android:layout_height="fill_parent"
  android:layout_margin="@dimen/activity_horizontal_margin"
  android:padding="@dimen/activity_horizontal_margin" >

  <TextView
    android:id="@+id/textViewMonth"
    android:layout_width="wrap_content"
    android:layout_height="wrap_content"
    android:layout_alignParentLeft="true"
    android:layout_alignParentRight="true"
    android:layout_alignParentTop="true"
    android:gravity="center"
    android:text="textViewMonth"
    android:textAppearance="?android:attr/textAppearanceLarge" />

  <TextView
    android:id="@+id/textViewDate"
    android:layout_width="wrap_content"
    android:layout_height="wrap_content"
    android:layout_alignParentLeft="true"
    android:layout_alignParentRight="true"
    android:layout_below="@+id/textViewMonth"
    android:gravity="center"
    android:text="textViewDate"
    android:textAppearance="?android:attr/textAppearanceMedium" />

  <TextView
    android:id="@+id/textViewTime"
    android:layout_width="wrap_content"
    android:layout_height="wrap_content"
    android:layout_alignParentLeft="true"
    android:layout_alignParentRight="true"
    android:layout_below="@+id/textViewDate"
    android:gravity="center"
    android:text="textViewTime"
    android:textAppearance="?android:attr/textAppearanceMedium" />

</RelativeLayout>
```

3. Create the custom Adapter class. From the src folder context menu, select
    New ➤ Class. Use the **Create Java Class** wizard to do the following:

    a. Enter **MasterGridDetail/src** as the Source folder.

    b. Enter **com.pdachoice.mastergriddetail** as the Package.

    c.   Enter **MasterGridAdapter** as the Name.

    d.   Enter **android.widget.BaseAdapter** as the Superclass (or browse).

    e.   Select the **Inherited abstract methods**.

    f.   Click the **Finish** button when done (see Listing 3-44).

Tip   Eclipse creates the class skeletons with the required abstract methods that need to be implemented. These method names seem fairly self-explanatory if you already know how to implement UITableViewDataSource in iOS. You will fill in the blanks.

Listing 3-44. Using BaseAdapter

```
package com.pdachoice.mastergriddetail;

import android.view.View;
import android.view.ViewGroup;
import android.widget.BaseAdapter;

public class MasterGridAdapter extends BaseAdapter {

  @Override
  public int getCount() {
    // TODO Auto-generated method stub
    return 0;
  }

  @Override
  public Object getItem(int position) {
    // TODO Auto-generated method stub
    return null;
  }

  @Override
  public long getItemId(int position) {
    // TODO Auto-generated method stub
    return 0;
  }

  @Override
  public View getView(int position, View convertView, ViewGroup parent) {
    // TODO Auto-generated method stub
    return null;
  }
}
```

4.   BaseAdapter is an abstract class that implements partial adapter contract/ interface. Instead of implementing the whole adapter interface, it is much simpler to extend the BaseAdapter class. Use it when you can (see Listing 3-45).

Listing 3-45. *MasterGridAdapter Constructor*

```java
public class MasterGridAdapter extends BaseAdapter {
  private List<Date>timestamps;
  private Activityactivity;

  public MasterGridAdapter(Activitycaller) {
    this.timestamps = new ArrayList<Date>();
    this.activity = caller;
  }
  ...
```

> **Tip**   In Java, you can think of the Abstract class as an intentional incomplete class that defines how to make it a complete class for its intended purpose, which is similar to the Java Interface. However, it also provides a valuable implementation that can be inherited from. The combination of a Java interface and an abstract class makes a perfect pair for the well-known GoF Template design pattern.
>
> In Objective-C, there is no such compile-time enforcement. You probably just use a naming convention.

    a.   Add some Java properties and a constructor.

    b.   Adapter manages the underlying data set naturally. For simplicity's sake, add a property to hold your data and timestamps.

    c.   Create a constructor with an argument caller, `Activity`. An activity has many utility methods, such as creating a view from a layout file. You will find it handy.

IOS ANALOGY

- (NSInteger) table View: (UI Table View *) table View number Of Rows In Section: (NSInteger) section

- (NSInteger) number Of Sections In Table View: (UI Table View *) table View

---

   5.   Complete the following abstract methods (and see Listing 3-46):

    a.   getCount: The number of items in the data set.

    b.   getItem(): The data item with the position in the data set.

    c.   getItemId(): The row id with the position.

    d.   getItemViewType(): If your `ListView` uses more than one type of list item view, you need to implement this method to return the specific type at the given position, such as an even or odd list item.

    e.   getViewTypeCount(): If your `ListView` uses more than one type of list item view, you need to implement this method to return the number of types.

Listing 3-46. BaseAdapter Abstract Methods

```
public class MasterGridAdapter extends BaseAdapter {
  ...
  @Override
  public int getCount() {
    return timestamps.size();
  }

  @Override
  public Object getItem(int position) {
    return timestamps.get(position);
  }

  @Override
  public long getItemId(int position) {
    return position;
  }
  ...
}
```

IOS ANALOGY

- (NSInteger) table View: (UIT able View *) table View cell For Row At Index Path: (NS Index Path *) index Path.

---

6. Implement getView(...) to return the View object with the data item
    (see Listing 3-47):

    a. The grid cells are recycled objects, meaning they can be reused to save
        memory. We should always check if it is null before creating one from the
        layout file.

    b. LayoutInflater is a helper class that creates the content view object from
        layout files. We can get one from application components, such as activity.

    c. Before returning to the grid cell, populate view widgets with business data.
        In this case, we want to fill three TextView widgets with a Date object.
        You also change the cell background color to demonstrate that you can
        manipulate the look and feel for each cell individually.

Listing 3-47. Adapter.getView

```
public class MasterGridAdapter extends BaseAdapter {
  ...
  @Override
  public View getView(int position, View view, ViewGroup parent) {

    if (view == null) { // check null first before recycled object.
      view = activity.getLayoutInflater().inflate(R.layout.date_grid_cell, null);
    }
```

```
                   // manipulate the view widgets and display data
                   if (position % 2 == 0) {
                     view.setBackgroundColor(Color.argb(32, 0, 128, 128));
                   } else {
                     view.setBackgroundColor(Color.argb(0, 0, 0, 0));
                   }

                   Date ts = timestamps.get(position);

                   TextView textViewMonth = (TextView)view.findViewById(R.id.textViewMonth);
                   textViewMonth.setText(DateFormat.format("MMMM yyyy", ts));

                   TextView textViewDate = (TextView) view.findViewById(R.id.textViewDate);
                   textViewDate.setText(DateFormat.format("EEEE, MMMM dd", ts));

                   TextView textViewTime = (TextView) view.findViewById(R.id.textViewTime);
                   textViewTime.setText(DateFormat.format("h:mmaa", ts));

                   return view;
                 }
                 ...
             }
```

7. Use the newly created MasterGridAdapter class. Modify
    src/MasterGridFragment.java in the Java editor, replacing all occurrences
    of ArrayAdapter<String> with MasterGridAdapter (see Listing 3-48).

Listing 3-48. Using MasterGridAdapter

```java
public class MasterGridFragment extends Fragment implements OnItemClickListener {
  ...
  MasterGridAdapter mGridAdapter;

  @Override
  public void onCreate(Bundle savedInstanceState) {
    ...
    // setup ListView data source
    mGridAdapter = new MasterGridAdapter(getActivity());
    ...
  }
  ...
```

> **Note**   You will get two trivial compilation errors. You can read the error descriptions in the Problems view.
> See Figure 3-32.

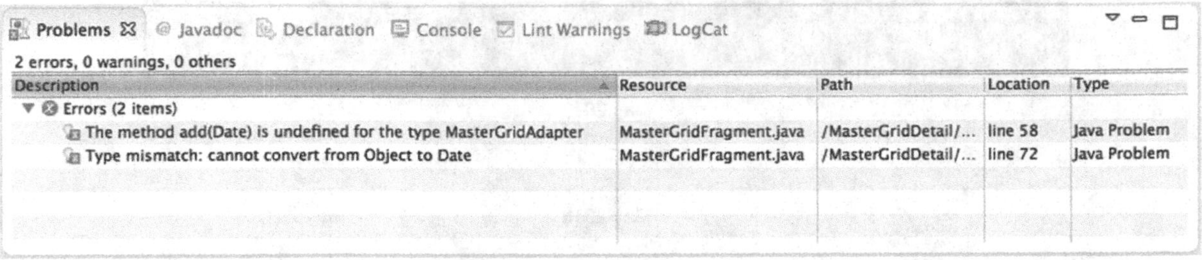

Figure 3-32. Problems view

8. Fix any compilation errors in the `MasterGridAdapter` class as shown in Listing 3-49:

   a. Create the `add(Date)` method.

   b. Change the return type of `getItem(...)` to **Date**.

Listing 3-49. Fix Errors

```java
public class MasterGridAdapter extends BaseAdapter {
  ...
  // the data item with the position in the data set
  @Override
  public Date getItem(int position) {
    return timestamps.get(position);
  }
  ...
  public void add(Date time) {
    timestamps.add(time);
  }
  ...
}
```

9. That's all! Build and run the MasterGridDetail ADT project to see the live app in action, as shown in Figure 3-33.

Figure 3-33. GridView with custom Adapter view

It looks like a chessboard, but I hope it gets my points across.☺

Navigation Tabs

Navigation tabs are another very common and popular UX design pattern. Apple's *iOS Human Interface Guidelines* suggest using a tab bar to give users access to different perspectives on the same set of data or on different subtasks related to the overall function of your app. Each tab (navigation tab) is associated with a view controller (fragment). When the user selects a specific tab, the associated view controller (fragment) presents its own content view (layout), replacing any previous views.

The iOS app shown in Figure 3-34 was created using the Xcode Tabbed Application project template. In ADT, there is also a project template to create apps with fixed or scrollable tabs. For learning purposes, you are going to create an Android version from scratch.

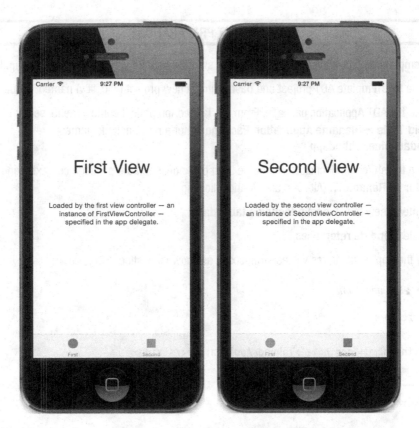

Figure 3-34. iOS tabbed app

Just like iOS tabs, each tab is associated with a `UIViewController`. Each navigation tab on the action bar is associated with a fragment. In iOS, you use a system framework container view controller, `UITabbarController`, to manage the children. We need to update `MainActivity` to fulfill the same responsibility:

1. Enable the navigation tabs area in the ActionBar.

2. For each navigation tab, add a `Tab` object to `ActionBar`.

3. Set the tab appearance, such as the title and an optional tab icon.

4. Set the tab listener that responds to events when the tab is selected, deselected, and reselected. Upon the tab being selected, switch to the right screen.

ADT PROJECT PREPARATIONS

Let's use the MvcTemplate project that we created earlier to start the Android version of the tabbed application.

1. Copy the MvcTemplate ADT project and paste it into a new project (⌘c, ⌘v) named **TabbedApp**.

2. Rename the ADT Application package. From the TabbedApp project context menu, select **Android Tools ➤ Rename Application Package**. Enter a new package name: **com.pdachoice.tabbedapp**.

3. Rename the src/com.pdachoice.renameme Java package. From the package context menu, select **Refactor ➤ Rename…** (Alt+⌘r) and do the following:

   a. Enter a new name: **com.pdachoice.tabbedapp**.

   b. Select **Update references**.

4. Modify the app_name in res/values/strings.xml, as shown in Listing 3-50.

   Listing 3-50. *app_name*

```
<resources>

    <string name="app_name">Tabbed Application</string>
    ...

</resources>
```

5. You may build and run the prep project to make sure you have a clean start.

ActionBar

IOS ANALOGY

UITabBarController

The Android *action bar* is an important addition since API Level 11. It provides the navigation tabs that we need now, but it is actually more than the iOS tab bar. In a nutshell, it offers the following UX components (see Figure 3-35) consistently across the whole app. We will revisit other components later. For now, the navigation tabs are all we need.

Figure 3-35. *Action bar components*

1. The **app icon** on the left to show your application identity.

2. **Navigation tabs** for content views, the main objective of this chapter.

3. **Action items** for important actions of the apps.

4. An **overflow menu** button for actions that are used less often.

If you run the TabbedApp project now, it should look like the MvcTemplate app. We haven't done anything about navigation tabs yet. We only renamed the project files without changing layouts. Of course, there is no tab either. It is time to start working on our main topic.

To add two navigation tabs and switch to the content view/fragment view controller accordingly when each tab is selected, follow these steps:

1. Enable the navigation tabs area by setting the proper navigation mode. To save some space, you can choose to disable the whole title bar in the actionbar, as shown in Listing 3-51.

   Listing 3-51. Enable Navigation Tabs

   ```
   public class MainActivity extends ActionBarActivity {
     @Override
     protected void onCreate(Bundle savedInstanceState) {
       super.onCreate(savedInstanceState);
       setContentView(R.layout.activity_main);

       // enable the Navigation Tabs in ActionBar
       ActionBar actionBar = getSupportActionBar();
       actionBar.setNavigationMode(ActionBar.NAVIGATION_MODE_TABS);
       actionBar.setDisplayShowTitleEnabled(false);
       actionBar.setDisplayShowHomeEnabled(false);
       ...
     }
     ...
   ```

2. For each tab, create a tab instance using `actionBar.newTab()`. Set the tab appearance and tab listener accordingly (see Listing 3-52).

   a. Declare `MainActivity` to implement `TabListener`.

   b. Implement methods defined in `TabListener`.

   c. Set the tab listener to `this`.

   d. Add tabs to the action bar.

Tip   Don't worry about remembering the interface methods names and signatures (see Figure 3-15).

Listing 3-52. Add Tabs

```java
public class MainActivity extends ActionBarActivity implements TabListener {

  @Override
  protected void onCreate(Bundle savedInstanceState) {
    ...
    // create and add First tab, with label, icon
    Tab tab1 = actionBar.newTab().setText("First")
      .setIcon(android.R.drawable.ic_dialog_alert).setTabListener(this);
    actionBar.addTab(tab1);

    // create and add Second tab, with label, icon and listener
    Tab tab2 = actionBar.newTab().setText("Second")
      .setIcon(android.R.drawable.ic_dialog_info).setTabListener(this);
    actionBar.addTab(tab2);
  }

  // ActionBar.TabListener implementations
  @Override
  public void onTabSelected(Tab tab, FragmentTransaction arg1) {
    // TODO ...
  }

  @Override
  public void onTabReselected(Tab t, FragmentTransaction arg1) {
    // do nothing
  }
  @Override
  public void onTabUnselected(Tab arg0, FragmentTransaction arg1) {
    // do nothing
  }
  ...
```

3. To switch fragments, the same method, pushViewController(...), still works (see Listing 3-53):

   a. Call findFragmentByTag(...) to retrieve the existing fragment from the FragmentManager back stack.

   b. Call pushViewController(...).

Listing 3-53. Tabs Navigation

```java
public class MainActivity extends ActionBarActivity {
  ...
  @Override
  public void onTabSelected(Tab tab, FragmentTransaction arg1) {
    int position = tab.getPosition();
```

```java
FragmentManager manager = getSupportFragmentManager();
Fragment toFragment = null;
switch (position) {
case 0:
  toFragment = manager.findFragmentByTag(
      ScreenOneFragment.class.getSimpleName());
  if (toFragment == null) {
    toFragment = new ScreenOneFragment();
  }
  break;
case 1:
  toFragment = manager.findFragmentByTag(
      ScreenTwoFragment.class.getSimpleName());
  if (toFragment == null) {
    toFragment = new ScreenTwoFragment();
  }
  break;
}

pushViewController(toFragment, true);
}

@Override
public void onBackPressed() {
  // this is the back button callback.
  // prevent back event to make tab navigation strictly
}
...
```

> **Note** In iOS apps, you normally don't mix tabs with the Back button. To make it behave similarly to the iOS app, you can disable the system Back button by overriding the Back button pressed callback method, onBackPressed(), without doing anything. However, it doesn't seem graceful to disable system behaviors/the Back button completely because it is a system button, and Android users might expect the default system behavior (go back) or for it do something. The previous suggestion was just for simplicity. Specifically it was to mimic the iOS behavior which doesn't have a system Back button. You will probably want to write some code to respond to the system Back button. For example, some apps do go back to the previous tab and prompt users if they want to leave the app when the Back button is pressed repeatedly. It might not look as strange as it would in iOS. It is a UX topic—choose it wisely.

4. There is nothing to do for onTabUnselected(...) or onTabReselected(...) methods for this purpose. In some apps, you may want to refresh data for onTabReselected.

5. Most likely, you want to use the appcompat_v7 Support Library to support devices with API Level 7+. This is already done in the ADT Blank Activity template. You should take a look at how this is done in case you need to do it yourself manually (for older projects):

   a. Your Activity class, MainActivity, needs to extend from ActionBarActivity instead of the Activity class.

   b. Specify the theme of the app in res/values/styles.xml.
   Use Theme.AppCompat (or its descendant): <style name="AppBaseTheme" parent="Theme.AppCompat.Light">.

   c. The menu item showAsAction attributes in res/menu/main.xml need to be defined in a different namespace: xmlns:app=http://schemas.android.com/apk/res-auto.

6. Build and run the TabbedApp project. The tabs should work as expected. However, the content views do not look like the iOS version (see Figure 3-34) yet; they look more like the screens in our MvcTemplate app with navigation tabs because they are copied from MvcTemplate project. ☺

FINAL TOUCH

You have completed the main topics in this ADT project, comparing the Android app with the iOS app look and feel. Optionally, you can tighten some minor loose ends by updating the layouts and doing some clean up.

1. Modify res/values/strings.xml, as shown in Listing 3-54.

   a. Modify app_name, label_screenone, and label_screentwo.

   b. Add two more strings that appear on first and second tab. You will use them.

Listing 3-54. String Resources for TabbedApp

```xml
<?xml version="1.0" encoding="utf-8"?>
<resources>

    <string name="app_name">Tabbed Application</string>
    <string name="action_settings">Settings</string>
    <string name="hello_world">Hello world!</string>
    <string name="label_screenone">First View</string>
    <string name="label_screentwo">Second View</string>
    <string name="description_screenOne">Loaded by the first view controller –
    an instance of FirstViewController – specified in the app delegate.</string>
    <string name="description_screenTwo">Loaded by the second view controller –
    an instance of SecondViewController – specified in the app delegate.</string>

</resources>
```

2. You only need two screens. Delete the Screen Three fragment (command shortcut key: fn+Delete).

   a. Delete src/ScreenThreeFragment.java.

   b. Delete res/layout/screenthree_fragment.xml.

3. You only need two TextView for both layouts. For First View, modify res/layout/screenone_fragment.xml (see Listing 3-55).

Listing 3-55. TabbedApp screenone_fragment.xml

```xml
<?xml version="1.0" encoding="utf-8"?>
<RelativeLayout xmlns:android="http://schemas.android.com/apk/res/android"
  android:layout_width="match_parent"
  android:layout_height="match_parent">

  <TextView
    android:id="@+id/textViewLabel"
    android:layout_width="wrap_content"
    android:layout_height="wrap_content"
    android:layout_alignParentTop="true"
    android:layout_centerHorizontal="true"
    android:layout_marginTop="@dimen/label_marginTop"
    android:text="@string/label_screenone"
    android:textAppearance="?android:attr/textAppearanceLarge"
    android:textSize="@dimen/label_textsize" />

  <TextView
    android:id="@+id/textViewDescription"
    android:layout_width="wrap_content"
    android:layout_height="wrap_content"
    android:layout_centerHorizontal="true"
    android:layout_centerVertical="true"
    android:layout_marginLeft="@dimen/activity_horizontal_margin"
    android:layout_marginRight="@dimen/activity_horizontal_margin"
    android:gravity="center"
    android:text="@string/description_screenone"
    android:textAppearance="?android:attr/textAppearanceSmall" />

</RelativeLayout>
```

4. For Second View, modify res/layout/screentwo_fragment.xml (see Listing 3-56).

Listing 3-56. TabbedApp screentwo_fragment.xml

```xml
<?xml version="1.0" encoding="utf-8"?>
<RelativeLayout xmlns:android="http://schemas.android.com/apk/res/android"
  android:layout_width="match_parent"
  android:layout_height="match_parent">
```

```xml
    <TextView
        android:id="@+id/textViewLabel"
        android:layout_width="wrap_content"
        android:layout_height="wrap_content"
        android:layout_alignParentTop="true"
        android:layout_centerHorizontal="true"
        android:layout_marginTop="@dimen/label_marginTop"
        android:text="@string/label_screentwo"
        android:textAppearance="?android:attr/textAppearanceLarge"
        android:textSize="@dimen/label_textsize" />

    <TextView
        android:id="@+id/textViewDescription"
        android:layout_width="wrap_content"
        android:layout_height="wrap_content"
        android:layout_centerHorizontal="true"
        android:layout_centerVertical="true"
        android:layout_marginLeft="@dimen/activity_horizontal_margin"
        android:layout_marginRight="@dimen/activity_horizontal_margin"
        android:gravity="center"
        android:text="@string/description_screenTwo"
        android:textAppearance="?android:attr/textAppearanceSmall" />

</RelativeLayout>
```

5. Fragment classes should have some trivial errors after changing the layout files because there is no longer a nextButton. Remove or comment out any code related to nextButton in Screen One Fragment.java, as shown in Listing 3-57.

Listing 3-57. TabbedApp ScreenOneFragment.java

```java
public class ScreenOneFragment extends Fragment /* implements OnClickListener */{
    private View contentView;

    // private View nextButton;

    @Override
    public View onCreateView(LayoutInflater inflater, ViewGroup container,
                             Bundle savedInstanceState) {
        contentView = inflater.inflate(R.layout.screenone_fragment, container,
            false);

        // nextButton = contentView.findViewById(R.id.buttonNext);
        // nextButton.setOnClickListener(this); // Delegate button OnClick events
        return contentView;
    }
```

```
    // provide the interface implementation
    // @Override
    // public void onClick(View v) {
    // // Step E: delegate to MainActivity
    // ScreenTwoFragment frag = new ScreenTwoFragment();
    // ((MainActivity) getActivity()).pushViewController(frag, true);
    // }
}
```

6. Remove the code related to nextButton in ScreenTwoFragment.java, as shown in Listing 3-58.

Listing 3-58. TabbedApp ScreenTwoFragment.java

```java
public class ScreenTwoFragment extends Fragment {
  private View contentView;

  @Override
  public View onCreateView(LayoutInflater inflater, ViewGroup container,
                           Bundle savedInstanceState) {
    contentView = inflater.inflate(R.layout.screentwo_fragment, container, false);

    return contentView;
  }
}
```

7. Build and run the project to see the live app in action, as shown in Figure 3-36.

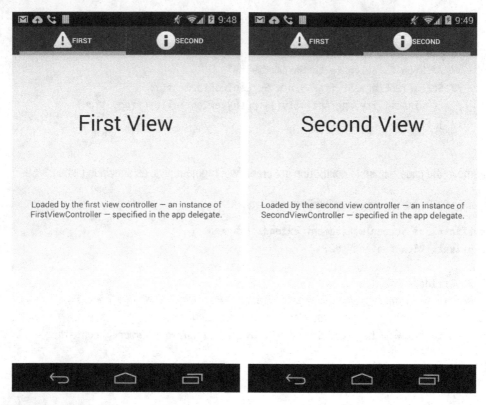

Figure 3-36. Android TabbedApp

The navigation tabs appear on top of the screen, which is different from the iOS TabbedApp. In general, you want to maintain your mobile app UX consistencies across platforms when it makes sense. You need to make your mobile app UX-consistent with system apps and compliant with platform UX guidelines. When there are conflicts, you either need to be more creative or make educated decisions. In general, platform UX guidelines should never be overlooked. Keep the navigation tabs on the top, which is where most of the Android users expect to see them.

Swipe Views

IOS ANALOGY

UIPageViewController

The *swipe view* is another very common and popular UX design pattern. You use this pattern to display content, page by page, using horizontal swipe gestures. It allows the user to move from item to item efficiently. With built-in page transitions animation effects, the app offers a more enjoyable viewing experience without much coding effort. Both iOS and Android provide framework classes, as well as a project creation template to promote this page-by-page navigation UX pattern.

Figure 3-37 shows the PageByPage iOS app that was created using the Xcode Page-Based Application template. You are going to port this iOS app to Android platform.

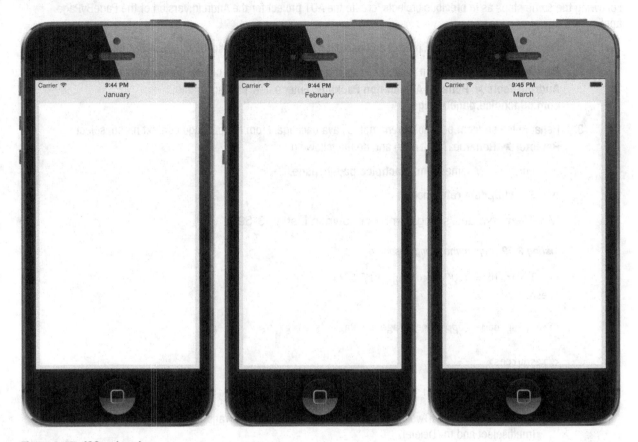

Figure 3-37. iOS swipe views

For learning purposes, you are going to create the Android version from the MvcTemplate project:

1. Create one `Fragment` class with a property to hold the month. Instantiate each fragment object for each month.

2. Use **ViewPager** to switch fragments page by page.

There is a more sophisticated project template that creates Tabs + Swipe apps, too. After you obtain an understanding of the key framework class, you should take it one step further by creating and reading the project created using the ADT Tabs + Swipe template.

ADT PROJECT PREPARATIONS

Following the same steps as in previous projects, create the ADT project for the Android version of the PageByPage application.

1. Copy the MvcTemplate ADT project and paste it into a new project (⌘c, ⌘v) named **PageByPage**.

2. Rename the ADT Application package. From the PageByPage project context menu, select **Android Tools ➤ Rename Application Package**. Enter a new package name: **com.pdachoice.pagebypage**.

3. Rename the src/com.pdachoice.renameme Java package. From the package context menu, select **Refactor ➤ Rename…** (Alt+⌘r) and do the following:

    a. Enter a new name: **com.pdachoice.pagebypage**.

    b. Select **Update references**.

4. Modify res/values/strings.xml as shown in Listing 3-59.

    Listing 3-59. app_name String Resource

    ```xml
    <?xml version="1.0" encoding="utf-8"?>
    <resources>

        <string name="app_name">Page by Page</string>
        ...
    </resources>
    ```

5. You only need one fragment, so do the following:

    a. Delete the src/ScreenTwoFragment.java and src/ScreenThreeFragment.java classes (multiselect and fn+Delete).

    b. Delete the res/layout/screentwo_fragment.xml and res/layout/screenthree_fragment.xml files (fn+Delete).

    c. Rename the ScreenOneFragment.java class (Alt+⌘r) as **MonthFragment**.

    d. Rename the res/layout/screenone_fragment.xml resource (Alt+⌘r) as **month_fragment**.

    e. Remove code related to the nextButton in ScreenOneFragment.java (see Listing 3-60). You don't need the button.

Listing 3-60. *MonthFragment*

```
public class MonthFragment extends Fragment {
  private View contentView;

  @Override
  public View onCreateView(LayoutInflater inflater, ViewGroup container,
                           Bundle savedInstanceState) {
    contentView = inflater.inflate(R.layout.month_fragment, container, false);

    return contentView;
  }
}
```

ViewPager

```
                              IOS ANALOGY

UIPageViewController
```

The key to implementing the swipeable page-by-page pattern is to use the framework ViewPager class. Just like the ListFragment class, it needs a PagerAdapter to supply page views with data.

Here's a quick overview of ViewPagerusage:

- MainActivity, the container view controller, uses ViewPager as the container root element in its layout file.
- Creates fragment(s) for the page view(s).
- Creates a PagerAdapter class that supplies page views with data.

Continue by doing the following in the PageByPage Android project:

1. ViewPager is a ViewGroup. Use it as the view container instead of FrameLayout. Modify the res/layout/activity_main.xml file, as shown in Listing 3-61.

    Listing 3-61. *ViewPager*

    ```
    <android.support.v4.view.ViewPager

      xmlns:android="http://schemas.android.com/apk/res/android"
        android:id="@+id/fragment_container"
        android:layout_width="match_parent"
        android:layout_height="match_parent">

    </android.support.v4.view.ViewPager>
    ```

2. You need a custom PagerAdapter that supplies the ViewPager page views with page data. It is the same adapter pattern used by ListView. Use the **Create Java Class** wizard to create the Java class. From the project src folder or Java package context menu, select **New ➤ Class** and do the following:

    a. Enter **PageByPage/src** as the Source folder.

    b. Enter **com.pdachoice.pagebypage** as the Package.

    c. Enter **MonthViewPagerAdapter** as the Name.

    d. Enter **android.widget.FragmentPagerAdapter** as the Superclass (or browse).

    e. Select **Constructors** from the Superclass.

    f. Select **Inherited abstract methods**.

    g. Click the **Finish** button when done. Eclipse creates the class skeleton with the required abstract methods that need to be implemented as shown in Listing 3-62. You will fill in the blanks.

Listing 3-62. PagerAdapter

```
package com.pdachoice.pagebypage;

import android.support.v4.app.Fragment;
import android.support.v4.app.FragmentManager;
import android.support.v4.app.FragmentPagerAdapter;

public class MonthViewPagerAdapter extends FragmentPagerAdapter {

  public MonthViewPagerAdapter(FragmentManager fm) {
    super(fm);
    // TODO Auto-generated constructor stub
  }

  @Override
  public Fragment getItem(int pos) {
    // TODO Auto-generated method stub
    return null;
  }

  @Override
  public int getCount() {
    // TODO Auto-generated method stub
    return 0;
  }
}
```

> **Note** FragmentPagerAdapter is an abstract class that implements a partial PagerAdapter contract/interface. Instead of implementing the whole PagerAdapter interface, it is much simpler to extend the FragmentPagerAdapter class.

> **Tip** Regarding Eclipse and Java, if you did not select the **Constructor from superclass** check box, you will get a compilation error. Click the red error indicator—the little red circle with a cross, or the red underlining—and choose the appropriate suggestion as shown in Figure 3-38.

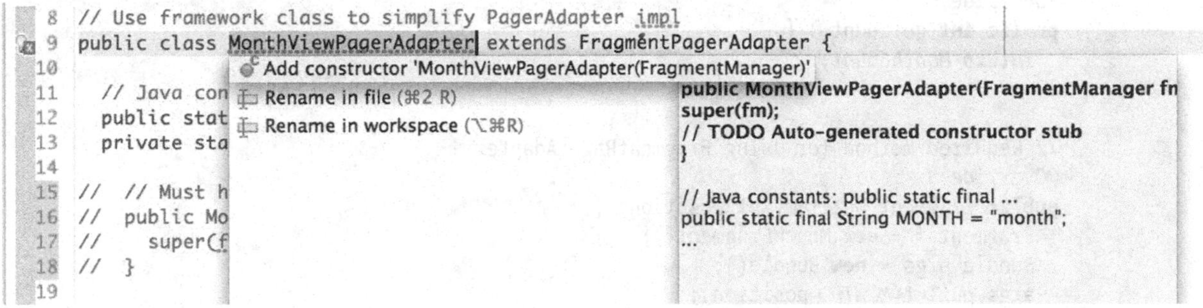

```
 8   // Use framework class to simplify PagerAdapter impl
 9   public class MonthViewPagerAdapter extends FragmentPagerAdapter {
10
11       // Java con   [⚙] Add constructor 'MonthViewPagerAdapter(FragmentManager)'
12       public stat   [▭] Rename in file (⌘2 R)          public MonthViewPagerAdapter(FragmentManager fn
13       private sta   [▭] Rename in workspace (⌥⌘R)      super(fm);
14                                                        // TODO Auto-generated constructor stub
15   //   // Must h                                       }
16   //   public Mo
17   //     super(f                                       // Java constants: public static final ...
18   //   }                                               public static final String MONTH = "month";
19                                                        ...
```

Figure 3-38. Add constructor

> **Tip** There is a Java rule that if the superclass defines a nondefault constructor, the subclass must define a constructor. If you did not define a constructor, hover over the red line to see the suggestion.

3. Complete the following abstract methods as shown in Listing 3-63:

    a. getCount(...): The number of page views in ViewPager.

    b. getItem(...): Returns the fragment object that manages the pager view.

    c. As a rule of thumb, to pass data to a fragment, an activity, or any application component, you need to do setArgument(...). This is because these application components go through component lifecycles. Do not use properties. They get lost when the activity or fragment restarts.

Listing 3-63. Implement PagerAdapter

```java
// Use framework class to simplify PagerAdapter impl
public class MonthViewPagerAdapter extends FragmentPagerAdapter {

    // constants in Java: public static final ...
    public static final String MONTH = "month";
    private static final int MonthCount = 12;

    // Must have at least one constructor if parent has non-default constructor
    public MonthViewPagerAdapter(FragmentManager fm) {
        super(fm);
    }

    // Required method for using FragmentPagerAdapter
    @Override
    public int getCount() {
        return MonthCount;
    }

    // Required method for using FragmentPagerAdapter
    @Override
    public Fragment getItem(int position) {
        Fragment f = new MonthFragment();
        Bundle args = new Bundle();
        args.putInt(MONTH, position);
        f.setArguments(args);
        return f;
    }
}
```

4. Use the newly created `MonthViewPagerAdapter` class in `MainActivity.java` (see Listing 3-64).

    a. Create an instance and assign it to be the `ViewPager` adapter.

    b. ViewPager takes care of screen navigation by swiping the screen horizontally. You don't need to `pushViewController(...)`, and so forth. Remove this code.

Listing 3-64. Set ViewPager Adapter

```java
public class MainActivity extends ActionBarActivity {

    private ViewPager viewPager;

    @Override
    protected void onCreate(Bundle savedInstanceState) {
        super.onCreate(savedInstanceState);

        // setup the content view.
        setContentView(R.layout.activity_main);
```

```
    viewPager = (ViewPager) findViewById(R.id.fragment_container);

    // set a custom adapter to supply view with data per page
    PagerAdapter adapter =
      new MonthViewPagerAdapter(getSupportFragmentManager());
    viewPager.setAdapter(adapter);
  }
  ...
```

5. Build and run the ADT PageByPage project. You should see the page-by-page swipe views in action! However, the 12-month page views are still showing the familiar content view copied from the MvcTemplate project. That is the beauty of using the MVC framework: you can modify the view and its view controller code independently.

FINAL TOUCH

You have completed the main topics in this ADT project, comparing the Android app with the iOS app look and feel. Optionally, you can tighten some minor loose ends. To update the MonthFragment to display the month name in its view, do the following:

1. Use the layout editor to draw your layout, res/layout/month_fragment.xml. To mimic the iOS view, all you need is one TextView and an empty container widget with a white background. (See Listing 3-65.)

Listing 3-65. month_fragment.xml

```
<?xml version="1.0" encoding="utf-8"?>
<RelativeLayout
  xmlns:android="http://schemas.android.com/apk/res/android"
  android:layout_width="match_parent"
  android:layout_height="match_parent"
  android:background="#FE9A2E">

  <TextView
    android:id="@+id/textViewLabel"
    android:layout_width="wrap_content"
    android:layout_height="wrap_content"
    android:layout_alignParentTop="true"
    android:layout_centerHorizontal="true"
    android:layout_marginTop="@dimen/button_marginEnd"
    android:text="@string/label_screenone"
    android:textAppearance="?android:attr/textAppearanceLarge" />
```

```
<RelativeLayout
    android:layout_width="fill_parent"
    android:layout_height="fill_parent"
    android:layout_below="@+id/textViewLabel"
    android:layout_centerHorizontal="true"
    android:layout_margin="@dimen/activity_horizontal_margin"
    android:background="@android:color/white" />

</RelativeLayout>
```

2. Colors are an Android resource. You should externalize color code in res/values/colors.xml as shown in Listing 3-66.

Listing 3-66. *colors.xml Color Resource*

```xml
<?xml version="1.0" encoding="utf-8"?>
<resources>
    <color name="monthViewBackground">#FE9A2E</color>
</resources>
```

3. You can use android:background="@color/monthViewBackground" in your res/layout/month_fragment.xml layout file.

4. Update src/MonthFragment.java to populate the content view with data, as shown in Listing 3-67.

Listing 3-67. *Render MonthFragment View*

```java
public class MonthFragment extends Fragment {  ...
    @Override
    public View onCreateView(LayoutInflater inflater, ViewGroup container,
                              Bundle savedInstanceState) {

        ...
        int month = this.getArguments().getInt(MonthViewPagerAdapter.MONTH);

        String monthName = new DateFormatSymbols().getMonths()[month];
        TextView label = (TextView) contentView.findViewById(R.id.textViewLabel);
        label.setText(monthName);
        ...
    }
}
```

5. Rebuild and run the PageByPage ADT project to see the live app in action, as shown in Figure 3-39.

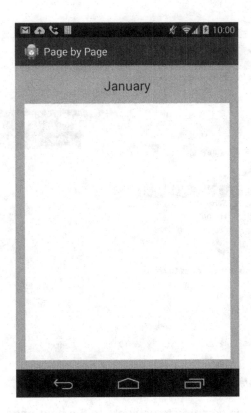

Figure 3-39. Android swipe views

This works fine by design, and it closely resembles the iOS app look and feel and the swiped view behaviors. Everything looks OK from iOS eyes, but it appears to be missing something in Android eyes. Apparently, there is a more popular variant, Tabs + Swipe, in Android. There are two Tabs + Swipe ADT templates. Let's try to visualize its usage (see Figure 3-40).

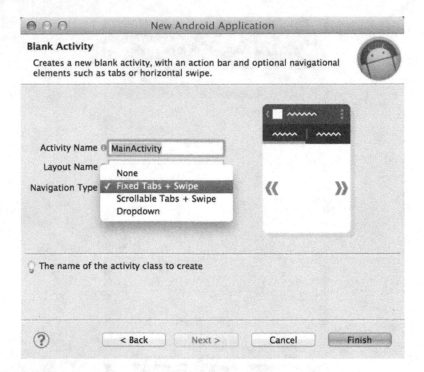

Figure 3-40. ADT Tabs + Swipe template

This template project offers *swipe gestures* to navigate to the next page. It also provides navigation tabs to change the page. The navigation tabs' title shows the page title, naturally. It should look like Figure 3-41.

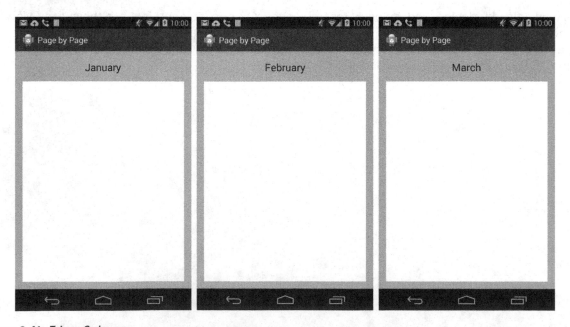

Figure 3-41. Tabs + Swipe app

Take some time to read the template code. I already introduced the required techniques. To apply this beautiful UX pattern, you can continue working with your TabbedApp project. All you need to do extra is add navigation tabs, and programmatically change tabs or change the page via the appropriate selected tab or page change events.

Sliding Menu

The *sliding menu* is a panel that displays the app's menu on the left edge of the screen. It is hidden and only revealed when the user swipes a finger from the left edge of the screen. Many popular apps on iOS and Android use this navigation pattern, including Facebook and most of the Google mobile apps like YouTube, Gmail, Google Map, and so forth. Although there is no direct support in the iOS SDK, many iOS developers simply handcraft it or use some open source libraries to achieve the same purpose. Most of the iOS developers call it sliding menu. On the Android platform, it is called the *navigation drawer*, and you can easily implement this UX pattern using the framework API.

ADT PROJECT PREPARATIONS

As usual, let's use the MvcTemplate project to create an ADT project:

1. Copy the MvcTemplate ADT project and paste it into a new project (⌘c, ⌘v) named **SlidingMenu**.

2. Rename the Android application package. From the newly created SlidingMenu project context menu, select **Android Tools ➤ Rename Application Package** and enter a new package name: **com. pdachoice.slidingmenu**.

3. Rename the src/com.pdachoice.renameme Java package. From the package context menu, select **Refactor ➤ Rename...** (Alt+⌘r) and do the following:

   a. Enter a new name: **com.pdachoice.slidingmenu**.

   b. Select **Update references**.

4. Modify res/values/strings.xml, as shown in Listing 3-68.

   Listing 3-68. app_name

```xml
<?xml version="1.0" encoding="utf-8"?>
<resources>

    <string name="app_name">Sliding Menu</string>
    ...

</resources>
```

DrawerLayout

In Android, you can simply implement the navigation drawer using the `DrawerLayout` API, as follows:

1. As usual, modify the `MainActivity` container view controller to manage the child fragments. Modify `res/layout/main_activity.xml`. The following shows a very common usage using `DrawerLayout` (see Listing 3-69).

    a. The main content view, `FrameLayout`, must be the first child in the `DrawerLayout` because the XML order implies z-ordering and the drawer must be on top of the content.

    b. The main content view is set to match the parent view's width and height, because it represents the entire UI when the navigation drawer is hidden.

    c. The drawer view, the `ListView`, must specify its horizontal gravity with the `android:layout_gravity` attribute. To support right-to-left (RTL) languages, specify the value with `"start"`.

    d. The drawer view specifies its width in density-independent pixel (dp) units, and the height matches the parent view. The drawer width should be no more than 320dp so that the user can always see a portion of the main content.

Listing 3-69. DrawerLayout

```
<android.support.v4.widget.DrawerLayout
xmlns:android="http://schemas.android.com/apk/res/android"
    android:id="@+id/drawer_layout"
    android:layout_width="match_parent"
    android:layout_height="match_parent">

    <!-- The main content view from child fragments -->
    <FrameLayout
        android:id="@+id/fragment_container"
        android:layout_width="match_parent"
        android:layout_height="match_parent"/>

    <!-- The navigation drawer -->
    <ListView
        android:id="@+id/leftDrawer"
        android:layout_width="240dp"
        android:layout_height="match_parent"
        android:layout_gravity="start"
        android:background="@android:color/background_light"
        android:choiceMode="singleChoice"
        android:divider="@android:color/background_dark"
        android:dividerHeight="0dp"/>

</android.support.v4.widget.DrawerLayout>
```

2. The drawer view is a `ListView`. As usual, set the adapter for list items, and delegate list item clicked events—`setOnItemClickListener(...)`—to this. Also, make `ScreenOneFragment` the first screen, as shown in Listing 3-70.

Listing 3-70. Drawer View

```
public class MainActivity extends ActionBarActivity implements OnItemClickListener {

    private static final List<String>items =
        Arrays.asList("1st view",  "2nd view", "3rd view");

    private View contentView;
    private ListView leftDrawer;
    private ArrayAdapter<String>mListAdapter;

    @Override
    protected void onCreate(Bundle savedInstanceState) {
        super.onCreate(savedInstanceState);

        // setup the content view.
        setContentView(R.layout.activity_main);

        contentView = findViewById(R.id.drawer_layout);

        leftDrawer = (ListView) contentView.findViewById(R.id.leftDrawer);

        mListAdapter = new ArrayAdapter<String>(
            this, android.R.layout.simple_list_item_1, items);

        leftDrawer.setAdapter(mListAdapter);
        leftDrawer.setOnItemClickListener(this);

        pushViewController(new ScreenOneFragment(), false);
    }

    @Override
    public void onItemClick(AdapterView<?> lv, View li, int pos, long id) {
        // TODO
    }
    ...
```

3. Implement onItemClick(...) to handle the list item selected events (see Listing 3-71):

   a. Close the drawer (the sliding menu).

   b. Set the title on the action bar.

   c. Navigate to the selected fragment using the same FragmentManager API.

Listing 3-71. onItemClick

```java
public class MainActivity extends ActionBarActivity implements OnItemClickListener {
  ...
  @Override
  public void onItemClick(AdapterView<?> lv, View li, int pos, long id) {
    // Close the sliding menu, and set the title.
    ((DrawerLayout) contentView).closeDrawer(leftDrawer);
    getSupportActionBar().setTitle(items.get(pos));

    // Navigate to the selected Fragment.
    FragmentManager manager = getSupportFragmentManager();
    Fragment toFragment = null;
    switch (pos) {
    case 0:
      toFragment = manager.findFragmentByTag(ScreenOneFragment.class
        .getSimpleName());
      if (toFragment == null) {
        toFragment = new ScreenOneFragment();
      }
      break;
    case 1:
      toFragment = manager.findFragmentByTag(ScreenTwoFragment.class
        .getSimpleName());
      if (toFragment == null) {
        toFragment = new ScreenTwoFragment();
      }
      break;
    case 2:
      toFragment = manager.findFragmentByTag(ScreenThreeFragment.class
        .getSimpleName());
      if (toFragment == null) {
        toFragment = new ScreenThreeFragment();
      }
      break;
    }

    pushViewController(toFragment, true);
  }
  ...
```

FINAL TOUCH

The sliding menu works just fine when you swipe your finger from the left edge of the screen. You have completed the main topics in this ADT project. However, most of those apps also offer toggling the drawer when you tap on a revealing button. On Android, you have a free widget you can use: the *action bar app icon* that appears on the top-left corner of the screen, as shown in Figure 3-35. Precisely speaking, it is the app icon enabled as an Up button that has a look and feel slightly different from the pure app icon. As I mentioned, the action bar is an important addition since API 11+. We used it to create navigation tabs earlier. We are using it as a navigational Up button. We will talk about it again later. Optionally, you may use the code shown in Listing 3-72 to enable the app icon as an Up button and toggle the sliding menu.

Listing 3-72. App Icon As Up Button

```
public class MainActivity extends ActionBarActivity implements OnItemClickListener {
  ...
  @Override
  protected void onCreate(Bundle savedInstanceState) {
    ...
    // enable App Icon as Up button
    getSupportActionBar().setDisplayHomeAsUpEnabled(true);
  }

  @Override
  public boolean onSupportNavigateUp() {
    if(((DrawerLayout) contentView).isDrawerOpen(leftDrawer)) {
      ((DrawerLayout) contentView).closeDrawer(leftDrawer);
    } else {
      ((DrawerLayout) contentView).openDrawer(leftDrawer);
    }
    return true;
  }
  ...
```

I also deleted the nextButton buttons from res/layout/screenone_fragment.xml and res/layout/screentwo_fragment.xml.

Build and run the app to see the live app in action again. Figure 3-42 shows the sliding menu from being opened to completely closed. The main content view background color alpha value was gradually increased by the framework API. If you are handcrafting the sliding menu in your iOS app, you should animate the background alpha value like the Android framework does.

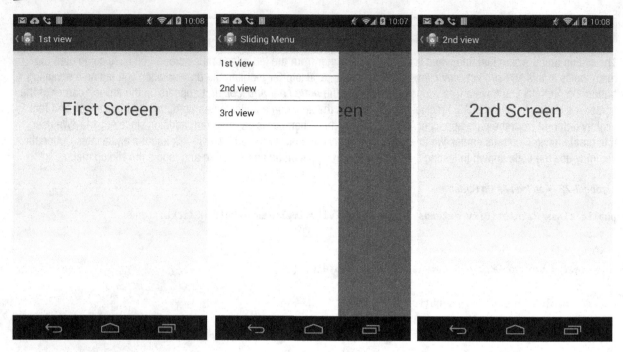

Figure 3-42. Sliding menu

Dialogs

Dialogs are widely used to display important information to users, such as confirmations, warnings, errors, and so forth. Many apps also use it to request user input. Dialogs normally sit on top of the current screen while that screen remains partially visible or dimmed. This creates a visual effect that is meant to get more user attention.

In general, you apply this UX pattern to give mobile users quick feedback or to request simple confirmation or choices. In Android, you can also create more sophisticated custom layouts to collect user input before continuing with the current task. The Android Dialog API is actually more than the iOS `UITableView` with richer functionalities.

AlertDialog

Figure 3-43 pretty much depicts all you need to know about the `AlertDialog` usages.

Figure 3-43. *Dialog anatomy*

The pointers in Figure 3-43 show the following:

1. **Title**: This is optional and should be used only when the content area is occupied by a detailed message, list, or custom layout. If you need to state a simple message or question, conventionally you don't need a title.

2. **Content area**: This can display a message, list, or custom layout.

3. **Action buttons**: There should be no more than three action buttons in a dialog.

The iOS app in Figure 3-44 shows the standard UIAlertView usage: a title, a message, and two buttons. It presents a message to users with a concise look and feel. Let's port it to Android to see the Android dialog in action.

Figure 3-44. iOS UIAlertView

ADT PROJECT PREPARATIONS

Use the MvcTemplate project to create an ADT project for the Android version of the Dialogs application.

1. Copy the MvcTemplate ADT project and paste it into a new project (⌘c, ⌘v) named **Dialogs**.

2. Rename the Android application package. From the Dialogs project context menu, select **Android Tools ➤ Rename Application Package**. Enter a new package name: **com.pdachoice.dialogs**.

3. Rename the src/com.pdachoice.renameme Java package. From the package context menu, select **Refactor ➤ Rename…** (Alt+⌘r) and do the following:

   a. Enter a new name: **com.pdachoice.dialogs**.

   b. Select **Update references**.

4. Modify res/values/strings.xml, as shown in Listing 3-73.

    Listing 3-73. app_name in strings.xml

    ```xml
    <?xml version="1.0" encoding="utf-8"?>
    <resources>
        <string name="app_name">Dialogs</string>
        <string name="action_settings">Settings</string>
        <string name="popup">Popup</string>
        <string name="alert">Alert</string>
    </resources>
    ```

5. You only need one fragment: keep ScreenOneFragment and delete the other two, as follows:

    a. Delete the src/ScreenTwoFragment.java and src/ScreenThreeFragment.java classes (multiselect and fn+Delete).

    b. Delete the res/layout/screentwo_fragment.xml and res/layout/screenthree_fragment.xml files (fn+Delete).

6. Modify res/layout/screenone_fragment.xml, as shown in Listing 3-74. You need a Button widget to show an alert view. Rename buttonNext as **buttonAlert** (Alt+⌘r).

    Listing 3-74. screenone_fragment.xml

    ```xml
    <?xml version="1.0" encoding="utf-8"?>
    <RelativeLayout
    xmlns:android="http://schemas.android.com/apk/res/android"
        android:layout_width="match_parent"
        android:layout_height="match_parent">

        <Button
            android:id="@+id/buttonAlert"
            android:layout_width="wrap_content"
            android:layout_height="wrap_content"
            android:layout_alignParentTop="true"
            android:layout_centerHorizontal="true"
            android:layout_marginTop="@dimen/label_marginTop"
            android:text="@string/alert" />

    </RelativeLayout>
    ```

7. Modify src/ScreenOneFragment.java (see Listing 3-75):

    a. Delete the code in the onClick(…) method. When the button is tapped, you want to show an alert view. You will fill in the blank later.

    b. Rename nextButton as **alertButton** (Alt+⌘r).

Listing 3-75. ScreenOneFragment.java

```java
public class ScreenOneFragment extends Fragment implements OnClickListener {
    private View contentView;
    private View alertButton;

    @Override
    public View onCreateView(LayoutInflater inflater, ViewGroup container, Bundle
                             savedInstanceState) {
        contentView = inflater.inflate(R.layout.screenone_fragment, container, false);

        alertButton = contentView.findViewById(R.id.buttonAlert);
        alertButton.setOnClickListener(this); // Delegate button OnClick events
        return contentView;
    }

    // provide the interface implementation
    @Override
    public void onClick(View v) {
        // TODO: show an Alert view
    }
}
```

8. Build and run the ADT project, just to make sure it works.

Among all the AlertDialog usages, this alert is the simplest: it informs the user about a situation that requires a simple choice based on the dialog confirmation message or acknowledgement. When implementing this type of alert, you can use a title, a message, and an icon to show the message with severity. It only uses a message text in the *content area*. The *title area* is optional; it can be any text or icon but it is primarily used to show severities or appropriate categories that users immediately understand.

In the Dialogs app, show an alert view when the alertButton is tapped. The following is an AlertDialog usage quick overview:

- Use AlertDialog.builder to create an AlertDialog instance.
- Set the **Title** text.
- Set the **Message** text.
- Add **Buttons** (max three).
- Handle the button OnClick events.

Now, try the following:

1. Instead of creating the AlertDialog instance directly, create a builder instance first (the GoF Builder Creational pattern).

   a. To set the AlertDialog properties, do it via the builder instance.

   b. Title with an icon.

   c. Content area using a simple text string.

2. Implement action buttons: one positive and one negative button. Make the this fragment handle the dialog button OnClick events (see Listing 3-76):

   a. Declare the ScreenOneFragment class to implement DialogInterface. OnClickListener.

   b. Provide a DialogInterface.OnClickListener implementation: onClick(...).

   c. Make it a modal dialog like iOS UIAlertView.

   d. Use the builder instance to create and show the dialog instance.

Listing 3-76. AlertDialog

```
public class ScreenOneFragment extends Fragment implements OnClickListener,
    DialogInterface.OnClickListener {
  ...
  @Override
  public void onClick(View v) {
    // create builder instance.
    AlertDialog.Builder builder = new AlertDialog.Builder(getActivity());

    // set alert dialog content view, Title with an icon
    builder.setTitle("Attention").setIcon(android.R.drawable.ic_menu_help);

    // content area message.
    builder.setMessage("Standard User Alert");

    //  max 3 buttons.
    builder.setPositiveButton("Ok", this);
    builder.setNegativeButton("Cancel", this);

    // make it a modal dialog
    builder.setCancelable(false);

    // create the dialog instance and show it.
    AlertDialog dialog = builder.create();
    dialog.show();
  }
```

```
        // DialogInterface.OnClickListener interface impl.
        @Override
        public void onClick(DialogInterface dialog, int id) {
          if (id == DialogInterface.BUTTON_POSITIVE)
              Log.d("", "AlertDialog.onClick: " + "OK'd");
          else
              Log.d("", "AlertDialog.onClick: " + "Canceled");
        }
        ...
        }
```

3. This is all about alert usages. Build and run the ADT Dialogs app to see the app in action, as shown in Figure 3-45.

Figure 3-45. Android AlertDialog

DialogFragment

A `DialogFragment` can do everything that the `AlertDialog` can do. Particularly, to make the dialog more modular/reusable or to use a custom layout for more sophisticated dialog designs, you should create a custom `DialogFragment` class. Many times, I choose to use it just to minimize potential refactoring efforts that might occur later, simply because it is more versatile. For example, there are situations when a full screen is more suitable on smaller devices; however, for the same app, it might make more sense to use partial screens on tablets. In this case, I can present the same layout within a modal dialog that occupies a partial screen, or I can just treat it as a regular fragment and use the Fragment API to manage the lifecycle or screen navigations in tabs or stacks.

It also gives developers more controls to customize the content area, if needed. It is definitely more MVC-oriented. I found myself only using AlertDialog for the alert style with a simple text message introduced earlier.

Let's use the DialogFragment for the second Android dialog UX pattern: *popups*. These are lightweight version of dialogs that require a single selection from the user. Popups don't have to have specific buttons that accept or cancel the operation. Instead, making a selection advances the workflow, and simply touching outside the popup dismisses it.

IOS ANALOGY

UIPopoverController—for the iPad only.

The closest iOS framework class is the UIPopoverController for iPad (see Figure 3-46). On iPhone, I would probably just create a UIView overlay to create the UX look and feel, or simply use UITableViewController to prompt the selections.

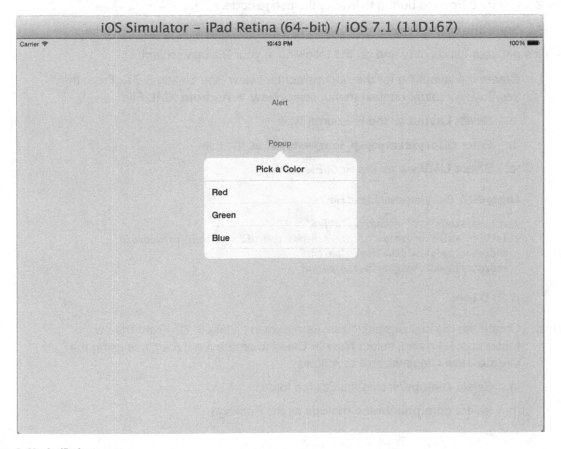

Figure 3-46. An iPad popover

Continue with the previous ADT Dialogs project. Let's modify the app to demonstrate the popups usage. A dialog contains a `ListView` that users can make a selection from.

`DialogFragment` is a dialog and it is also a fragment. You create it as a fragment with a layout file. You treat it as a dialog so that you can take advantage of the Dialog API and the UX.

There are two options to create a `DialogFragment`:

- Like the way you create custom `Fragment` classes, override `onCreateView(...)`, which returns a view from a custom layout file.

- You can also override `onCreateDialog(...)`, which returns a `Dialog` object.

It is allowed—but it is not a good idea—to mix both by implementing them in the same class, in my opinion. You can do it for some rare situations that I personally feel are not practical. I am going to show the second approach simply because you have already seen `onCreateView(...)` so many times that you should know how to do it already.

You only need to add a button to demo the popups usage code. The following is a `DialogFragment` task quick overview:

1. Create a custom `DialogFragment` class.

2. Create a Popups button to invoke the usage code.

3. Show the `DialogFragment` the same way you showed `AlertDialog` previously.

Now, let's get your hands dirty and do the following in your Dialogs project:

1. Create the layout file for the popups content view (see Listing 3-77). From the res/layout/ folder context menu, select **New ➤ Android XML File**:

   a. Select **Layout** as the Resource Type.

   b. Enter **colorpickerpopup_fragment.xml** as the File.

   c. Select **ListView** as the Root Element.

Listing 3-77. DialogFragment Layout File

```
<?xml version="1.0" encoding="utf-8"?>
<ListView xmlns:android="http://schemas.android.com/apk/res/android"
  android:layout_width="match_parent"
  android:layout_height="match_parent">

</ListView>
```

2. Create the `DialogFragment` class, as shown in Listing 3-78. From the src folder context menu, select **New ➤ Class** to create the Java class using the **Create Java Class** wizard, as follows:

   a. Select **Dialogs/src** as the Source folder.

   b. Select **com.pdachoice.dialogs** as the Package.

    c. Enter **ColorPickerPopupFragment** as the Name.

    d. Enter **android.support.v4.app.DialogFragment** or browse Superclass.

Listing 3-78. Custom DialogFragment Class

```
import android.support.v4.app.DialogFragment;

public class ColorPickerPopupFragment extends DialogFragment {

}
```

3. Create a ListAdapter instance that supplies the list items for the
ListView, as shown in Listing 3-79. The system class ArrayAdapter with
android.R.layout.simple_list_item_1 is perfect for simple usage like this.
This was covered in the "ListFragment" section.

Listing 3-79. ListAdapter for Popup List

```
public class ColorPickerPopupFragment extends DialogFragment {

    private ArrayAdapter<String>mListAdapter;

    @Override
    public void onCreate(Bundle savedInstanceState) {
      super.onCreate(savedInstanceState);

      mListAdapter = new ArrayAdapter<String>(
          getActivity(),
          android.R.layout.simple_list_item_1,
          new String[] { "Red", "Green", "Blue" });
    }
    ...
```

4. To show the DialogFragment content view as a popup, implement the
onCreateDialog(...) method that returns a Dialog instance
(see Listing 3-80):

    a. Set the ListAdapter that provides the color list items.

    b. Create the AlertDialog instance using the framework builder class.

    c. Instead of setting a dialog content area with message text, use
setView(mListview) to provide a dialog content area with our custom
layout, mListview.

Listing 3-80. onCreateDialog(...)

```
public class ColorPickerPopupFragment extends DialogFragment {

    private ArrayAdapter<String>mListAdapter;
    private ListView mListview;
    ...
```

```
        @Override
        public Dialog onCreateDialog(Bundle savedInstanceState) {

            LayoutInflater inflater = getActivity().getLayoutInflater();

            // set list item Adapter that supplies list view items
            mListview = (ListView) inflater.inflate(R.layout.colorpickerpopup_fragment, null);
            mListview.setAdapter(mListAdapter);
            // mListview.setOnItemClickListener(this);

            // Same as previous Alert, the framework use Builder design pattern
            AlertDialog.Builder builder = new AlertDialog.Builder(getActivity());

            // AlertDialog title and icon.
            builder.setTitle("Pick a color");
            builder.setIcon(android.R.drawable.ic_menu_directions);

            // AlertDialog custom layout in AlertDialog content area
            builder.setView(mListview);

            // Create the AlertDialog instance and return it.
            AlertDialog dialog = builder.create();
            return dialog;
        }
    }
```

5. When a color is selected from the Color Picker popup, log a text to LogCat
    view (see Listing 3-81):

    a. Declare ColorPickerPopupFragment to implement OnItemClickListener.

    b. Set the color item OnItemClickListener to the PopupColorsDialogFragment, this.

    c. Provide OnItemClickListener implementation that logs a text.

Listing 3-81. Implement Popup List OnItemClickListener

```
public class ColorPickerPopupFragment extends DialogFragment implements OnItemClickListener {
    ...
    @Override
    public Dialog onCreateDialog(Bundle savedInstanceState) {
        ...
        mListview.setOnItemClickListener(this);
        ...
    }

    @Override
    public void onItemClick(AdapterView<?> parent, View v, int position, long id) {
        Log.d("onClick", "position: " + position + "id: " + id);
    }
    ...}
```

6. To show the new Color Picker popup, add a button to the layout file. Open
    res/layout/screenone_fragment.xml in the ADT graphical layout editor to
    add a <button> widget, as shown in Listing 3-82.

Listing 3-82. Add a Simple Button

```
<RelativeLayout ...>

  ...
  <Button
    android:id="@+id/buttonPopup"
    android:layout_width="wrap_content"
    android:layout_height="wrap_content"
    android:layout_centerHorizontal="true"
    android:layout_below="@+id/buttonAlert"
    android:layout_marginTop="@dimen/label_marginTop"
    android:text="@string/popup"/>

</RelativeLayout>
```

7. Implement the onClick(...) behavior when the new buttonPopup widget
    is selected (see Listing 3-83). Set the button OnClickListener to the
    ScreenOneFragment, this.

Listing 3-83. Implement Button OnClickListener

```
public class ScreenOneFragment extends Fragment implements OnClickListener,
DialogInterface.OnClickListener {
  ...
  private View buttonPopup;

  @Override
  public View onCreateView(LayoutInflater inflater, ViewGroup container,
                           Bundle savedInstanceState) {
    ...
    buttonPopup = contentView.findViewById(R.id.buttonPopup);
    buttonPopup.setOnClickListener(this); // Delegate button OnClick events
    ...
  }
  ...
```

8. The onClick(...) method will need to respond to two buttons. To make
    the code cleaner, move the current code in onClick(...) to a new method,
    showAlert(), as shown in Listing 3-84.

Listing 3-84. showAlert()

```
public class ScreenOneFragment extends Fragment implements OnClickListener,
DialogInterface.OnClickListener {
  ...
  @Override
  public void onClick(View v) {
    showAlert();
  }
```

```java
    private void showAlert() {
      // create builder instance.
      AlertDialog.Builder builder = new AlertDialog.Builder(getActivity());

      //  set alert dialog content view, title with an icon
      builder.setTitle("Attention").setIcon(android.R.drawable.ic_menu_help);

      // content area message.
      builder.setMessage("Standard User Alert");

      // max 3 buttons.
      builder.setPositiveButton("Ok", this);
      builder.setNegativeButton("Cancel", this);

      // make it a modal dialog
      builder.setCancelable(false);

      // create the dialog instance and show it.
      AlertDialog dialog = builder.create();
      dialog.show();
    }
    ...
```

> **Tip**   In Eclipse, you can do this manually. Or in the Java editor, highlight any code you want to extract to a new method; and then from the context menu, select **Refactor ➤ Extract Method…** (Alt+⌘m).

9.   Create a new showPopup() method that shows ColorPickerPopupFragment as a dialog (see Listing 3-85).

Listing 3-85. showPopup()

```java
public class ScreenOneFragment extends Fragment implements OnClickListener,
DialogInterface.OnClickListener {
  ...
  // same Dialog.show(...) API to show the dialog.
  private void showPopup() {
    ColorPickerPopupFragment dialog = new ColorPickerPopupFragment();
    dialog.show(getFragmentManager(), dialog.getClass().getSimpleName());
  }
  ...
```

10.   Modify the onClick(...) method to handle both the alert and the popup buttons, as shown in Listing 3-86.

Listing 3-86. onClick Handler for Two Buttons

```java
public class ScreenOneFragment extends Fragment implements OnClickListener,
DialogInterface.OnClickListener {
  ...
  @Override
  public void onClick(View v) {
    int btnViewId = v.getId();
    if (btnViewId == R.id.buttonAlert) {
      showAlert();
    } elseif (btnViewId == R.id.buttonPopup) {
      showPopup();
    }
  }
  ...
```

11. Build and run the modified Dialogs ADT project to see the code in action, as shown in Figure 3-47.

Figure 3-47. Android DialogFragment

Everything behaves as expected. When a color is selected, log the user choice in LogCat view. It works, but it is not too user-friendly yet. Your users are not going to see the LogCat output. You need to provide some visual feedback for your app users.

Toasts

In Figure 3-47 we did not do anything to show the user color selection, except the logging code. If all you want to do is give users quick feedback or information without much interruption, you can use an Android *Toast*, which shows text in a popup near the bottom of the screen and automatically dismisses itself after a short period of time. A toast has a very simple API; just make sure it is called from the UI thread.

Please modify `ColorPickerPopupFragment.onItemClick(...)` to give users a quick visual feedback using the `Toast` object (see Listing 3-87).

Listing 3-87. Use Toast

```
public class ColorPickerPopupFragment extends DialogFragment implements OnItemClickListener {
  ...
  @Override
  public void onItemClick(AdapterView<?> parent, View v, int position, long id){
    ...
    Toast.makeText(getActivity(), mListAdapter.getItem(position),Toast.LENGTH_LONG).show();
    ...
  }
  ...
```

Build and rerun the Dialogs ADT project again. When a color is selected from the Popup dialog, a toast is shown near the bottom of the screen. It gets dismissed shortly thereafter (see Figure 3-48).

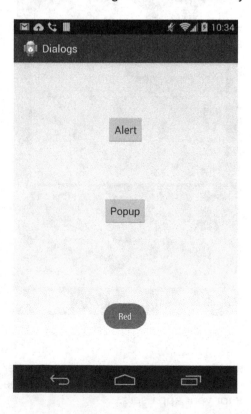

Figure 3-48. Show toast

A simple toast makes for a much better user experience. ☺

Summary

To port iOS to an Android app in a top-down fashion, from class design to low-level programming methods, structuring your Android app in the iOS-like MVC design is essentially the key step. Not only for porting purposes, it is always good to apply the MVC design pattern to break dependencies.

Simply use an iOS app as the UI mock-up, and early on, implement the screen navigation patterns that connect all the screens—just like the iOS storyboard does. The result is a set of MVC classes that map to iOS counterparts. Compared with the iOS SDK, what's missing in the Android SDK are the iOS-like container view controller (i.e., UINavigationController, and so forth). By implementing the iOS-like container view controller responsibility in the MainActivity class, your Activity class naturally glues the whole thing together—just like those iOS container view controllers do. The content view and view controller mappings between iOS and Android remain trivial. We will dive into the details of each screen in Chapter 4.

CHECKPOINT

To port your iOS apps to Android, you have done the following—repeatedly—for each screen navigation pattern:

1. Used the counterpart iOS app as the precise UI prototype for your Android app.

2. Implemented the screen navigation code that connects all the screens—just as they are connected in the iOS app.

3. Learned that MainActivity is the natural candidate to manage child fragments and act as the iOS-like container view controller.

Can you name the mobile screen navigation patterns that were introduced?

These exercise projects all ended up with a collection of layout-fragment paired skeletons that closely resemble their counterparts in iOS storyboard scene–UIViewController pairs.

Chapter 4

Implement Piece by Piece

In the previous chapter, you followed the iOS top-down approach to lay down the groundwork, implementing the iOS-like storyboard using Android navigation pattern guidelines. It resulted in a set of connected Fragment classes in MVC fashion that mapped to iOS counterpart classes.

In this chapter, after you have created an iOS-like storyboard and your app is structured in the desired MVC fashion, you are going to implement each fragment, one piece at a time, with a detailed user interface and business logic that should already be presented in the counterpart of the iOS UIViewController and the storyboard scene. You will also focus on the following programming tasks for the most common app component mappings from iOS to Android:

- User interface and common UI widgets
- Persistent storages options
- Network and remote service with JSON

User Interface

All those screen layouts that we created for the screen navigation patterns in Chapter 3 were intentionally very simple. Obviously, a useful mobile app provides rich content and offers better functionality to gracefully interact with users. User interface certainly plays an important role in the overall UX design.

In general, I choose to do a top-down approach to get screen flows and a storyboard in place first, and then I revisit each screen to detail a more sophisticated look and feel (L&F) and to add dynamic runtime behaviors based on the business rules of the project.

IOS ANALOGY

After you have the storyboard in place, you naturally start to detail each scene in the storyboard and add code to the custom UIViewController.

The techniques and vocabularies used to create meaningful screens for an Android project are definitely different from those for iOS. UI components are normally platform dependent. You just need to know the usages of the UI widgets and where to look up the specific widget specifications.

In general, there are similarities among many UI frameworks. Both iOS and Android views/parent views are structured as a container view model, which has been in the industry for a long time. In Android, user interface widgets are View or ViewGroup objects. A View is an object that draws something on the screen that the user can interact with. A ViewGroup is an object that holds other View (or ViewGroup) objects to define the layout of the user interface.

The iOS and Android UI frameworks are different in many aspects. There are fundamental differences in how to layout/position a UI widget within its parent view or relative to siblings. Android uses the "layout manager" concept to facilitate these UI tasks, whereas iOS uses AutoLayout.

Because the layout of the screen is stored in an XML file and used in Java code as well, the same type of thing may have a different term in an XML element vs. a Java class. A View object in Java normally refers to a UI widget element in an XML file; and ViewGroup in Java normally refers to a Layout element in an XML layout file. I normally try to stay with the Java terminologies, but you do want to keep in mind that a View object and a widget element, or a ViewGroup and a layout could be used interchangeably in some documents.

Layout and View Anatomy

We have been using the *graphical layout editor* (see "ADT Graphical Layout Editor" in Chapter 3) to create screen layout files. The view hierarchy is stored in a layout file in XML syntax. You can also declare the layout of the screen by instantiating each Java view object in Java code and then building the Java view object hierarchy. However, it is preferable to define screen layouts in an XML file.

After creating the layout files, you can visualize the L&F of the screen layouts in the editor before you run the app. The presentation layer is greatly separated from view controllers and domain models. This is a very important aspect of MVC. It is definitely a big plus to use the graphical layout editor.

The View object is the basic building block for user interface components. It is the base class for all widgets; for example, those common widgets like Button and TextView. It is also the base class for the parent container view called ViewGroup.

IOS ANALOGY

UIView is the base class of all iOS UI widgets. It can contain other UI widgets as a view container as well.

A visible View occupies a rectangular area on the screen and is responsible for drawing and event handling.

ViewGroup is a subclass of View, which is a view container that holds other View elements. It is also responsible for how to position/layout the child view elements in it. They may not be visible, but you need one to manage the positions of the view elements. This view hierarchy, as shown in Figure 4-1, forms the well-known view container model.

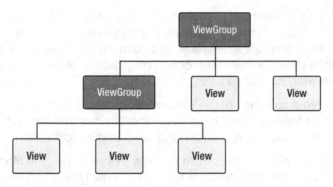

Figure 4-1. Android View-ViewGroup container model

This sample Android view hierarchy is translated into a layout file in XML format in Listing 4-1.

Listing 4-1. Layout XML Syntax

```xml
<?xml version="1.0" encoding="utf-8"?>
<ViewGroup xmlns:android="http://schemas.android.com/apk/res/android"
    android:id="@+id/xxx"
    android:layout_width="match_parent"
    android:layout_height="match_parent" >

    <ViewGroup
        android:layout_width="match_parent"
        android:layout_height="wrap_content" >

        <View
            android:id="@+id/xxx"
            android:layout_width="wrap_content"
            android:layout_height="wrap_content" />

        <View
            android:id="@+id/xxx"
            android:layout_width="wrap_content"
            android:layout_height="wrap_content" />

        <View
            android:id="@+id/xxx"
            android:layout_width="wrap_content"
            android:layout_height="wrap_content" />

    </ViewGroup>

    <View
        android:id="@+id/xxx"
        android:layout_width="wrap_content"
        android:layout_height="wrap_content" />

    <View
        android:id="@+id/xxx"
        android:layout_width="wrap_content"
        android:layout_height="wrap_content" />

</ViewGroup>
```

- Each layout file must start with one *root* ViewGroup element, which is normally a Layout element. The RelativeLayout and FrameLayout used earlier are examples of ViewGroup. From the root ViewGroup, you build the view hierarchy that may simply contain a UI widget element, or you may nest another ViewGroup that groups certain widgets and so forth.

- All UI widgets are a subclass of the View object, such as Button, TextView, EditText, and so forth. They all have specific attributes that define the L&F or behaviors; for example, color, background, text, and so forth.

- Children always inherit attributes from parents. For example, the ultimate based View class has a handful of attributes that apply to all UI widgets and ViewGroup elements.

- A set of attributes called *layout parameters* determine the positioning rules of the entire layout. Named android:layout_xxx, they are interrelated between the parents and children, meaning that a child element must define the appropriate layout parameters of how its parent ViewGroup's layout parameters are defined.

- Layout files are application resources that need to be saved in the $PROJ/res/layout folder.

In general, the View element names correspond to Java class names, and the XML attributes correspond to Java properties. For example, the View element has a background attribute that corresponds to Java View.setBackground(...) and View.getBackground() methods. Since View is the super class of any UI widget class, the background attribute is also inherited by any UI widgets and ViewGroup elements as well.

View has a handful of attributes you can use. This chapter describes those common attributes and important ones that you most likely will encounter or that are just good to know earlier. For the complete list of the View attributes, go to the online reference from the official Android Developers site: http://developer.android.com/reference/android/view/View.html.

ID

IOS ANALOGY

- (UIView *) viewWithTag: (NSInteger)tag

All View and ViewGroup elements have an optional ID attribute, android:id, that is unique within the container view hierarchy (within the layout file). Although it is optional, you need to set it when you need to reference to the View element from your Java code.

> **Note** Whenever you need to reference any widget from Java, you want to define an ID for the widget and use R.id.xxx to reference to the view element.

Recall in the Dialogs ADT project, the Alert button id is set as +@id/buttonAlert. The ADT SDK tool compiles the layout file and creates two references under the hook: one in Java syntax to be used in Java code, and the other to be used in an XML file, as shown in Listing 4-2.

Listing 4-2. Assign View id

```
<Button
    android:id="@+id/buttonAlert"
    ...
/>
```

- +@id/ creates a new ID application resource if one does not exist. (Pay attention to the plus sign (+). It instructs the ADT SDK tool to create the ID if it does not exist yet.)

- To reference to ID application resources, use @id/xxx from an XML file. Use the R.id.xxx identifier in Java code.

The Fragment.onCreateView(...) code in Listing 4-3 shows typical usages in almost every GUI app that keeps a convenient object reference to a UI widget:

- To get the object reference to the root container ViewGroup, use inflater. inflate(...).

- Use R.id.buttonAlert to id the Button widget.

- To get any child view element in a ViewGroup, use ViewGroup.findViewById (R.id.buttonAlert).

- With the View object reference, you can do what's needed, such as setOnClickListener(this).

Listing 4-3. findViewById

```
@Override
public View onCreateView(LayoutInflater inflater, ViewGroup container, Bundle savedInstanceState) {
  contentView = inflater.inflate(R.layout.screenone_fragment, container, false);

  alertButton = contentView.findViewById(R.id.buttonAlert);
  alertButton.setOnClickListener(this); // Delegate button OnClick events
  ...
}
```

IOS ANALOGY

In Xcode, you use IBOutlet to connect the view widget to your Object-C properties. findViewById() is what you need to reference to the widgets in the layout file.

To reference to other View elements from within the same XML file, you use @id/xxx to identify the targeting widget. For example, in the RelativeLayout element, the positions of child widgets are most likely relative to other widgets. We actually used RelativeLayout a lot in previous chapters.

For example, in the `RelativeLayout` element that we have used in the `screenone_fragment.xml` file in previous ADT Dialogs project, the Popup button is positioned relative to the Alert button (see Listing 4-4).

Listing 4-4. *Reference to Other View Elements in Layout File*

```
<Button
    android:id="@+id/buttonPopup"
    ...
    android:layout_below="@+id/buttonAlert"

    .../>
```

Geometry: Location and Size

IOS ANALOGY

UIView.frame

The `View` elements define a rectangular area that is anchored at the upper-left corner relative to its parent `ViewGroup` and a pair of width and height dimensions. The geometry parameters can be retrieved using the `View` class methods `getLeft()`, `getTop()`, `getWidth()`, and `getHeight()` in the runtime. However, in most of cases, you cannot assign these attributes directly to change the geometry of the element. The view rendering process dictates the final location and size of the view rectangle area, which is computed using the layout parameters of the parent `ViewGroup` and child `View` elements.

Margins and padding can also visually affect the geometry location. They are not mandatory layout parameters but are commonly used.

Common Layout Managers

`ViewGroup` is a type of view that is designed to layout its child views in a certain way. The `ViewGroup` class is the ultimate super class of all `ViewGroup` elements. For example, you have seen `RelativeLayout`, `FrameLayout`, and `ViewPager`. They all lay out their child `View` elements in different ways. `ViewGroup` and it child `View` elements have interrelated layout parameters that define all the layout rules together. The parent `ViewGroup` defines attributes that affect all child `View` elements. The child `View` elements must define the layout parameters that are appropriate for its parent. This forms a parallel `LayoutParams` class hierarchy. It requires many sentences to explain the parallel relationship, but is quickly depicted in Figure 4-2, which is excerpted from the official Android Developers site at `http://developer.android.com/guide/topics/ui/declaring-layout.html`.

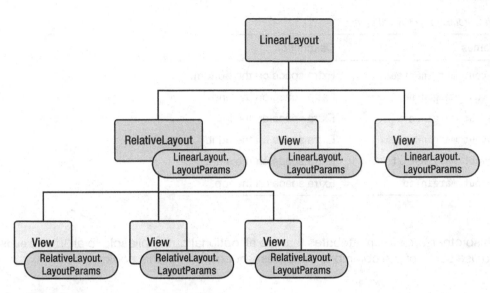

Figure 4-2. Layout parameters

As you can see in Figure 4-2, different types of ViewGroup elements are associated with different types of layout parameters, such as LinearLayout.LayoutParms vs. RelativeLayout.LayoutParms. The contained view elements must define its own LayoutParms for its parent. They are a subclass of the ViewGroup.LayoutParms class that defines the android:layout_width and android:layout_height attributes. Each View and ViewGroup element is required to define them. You can specify width and height with exact measurements by pixel, though you probably don't want to do this often. Instead, you specify relative measurements such as density-independent pixel units (dp). More often, you will use one of the following constants to set the width or height:

- wrap_content tells your View element to size itself to the dimensions required by its content.

- fill_parent (renamed match_parent in API Level 8) tells the View element to become as big as its parent View group will allow.

> **Tip** In the Eclipse layout editor, use Ctrl+<space> for type-ahead with autocompletion to find the valid values.

Using appropriate values helps ensure that your application will display properly across a variety of device screen sizes.

The layout ViewGroup defines a specific type of layout parameters. The height and width attributes are inherited by all types of LayoutParms. Margins and borders (defined in ViewGroup.MarginLayoutParms subclassed from ViewGroup.LayoutParams) are optional, but are common attributes inherited by many subclasses, as shown in Table 4-1.

Table 4-1. ViewGroup.MarginLayoutParams

Attribute Names	Description
android:layout_marginBottom	Extra space on the bottom.
android:layout_marginEnd	Extra space on the end.
android:layout_marginLeft	Extra space on the left.
android:layout_marginRight	Extra space on the right.
android:layout_marginStart	Extra space on the start.
android:layout_marginTop	Extra space on the top.

There are also other ViewGroup attributes that are all optional but applicable to all ViewGroups. You will learn to use some of the commons attributes—but not all—in this book.

> **Note**   For more information about the ViewGroup attributes listed in Table 4-1, see the online reference at the Android Developers site (http://developer.android.com/reference/android/view/ViewGroup.html).

RelativeLayout

IOS ANALOGY

AutoLayout. Being an iOS developer, I found myself using RelativeLayout more frequently. The syntax definitely is different, but they seem to have similar usages. RelativeLayout has proven to be a very capable layout manager for common usages.

Among all the Android Layouts, the RelativeLayout usage is the closest to iOS AutoLayout. You have seen it and used it in previous chapters. RelativeLayout is a ViewGroup that lets child views specify their positions relative to the parent view or to each other (specified by ID). So you can align two elements by their right borders, or make one below the other, or centered in the screen, or centered left, and so on. A RelativeLayout is very powerful for designing a user interface because it can eliminate nested view groups and keep your layout hierarchy flat, which improves performance. If you find yourself using several nested LinearLayout groups, you may be able to replace them with a single RelativeLayout. By default, all child View elements are drawn at the top-left of the layout. You must define the position of each view using the various View element attributes. See Table 4-2 and Table 4-3 for details.

Table 4-2. *RelativeLayout XML Attributes*

android:gravity	android:ignoreGravity

Table 4-3. *Child View Element RelativeLayout.LayoutParms XML Attributes*

Attribute Names

android:layout_above	android:layout_alignStart
android:layout_alignBaseline	android:layout_alignTop
android:layout_alignBottom	android:layout_alignWithParentIfMissing
android:layout_alignEnd	android:layout_below
android:layout_alignLeft	android:layout_centerHorizontal
android:layout_alignParentBottom	android:layout_centerInParent
android:layout_alignParentEnd	android:layout_centerVertical
android:layout_alignParentLeft	android:layout_toEndOf
android:layout_alignParentRight	android:layout_toLeftOf
android:layout_alignParentStart	android:layout_toRightOf
android:layout_alignParentTop	android:layout_toStartOf
android:layout_alignRight	android:layout_alignStart

As usual, the interrelated Layout parameters dictate the layout process: the RelativeLayout view group defines the overall attributes that apply to all view elements, while the child View elements must supply the appropriate layout parameters, defined in RelativeLayout.LayoutParms.

Table 4-2 lists the names of the RelativeLayout XML attributes. RelativeLayout also inherits the ViewGroup attributes.

Table 4-3 lists the names of the RelativeLayout.LayoutParms attributes. RelativeLayout also inherits layout_height and layout_width and all the border and margin–related attributes from its super class.

> **Note**   For more information about RelativeLayout.LayoutParms attributes, see the online reference at the Android Developers site (http://developer.android.com/reference/android/widget/RelativeLayout.html).

LinearLayout

LinearLayout is a ViewGroup that lines up all child view elements one after another, vertically or horizontally, specified by the android:orientation attribute. You can also specify gravity, which states the alignment of all the child elements.

To determine the space each child view element occupies, LinearLayout honors the space claimed by each child, then distributes the remaining space to child View elements by the android:layout_weight attribute specified in the child view elements. A larger weight value allows the child view element to expand to fill any remaining space in the parent view. Child view elements can specify a weight value, and then any remaining space in the view group is assigned to children in proportion to their declared weight. The default weight is zero.

You can divide a screen into smaller blocks and nest LinearLayout inside another LinearLayout. It may seem a flexible solution to lay out the view elements with this modular approach in many situations. While it does provide a very flexible solution, you want to keep in mind the potential performance penalties in Android from rendering deeper hierarchical nested layouts. In many cases, the relative layout introduced earlier can be an alternative approach to the nested LinearLayout approach, just like you have using relative layout. When porting an iOS storyboard scene, I have no problem manually converting the iOS AutoLayout constraints to Android RelativeLayout in most cases.

Table 4-4 lists the names of the LinearLayout XML attributes. android:orientation and child android:layout_weight attributes are for sure the most important ones among all attributes. It also inherits all the attributes from its super class, ViewGroup.

Table 4-4. LinearLayout XML Attributes

Attribute Name	
android:baselineAligned	android:measureWithLargestChild
android:baselineAlignedChildIndex	android:orientation
android:divider	android:weightSum
android:gravity	

Table 4-5 lists the names of the LinearLayout.LayoutParms. Just like most of the LayoutParms, the LinearLayout.LayoutParms class inherits layout_height and layout_width from the ViewGroup class. It also inherits the attributes from its direct super class, MarginLayoutParms (see Table 4-1).

Table 4-5. LinearLayout Child LayoutParams Attributes

Attribute Name	Description
android:layout_gravity	Standard gravity constant that a child supplies to its parent.
android:layout_weight	Indicates how much of the remaining space in the LinearLayout will be allocated.

Note   For more information about these attributes, see the online reference at the Android Developers site (http://developer.android.com/reference/android/widget/LinearLayout.html).

FrameLayout

In FrameLayout, child View elements are drawn in a stack, with the most recently added child View on top. If you add two views to the parent FrameLayout, only the last one on top is visible (imagine a poker card deck, where each card is stacked on top of another and only the top card is visible). Although only the top view is visible, the size of the FrameLayout is actually the size of its largest child (plus padding), visible or not.

Generally, FrameLayout is the best choice to reserve an area on the screen to display a single View or ViewGroup as a whole. For example, in the MvcTemplate project, you use a FrameLayout in the MainActivity layout file to house the entire content view from a child fragment so that you can simply add or replace the entire content view. Since you replace instead of add a fragment content view, you actually can use another layout if you want to.

Table 4-6 and Table 4-7 list the names of the XML attributes of the FrameLayout and its children's LayoutParms. This is a simple Layout; you only use it in the MainActivity to house the child fragment's content view to take up the entire screen. You will not experience other XML attributes in this book.

Table 4-6. *FrameLayout Layout Parms*

Attribute Name		
android:foreground	android:measureAllChildren	android:foregroundGravity

Table 4-7. *FrameLayout Child LayoutParms*

Attribute Name
android:layout_gravity

> **Note**   For more information about these XML attributes, see the online reference at the Android Developers site (http://developer.android.com/reference/android/widget/FrameLayout.html).

ScrollView

IOS ANALOGY

UIScrollView

Due to the nature of the smaller screen size on mobile devices, ScrollView is very useful for displaying a content view larger than the physical display. On mobile devices, you want to offer users the ability to scroll the content view vertically or horizontally with swipe gestures.

ScrollView is a subclass of FrameLayout, meaning you should only place one child in it, containing the entire content view to scroll; for example, another ViewGroup element that you use to manage a complex view hierarchy or maybe a simple image view for a large picture.

There are two flavors: ScrollView for vertical scrolling and HorizontalScrollView for horizontal scrolling. To scroll in both directions, you can embed the vertical ScrollView in HorizontalScrollView, as shown in Listing 4-5.

Listing 4-5. *Vertical ScrollView in HorizontalScrollView*

```xml
<?xml version="1.0" encoding="utf-8"?>
<HorizontalScrollView xmlns:android="http://schemas.android.com/apk/res/android"
    xmlns:tools="http://schemas.android.com/tools"
    android:layout_width="wrap_content"
    android:layout_height="wrap_content" >

    <ScrollView
        android:layout_width="wrap_content"
        android:layout_height="wrap_content" >

        <LinearLayout
            android:layout_width="wrap_content"
            android:layout_height="0dp"
            android:orientation="vertical" >

            <!-- a very long and wide content view -->

        </LinearLayout>
    </ScrollView>

</HorizontalScrollView>
```

> **Note**   Based on my experience, embedding HorizontalScrollView in ScrollView doesn't seem to work.

Since ScrollView scrolls the content view by handling swipe gesture events internally, you might encounter unexpected behaviors when embedding certain scrollable widgets that seem to compete with the same gesture events. You should avoid designing your layout using ListView in the vertical ScrollView, or using ViewPager, the horizontal slider, in HorizontalScrollView, and so forth.

Generally, you use ScrollView for scrolling purposes only. There is only one attribute defined, as shown in Table 4-8.

Table 4-8. *ScrollView Parent XML Attribute*

Attribute Name	Description
android:fillViewport	Indicates whether the ScrollView stretches its content to fill the viewport.

ScrollView inherits attributes from the super class FrameLayout (see Table 4-6).

There is no particular layout parameter that a child View element has in respect to a ScrollView parent. Only the attributes available to FrameLayout.LayoutParms (see Table 4-7) are applicable to ScrollView.

Common UI Widgets

Generally, UI widgets are the interactive UI control components in the application's user interface, such as buttons, text fields, and so forth. Generally speaking, you create screens that contain the appropriate UI widgets to interact with users, or to collect information from users, and/or to show information.

The Android framework provides rich system UI widgets as application resources. You can also use the corresponding Java classes from the SDK to create the View elements from Java code in the runtime; but most likely, you create the UI widgets from the XML layout file and reference the UI widgets from your Java code in the runtime. Actually, in previous chapters you created the linkages between the content view layout file and the fragment view controller. Although those layout files and the UI widgets were intended to be simple, the concept and steps are still the same: IBOutlet in iOS. In this chapter, you are going to dive into detailed usages for common UI widgets provided in the Android SDK.

The XML vocabulary for declaring UI widget elements closely follows the structure and naming of Java classes and methods, where View element names correspond to View class names, and the XML attribute names correspond to methods. For example, the TextView element has the android:visibility attribute, and there is a corresponding TextView Java class and method, setVisibility(...). To define the initial visibility, you assign android:visibility="visible" in the layout XML file. To change the widget visibility in the runtime, you call setVisibility(...) in your Java code, as shown in Listing 4-6.

Listing 4-6. Java Getter/Setter Corresponding to XML Visibility Attribute

```
TextView label = (TextView) contentView.findViewById(R.id.textViewLabel);
label.setVisibility(View.INVISIBLE);
```

The rest of this section shows you the common Android UI widgets by example. Let's create an ADT project to visualize the most common Android UI widgets. The iOS app in Figure 4-3 shows the common iOS UI elements. From top to bottom, there are 13 UI elements in UIScrollView. All of them are of different types: UILabel, UITextField, UITextView, UIButton, UISegmentedControl, UISlider, UIProgressIndicator, UISwitch, UIProgressView, UIImageView, a UIView for video, and UIPickerView. On the top of the screen, there is UIBarButtonItem in UINavigationBar.

Figure 4-3. iOS CommonWidgets app

ADT PROJECT PREPARATIONS

Same as usual, let's use the MvcTemplate project to create the ADT project for the Android CommonWidgets application.

1. Copy the MvcTemplate ADT project and paste it into a new project (⌘c, ⌘v) named **CommonWidgets**.

2. Rename the Android application package. From the newly created CommonWidgets project context menu, select **Android Tools ➤ Rename Application Package**. Enter a new package name: **com.pdachoice.commonwidgets**.

3. Rename the CommonWidgets/src/com.pdachoice.renameme Java package. From the package context menu, select **Refactor ➤ Rename...** (Alt+⌘r) and do the following:

    a. Enter a new name: **com.pdachoice.commonwidgets**.

    b. Select **Update references**.

4. Modify res/values/strings.xml (see Figure 4-7). You will need some text, as shown in the iOS app in Figure 4-3.

Listing 4-7. CommonWidgets String Resources

```xml
<?xml version="1.0" encoding="utf-8"?>
<resources>

    <string name="app_name">Common Widgets</string>
    <string name="action_settings">Settings</string>
    <string name="labelText">Simple text Label</string>
    <string name="textfieldHints">Hint: one-line text input</string>
    <string name="textfieldMultipleLine">Hint: multiple-line text input</string>
    <string name="buttonTitle">Action Button</string>
    <string name="segmentControl_1">First</string>
    <string name="segmentControl_2">Second</string>
    <string name="segmentControl_3">Third</string>
    <string name="barButtonTitle">Action Sheet</string>
    <string name="contextMenuItem1">Context Action 1</string>
    <string name="contextMenuItem2">Context Action 2</string>
    <string name="contextMenuItem3">Context Action 3</string>
    <string name="popupMenuItem1">Popup Action 1</string>
    <string name="popupMenuItem2">Popup Action 2</string>
    <string name="popupMenuItem3">Popup Action 3</string>

    <string-array name="spinnerItems">

        <item>Item 0</item>
        <item>Item 1</item>
        <item>Item 2</item>
        <item>Item 3</item>
        <item>Item 4</item>
    </string-array>


</resources>
```

5. You only need one fragment: keep ScreenOneFragment and delete the other two.

    a. Delete the src/ScreenTwoFragment.java and src/ScreenThreeFragment.java classes (multiselect and fn+Delete).

    b. Delete the res/layout/screentwo_fragment.xml and res/layout/screenthree_fragment.xml files (fn+Delete).

6. Modify res/layout/screenone_fragment.xml as shown in Figure 4-8. You will add one widget at time, and it will become very long. You need ScrollView to house all the UI widgets in one screen.

Listing 4-8. screenone_fragment Layout File

```xml
<?xml version="1.0" encoding="utf-8"?>
<ScrollView xmlns:android="http://schemas.android.com/apk/res/android"
    android:layout_width="match_parent"
    android:layout_height="wrap_content" >

    <RelativeLayout
        android:id="@+id/layoutContainer"
        android:layout_width="match_parent"
        android:layout_height="wrap_content" >

        <!-- a very long content view -->

    </RelativeLayout>
</ScrollView>
```

7. Clean up src/ScreenOneFragment.java, as shown in Listing 4-9.

    a. Delete lines with errors in the onClick(...) method.

    b. Delete the code related to nextButton. It was deleted from the layout file already.

Listing 4-9. ScreenOneFragment Class

```java
public class ScreenOneFragment extends Fragment implements OnClickListener {
  private View contentView;

  @Override
  public View onCreateView(LayoutInflater inflater, ViewGroup container,Bundle
savedInstanceState) {
     contentView = inflater.inflate(R.layout.screenone_fragment, container, false);

     return contentView;
  }

  // provide the OnClickListener implementation
  @Override
  public void onClick(View v) {
    // TODO
  }
}
```

8. Build and run the ADT project, just to make sure it is good. The Android app should display a screen with nothing in it. We will add UI widgets one at a time.

TextView

In iOS, UILabel displays static text. In Android, TextView should be your first choice. You commonly use this widget to draw one or multiple lines of static text, such as those you might use to identify other parts of your user interface.

To translate the iOS UILabel in the iOS CommonWidgets app, do the following:

1. Modify res/layout/screenone_fragment.xml by adding a TextView element. You can use the graphical layout editor, but to learn these XML attributes, please switch to a text editor and simply code the layout file, as shown in Listing 4-10.

   a. To position the element on top of the parent RelativeLayout, you specify layout_alignParentTop and layout_centerHorizontal.

   b. Text strings are an application resource and defined in the $PROJ/res/values/strings.xml file. To set the text, simply specify the value in the android:text attribute.

   c. textAppearance is more than a single value attribute. It is used to specify a text *style* that defines color, typeface, size, style, and so forth. It is also a type of application resource. To reference a predefined style application resource in the SDK, use a question mark (?android:attr) instead of the @ symbol (@android).

Listing 4-10. TextView Widget

```xml
<?xml version="1.0" encoding="utf-8"?>
<ScrollView ... >

    <RelativeLayout ... >

        <!-- a very long content view -->
        <TextView
            android:id="@+id/textViewLabel"
            android:layout_width="wrap_content"
            android:layout_height="wrap_content"
            android:layout_alignParentTop="true"
            android:layout_centerHorizontal="true"
            android:text="@string/labelText"
            android:textAppearance="?android:attr/textAppearanceLarge" />
        ...
    </RelativeLayout>
</ScrollView>
```

2. As usual, you can access the TextView text in in Java code as shown in Listing 4-11. Recall that the View XML element names correspond to Java class names, and the XML attribute names correspond to Java accessors, such as android:text XML attribute vs. Java getText() and setText() methods.

Listing 4-11. TextView.setText/getText

```
public class ScreenOneFragment extends Fragment implements OnClickListener {
    ...
    private TextView mTextView;

    @Override
    public View onCreateView(LayoutInflater inflater, ViewGroup container, Bundle
savedInstanceState) {
        ...
        // TextView
        mTextView = (TextView) contentView.findViewById(R.id.textViewLabel);
        mTextView.setText("My " + mTextView.getText());
        ...
    }
    ...
}
```

3. You may build and run the CommonWidgets ADT app to make sure it is working.

Just like the iOS UILabel, TextView is fairly simple and straightforward. You only need to use some common TextView attributes in this project. However, it has a number of optional attributes, which are listed in Table 4-9.

Table 4-9. TextView

Attribute Names		
android:autoLink	android:lines	android:textIsSelectable
android:autoText	android:linksClickable	android:textScaleX
android:bufferType	android:marqueeRepeatLimit	android:textSize
android:capitalize	android:maxEms	android:textStyle
android:cursorVisible	android:maxHeight	android:typeface
android:digits	android:maxLength	android:width
android:drawableBottom	android:maxLines	android:imeActionId
android:drawableEnd	android:maxWidth	android:imeActionLabel
android:drawableLeft	android:minEms	android:imeOptions
android:drawablePadding	android:minHeight	android:includeFontPadding
android:drawableRight	android:minLines	android:inputMethod
android:drawableStart	android:minWidth	android:inputType
android:drawableTop	android:numeric	android:lineSpacingExtra
android:editable	android:password	android:lineSpacingMultiplier
android:editorExtras	android:phoneNumber	android:lines
android:ellipsize	android:privateImeOptions	android:linksClickable

(continued)

Table 4-9. (*continued*)

Attribute Names

android:ems	android:scrollHorizontally	android:marqueeRepeatLimit
android:fontFamily	android:selectAllOnFocus	android:maxEms
android:freezesText	android:shadowColor	android:maxHeight
android:gravity	android:shadowDx	android:maxLength
android:height	android:shadowDy	android:maxLines
android:hint	android:shadowRadius	android:maxWidth
android:imeActionId	android:singleLine	android:minEms
android:imeActionLabel	android:text	android:minHeight
android:imeOptions	android:textAllCaps	android:minLines
android:includeFontPadding	android:textAppearance	android:minWidth
android:inputMethod	android:textColor	android:numeric
android:inputType	android:textColorHighlight	android:password
android:lineSpacingExtra	android:textColorHint	
android:lineSpacingMultiplier	android:textColorLink	

Note   For more information about these XML attributes, see the online reference at the Android Developers site (http://developer.android.com/reference/android/widget/TextView.html).

EditText

IOS ANALOGY

UITextField for a single line and UITextView for multiple lines.

In iOS, UITextField accepts a single line of user input and placeholder text when the user input is still empty. UITextView accepts and displays multiple lines of text. In Android, you use the EditText widget for both.

To learn by example, do the following to use EditText in the CommonWidgets project.

1. Modify res/layout/screenone_fragment.xml by adding the following EditText elements (also see Listing 4-12):

    a. The android:hint attribute is just like the UITextField placeholder.

    b. To specify font size, use the android:textSize attribute.

c. You can specify android:lines to display area height. Otherwise, it defaults to a single line.

d. To enforce a one-line-only text input, you can specify proper android:inputType, such as text. Without it, or by specifying "none", the Return key will insert a new line.

e. android:inputType specifies the type of keyboard. Here are some of the common values:

   ▪ "text": Normal text keyboard.

   ▪ "textEmailAddress": Normal text keyboard with the @ character.

   ▪ "textUri": Normal text keyboard with the / character.

   ▪ "number": Basic numbers keypad.

   ▪ "phone": Phone-style keypad.

f. android:imeOptions specifies certain keyboard behaviors. Here are some of the common input type values.

   ▪ "textCapSentences": Normal text keyboard that capitalizes the first letter of each new sentence.

   ▪ "textCapWords": Normal text keyboard that capitalizes every word. Good for titles or a person's name.

   ▪ "textAutoCorrect": Normal text keyboard that corrects commonly misspelled words.

   ▪ "textPassword": Normal text keyboard, but the characters entered turn into dots.

   ▪ "textMultiLine": Normal text keyboard that allows users to input long strings of text that include line breaks (carriage returns).

   ▪ It also allows bitwise combinations so that you can specify both a keyboard layout and one or more behaviors at once.

Listing 4-12. EditText Widget

```xml
<?xml version="1.0" encoding="utf-8"?>
<ScrollView ... >
    <RelativeLayout ... >
        ...
        <EditText
            android:id="@+id/editTextOneLine"
            android:layout_width="wrap_content"
            android:layout_height="wrap_content"
            android:layout_alignParentLeft="true"
            android:layout_alignParentRight="true"
            android:layout_below="@id/textViewLabel"
            android:textSize="20sp"
```

```
            android:hint="@string/textfieldHints"
            android:imeOptions="actionNext"
            android:inputType="text" />

        <EditText
            android:id="@+id/editTextFourLine"
            android:layout_width="wrap_content"
            android:layout_height="wrap_content"
            android:layout_alignParentLeft="true"
            android:layout_alignParentRight="true"
            android:layout_below="@id/editTextOneLine"
            android:textSize="20sp"
            android:gravity="top"
            android:hint="@string/textfieldMultipleLine"
            android:lines="4" />

    </RelativeLayout>
</ScrollView>
```

2. To access the text, use the same API that accesses TextView, as shown in Listing 4-13.

Listing 4-13. TextView Get and Set Text

```java
public class ScreenOneFragment extends Fragment implements OnClickListener {
    ...
    private EditText mEditTextOneLine;
    private EditText mEditTextFourLine;

    @Override
    public View onCreateView(LayoutInflater inflater, ViewGroup container, Bundle savedInstanceState) {

        ...
        // EditText
        mEditTextOneLine =
            (EditText) contentView.findViewById(R.id.editTextOneLine);
        mEditTextFourLine =
            (EditText) contentView.findViewById(R.id.editTextFourLine);

        String tmp = mEditTextOneLine.getText().toString();
        mEditTextOneLine.setText(tmp);
        ...
    }
    ...
}
```

Note   The EditText class inherits from TextView. It simply inherits the methods.

3. You can set the action event listener when the keyboard button is pressed (see Listing 4-14). You often do this to intercept certain key presses, such as the Return key.

   a. Declare the listener class to conform to the OnEditorActionListener interface.

   b. Register the listener object this to handle the action events.

   c. Provide the OnEditorActionListener interface implementation.

Listing 4-14. Implement TextView OnEditorActionListener

```
public class ScreenOneFragment extends Fragment implements ... ,
   OnEditorActionListener {
  ...
  private EditText mEditTextOneLine;
  private EditText mEditTextFourLine;

  @Override
  public View onCreateView(LayoutInflater inflater, ViewGroup container, Bundle
savedInstanceState) {
    ...
    mEditTextOneLine.setOnEditorActionListener(this);
    ...
  }

  @Override // implements interface methods
  public boolean onEditorAction(TextView textView, int actionId, KeyEvent key) {
    if (textView.getId() == R.id.editTextOneLine) {
      mEditTextFourLine.setText(mEditTextOneLine.getText());
    }
    return true;
  }
  ...
}
```

4. Build and run the CommonWidgets Android app to make sure it is working. The preceding two EditTexts do not do anything meaningful actually. I simply put the text from the first EditText in the second one, just to show you some quick and simple EditText widget usages.

EditText doesn't have extra attributes except those inherited from TextView (see Table 4-9). For example, you can use android:text to set initial text and use View.getText() and View.setText(...) to get or set the text in the runtime from your Java code.

Button

Button is another common UI widget, just like UIButton in iOS. It intercepts touch events and sends an action message to the delegate or the so-called action event listener when tapped. The Android Button consists of the title text or an icon (or both text and an icon).

To learn by example, do the following to translate the iOS UIButton to the Android Button in the CommonWidgets app.

1. Add the Button element to the res/layout/screenone_fragment.xml layout file (see Listing 4-15). To specify the title text on the button, specify android:text.

> **Note** Doesn't android:text seem familiar? Yes, you saw the attribute in the TextView element. Both Button and EditText are extended from TextView! This is why you see a lot of TextView attributes but very few in Button and EditText.

Listing 4-15. *Button in Layout File*

```xml
<?xml version="1.0" encoding="utf-8"?>
<ScrollView ... >
    <RelativeLayout ... >

        ...
        <Button
            android:id="@+id/buttonAction"
            android:layout_width="wrap_content"
            android:layout_height="wrap_content"
            android:layout_alignParentLeft="true"
            android:layout_alignParentRight="true"
            android:layout_below="@+id/editTextFourLine"
            android:text="@string/buttonTitle" />

    </RelativeLayout>
</ScrollView>
```

2. Optionally, you can specify an image icon (or multiple icons) by using the attributes. Table 4-10 lists the attribute names.

Table 4-10. Button Image Icons

Attribute Names

android:drawableBottom	android:drawablePadding	android:drawableTop
android:drawableEnd	android:drawableRight	
android:drawableLeft	android:drawableStart	

Note   For example, to have an icon on the left side of a button, you can write the following:

android:drawableLeft="@android:drawable/ic_input_get"

These attributes are actually inherited from the TextView element (see Table 4-9). This was surprising to me: you can do the same to TextView and its subclasses, such as EditText. It might not look common though.

BUTTON VS IMAGEBUTTON

To create an image-only button (one without text) with an image that takes up the entire rectangular area of the button, you should use ImageButton element. You only need to use android:src to specify the source of the drawable, as shown in Listing 4-16 for example.

Listing 4-16. ImageButton

```
<ImageButton
    android:layout_width="wrap_content"
    android:layout_height="wrap_content"
    android:src="@android:drawable/btn_star_big_on" />
```

Note ImageButton is a subclass of ImageView, not Button. All attributes from ImageView apply, too. You will see ImageView XML attributes soon.

---

3. Follow the same repeated event-delegation pattern to delegate the Button OnClick events (as shown in Listing 4-17).

   a. Declare the listener class to conform to the OnClickListener interface.

   b. Register the listener object this, which handles the OnClick events.

   c. Provide the OnClickListener.onClick(...) interface implementation.

Listing 4-17. Implement Button onClicked Event

```
public class ScreenOneFragment extends Fragment implements ... ,
    OnClickListener {
  ...
  private Button mButton;

  @Override
  public View onCreateView(LayoutInflater inflater, ViewGroup container, Bundle
savedInstanceState) {
    ...
    // Button
    mButton = (Button) contentView.findViewById(R.id.buttonAction);
    mButton.setOnClickListener(this);
    ...
  }

  // provide the OnClickListener implementation
  @Override
  public void onClick(View v) {
    if (v.getId() == R.id.buttonAction) {
      Log.d("ScreenOneFragment", "My Button is pressed");
    }
  }
  ...
}
```

> **Note**   The onClick event is inherited from the View class. You can actually set up the behavior on any View element, such as TextView or any widget, because View is the super class of any UI widget.

The Button element inherits from TextView and no extra XML attributes are defined.

4. Build and run the Android CommonWidgets app to make sure everything is good. When the button is pressed, it simply logs some text in LogCat.

RadioGroup

```
                        IOS ANALOGY
```

UISegmentedControl

In iOS, UISegmentedControl is a linear set of segments, each of which functions as an action button that can display a different view. It offers closely related, but mutually exclusive choices. In Android, RadioGroup can offer the same usage, although the L&F is more of a traditional desktop app or web page style. In many cases, RadioGroup is a very reasonable choice for the stated purpose.

To translate iOS `UISegmentedControl` to the Android `RadioGroup`, do the following in the CommonWidgets app.

1. Modify `res/layout/screenone_fragment.xml` by adding the parent `RadioGroup`, which contains `RadioButton` elements for each segment, as shown in Listing 4-18.

   a. By wrapping `RadioButton` elements in one `RadioGroup`, the choice becomes mutually exclusive.

Note   RadioGroup contains children elements. It must be a type of ViewGroup. In fact, it is subclassed from LinearLayout.

---

   b. Just like `LinearLayout`, use `android:orientation` to show the choices horizontally or vertically.

   c. `RadioButton` is a subclass of `CompoundButton` and has two states. It inherits all attributes from `Button`, which is a subclass of `TextView`.

Note   Whenever you specify the attributes from super, be cautious and use common sense. For example, the circle radio icon probably is the Left image icon specified by android:drawableLeft attribute in the super attribute. It is allowed to override the Left image icon, but you might be surprised by the result.

Listing 4-18. RadioGroup

```xml
<?xml version="1.0" encoding="utf-8"?>
<ScrollView ... >
    <RelativeLayout ... >
        ...
        <RadioGroup
            android:id="@+id/radioGroup"
            android:layout_width="wrap_content"
            android:layout_height="wrap_content"
            android:layout_alignParentLeft="true"
            android:layout_alignParentRight="true"
            android:layout_below="@+id/buttonAction"
            android:orientation="horizontal" >

            <RadioButton
                android:id="@+id/radio0"
                android:layout_width="wrap_content"
                android:layout_height="wrap_content"
                android:checked="true"
                android:text="@string/segmentControl_1" />
```

```
            <RadioButton
                android:id="@+id/radio1"
                android:layout_width="wrap_content"
                android:layout_height="wrap_content"
                android:text="@string/segmentControl_2" />

            <RadioButton
                android:id="@+id/radio2"
                android:layout_width="wrap_content"
                android:layout_height="wrap_content"
                android:text="@string/segmentControl_3" />
        </RadioGroup>

    </RelativeLayout>
</ScrollView>
```

2. In the runtime from Java code, you can retrieve the selection using getCheckedRadioButtonId(). More often, you register a RadioGroup. OnCheckedChangeListener to respond to the UI events when users make a selection. The following Java code shows the same repeated UI event-handling pattern (see Listing 4-19).

   a. Declare ScreenOneFragment to conform to the RadioGroup. OnCheckedChangeListener interface.

   b. Register the listener object this to handle the onChecked events.

   c. Provide OnCheckedChangeListener.onCheckedChanged(...) implementation.

Listing 4-19. RadioGroup onCheckedChangeListener

```java
public class ScreenOneFragment extends Fragment implements ... ,
    RadioGroup.OnCheckedChangeListener {
  ...
  private RadioGroup mRadioGroup;

  @Override
  public View onCreateView(LayoutInflater inflater, ViewGroup container, Bundle
savedInstanceState) {
    ...
    // RadioButton
    mRadioGroup = (RadioGroup) contentView.findViewById(R.id.radioGroup);
    mRadioGroup.setOnCheckedChangeListener(this);
    ...
  }

  @Override
  public void onCheckedChanged(RadioGroup group, int checkedId) {
    CharSequence label =
        ((RadioButton)group.findViewById(checkedId)).getText();
    Log.d("ScreenOneFragment", String.format("%s is pressed", label));
  }
  ...
}
```

3. You may build and run the Android CommonWidgets app to make sure everything is in place.

RadioGroup inherits all attributes from LinearLayout. Most frequently, you use android:orientation to make it horizontal or vertical. You can also use android:checkedButton to specify the id of the child radio button that should be checked.

SeekBar

IOS ANALOGY

UISlider

In iOS, UISlider allows users to make adjustments to a value or to progress throughout a range of allowed values. In Android, you use SeekBar. Users drag left or right to set the value. The interactive nature of the slider makes it a great choice for settings that reflect intensity levels, such as volume, brightness, or color saturation.

To translate the iOS UISlider to the Android SeekBar, do the following in the CommonWidgets app.

1. Modify ComomnWidgets/res/layout/screenone_fragment.xml, as shown in Listing 4-20.

2. Just to visualize the SeekBar android:progress attribute, let's create a label to display the progress value explicitly.

    a. Set the initial progress value using the android:progress attribute.

    b. Set the max value using the android:max attribute. The default is 100.

    c. Unlike iOS UISlider, there is no attribute to set the minimum value. It defaults to zero. You can simply write your own offset logic when needed.

Listing 4-20. SeekBar

```xml
<?xml version="1.0" encoding="utf-8"?>
<ScrollView ... >
    <RelativeLayout ... >
        ...
        <TextView
            android:id="@+id/textViewSlider"
            android:layout_width="wrap_content"
            android:layout_height="wrap_content"
            android:layout_alignParentLeft="true"
            android:layout_below="@+id/radioGroup"
            android:textAppearance="?android:attr/textAppearanceLarge" />
```

```
    <SeekBar
        android:id="@+id/seekBar"
        android:layout_width="match_parent"
        android:layout_height="wrap_content"
        android:layout_alignParentRight="true"
        android:layout_below="@+id/radioGroup"
        android:layout_toRightOf="@id/textViewSlider"
        android:max="100"
        android:progress="10" />

    </RelativeLayout>
</ScrollView>
```

3. In the runtime from Java code, you can retrieve the progress value from SeekBar, using the android:progress attribute getProgress() Java method. More often, you register a SeekBar.OnSeekBarChangeListener to respond to the UI events when a user drags his thumb to change the value (see Listing 4-21).

    a. Declare ScreenOneFragment to conform to the OnSeekBarChangeListener interface.

    b. Register the listener object this to handle the OnSeekBarChange events.

    c. Provide OnSeekBarChangeListener interface implementation.

Listing 4-21. Implement OnSeekBarChangeListener

```java
public class ScreenOneFragment extends Fragment implements ... ,
    OnSeekBarChangeListener {
    ...
    private SeekBar mSeekBar;
    private TextView mTextViewSlider;

    @Override
    public View onCreateView(LayoutInflater inflater, ViewGroup container, Bundle
savedInstanceState) {
        ...
        // SeekBar
        mSeekBar = (SeekBar) contentView.findViewById(R.id.seekBar);
        mSeekBar.setOnSeekBarChangeListener(this);

        mTextViewSlider = (TextView) contentView.findViewById(R.id.textViewSlider);
        mTextViewSlider.setText(String.valueOf(mSeekBar.getProgress()));
        ...
    }

    // implement OnSeekBarChangeListener
    @Override
    public void onProgressChanged(SeekBar seekBar, int progress, boolean user) {
        mTextViewSlider.setText(String.valueOf(progress));
    }
```

```java
    @Override
    public void onStartTrackingTouch(SeekBar seekBar) {
      mSeekBar.setBackgroundColor(Color.YELLOW);
    }

    @Override
    public void onStopTrackingTouch(SeekBar seekBar) {
      mSeekBar.setBackgroundColor(Color.TRANSPARENT);
    }
    ...
  }
```

4.   Build and run the ADT project to make sure everything is good.

To customize the draggable thumb, you can use `android:thumb` to specify the thumb drawable. SeekBar also inherits all attributes from ProgressBar (see Table 4-12). Override the inherited attributes with caution because some are used internally for the default L&F. Overriding inherited attributes might mess up the SeekBar L&F or behaviors, based on my experience.

ProgressBar

IOS ANALOGY

UIActivityIndicatorView or UIProgressView

In iOS, `UIActivityIndicatorView` displays a "busy" activity indicator for a task or something that is in progress. If the task or process has a known duration, use `UIProgressView` to show how far the task has progressed. With this, users can better anticipate how long an activity has been in progress or how much longer until it completes.

In Android, you use `ProgressBar` for both usages. To translate `UIActivityIndicatorView` and `UIProgressView` to the Android `ProgressBar`, do the following in the CommonWidgets iOS app.

1.   Modify the `CommonWidgets/res/layout/screenone_fragment.xml` layout file by adding two `ProgressBar` elements at the end (see Listing 4-22). Use the `style` attribute to set the horizontal progress bar, or default to the circle cursor. The first `ProgressBar` element, `progressBar1`, displays a "busy" activity indicator. Normally, you simply show it when a task starts and hide it when the task ends.

Listing 4-22. ProgressBar

```xml
<?xml version="1.0" encoding="utf-8"?>
<ScrollView ... >
    <RelativeLayout ... >
        ...
        <ProgressBar
            android:id="@+id/progressBar1"
            android:layout_width="wrap_content"
            android:layout_height="wrap_content"
```

```
                    android:layout_alignParentLeft="true"
                    android:layout_below="@id/seekBar" />

            <ProgressBar
                android:id="@+id/progressBar2"
                style="?android:attr/progressBarStyleHorizontal"
                android:layout_width="wrap_content"
                android:layout_height="wrap_content"
                android:layout_alignParentLeft="true"
                android:layout_alignParentRight="true"
                android:layout_below="@id/progressBar1"
                android:max="100" />
        </RelativeLayout>
</ScrollView>
```

2. The Android system provides the progress bar styles shown in Table 4-11.

Table 4-11. ProgressBar Styles

Attribute Name	
progressBarStyle	progressBarStyleLargeInverse
progressBarStyleHorizontal	progressBarStyleSmall
progressBarStyleInverse	progressBarStyleSmallInverse
progressBarStyleLarge	progressBarStyleSmallTitle

3. To display how far the task has progressed in the horizontal ProgressBar
    element, the android:max and android:progress attributes affect
    the progress display. Let's modify OnSeekBarChangeListener.
    onProgressChanged(...) (see Listing 4-21) to update the horizontal
    ProgressBar progress attribute upon a SeekBar progress value change
    (see Listing 4-23).

Listing 4-23. ProgressBar setProgress()

```java
public class ScreenOneFragment extends Fragment implements ... ,
    OnSeekBarChangeListener {
  ...
  private ProgressBar mProgressBar1;
  private ProgressBar mProgressBar2;

  @Override
  public View onCreateView(LayoutInflater inflater, ViewGroup container, Bundle
savedInstanceState) {
    ...
    // ProgressBar
    mProgressBar1 = (ProgressBar) contentView.findViewById(R.id.progressBar1);
    mProgressBar2 = (ProgressBar) contentView.findViewById(R.id.progressBar2);
    ...
  }
```

```
                    // implement OnSeekBarChangeListener
                    @Override
                    public void onProgressChanged(SeekBar seekBar, int progress, boolean user) {
                      ...
                      mProgressBar2.setProgress(progress);
                    }
                    ...
                  }
```

> **Note**   The usage is actually the same as its subclass SeekBar, getProgress() and setProgress(...). One caveat is that these updates need to be performed in the UI main thread.

4.   Build and run the CommonWidgets Android app. Drag the SeekBar widgets and observe how both progress bars change.

In addition to the attributes inherited from the super View class, Table 4-12 lists the names of the ProgressBar XML attributes that you can use safely to modify its L&F.

Table 4-12. ProgressBar Attributes

Attribute Names		
animationResolution	indeterminateOnly	minHeight
indeterminate	interpolator	minWidth
indeterminateBehavior	max	progress
indeterminateDrawable	android:maxHeight	progressDrawable
indeterminateDuration	android:maxWidth	secondaryProgress

> **Note**   For more information about these XML attributes, see the online reference at the Android Developers site (http://developer.android.com/reference/android/widget/ProgressBar.html).

Switch

IOS ANALOGY

UISwitch

In iOS, UISwitch presents two mutually exclusive choices or states. It allows a user to change values by toggling or dragging her thumb between two states. Both Android and iOS provide system widgets for the switch-like UI elements. The switch-like widgets are very user-friendly for situations like the On/Off, Yes/No, or True/False inputs, and so forth.

In Android, the Switch element is not the only option. CompoundButton, the super class of Switch, is a type of Button with two states. It has three subclasses, each with a different L&F. All are capable of the same purpose (see Figure 4-4):

- **CheckBox** seems to be relatively more desktop or web page style, in my opinion.

- **ToggleButton** has a fairly compact L&F.

- **Switch** closely resembles the L&F of iOS UISwitch introduced in API Level 14. Toggle or drag to change values, just like the iOS UISwitch.

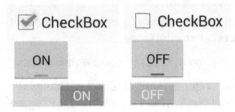

Figure 4-4. Android CompoundButton choices

To translate iOS UISwitch to Android, do the following in the CommonWidgets app.

1. Modify ComomnWidgets/res/layout/screenone_fragment.xml by adding a Switch or ToggleButton element (see Listing 4-24).

   a. If your device doesn't meet API Level 14 requirements, use the ToggleButton widget instead. The ToggleButton L&F doesn't look like the iOS UISwitch, but it has been available since API Level 1.

> **Note**   In Chapter 6 you will learn how to provide alternative layouts by showing Switch on devices with API Level 14+, while showing the ToggleButton or CheckBox on older devices.

   b. Use the android:checked attribute to set a value to true or false.

Listing 4-24. Android ToggleButton

```xml
<?xml version="1.0" encoding="utf-8"?>
<ScrollView ... >
    <RelativeLayout ... >
        ...
        <ToggleButton
            android:id="@+id/switchButton"
            android:layout_width="wrap_content"
            android:layout_height="wrap_content"
```

```
                    android:layout_alignBottom="@id/progressBar1"
                    android:layout_alignParentRight="true"
                    android:layout_alignTop="@id/progressBar1"
                    android:checked="true" />

        </RelativeLayout>
</ScrollView>
```

2. From your runtime Java code, you can use isChecked() to retrieve the state. More frequently, you want to delegate the OnCheckedChange events to an OnCheckedChangeListener delegate object to respond to the state changes (see Listing 4-25).

    a. Declare ScreenOneFragment to conform to CompoundButton.OnCheckedChangeListener interface.

    b. Register the listener object, this, to handle the events.

    c. Provide OnCheckedChangeListener.onCheckedChanged(...) implementation. Previously, you have created a ProgressBar to show an activity indicator. You can also use it to show/simulate on/off behavior. When the button is pressed/on, show the indicator. When the CompoundButton is off, hide the activity indicator.

Listing 4-25. Implement CompoundButton.OnCheckedChangeListener

```java
public class ScreenOneFragment extends Fragment implements ... ,
        CompoundButton.OnCheckedChangeListener{
    ...
    private CompoundButton mSwitchButton;

    @Override
    public View onCreateView(LayoutInflater inflater, ViewGroup container, Bundle
savedInstanceState) {
        ...
        // CompoundButton
        mSwitchButton =
            (CompoundButton)contentView.findViewById(R.id.switchButton);
        mSwitchButton.setOnCheckedChangeListener(this);
        ...
    }

    // implement OnCheckedChangeListener
    @Override
    public void onCheckedChanged(CompoundButton button, boolean isChecked) {
        mProgressBar1.setVisibility(isChecked ? View.VISIBLE : View.INVISIBLE);
    }
    ...
}
```

> **Note**   I personally don't use CheckBox often because it appears to be relatively nonmobile to me, but it can do the same things.

3. Build and run the CommonWidgets Android app to make sure everything works by design.

Among all the applicable attributes, the following three attributes are the most commonly used by me:

- ■ android:checked: This is the only attribute you used in the CommonWidgets project, which you will pretty much use at all times—regardless of the variants of CompoundButton.

- ■ android:textOff and android:textOn: These two are optional. They default to ON or OFF. You use them to specify the text showing on the widgets.

For your convenience, Tables 4-13 and 4-14 list and describe all the XML attributes syntax that you can use to customize the L&F.

Table 4-13. *ToggleButton Attributes*

Attribute Name	Description
android:disabledAlpha	Specifies the alpha to the indicator when disabled.
android:textOff	Specifies the text for the button not checked.
android:textOn	Specifies the text for the button checked.

Table 4-14. *Switch Attributes*

Attribute Name	Description
android:switchMinWidth	Specifies the minimum width.
android:switchPadding	Specifies the minimum space between the switch and the caption text.
android:switchTextAppearance	Specifies the TextAppearance style for text on the switch thumb.
android:textOff	Specifies the text when the switch is in the "off" state.
android:textOn	Specifies the text when the switch is in the "on" state.
android:textStyle	Specifies the style for the text.
android:thumb	Specifies the drawable "thumb" that switches back and forth.
android:thumbTextPadding	Specifies the padding on either side of the text within the switch thumb.
android:track	Specifies the drawable as the "track" that the switch thumb slides within.
android:typeface	Specifies the typeface for the text.

CheckBox doesn't have its own attributes. All attributes are inherited from `Button` and `TextView`.

> **Note**   All three subclasses of CompoundButton inherit attributes from Button and TextView. However, some attributes are used internally to achieve certain L&F and behaviors. Use common sense to decide whether you want to override the inherited attributes. Definitely keep an eye on the outcomes to make sure you don't mess up the widgets.

ImageView

IOS ANALOGY

UIImageView

In iOS, `UIImageView` displays one image or an animated series of images, such as a small icon or a large picture. In Android, you use the `ImageView` widget to load images from various image sources. For a simple usage like the CommonWidgets app, all you need to do is specify the image source and the attributes for how you want to render the image.

To translate the iOS `UIImageView` to Android, do the following in the CommonWidgets app.

1. Modify `ComomnWidgets/res/layout/screenone_fragment.xml` to add an `ImageView` element, as shown in Listing 4-26.

   a. Drag and drop an image file, `iosadt.jpg`, into the `CommonWidgets/res/drawable-mdpi` folder. This creates a drawable Android resource that can be referenced by `"@drawable/iosadt"` in Android XML resource files.

> **Note**   You can download the file from `http://pdachoice.com/me/iosadt.jpeg`.

   b. Use the `android:src` attribute to load the image from a drawable application resource, or specify a color value in the form of "#rgb", "#argb", "#rrggbb", or "#aarrggbb", as shown in Listing 4-26.

Listing 4-26. ImageView Widget

```
<?xml version="1.0" encoding="utf-8"?>
<ScrollView ... >
    <RelativeLayout ... >
        ...
        <ImageView
            android:id="@+id/imageView"
```

```
                  android:contentDescription="@android:string/unknownName"
                  android:layout_width="wrap_content"
                  android:layout_height="wrap_content"
                  android:layout_alignParentLeft="true"
                  android:layout_alignParentRight="true"
                  android:layout_below="@id/progressBar2"
                  android:adjustViewBounds="true"
                  android:scaleType="center"
                  android:src="@drawable/iosadt" />

        </RelativeLayout>
    </ScrollView>
```

2. android:scaleType is another frequently used attribute. It controls how the image should be resized or moved to match the size of the ImageView. Table 4-15 shows valid values and descriptions.

Table 4-15. ImageView Attributes

Constant	Description
matrix	Scale the ImageView using the image matrix.
fitXY	Compute a scale that will maintain the original image aspect ratio, but will also ensure that the image fits entirely inside ImageView. At least one axis (X or Y) will fit exactly. The result is centered inside ImageView.
fitStart	Compute a scale that will maintain the original image aspect ratio, but will also ensure that src fits entirely inside ImageView. At least one axis (X or Y) will fit exactly. START aligns the result to the left and top edges of ImageView.
fitCenter	Compute a scale that will maintain the original image aspect ratio, but will also ensure that the image fits entirely inside ImageView. At least one axis (X or Y) will fit exactly. The result is centered inside ImageView.
fitEnd	Compute a scale that will maintain the original image aspect ratio, but will also ensure that the image fits entirely inside ImageView. At least one axis (X or Y) will fit exactly. END aligns the result to the right and bottom edges of ImageView.
center	Center the image in the ImageView, with no scaling.
centerCrop	Scale the image uniformly (maintain the image's aspect ratio) so that both dimensions (width and height) of the image will be equal to or larger than the corresponding dimension of the ImageView (minus padding).
centerInside	Scale the image uniformly (maintain the image's aspect ratio) so that both dimensions (width and height) of the image will be equal to or less than the corresponding dimension of the ImageView (minus padding).

3. Often, you don't know the image size until it is fetched from the server. The following Java method ensures that an image is scaled to fit the width while not being cropped by ImageView height. Similar methods can be implemented to scale image to fit height or both.

```java
public class ScreenOneFragment extends Fragment implements ... {

  ...
  private ImageView mImageView;

  @TargetApi(Build.VERSION_CODES.HONEYCOMB_MR2)
  @SuppressWarnings("deprecation")
  @Override
  public View onCreateView(LayoutInflater inflater, ViewGroup container, Bundle
savedInstanceState) {
    ...
    // ImageView
    mImageView = (ImageView) contentView.findViewById(R.id.imageView);
    Bitmap bitmap = ((BitmapDrawable) getResources().getDrawable(R.drawable.iosadt)).getBitmap();

    Display display = getActivity().getWindowManager().getDefaultDisplay();

    int desireWidth;
    if (android.os.Build.VERSION.SDK_INT >=13) {
      Point out = new Point();
      display.getSize(out);
      desireWidth = out.x;
    } else {
      desireWidth = display.getWidth();
    }

    scaleToFitWidth(bitmap, mImageView, desireWidth);
    ...
  }

  void scaleToFitWidth(Bitmap bitmap, ImageView imageView, int desiredWidth) {
    int w = bitmap.getWidth();
    int h = bitmap.getHeight();

    float scale = (float) desiredWidth / w;
    int scaledW = (int) (w * scale);
    int scaledH = (int) (h * scale);

    imageView.getLayoutParams().width = scaledW;
    imageView.getLayoutParams().height = scaledH;
  }
  ...
}
```

Note   Display.getWidth() is deprecated since API Level 13. You can safely use getSize(outsize) if you target devices with API 13+. Otherwise, to support older devices, you are stuck with the deprecated methods. A better implementation would be to check the API version and call the right API conditionally, just in case an older device gets an OS upgrade *and* the deprecated API gets removed from the new API.

4.   You may build and run the CommonWidgets Android app to make sure it is working.

ImageView extends directly from View. In addition to the super class View attributes, it actually has a few attributes that help general image manipulation tasks, as shown in Table 4-16.

Table 4-16. ImageView Attributes

Attribute Name	Description
android:adjustViewBounds	True if you want the ImageView to adjust its bounds to preserve the aspect ratio of its drawable. Otherwise, false.
android:baseline	The offset of the baseline within this view.
android:baselineAlignBottom	True if the image view will be baseline aligned with based on its bottom edge. Otherwise, false.
android:cropToPadding	True if the image will be cropped to fit within its padding.
android:maxHeight	A maximum height for this view.
android:maxWidth	A maximum width for this view.
android:scaleType	How the image should be resized or moved to match the size of this ImageView.
android:src	A drawable as the content of this ImageView.
android:tint	A tint color for the image.

Menu

Menu is a user interface that provides quick access to frequently used actions. Generally, it is also presented consistently across screens. It is particularly common in desktop platforms. Although there is no such similarly named thing in the iOS SDK, UIBarButtonItem in UIToolbar or UINavigationBar serve a similar purpose as the menu system in the Android platform. In addition, Android also supports the context menu and the popup menu. I will demonstrate the usages for all three types of menus: the options menu, the context menu, and the popup menu.

Older devices prior to API 10 use a dedicated Menu button. Considering this small market share, you should implement the options menu provided by the activity action bar. We will get into the details, but I just wanted to let you know that we will be focusing on the action bar options menu implementation, and be using the v7 appcompat Support Library to port your code down to API Level 7.

Options Menu

```
                                    IOS ANALOGY
```

There are no specific menu widgets in iOS. However, the UIToolbar and the UIBarButtonItem serve similar purposes: quick access to frequently used action widgets.

Previously, you implemented navigation tabs using the action bar (see Figure 3-36 in Chapter 3). Recall that the action bar has four types of components:

1. **App icon** shows the application identity navigation tabs for content views, the main objective of this chapter.

2. **Navigation tabs** (see "Navigation Tabs" in Chapter 3).

3. **Action items** for an app's important actions.

4. **Overflow** menu items for actions that are less often used.

The options menu refers to both the action items (3) and the overflow (4), (see Figure 4-5). The iOS UIBarButtonItem serves a similar purpose as the action items in Android.

Figure 4-5. Android action bar components

A menu resource is a type of application resource that defines the options menu. Similar to but simpler than a layout resource, a menu resource is defined in an XML file in the res/menu folder. Just like the layout resource, the menu resource is defined in an XML file with XML tags and attributes to define the menu items. Listing 4-27 shows a generic menu resource XML structure.

Listing 4-27. Menu Resource Sample Structure

```xml
<menu xmlns:android="http://schemas.android.com/apk/res/android"
    xmlns:app="http://schemas.android.com/apk/res-auto" >

    <item
        android:id="@+id/item1"
        android:title="@android/item1"
        android:icon="@android:drawable/ic_menu_gallery"
        app:showAsAction="always|withText"/>

    <group android:id="@+id/group" >
        <item
            android:id="@+id/group_item1"
            android:title="@android/group_item1"
            android:icon="@android:drawable/ic_menu_agenda"
            app:showAsAction="always|withText"/>
        <item
            android:id="@+id/group_item2"
            android:title="@android/group_item2"
            android:icon="@android:drawable/ic_menu_agenda"
            app:showAsAction="always|withText"/>
    </group>
```

```
<item
    android:id="@+id/submenu"
    android:title="@android/submenu_title"
    android:icon="@android:drawable/ic_menu_help"
    app:showAsAction=" always|withText ">
    <menu>
        <item
            android:id="@+id/submenu_item1"
            android:title="@android/submenu_item1"
            android:icon="@android:drawable/ic_menu_info_details"
            app:showAsAction="always|withText"/>
    </menu>
</item>
</menu>
```

The preceding sample menu resource should render as shown in Figure 4-6.

Figure 4-6. *Sample menu resource*

Listing 4-27 doesn't use all the legitimate XML attributes in the menu resource file. It does show all the top XML elements and the frequently used common attributes, as follows:

■ The menu resource file must start with a menu root node (one and only one) that contains items or a group of items.

■ The item node can contain a menu node to form a submenu.

■ The group node is a logical grouping for related items such that you can apply the same attributes to the whole group. For example, you can make the whole group of items visible or invisible all at once.

■ Some new menu attributes come with action bar and can be ported to older devices using the v7 appcompat library. You need to prefix the v7 namespace to the appropriate attributes. You don't need to do this manually anymore because the Android Project template and our MvcTemplate already have it done. I just wanted to point it out to you in Listing 4-28.

Listing 4-28. *v7 namespace in Menu Resource*

```
<menu ...
    xmlns:app="http://schemas.android.com/apk/res-auto"
    ... >

    <item
        ...
        app:showAsAction="never"/>
</menu>
```

You are ready to write the menu code now. To port the iOS UIBarButtonItem in the CommonWidgets app, you create the activity action bar with action item.

1. ADT project templates give you a default menu, res/menu/main.xml. Let's modify it for one action item, as shown in Listing 4-29.

Listing 4-29. *Options Menu Resource File*

```
<menu xmlns:android="http://schemas.android.com/apk/res/android"
    xmlns:app="http://schemas.android.com/apk/res-auto" >

    <item
        android:id="@+id/menuAction"
        android:icon="@android:drawable/ic_menu_directions"
        android:title="@string/barButtonTitle"
        app:showAsAction="always|withText"/>

</menu>
```

2. <item> has the following common attributes:

   a. android:id: A unique resource ID for the item.

   b. android:icon: A drawable resource ID to use as the item's icon.

   c. android:title: A string resource ID to use as the item's title.

   d. android:showAsAction: Action items can appear in the options menu in different ways, as defined in Table 4-17. You can also specify multiple values using the pipe (|) letter.

Table 4-17. *Menu Item android:showAsAction Attribute*

Value	Description
ifRoom	Show this item in the action bar. If there isn't room for it, you can move it to the Overflow field.
withText	Include the title text with the action item. Note that the title text is defined by android:title.
never	Place item in the Overflow field instead of the action bar.
always	Place item in the action bar.
collapseActionView	The action view associated with this action item is collapsible.

e. use app:showAsAction: Supports devices all the way up to API Level 7
    (see Table 4-17).

Tip You don't need to memorize all the spellings. To find out the valid values of any given attributes, use
Ctrl+<space>.

Note Menu resource actually has a handful of XML attributes that I won't go into detail in this book. As long
as you understand the concepts, you can always look up the syntactical definitions from the official Android
Developers site at http://developer.android.com/guide/topics/resources/menu-resource.html.

---

3. Similar to loading a layout resource, the Android framework loads the menu
    resource in the designated activity or fragment lifecycle callback, as shown in
    Listing 4-30.

    a. Override onCreateOptionsMenu(...) by inflating the appropriate menu
        resource. The same option menu will be available to all the child
        fragments throughout the entire activity.

    b. Override the activity onOptionsItemSelected(...) callback method to
        handle the action item events.

Listing 4-30. Activity Options Menu

```java
public class MainActivity extends ActionBarActivity {
  ...
  @Override
  public boolean onCreateOptionsMenu(Menu menu) {
    getMenuInflater().inflate(R.menu.main, menu);
    return super.onCreateOptionsMenu(menu);
  }

  @Override
  public boolean onOptionsItemSelected(MenuItem item) {
    switch (item.getItemId()) {
    case R.id.menuAction:
      // do something ...
      return true;
    case R.id.menuAction1:
      // do something ...
      return true;
    default:
      return super.onOptionsItemSelected(item);
    }
  }
  ...
```

4. A fragment can append its own options menu to the activity options menu, but it is disabled by default. Do the following to create your fragment-specific options menu as shown in Listing 4-31:

    a. Call setHasOptionsMenu(true) in the onCreate(...) or onCreateView(...) lifecycle callback to enable the fragment options menu explicitly.

    b. Override onCreateOptionsMenu(...) so that you can inflate the appropriate menu resource. The fragment options menu overrides the options menu in the parent activity.

    c. Override the fragment onOptionsItemSelected(...) callback method to handle the action item events.

    d. Remove or comment out the code that creates the options menu in MainActivity.java (see Listing 4-30). The menu item event-handling code is also chained. Activity.onOptionsItemSelected(...) is called first, and then the Fragment.onOptionsItemSelected(...). It is legal, but you want to pay attention to the return value. For simplicity, please remove or comment out both methods in MainActivity.java.

Listing 4-31. Fragment Options Menu

```java
public class ScreenOneFragment extends Fragment implements  ... {
    ...
    @Override
    public View onCreateView(LayoutInflater inflater, ViewGroup container, Bundle
savedInstanceState) {
        ...
        // Options Menu
        setHasOptionsMenu(true); // need to enable it explicitly
        ...
    }

    @Override
    public void onCreateOptionsMenu(Menu menu, MenuInflater inflater) {
        super.onCreateOptionsMenu(menu, inflater);
        inflater.inflate(R.menu.main, menu);
    }

    @Override
    public boolean onOptionsItemSelected(MenuItem item) {
        switch (item.getItemId()) {
        case R.id.menuAction:
            // do something ...
            return true;

        default:
            return super.onOptionsItemSelected(item);
        }
    }
    ...
}
```

5. You may build and run the CommonWidgets Android app to make sure the code in Listing 4-31 has no errors.

Context Menu

```
                              IOS ANALOGY
```

ActionSheet might have the closest L&F. However, it is rare to encounter porting the iOS ActionSheet to the Android context menu because it seems uncommon to me to have different ActionSheets associated with different contexts in the same screen in iOS. It's technically possible though.

On the desktop, the context menu is a floating menu that appears when the user performs a right-click on an element. On Android, you get a similar floating menu through a long-click on a View element. The context menu implementations are very similar to the options menu.

To demonstrate Android context menu usage, let's create the floating context menu when users perform a long-click on the text label and action button in the CommonWidgets Android app.

1. Just like the options menu, you create a menu resource for the context menu in an XML file. Create an XML file named CommonWidgets/res/menu/contextmenu.xml, as shown in Listing 4-32.

Listing 4-32. Context Menu Layout File

```xml
<?xml version="1.0" encoding="utf-8"?>
<menu xmlns:android="http://schemas.android.com/apk/res/android" >

    <item
        android:id="@+id/contextMenuAction1"
        android:title="@string/contextMenuItem1"/>
    <item
        android:id="@+id/contextMenuAction2"
        android:title="@string/contextMenuItem2"/>
    <item
        android:id="@+id/contextMenuAction3"
        android:title="@string/contextMenuItem3"/>

</menu>
```

Note There is no item icon in the context menu.

2. Register the View widgets for the context menu, as shown in Listing 4-33.

Listing 4-33. Register for Context Menu

```java
public class ScreenOneFragment extends Fragment implements  ... {
  ...
  @Override
  public View onCreateView(LayoutInflater inflater, ViewGroup container, Bundle
savedInstanceState) {
    ...
    // Context Menu
    registerForContextMenu(mTextView);
    registerForContextMenu(mButton);
    ...
  }
  ...
}
```

3. Very similar to the options menu implementation, the menu resource needs
    to be inflated in an appropriate lifecycle callback, onCreateContextMenu(...).
    You also override onContextItemSelected(...) to respond to menu
    selections (see Listing 4-34). Individual View elements may have different
    context menus. Use View.getId() to identify the context and inflate
    individual menu resources accordingly.

Listing 4-34. Inflate Context Menu and Handle Callback Events

```java
public class ScreenOneFragment extends Fragment implements  ... {
  ...
  @Override
  public void onCreateContextMenu(ContextMenu menu, View v, ContextMenuInfo menuInfo) {
    super.onCreateContextMenu(menu, v, menuInfo);

    MenuInflater inflater = getActivity().getMenuInflater();

    // inflate individual menu resource respectfully
    switch (v.getId()) {
    case R.id.textViewLabel:
      // inflater.inflate(R.menu.contextmenu, menu);
      // break;
    case R.id.buttonAction:
      inflater.inflate(R.menu.contextmenu, menu);
      break;
    }
  }

  @Override
  public boolean onContextItemSelected(MenuItem item) {
    switch (item.getItemId()) {
    case R.id.contextMenuAction1:
```

```
            // TODO: do something ...
            break;
        case R.id.contextMenuAction2:
            // TODO: do something ...
            break;
        case R.id.contextMenuAction3:
            // TODO: do something ...
            break;
        default:
            break;
        }
        return true;
    }
    ...
}
```

4. Build and run the CommonWidgets Android app to visualize the context menu usages.

Popup Menu

IOS ANALOGY

UIActionSheet (similar usage but different L&F) or UITableView in UIPopoverController (iPad only).

In iOS, `UIActionSheet` displays a set of choices related to a task the user initiates. On the iPhone, it emerges from the bottom of the screen and hovers over the entire screen. The side edges of an action sheet are anchored to the sides of the screen, which reinforces its visual connection to the app and to the user's most recent action. On the iPad, an action sheet is always displayed within a popover.

Figure 4-7. iOS popover

Previously (see the "Dialogs" section in Chapter 3), we translated the iPad popover to Android using `DialogFragment`. It certainly works for the intended purpose, but I have to admit it may not be the best option to match the L&F in iOS. `DialogFragment` is more capable of providing a richer content view because it is a fragment and you can use it for full-screen navigations using the Fragment API. For simple choice of action, you can use `PopupMenu`, which displays a list of action items in a vertical list that's normally anchored to the view element that invokes the popup menu. It visually suggests to users the extended actions that relate to the triggering view element. The L&F and purpose is very similar to having a `UITableView` in a popover on the iPad.

Let's show a `PopupMenu` when an action item in the fragment options menu is selected in the CommonWidgets Android app.

1. For any Android menu, including `PopupMenu`, you need to create a menu resource in an XML file, such as `CommonWidgets/res/menu/popupmenu.xml` (see Listing 4-35).

    Listing 4-35. Android Popup Menu Layout File

    ```
    <?xml version="1.0" encoding="utf-8"?>
    <menu xmlns:android="http://schemas.android.com/apk/res/android" >

        <item
            android:id="@+id/popupAction1"
            android:title="@string/popupMenuItem1"/>
    ```

```
        <item
            android:id="@+id/popupAction2"
            android:title="@string/popupMenuItem2"/>
        <item
            android:id="@+id/popupAction3"
            android:title="@string/popupMenuItem3"/>
</menu>
```

2. Modify the previous options menu handler, onOptionsItemSelected(...) to create a PopupMenu (see Listing 4-36).

    a. The position of the PopupMenu is determined by a given View element. You want it to be anchored at the MenuItem. You can always use findViewById(...) to get the View object.

    b. Just like loading any menu, use MenuInflater to load the menu from the menu resource.

    c. Specify the v7 version using the appropriate import statement.

Listing 4-36. Create PopupMenu

```
import android.support.v7.widget.PopupMenu
...
public class ScreenOneFragment extends Fragment implements ... {
    ...
    @Override
    public boolean onOptionsItemSelected(MenuItem item) {
      switch (item.getItemId()) {
      case R.id.menuAction:
        // show iPad-like popover
        View anchorView = (View) getActivity().findViewById(R.id.menuAction);
        PopupMenu popup = new PopupMenu(getActivity(), anchorView);
        MenuInflater inflater = popup.getMenuInflater();
        inflater.inflate(R.menu.popupmenu, popup.getMenu());
        popup.show();
        return true;

      default:
      return super.onOptionsItemSelected(item);
    }
    ...
}
```

3. Implement the PopupMenu item event-handling code (see Listing 4-37).

    a. Declare ScreenOneFragment to conform to the OnMenuItemClickListener interface.

    b. Register the listener object this to handle the events.

    c. Provide OnMenuItemClickListener.onMenuItemClick(...) implementation.

Listing 4-37. Implement PopupMenu onMenuItemClick Callback

```java
public class ScreenOneFragment extends Fragment implements  ...
    OnMenuItemClickListener {
  ...
  @Override
  public boolean onOptionsItemSelected(MenuItem item) {
    Log.d("ScreenOneFragment", "" + item.getItemId());
    switch (item.getItemId()) {
    case R.id.menuAction:
      // show iPad-like popover
     ...
      popup.setOnMenuItemClickListener(this); // register handler
      break;

    default:
      return super.onOptionsItemSelected(item);
    }
  }


  @Override
  public boolean onMenuItemClick(MenuItem item) {
    Log.d("ScreenOneFragment", "onMenuItemClick: " + item.getItemId());
    switch (item.getItemId()) {
    case R.id.popupAction1:
      // TODO: do something ...
      break;
    case R.id.popupAction2:
      // TODO: do something ...
      break;
    case R.id.popupAction3:
      // TODO: do something ...
      break;
    default:
      break;
    }

    Toast.makeText(getActivity(), item.getTitle(), Toast.LENGTH_SHORT).show();
    return true;
  }
  ...
}
```

4. Build and run the CommonWidgets Android app to visualize how the Android PopupMenu works.

Spinner

UIPickerView

In iOS, `UIPickerView` displays a set of values from which the user selects. It provides a quick way to select one value from a spinning wheel–like list that shows all or part of the selections. The Android system provides a `Spinner` widget. One obvious difference is that it only shows the currently selected value. Touching the spinner displays a drop-down menu with all other available values, from which the user can select a new one. It is very similar to the drop-down list commonly seen in traditional desktop apps or web pages. If you really want to show users the currently selected value and other available selections without dropping the list down, you can always use a `ListView`.

`Spinner` is a type of `AdapterView`, just like `ListView` or `GridView`, which use the same `Adapter` pattern to bind item data with the item view. To learn by example, let's add a `Spinner` widget to our CommonWidgets app.

1. Add a `Spinner` element to the end of the `res/layout/screenone_fragment.xml` layout file, as shown in Listing 4-38.

    Listing 4-38. Spinner Widget

    ```xml
    <?xml version="1.0" encoding="utf-8"?>
    <ScrollView ... >
        <RelativeLayout ... >
            ...
            <Spinner
                android:id="@+id/spinner"
                android:layout_width="fill_parent"
                android:layout_height="wrap_content"
                android:layout_below="@+id/imageView" />

        </RelativeLayout>
    </ScrollView>
    ```

> **Note** We will set a spinner data source in Java code later. For a static list, you can simply define spinner items in res/values/strings.xml and assign the string array in in the layout file; for example
>
> android:entries="@array/spinnerItems"

2. Spinner uses the same Adapter pattern to bind item content with an item layout (see Listing 4-39).

    a. For a simple list item with a one-line text label, you can use ArrayAdapter with a simple_list_item_1 item layout from the Android SDK. If you need to, create your own custom Adapter class the same way you did for ListView (see Chapter 3).

    b. To access application resources, use getResources(). getStringArray(...), getString(...), getInteger(...), getDrawable(...), and so forth.

    c. The selected item layout is specified in the adapter.

    d. The item layout in the drop-down list can be specified by setDropDownViewResource(...). Otherwise, it defaults to the selected layout.

    e. You may set the initial selection.

Listing 4-39. Supply Spinner Items Using Adapter

```java
public class ScreenOneFragment extends Fragment implements  ... {
  ...
  private Spinner mSpinner;
  @Override
  public View onCreateView(LayoutInflater inflater, ViewGroup container, Bundle
savedInstanceState) {
    ...
    // Spinner and its Adapter
    mSpinner = (Spinner) contentView.findViewById(R.id.spinner);

    String[] datasource = getResources().getStringArray(R.array.spinnerItems);
    ArrayAdapter<String> adapter = new ArrayAdapter<String>(getActivity(),
        android.R.layout.simple_list_item_1, datasource);

    // The layout of the drop-down list items
    adapter.setDropDownViewResource(android.R.layout.simple_list_item_checked);

    // Set the adapter and initial selection.
    mSpinner.setAdapter(adapter);
    mSpinner.setSelection(1);
    ...
  }
  ...
}
```

3. Similar to all the action delegate code, do the following to handle the item selected action events (see Listing 4-40):

    a. Declare `ScreenOneFragment` to conform to the `OnItemSelectedListener` interface.

    b. Register the listener object `this` to handle the events.

    c. Provide `OnItemSelectedListener` interface implementation.

Listing 4-40. Implement Spinner OnItemSelectedListener

```java
public class ScreenOneFragment extends Fragment implements ...
    OnItemSelectedListener { // confront to interface
  ...
  private Spinner mSpinner;
  @Override
  public View onCreateView(LayoutInflater inflater, ViewGroup container, Bundle
savedInstanceState) {
    ...
    // Spinner and its Adapter
    ...
    mSpinner.setOnItemSelectedListener(this);
    ...
  }

  // provide OnItemSelectedListener interface impl
  @Override
  public void onItemSelected(AdapterView<?> list, View item, int pos, long id) {
    Log.d("MainActivity", "onItemSelected: " + mSpinner.getSelectedItem());
    // TODO do something
  }

  @Override
  public void onNothingSelected(AdapterView<?> arg0) {
    Log.d("MainActivity", "onNothingSelected: " + mSpinner.getSelectedItem());
    // do nothing, it could happen rarely, i.e., when adapter become empty
  }
  ...
}
```

The implementation is almost the same as implementing the `AdapterView` for `ListView` and `GridView` elements. The only difference is that you can also use `setDropDownViewResource(...)` to specify the list item style for the drop-down list.

Note   Being an iOS developer, I find I rarely use Spinner because it feels more like a desktop or web page drop-down widget. The Android ListView L&F is probably a better match to the iOS UIPickerView L&F in my opinion.

5. Build and run the CommonWidgets Android app to visualize this code in action.

Table 4-18 lists the name of the `Spinner` XML attributes. It is also inherits all the attributes from `ViewGroup` (see Table 4-1). Again, for the composite type of `View` elements, always be cautious when overriding the attributes from the inherited view element.

Table 4-18. *Spinner Attributes*

Attribute Names	
android:entries	android:gravity
android:dropDownHorizontalOffset	android:popupBackground
android:dropDownSelector	android:prompt
android:dropDownVerticalOffset	android:spinnerMode
android:dropDownWidth	

Note   For more information about these XML attributes, see the online reference on the Android Developers site (`http://developer.android.com/reference/android/widget/Spinner.html`).

VideoView

IOS ANALOGY

MPMoviePlayerController

Generally, you want to use a media player to play video. The media player is more than a UI widget. To play a video within your screen layout, you can use the `VideoView` widget to load videos from the local file system, remote server, or media resources bundled with the app. For playing media content in full-screen mode, you should always consider integrating your app with the device's existing media player, instead of reinventing the media player. We will discuss how to use an existing app in Chapter 7.

To learn how to use the `VideoView` element, do the following in the CommonWidgets Android app.

1. Add a `VideoView` element to the end of the `res/layout/screenone_fragment.xml` layout file, as shown in Listing 4-41.

Listing 4-41. *VideoView Widget*

```
<?xml version="1.0" encoding="utf-8"?>
<ScrollView ... >
    <RelativeLayout ... >
        ...
```

```
        <VideoView
            android:id="@+id/videoView"
            android:layout_width="190dp"
            android:layout_height="240dp"
            android:layout_below="@id/spinner"
            android:layout_centerInParent="true" />

    </RelativeLayout>
</ScrollView>
```

2.   All you need is a valid URI to a video source that can be used for a remote HTTP link, local files, or application resources bundled with the app (see Listing 4-42). Most likely, you want to attach a media player control to the VideoView with the MediaController object.

Listing 4-42. VideoView with MediaController

```
public class ScreenOneFragment extends Fragment implements ... {
    ...
    private VideoView mVideoView;
    @Override
    public View onCreateView(LayoutInflater inflater, ViewGroup container, Bundle savedInstanceState) {
        ...
        // VideoView
        mVideoView = (VideoView) contentView.findViewById(R.id.videoView);
        Uri demoUrl = Uri.parse("http://www.pdachoice.com/me/sample_mpeg4.mp4");
        mVideoView.setVideoURI(demoUrl);
        // set a media controller
        final MediaController mc = new MediaController(getActivity());
        mVideoView.setMediaController(mc);
        ...
    }
    ...
}
```

> **Note**   You can get the URI from local file Uri.fromFile(new File("/sdcard/demo.mp4")).
>
> You can also drag and drop a video file into the ADT project res/raw/ folder to create the raw application resource. Then, you can create the URI from the application resource as follows:
>
> Uri.parse("android.resource://" + getActivity().getPackageName() + "/" + R.raw.sample_mpeg4).

3.   MediaPlayer is the core class in the Android multimedia framework. You may not need to handle any VideoView lifecycle or rendering events by implementing the OnPreparedListener since the VideoView element already handles the most common usages. When you need to do more, you really need the MediaPlayer instance. Listing 4-43 shows one of the easiest ways to get a hold of the MediaPlayer instance.

a. Declare ScreenOneFragment to conform to the OnPreparedListener interface.

b. Register the listener object this so you can get the callback events.

c. Provide OnPreparedListener interface implementation. You will get the MediaPlayer instance in the callback.

d. The VideoView widget shows a black empty screen until any video frame is loaded. I use the seekTo(...) method to get rid of the black empty screen without playing the media. Generally, this is not a bulletproof solution because you might not always know where to seekTo. It is better to overlay a meaningful image and programmatically hide the image as soon as the video starts.

Listing 4-43. Implement VideoView OnPreparedListener

```
public class ScreenOneFragment extends Fragment implements ...
    OnPreparedListener { // confront to interface
  ...
  private VideoView mVideoView;
  @Override
  public View onCreateView(LayoutInflater inflater, ViewGroup container, Bundle
savedInstanceState) {
    ...
    // VideoView

    ...
    mVideoView.setOnPreparedListener(this);
    ...
  }


  // provide OnPreparedListener interface implementation
  @Override
  public void onPrepared(MediaPlayer mediaPlayer) {
    mProgressBar1.setVisibility(View.INVISIBLE);
    mSwitchButton.setChecked(false);

    // You can do more with the framework core class: MediaPlayer
    mediaPlayer.setLooping(true);
    int h = mediaPlayer.getVideoHeight();
    int w = mediaPlayer.getVideoWidth();

    Log.d("onPrepared", "w: " + w + " h: " + h);

    // to eliminate an empty black view
    mVideoView.seekTo(10);
//    mVideoView.start();
  }
  ...
}
```

4. To access the Internet or certain platform features from an Android app, you need to let users know by declaring the `uses-permission`. Modify the `AndroidManifest.xml` file to add the `uses-permission` request, as shown in Listing 4-44. Users will see the permission request when installing the app from the Google Play Store.

    Listing 4-44. *Declare uses-permission in Manifest.xml*

    ```
    <manifest ... >

        <uses-permission android:name="android.permission.INTERNET" />
        ...
    </manifest>
    ```

5. Build and run the CommonWidgets Android app to see the `VideoView` widget code in action.

> **Note**   You may encounter device fragmentation issues when dealing with multimedia. In general, you want to make sure the content format is supported on the intended devices. However, different API levels or certain devices may have different capabilities. For example, the HTTP Live Streaming protocol is not supported until Android 3.0. Normally, the newer devices are more capable of supporting different types of network protocols and more media formats. In general, you want to choose the content types that are more device-agnostic, for example, the sample video source sample_mpeg4.mp4 is of H.263 format, MPEG-4 file type—one of the most widely supported video formats. The Android Developers site lists the requirements per API level at `http://developer.android.com/guide/appendix/media-formats.html`.

`VideoView` doesn't have specific XML attributes. It inherits the XML attributes from the `View` element. Most of them actually don't seem to be useful on the `VideoView` element.

Extra Android Widgets

Whew! You have come a long way in translating almost all of the iOS UI widgets to the Android platform. There are a few Android system widgets that I have not covered yet. Apparently, the Android framework provides more system widgets out of box than iOS does. These extra widgets are handy when you need them. To explore further, simply drag and drop any widgets from the palette view in the graphical layout editor and try them out yourself. For example, drag the five-star element shown in Figure 4-8 onto the layout.

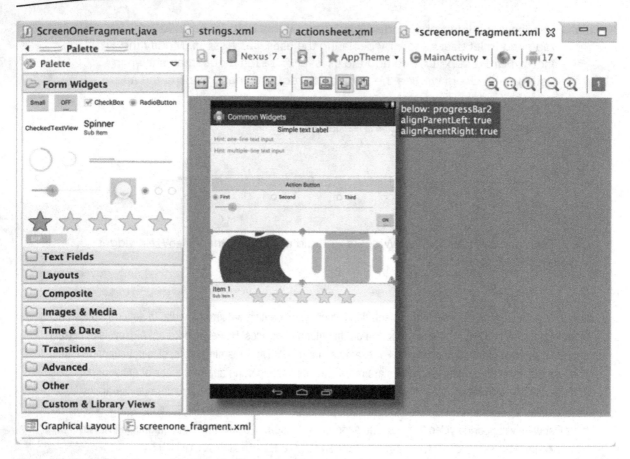

Figure 4-8. RatingBar in the graphical layout editor

By examining the XML layout file, you will see that it is called `RatingBar`. You can simply look up the class reference from official Android Developers site at `http://developer.android.com/reference/android/widget/RatingBar.html`.

Apparently, it is just a subclass of `SeekBar`. I think that you will visit the online API reference frequently when you are working on Android projects. Bookmark it!

FINAL TOUCH

You have completed all the topics in this chapter. If you have followed all the widget topics, the app should have the same functionality as the iOS app. Only the L&F is a little off. The iOS app has some padding around the UI elements. It also uses a white background to highlight input fields. To get the same L&F, you can add the following simple view attributes to adjust the appearance.

1. Set the background color on the entire screen. Instead of the hard-code color #33808080, create the color resource in $PROJ/res/values/strings.xml, as shown in Listing 4-45.

Listing 4-45. *Android Color Resource*

```xml
<?xml version="1.0" encoding="utf-8"?>
<resources>
    ...
    <color name="bgcolor">#33808080</string>
    ...
</resources>
```

Note   Color is a type of application resource specified with an RGB value and an alpha channel that you can define in an XML file in the res/values/ folder. Although the file name is arbitrary, it might be more organized to save all the project-specific colors in a separate file, such as res/values/colors.xml.

---

2.   Specify android:background on the parent layout RelativeLayout element (see Listing 4-46).

Listing 4-46. *android:background*

```xml
<?xml version="1.0" encoding="utf-8"?>
<ScrollView ... >
    <RelativeLayout
        ...
        android:background="@color/bgcolor" >
        ...
    </RelativeLayout>
</ScrollView>
```

3.   Create a measurement for border padding in $PROJ/res/values/dimens.xml, as shown in Listing 4-47.

Listing 4-47. *Android Measurement Resource*

```xml
<resources>
    ...
    <dimen name="borderPadding">3dp</dimen>
    ...
</resources>
```

4.   To create uniformed borders around all the widgets, add the borderPadding (see Listing 4-47) around the entire parent layout, and then bottom padding to all the child widget elements, as shown in Listing 4-48.

Listing 4-48. Add Border Paddings to Widgets

```xml
<?xml version="1.0" encoding="utf-8"?>
<ScrollView ... >
    <RelativeLayout ... android:padding="@dimen/borderPadding" >

        <!-- a very long content view -->

        <TextView  ... android:layout_marginBottom="@dimen/borderPadding" />
        <EditText  ... android:layout_marginBottom="@dimen/borderPadding" />
        <EditText  ... android:layout_marginBottom="@dimen/borderPadding" />
        <Button  ... android:layout_marginBottom="@dimen/borderPadding" />
        <RadioGroup  ... android:layout_marginBottom="@dimen/borderPadding" >
            ...
        </RadioGroup>
        <TextView  ... android:layout_marginBottom="@dimen/borderPadding" />
        <SeekBar  ... android:layout_marginBottom="@dimen/borderPadding" />
        <ProgressBar  ... android:layout_marginBottom="@dimen/borderPadding" />
        <ProgressBar  ... android:layout_marginBottom="@dimen/borderPadding" />
        <ToggleButton  ... android:layout_marginBottom="@dimen/borderPadding" />
        <ImageView  ... android:layout_marginBottom="@dimen/borderPadding" />
        <Spinner  ... android:layout_marginBottom="@dimen/borderPadding" />
        <VideoView  ... android:layout_marginBottom="@dimen/borderPadding" />
    </RelativeLayout>
</ScrollView>
```

5. Set a white background color on EditText, RadioGroup, and Spinner elements, as shown in
    Listing 4-49.

Listing 4-49. Add Background Colors

```xml
<?xml version="1.0" encoding="utf-8"?>
<ScrollView ... >
    <RelativeLayout ... >
        ...
        <EditText  ... android:background="@android:color/white" />
        <EditText  ... android:background="@android:color/white" />
        ...
        <RadioGroup  ... android:background="@android:color/white" >
            ...
        </RadioGroup>
        ...
        <Spinner  ... android:background="@android:color/white" />
    </RelativeLayout>
</ScrollView>
```

6. Build and run the CommonWidgets Android app. Does your app look like Figure 4-9?

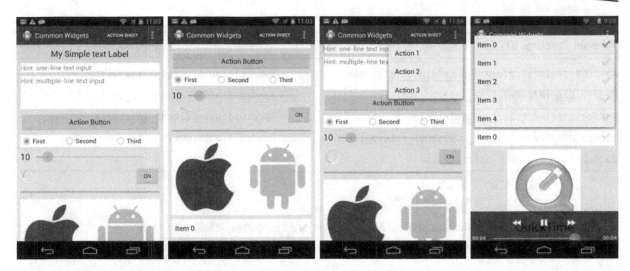

Figure 4-9. Android CommonWidgets app

Screen Animations

Back in the old days developing mobile apps for Blackberry or Windows Mobile, I really cared less about the animation effects between screen transitions. I think iOS evolution definitely raised the bar higher. On the Android platform, the animations framework makes it simple, but you have choices to make in terms of compatibility. The newer API is easier and you can do more. The old view animation framework covers all Android devices. In addition to considering target audiences, you also need to know the capacities. It might sound messy, but it is actually not that bad. The key classes are different but the framework usages are similar.

We will talk about both frameworks: the property animation framework and the view animation framework. You always want to learn new techniques for sure. For this topic, the old way cannot be completely abandoned yet because it still covers a fairly large number of devices that are out there. Both frameworks take three parameters to animate a View:

- **Animation duration:** The length of the animation in milliseconds.

- **Drawing attributes:** The view attributes that are being animated over the duration, such as alpha, scale, translate, rotate, and so forth.

- **Animation interpolator:** Changes to the drawing attributes during the animation duration, such as animating a ball movement from point A to point B. You use this factor to specify a constant linear movement or acerbated speed, or bouncing up and down, and so forth. Instead of implementing your own interpolator, Table 4-19 lists the available animation interpolator resource IDs that you can use right out of the box from the Android SDK. I think it covers the most common cases.

Table 4-19. Animation Framework Interpolators

Android Resource ID	
`@android:anim/accelerate_decelerate_interpolator`	`@android:anim/cycle_interpolator`
`@android:anim/accelerate_interpolator`	`@android:anim/decelerate_interpolator`
`@android:anim/anticipate_interpolator`	`@android:anim/linear_interpolator`
`@android:anim/anticipate_overshoot_interpolator`	`@android:anim/overshoot_interpolator`
`@android:anim/bounce_interpolator`	

> **Note**   For more information about these XML attributes, see the Android Developers site at
> `http://developer.android.com/guide/topics/resources/animation-resource.html`.

Other than the key classes being in different packages, both frameworks and API usages are fairly similar.

View Animations: API Level 1

Since API Level 1, you can attach an `Animation` object to a `View` element to alter the drawing attributes of the `View` object, including the containing child view elements over time.

This old style animation objects only affect where and how the view is rendered, *not* the actual `View` attributes. This works fine in most cases if the `View` element doesn't need to interact with users after animation; for example, a bouncing ball, or an icon that does nothing except show decorative visual effects, or when the entire content view is faded out. The best part is that it covers all Android devices since API Level 1.

In the view animation framework, all the interpolators (see Table 4-19) are applicable. For the animation drawing attributes, you can apply the following XML attributes:

- `<alpha />`: Fade-in or fade-out animation
- `<scale />`: Resizing animation
- `<translate />`: Motion animation
- `<rotate />`: Rotation animation

To show animation visual effects when switching views, you can safely use the view animations framework.

ADT PROJECT PREPARATIONS

Same steps: use the MvcTemplate project to create an ADT project.

1. Copy MvcTemplate ADT project and paste it to a new project (⌘c, ⌘v) named **Animations**.

2. Rename the Android application package. From the Dialogs project context menu, select **Android Tools ➤ Rename Application Package**. Enter a new package name: **com.pdachoice.animations**.

3. Rename the src/com.pdachoice.renameme Java package. From the package context menu, select **Refactor ➤ Rename...** (Alt+⌘r) and do the following:

   a. Enter a new name: **com.pdachoice.animations**.

   b. Select **Update references**.

4. Modify res/values/strings.xml, as shown in Listing 4-50.

   Listing 4-50. *app_name*

   ```
   <?xml version="1.0" encoding="utf-8"?>
   <resources>
       <string name="app_name"> Animations</string>
       ...
   </resources>
   ```

5. You may build and run the prep app to make sure you have a clean start.

View Animation Resources

Animation is a type of application resource, just like string or layout resources, and so forth. You can also write pure Java code to achieve the same purpose. You should always consider defining animations as Android animation resources in the XML file. Doing so allows you to provide alternative application resources for different screen sizes, locales, internationalization, and so forth. We will talk about alternative application resources in Chapter 6.

Earlier, we used the MvcTemplate to create projects with different navigation patterns. One thing doesn't look exactly like an iOS app: there are no screen transition animations. To learn by example, let's add a screen transition animation to the newly created ADT Animations project.

1. View animation resources need to be saved in the res/anim folder, and you will reference the animation resource using R.anim.xxx in Java code. Create an animation resource XML file that defines the animation attributes.

   a. From the Animations/res folder context menu, select **New ➤ Folder** to create the res/anim folder.

   b. From the newly created res/anim folder context menu, select **New ➤ Android XML File** to create an application resource named res/anim/screentransition.xml.

2. Modify the newly created `screentransition.xml` file (as shown in Listing 4-51), particularly the following attributes :

    a. Use `android:interpolator` to specify the interpolator.

Tip   In the Eclipse XML editor, use Ctrl+<space> to see the available interpolator (see Table 4-19).

---

    b. Use `android:duration` to specify the duration in milliseconds.

    c. To fade-in a screen, specify the `alpha` attribute. Just for fun, you can fade-in with rotation, too.

Listing 4-51. View Animation Resource File

```xml
<?xml version="1.0" encoding="utf-8"?>
<set xmlns:android="http://schemas.android.com/apk/res/android"
    android:interpolator="@android:anim/bounce_interpolator"
    android:shareInterpolator="true"
    android:duration="3000">

    <alpha
        android:fromAlpha="0"
        android:toAlpha="1" />

    <rotate
        android:fromDegrees="0"
        android:pivotX="50%"
        android:pivotY="50%"
        android:toDegrees="360" />

</set>
```

3. Create a convenient utility method in `MainActivity.java` that loads the animation resource, and then apply it to a given `View` element (the `applyViewAnimation(...)` method in Listing 4-52).

    a. To load the animation resource, use `AnimationUtils.loadAnimation(...)`.

    b. Use `View.startAnimation(...)` to attach the `Animation` object to a view object.

Listing 4-52. Load Animation Resource File

```java
public class MainActivity extends FragmentActivity {
  ...
  public void applyViewAnimation(View view) {
    Animation screentransition =
        AnimationUtils.loadAnimation(this,  R.anim.screentransition);
    view.startAnimation(screentransition);
  }
  ...
}
```

4. You can animate a single `View` element or the whole content view. To animate screen transitions when the new view is appearing, call the method (see Listing 4-42) in the `onCreateView(...)` with the entire content view for all three Fragment classes (see Listing 4-53).

Listing 4-53. *Activity.applyViewAnimation*

```
@Override
public View onCreateView(LayoutInflater inflater, ViewGroup container, Bundle
savedInstanceState) {
    ...
    ((MainActivity)getActivity()).applyViewAnimation(contentView);
    return contentView;
}
```

> **Note**   You want to do the same for all three Fragment classes. Since you want to apply the same method to the lifecycle callback in all Fragment classes, you might consider creating a super class and do it in there.

5. Build and run the Animations app. You should see a funny animated fade-in and bouncing screen transition.

It is preferable to define an animation resource in the XML resource file because you can use the application resource guideline to create different animations for different types of devices or locales. If you don't need to worry about localizing the animation resource, you can write equivalent Java code without the `screentransition.xml` file. You want to do so particularly when you need to define animation logics in the runtime.

The `applyViewAnimation(...)` method in Listing 4-54 does the same thing without using an animation resource XML file.

Listing 4-54. *Create Animation in Runtime*

```
public class MainActivity extends FragmentActivity {
    ...
    void applyViewAnimation(View view) {
        AnimationSet screentransition = new AnimationSet(true);

        Animation fadeOut = new AlphaAnimation(0, 1);
        Animation rotate = new RotateAnimation(0f, 360f,
            Animation.RELATIVE_TO_PARENT, 0.5f,
            Animation.RELATIVE_TO_PARENT, 0.5f);

        screentransition.setInterpolator(new BounceInterpolator());
        screentransition.addAnimation(fadeOut);
        screentransition.addAnimation(rotate);
```

```
                 screentransition.setDuration(3000);
    //       Animation screentransition = AnimationUtils.loadAnimation(this,  R.anim.screentransition);

                 view.startAnimation(screentransition);
        }
        ...
    }
```

You can play with different animation attributes to see how they look. You can also try the nextButton element instead of the entire content view.

Property Animations: API Level 11

In API Level 11, Android introduced a newer and more robust animation framework, *property animation*. If backward-compatibility is not your concern, you should use this framework instead of the older animation method. Not only does this framework affect how View elements are rendered visually, it also changes the target object properties with the defined animation methods.

To elaborate the potential problem of using the older view animation framework, let's say that a button appears to be moved or resized due to the animation code, but the View geometry attributes actually remain unchanged, meaning the onClick region remains the same while the button appears in a different place. This isn't good when the app needs to keep track of the View attributes for various reasons. In fact, the property animation framework can be applied not only on the View objects, but to any object.

To compare, let's create the same screen transition animation effects using the property animation framework, as opposed to the view animation framework used earlier. Continue working on the Animations ADT project by doing the following:

1. Property animation resources are conventionally saved in the res/animator/ folder, and you will reference the animation resource from your Java code using R.animator.xxx.

2. Create a res/animator/screentransition.xml XML file to define the property animation attributes (see Listing 4-55).

    a. Use <ObjectAnimator> elements and specify the propertyName of the target view to animate.

Note   Compared with the view animation XML syntax that uses different XML elements for different animation attributes, don't you like this way better?

---

    b. Optionally, you can use the <set> element to group multiple animators together. The grouped animators can start "sequentially" or "together".

    c. All the `android:interpolator` used in previous view animation frameworks (see Table 4-19) are applicable here.

    d. Set `android:duration`, the same way you did in view animation.

> **Note**   Based on my experience with API 19 Nexus devices, it seems that the duration and interpolator animation attributes need to be specified in <ObjectAnimator> attributes instead of <set>. You might want to keep an eye on this.

Listing 4-55. *Property Animation Resource File*

```xml
<?xml version="1.0" encoding="utf-8"?>
<set xmlns:android="http://schemas.android.com/apk/res/android"
    android:ordering="together" >

    <objectAnimator
        android:duration="3000"
        android:interpolator="@android:anim/linear_interpolator"
        android:propertyName="alpha"
        android:valueFrom="0"
        android:valueTo="1" />
    <objectAnimator
        android:duration="3000"
        android:interpolator="@android:anim/bounce_interpolator"
        android:propertyName="rotation"
        android:valueFrom="0"
        android:valueTo="360" />
</set>
```

3.   Create another convenient utility method in `MainActivity.java` that loads the property animation resource and applies it to a given `View` element. To load animation resource files, use `AnimatorInflater.loadAnimator(...)`, as shown in Listing 4-56.

Listing 4-56. *Apply Property Animation Resource File*

```java
public class MainActivity extends FragmentActivity {
  ...
  void applyPropertyAnimation(View view) {
    Animator screentransition =
        AnimatorInflater.loadAnimator(this, R.animator.screentransition);

    screentransition.setTarget(view);
    screentransition.start();
  }
  ...
}
```

4. The property animation framework requires Android API Level 11+. You should get a compilation error unless you have changed the `minSdkVersion`. Read the Problems view (see Figure 4-10); it clearly tells the problem.

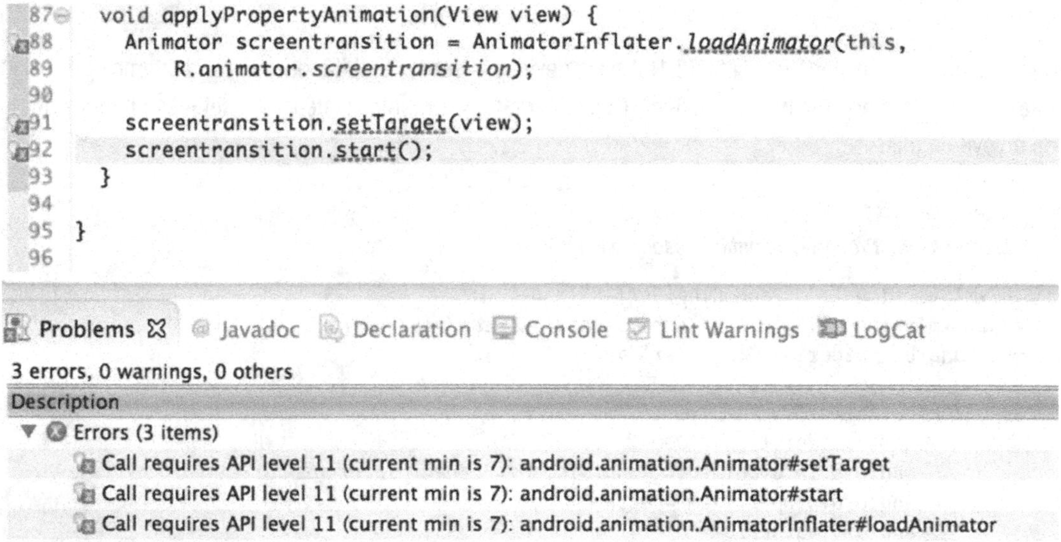

```
87⊖    void applyPropertyAnimation(View view) {
88        Animator screentransition = AnimatorInflater.loadAnimator(this,
89            R.animator.screentransition);
90
91        screentransition.setTarget(view);
92        screentransition.start();
93    }
94
95 }
96
```

Problems ⊠   Javadoc   Declaration   Console   Lint Warnings   LogCat

3 errors, 0 warnings, 0 others

Description

▼ ⊗ Errors (3 items)

    Call requires API level 11 (current min is 7): android.animation.Animator#setTarget

    Call requires API level 11 (current min is 7): android.animation.Animator#start

    Call requires API level 11 (current min is 7): android.animation.AnimatorInflater#loadAnimator

Figure 4-10. *API Level 11 required in Problem view*

5. Modify the `AndroidManifest.xml` file to change `minSdkVersion` to the required level, as shown in Listing 4-57.

Listing 4-57. *minSdkVersion*

```
<manifest ... >
    ...
    <uses-sdk
        android:minSdkVersion="11"
        ... />
    ...
</manifest>
```

6. Call the method (see Listing 4-57) in the `onCreateView(...)` with the whole content view for all three Fragment classes (see Listing 4-58).

Listing 4-58. *Apply Property Animation Resource*

```
@Override
public View onCreateView(LayoutInflater inflater, ViewGroup container, Bundle
savedInstanceState) {
    ...
//    ((MainActivity)getActivity()).applyViewAnimation(contentView);
    ((MainActivity)getActivity()).applyPropertyAnimation(contentView);
    return contentView;
}
```

7. Build and run the Animations app. You should see the same screen transition animation.

As with view animation, you can write pure Java code that creates the same property animations without the animation resource method, as shown in Listing 4-59.

Listing 4-59. Create Property Animation in Java

```java
void applyPropertyAnimation(View view) {

  AnimationSet screentransition = new AnimationSet(true);

  Animation fadeOut = new AlphaAnimation(0, 1);
  Animation rotate = new RotateAnimation(0f, 360f,
      Animation.RELATIVE_TO_PARENT, 0.5f, Animation.RELATIVE_TO_PARENT, 0.5f);

  screentransition.setInterpolator(new BounceInterpolator());
  screentransition.addAnimation(fadeOut);
  screentransition.addAnimation(rotate);

  screentransition.setDuration(3000);

  // Animation screentransition = AnimationUtils.loadAnimation(this, R.anim.screentransition);
  view.startAnimation(screentransition);
}
```

Property Animations: API Level 12

An animator called ViewPropertyAnimator was introduced in API Level 12. It provides a simple way to animate several properties of a View *in parallel* using a single underlying Animator object. It behaves much like an ObjectAnimator because it modifies the actual values of the view's properties, but is more efficient when animating many properties at once.

To use ViewPropertyAnimator animation, do the following:

1. Modify the AndroidManifest.xml file to change minSdkVersion to the required Level 12 or above.

2. Use the method shown in Listing 4-60, which does the same animation.

    Listing 4-60. Use ViewPropertyAnimation

    ```java
    void applyViewPropertyAnimation(View view) {
      ViewPropertyAnimator animator = view.animate();
      animator.setDuration(2000).setInterpolator(
          new BounceInterpolator()).alpha(1).rotation(360);
    }
    ```

The ViewPropertyAnimator offers simple and concise API usage and is easy to read. From this exercise, you can clearly see the simplicity of using it without an animation resource file.

A quick look at the Android Dashboards (`https://developer.android.com/about/dashboards/index.html`) shows that only 0.1% of distributions for Honeycomb ranged from Levels 11 to 13. Compatibility seems to not be a practical factor if you choose the Level 12 API. While this new API offers better performance and easier to use, it is limited to parallel usage: all the animators have to be played at the same time.

Fragment Animations

While the view animation and property animation frameworks can be applied to any UI widgets, including the entire screen, Android provides the fragment animations API that only applies to whole fragment navigations in APIs 11 and 13. Android must have realized the importance of a screen navigation animation UX by introducing a convenient animation API. It also works with the v7 Support Library!

> **Note**   To work with the v7 Support Library, you cannot use ObjectAnimator from the property animation framework.

The fragment animation API makes screen navigation animation really easy! Let's do the following to embed the fragment animations code in the MvcTemplate project so that it will carry the screen animations to your future projects. You will start by defining four view animation resources.

1. Create a view animation resource for entering the screen, as shown in Listing 4-61.

    Listing 4-61. slide_left_enter.xml

    ```xml
    <?xml version="1.0" encoding="utf-8"?>
    <set xmlns:android="http://schemas.android.com/apk/res/android"
        android:duration="3000"
        android:interpolator="@android:anim/accelerate_decelerate_interpolator"
        android:shareInterpolator="true" >

        <translate
            android:fromXDelta="100%p"
            android:toXDelta="0%p" />
        <alpha
            android:fromAlpha="0"
            android:toAlpha="1" />
    </set>
    ```

2. Create a view animation resource for exiting the screen, as shown in Listing 4-62.

Listing 4-62. *slide_left_exit.xml*

```xml
<?xml version="1.0" encoding="utf-8"?>
<set xmlns:android="http://schemas.android.com/apk/res/android"
    android:duration="3000"
    android:interpolator="@android:anim/accelerate_decelerate_interpolator"
    android:shareInterpolator="true" >

    <translate
        android:fromXDelta="0%p"
        android:toXDelta="-100%p" />

    <alpha
        android:fromAlpha="1"
        android:toAlpha="0" />

</set>
```

3. Create a view animation resource for reentering the screen using the Back button, as shown in Listing 4-63.

Listing 4-63. *slide_right_enter.xml*

```xml
<?xml version="1.0" encoding="utf-8"?>
<set xmlns:android="http://schemas.android.com/apk/res/android"
    android:duration="3000"
    android:interpolator="@android:anim/accelerate_decelerate_interpolator"
    android:shareInterpolator="true" >

    <translate
        android:fromXDelta="-100%p"
        android:toXDelta="0%p" />

    <alpha
        android:fromAlpha="0"
        android:toAlpha="1" />

</set>
```

4. Create a view animation resource for exiting the screen using the Back button, as shown in Listing 4-64.

Listing 4-64. *slide_right_exit.xml*

```xml
<?xml version="1.0" encoding="utf-8"?>
<set xmlns:android="http://schemas.android.com/apk/res/android"
    android:duration="3000"
    android:interpolator="@android:anim/accelerate_decelerate_interpolator"
    android:shareInterpolator="true" >

    <translate
        android:fromXDelta="0%p"
        android:toXDelta="100%p" />

    <alpha
        android:fromAlpha="1"
        android:toAlpha="0" />

</set>
```

5. Use the fragment animation API where you make a screen navigation prior to the `transaction.replace(...)`, as shown in Listing 4-65.

    Listing 4-65. transaction.setCustomAnimations

    ```java
    public class MainActivity extends ActionBarActivity {
        ...
        // to be called when you want to show the toFragments in Activity
        void pushViewController(Fragment toFragment, boolean addToStack) {
            ...
            transaction.setCustomAnimations(
                    R.anim.slide_left_enter,  R.anim.slide_left_exit,
                    R.anim.slide_right_enter, R.anim.slide_right_exit);

            // 2: tug in this toFragment into Activity ViewGroup
            transaction.replace(...);
            ...
        }
        ...
    }
    ```

6. The `transaction.setCustomAnimations(...)` one-liner is all you need. The key implementation is how you create the view animation resource. The animation duration is purposely very slow. You should modify it based on your needs. Build and run the new MvcTemplate project to see how the screen animation works.

Save Data

Saving data is an essential programming task in most programming platforms. In additional to transactional data, most of the mobile apps also save application states and user preferences so that users can resume their tasks later. Both iOS and Android provide several persistent storage options. There are the following choices from the Android SDK:

- SharedPreferences storage
- File storage
- SQLite databases

Before we start diving into each option, let's create an ADT project so that you can write code and visualize how these options work.

ADT PROJECT PREPARATIONS

Use the MvcTemplate project to create another ADT project.

1. Copy the MvcTemplate ADT project and paste it to a new project (⌘c, ⌘v) named **SaveData**.

2. Rename the Android application package. From the newly created SaveData project context menu, select **Android Tools ➤ Rename Application Package**. Enter a new package name: **com.pdachoice.savedata**.

3. Rename the Savedata/src/com.pdachoice.renameme Java package. From the package context menu, select **Refactor ➤ Rename...** (Alt+⌘r) and do the following:

    a. Enter a new name: **com.pdachoice.savedata**.

    b. Select **Update references**.

4. Modify res/values/strings.xml for the string resource to be used in the app (see Listing 4-66).

    Listing 4-66. *app_name in strings.xml*

    ```
    <?xml version="1.0" encoding="utf-8"?>
    <resources>
        <string name="app_name">Save Data</string>
        <string name="action_settings">Delete</string>
    </resources>
    ```

5. You only need one fragment: keep ScreenOneFragment and delete the other two.

    a. Delete the src/ScreenTwoFragment.java and src/ScreenThreeFragment.java classes (multiselect and fn+Delete).

    b. Delete the res/layout/screentwo_fragment.xml and res/layout/screenthree_fragment.xml files (multiselect and fn+Delete).

6. Modify res/layout/screenone_fragment.xml, as shown in Listing 4-67. You only need an EditText for user input.

    Listing 4-67. *screenone_fragment.xml*

    ```
    <?xml version="1.0" encoding="utf-8"?>
    <RelativeLayout xmlns:android="http://schemas.android.com/apk/res/android"
        android:layout_width="match_parent"
        android:layout_height="match_parent" >

        <EditText
            android:id="@+id/editTextInput"
            android:layout_width="wrap_content"
            android:layout_height="wrap_content"
            android:layout_alignParentTop="true"
    ```

```
            android:layout_centerHorizontal="true"
            android:layout_marginTop="@dimen/label_marginTop"
            android:ems="10"
            android:inputType="none" >

            <requestFocus />
        </EditText>

</RelativeLayout>
```

7. Modify src/ScreenOneFragment.java. Remove unnecessary code and enable the options menu, as shown in Listing 4-68.

   Listing 4-68. Enable Options Menu

```java
public class ScreenOneFragment extends Fragment {
  private View contentView;
  private EditText editTextInput;

  @Override
  public View onCreateView(LayoutInflater inflater, ViewGroup container, Bundle
savedInstanceState) {
     contentView = inflater.inflate(R.layout.screenone_fragment, container, false);
     setHasOptionsMenu(true);
     editTextInput = (EditText) contentView.findViewById(R.id.editTextInput);
     return contentView;
  }

  @Override
  public void onCreateOptionsMenu(Menu menu, MenuInflater inflater) {
     super.onCreateOptionsMenu(menu, inflater);
     inflater.inflate(R.menu.main, menu);
  }

  @Override
  public boolean onOptionsItemSelected(MenuItem item) {
     Log.d(">>>onOptionsItemSelected", item.getTitle().toString());
     return super.onOptionsItemSelected(item);
  }
}
```

8. Build and run the app just to make sure it is good. Nothing is new yet and the Android app should display a screen with an input text field and options menu (see Figure 4-11).

Figure 4-11. SaveData app

9. This new project exhibits a common problem that can be observed in the following three steps:

    a. Enter something in the input text field.

    b. Press the Back key to leave the app.

    c. Relaunch the app. The previous input is gone!

For typical app settings or user preferences, users are not happy if they need to enter data every time they launch the app. The app needs to save the data and load it back when the app restarts.

SharedPreferences

IOS ANALOGY

NSUserDefaults

You can use the Android SharedPreferences framework to save key-value pairs of primitive data types: booleans, floats, ints, longs, and strings. It has very simple API usages that are meant for small amounts of data, such as applications settings. The Android SharedPreferences framework takes care of the data caching and syncing for developers. It is easy to use and the performance is already optimized.

The Android SharedPreferences class usage and purposes are fairly similar to iOS NSUserDefaults. It provides a set of APIs to save and retrieve key-value pairs. Under the hood, the data is actually saved in a file.

Continue with the SaveData ADT prep project. You are going to fix the problem we observed earlier. In iOS, you most likely use NSUserDefaults to save user input and load it back when the app relaunches. In Android, you use the SharedPreferences API to save user input when Fragment.onStop(...), and load it back when Fragment.onCreateView(...).

1. Create the convenient methods that save, retrieve, and delete data using SharedPreferences API in ScreenOneFragment.java (see Listing 4-69).

   a. Get the SharedPreferences object from activity.

   b. You can specify MODE_WORLD_WRITEABLE mode to share data with other apps. It is discouraged for security reasons. iOS developers are probably already used to this.

   c. Use the Editor object to cache and batch the changes.

   d. Use commit() to send the batched updates to the SharedPreferences storage.

Listing 4-69. Save, Retrieve, and Delete in SharedPreferences

```
public class ScreenOneFragment extends Fragment {
    ...
    private static final String PREFS_NAME = "MyPrefs";
    private static final int MODE = Context.MODE_PRIVATE; // MODE_WORLD_WRITEABLE
    private static final String KEY_NAME = "name";

    ///////// SharedPreferences usage ///////////////////////
    private void saveSharedPref(String key, String data) {
        // get a handle to SharedPreferences object from Context, i.e., Activity
        SharedPreferences sharedPrefs =
            getActivity().getSharedPreferences(PREFS_NAME, MODE);
        // We need an Editor object to make preference changes.
        SharedPreferences.Editor editor = sharedPrefs.edit();
        // changes are cached in Editor first.
        editor.putString(key, data);
        // Commit all the changes from Editor all at once.
        editor.commit();
    }
```

```
    private String retrieveSharedPref(String key) {
      // get a handle to SharedPreferences object from Context.
      SharedPreferences sharedPrefs =
          getActivity().getSharedPreferences(PREFS_NAME, MODE);
      // use appropriate API to get the value by key.
      String data = sharedPrefs.getString(key, "");
      return data;
    }

    private void deleteSharedPref(String key) {
      SharedPreferences sharedPrefs =
          getActivity().getSharedPreferences(PREFS_NAME, MODE);
      SharedPreferences.Editor editor = sharedPrefs.edit();
      editor.remove(key);
      editor.commit();
    }
    ...
}
```

2. Use the convenient methods (see Listing 4-69) in the appropriate fragment lifecycle callback methods (see Listing 4-70), as follows:

a. Save the data in `Fragment.onStop()` and load the saved data in `Fragment.onCreateView(...)`.

b. Delete the user preferences when the Delete action is selected from the options menu. It is a good idea to give users a choice to delete any persistent data they created.

Listing 4-70. Save and Delete Data from SharedPreferences

```
public class ScreenOneFragment extends Fragment {
  ...
  @Override
  public View onCreateView(LayoutInflater inflater, ViewGroup container, Bundle
savedInstanceState) {
    ...
    String data = null;
    data = retrieveSharedPref(KEY_NAME);
    editTextInput.setText(data);
    ...
  }

  @Override
  public void onStop() {
    super.onStop();
    String data = editTextInput.getText().toString();
    if (data != null && data.length() > 0) {
      saveSharedPref(KEY_NAME, data);
    }
  }
}
```

```java
@Override
public boolean onOptionsItemSelected(MenuItem item) {
    Log.d(">>>onOptionsItemSelected", item.getTitle().toString());
    this.deleteSharedPref(KEY_NAME);
    editTextInput.setText(null);
    return super.onOptionsItemSelected(item);
}
...
}
```

3. Relaunch the SaveData project and repeat the failed test case. You should
    not need to reenter the name when reopening the app.

Object Serialization with File Storage

IOS ANALOGY

Archive and Serialization

You can take advantage of the Java serialization framework to save and retrieve *arbitrary* serializable Java objects in the Android file system. Technically speaking, this is just a common programming technique applicable to almost all of the Java platforms. Java serialization allows Java objects to be converted into bytes and the serialized bytes can be deserialized to restore to Java objects later. The Java serialization framework and Files API apply to the Android platform as well.

Previously, we used SharedPreferences to save and retrieve one simple text. It is the best choice for a small amount of key-value pairs. However, it is very common that more complex data is already encapsulated in an object. In this case, you want to save and retrieve the whole object.

ADT PROJECT PREPARATIONS

We can reuse the SaveData ADT project. Since we are going to save a whole Java object, let's create a new class. As usual, you can use the New Class wizard to create a new class that can hold the input from EditText. Give it a good name, such as Person, as shown in Listing 4-71.

Listing 4-71. Person Class

```java
package com.pdachoice.savedata;

public class Person {
    private String name;

    public Person(String name) {
        super();
        this.name = name;
    }
}
```

```java
public String getName() {
    return name;
}

public void setName(String name) {
    this.name = name;
}
}
```

Save the whole Person object as opposed to key-value pairs in SharedPreferences.

Java Serializable Object

Object serialization is the process of converting an object and its states to a byte stream. A Java object is serializable if its class implements the java.io.Serializable interface. *Deserialization* is the process of converting the serialized form of an object back into a copy of the Java object.

IOS ANALOGY

NSCoding

To make the preceding Person class serializable, do the following:

1. Mark the class to be Serializable by implementing the serializable interface, as shown in Listing 4-72.

   Listing 4-72. Java Serializable

   ```java
   import java.io.Serializable;

   public class Person implements Serializable {
       ...
   }
   ```

It is a very simple pattern, just mark the class with a serializable interface that doesn't define any method.

Note   java.io.Serializable is a type of interface that doesn't define any contract. This is a so-called *marker interface* design pattern.

File API

You can use the Java File API to read and write data from files for various data sources, including Java Serializable objects.

1. Create a convenient method that saves the whole object in file storage in ScreenOneFragment.java (see Listing 4-73):

    a. Open a FileOutputStream to the file storage. You can specify MODE_WORLD_WRITEABLE mode to share data with other apps. It is discouraged for security reasons. iOS developers are probably already used to this.

    b. To write the Serializable object to the file storage, wrap the object in ObjectOutputStream and chain it up with the FileOutputStream object.

    c. Always close streams in or out.

Listing 4-73. Java File API

```java
public class ScreenOneFragment extends Fragment {
  ...
  private static final String FILE_NAME = "person.ser";
  private void saveObjectToFile(Serializable obj) {

    // use File API to write to file
    ObjectOutputStream out = null;
    try {
      // use File API to write to file
      FileOutputStream fileOut = getActivity().openFileOutput(FILE_NAME, MODE);
      out = new ObjectOutputStream(fileOut);

      out.writeObject(obj);
      out.close();
      fileOut.close();
    } catch (IOException i) {
      i.printStackTrace();
    } finally {
      if (out != null) {
        try {
          out.close();
        } catch (IOException i) {
          i.printStackTrace();
        }
      }
    }
  }
  ...
}
```

2. To read the file content into a Java object, create a convenient method in
    ScreenOneFragment.java, as shown in Listing 4-74.

Listing 4-74. Convert File Content to Java Object

```
public class ScreenOneFragment extends Fragment {
  ...
  private Object retrieveFromFile() {
    Object obj = null;
    try {
      // use File API to read bytes from File
      FileInputStream fileIn = getActivity().openFileInput(FILE_NAME);
      ObjectInputStream in = new ObjectInputStream(fileIn);
      obj = in.readObject();
      in.close();
      fileIn.close();
    } catch (IOException i) {
      i.printStackTrace();
    } catch (ClassNotFoundException e) {
      e.printStackTrace();
    }

    return obj;
  }
  ...
}
```

3. To delete the file content, create a convenient method in ScreenOneFragment.
    java, as shown in Listing 4-75.

Listing 4-75. Delete File

```
public class ScreenOneFragment extends Fragment {
  ...
  private void deleteObjectFromFile() {
    // simply delete the file, or write empty content
    File dir = getActivity().getFilesDir();
    File f = new File(dir, FILE_NAME);
    boolean b = f.delete();
    Log.d("File.delete: ", b ? "deleted" : "failed");
  }
  ...
}
```

4. Instead of using the SharedPreferences API, use the convenient methods
    (see Listing 4-75) that save and retrieve serializable objects, as shown in
    Listing 4-76.

Listing 4-76. Use the Convenient Java Methods

```java
public class ScreenOneFragment extends Fragment {
  ...
  @Override
  public View onCreateView(LayoutInflater inflater, ViewGroup container, Bundle
savedInstanceState) {
    ...
    String data = null;
    // data = retrieveSharedPref(KEY_NAME);
    Person obj = (Person) retrieveFromFile();
    if (obj != null) {
      data = obj.getName();
    }
    ...
  }

  @Override
  public void onStop() {
    ...
    // saveSharedPref(KEY_NAME, data);
    saveObjectToFile(new Person(data));
    ...
  }

  @Override
  public boolean onOptionsItemSelected(MenuItem item) {
    ...
    // this.deleteSharedPref(KEY_NAME);
    this.deleteObjectFromFile();
    ...
  }
  ...
}
```

5. Retest the SaveData project and repeat the failed test case. It should work
    the same as using the SharedPreferences API; there is no need to reenter the
    EditText.

JSON and Saving a JSON Document

IOS ANALOGY

NSJSONSerialization

For the subtopic, I am actually not introducing a new persistent storage API. You may choose SharedPreferences, file persistent storage, or perhaps advanced storage options for your own purpose. The only thing new in this subtopic is JSONObject and JSON message serialization. This probably deserves a section to itself since it is more commonly used for interfacing with remote services (see the "Consume RESTFul Web Services" section). I just want to explicitly show that saving a JSON message is a practical usage in many use cases because most of the remote messages are in JSON format nowadays. Saving remote messages locally enables offline usages. Even when real-time data is mandatory, I often choose to render the most recently saved data first while fetching new data from the server to avoid a blank screen.

Just like iOS programming, you can easily convert JSON message strings to JSONObject back and forth on Android platforms. The JSONObject is already a class that contains structured data, which is a perfectly legitimate choice as opposed to creating custom POJO classes. Object serialization is simple, too. JSONObject objects are naturally serialized into JSON strings. Strings are a perfect data type for both File or SharedPreferences persistent storages. Unless you are looking for remote binary messages, which seems relatively rare, JSON is a very popular choice.

Java JSONObject usage is very similar to iOS NSDictionary. You basically call put(...) and get(...) to access the data in JSONObject by key.

IOS ANALOGY

NSDictionary/NSArray

To show what I am talking about and to learn by example, let's do the following exercise.

1. To save the input text in EditText, put the input text in a JSONObject, and save the whole JSONObject, as shown in Listing 4-77.

    a. To put data into an JSONObject, simply use put(key, value). Note that you cannot put a null key or value. You can also use putOpt(key, data) to suppress an error if the key or value is null.

    b. To serialize the JSONObject object, simply call toString(), which converts the Java object into a JSON string representation.

    c. To save the JSON string in SharedPreferences storage, use the saveSharedPref method you created earlier.

Note   The Java toString() method is similar to the iOS NSObject description method.

Listing 4-77. Serialize JSONObject

```
public class ScreenOneFragment extends Fragment {
  ...
  @Override
  public void onStop() {
    super.onStop();
    ...
    // saveSharedPref(KEY_NAME, data);
    // saveObjectToFile(new Person(data));

    // create JSONObject and use the generic setter, put(...)
    try {
      JSONObject jo = new JSONObject();
      jo.put(KEY_NAME, data);
      String jsonStr = jo.toString();
      saveSharedPref(KEY_NAME, jsonStr);
    } catch (JSONException e) {
      // TODO Auto-generated catch block
    }
    ...
  }
  ...
}
```

2. To restore the user input, retrieve the JSON string from SharedPreferences storage and convert the JSON string to a JSONObject (see Listing 4-78).

  a. Retrieve the saved JSON string from SharedPreferences storage.

  b. To deserialize the JSON string, use a constructor to create the JSONObject.

  c. Get the user input from the JSONObject.

Listing 4-78. Deserialize JSONObject

```
public class ScreenOneFragment extends Fragment {
  ...
  @Override
  public View onCreateView(LayoutInflater inflater, ViewGroup container, Bundle
savedInstanceState) {
    ...
    String data = null;
    // data = retrieveSharedPref(KEY_NAME);
    // Person obj = (Person) retrieveFromFile();
    // if (obj != null) {
    //   data = obj.getName();
    // }
```

```
            // create the JSONObject from the saved JSON string
            data = retrieveSharedPref(KEY_NAME);
            try {
                JSONObject jo = new JSONObject(data);
                // use JSONObject getters: getString, getInt, etc.
                String aName = jo.getString(KEY_NAME);
                this.editTextInput.setText(aName);
            } catch (JSONException e) {
                // TODO Auto-generated catch block
                e.printStackTrace();
            }
            ...
        }
        ...
    }
```

3. To delete the user input, call the deleteSharedPref(...) method, as shown
    in Listing 4-79, because the data is saved in SharedPreferences storage.

    Listing 4-79. Delete from SharedPreferences

```
public class ScreenOneFragment extends Fragment {
    ...
    @Override
    public boolean onOptionsItemSelected(MenuItem item) {
        ...
        this.deleteSharedPref(KEY_NAME);
        // this.deleteObjectFromFile();
        ...
    }
    ...
}
```

It is also perfectly legitimate to use file storage to save the whole JSONObject. However, JSONObject
is not java.io.Serializable. You can choose to create a custom class that extends JSONObject, and
then mark it as javao.io.Serializable to get around it. In my opinion, if the JSONObject is not too
big, storing the JSON string in SharedPreferences storage is just fine.

4. Retest the SaveData project. It should work the same as the previous two
    solutions.

Let's compare creating custom classes to encapsulate internal states: NSDictionary or JSONObject
are more flexible when you don't know the data structure of the data at compile time. This is often
the case when data is originally from the server. There are some legitimate arguments regarding
the parsing overhead. In my opinion, the performance penalties can be neglected when the
bottleneck is on the much heavier I/O or remote operations. For persistent storage programming
tasks, this is a very good choice in many practical use cases, particularly when the JSON
document is not large.

SQLite Database

If your mobile apps are heavily data-driven and require transactional data management with queries and search capabilities on large amounts of data, this is your best choice. Android provides a built-in SQLite database for you to read and write structured data, as well as query and search using the database API.

> **Note**   Both File and SharedPreferences do not have an API to query content directly from the file storage. I think that is a key differentiator.

If you are converting an iOS app using the Core Data Framework, you definitely want to look into the Android SQLite database.

SQLite Database API

Let's continue with the SaveData ADT project by doing the following:

1. Just like most of the database management systems, you need to create a database and tables to hold records in terms of data. On the Android platform, you create a subclass of SQLiteOpenHelper to create the database and describe the tables. The following class, SimpleSQLiteOpenHelper, shows a very simple usage that creates a database if one does not exist, and creates a table, if it does not exist (see Listing 4-80).

    a. Extend SQLiteOpenHelper. The super constructor takes care of database creation if it does not exist.

    b. The onCreate(...) lifecycle method is called to create the tables if it does not exist yet.

    c. The onUpgrade(...) lifecycle method is called when the version changes. You provide the implementation when the database or table scheme changes.

Listing 4-80. SQLiteDatabase Create and Update Table

```
public class SimpleSQLiteOpenHelper extends SQLiteOpenHelper {

    private static final String DB_NAME = "simple.db";
    private static final int DB_VERSION = 1;
```

```java
    static final String TABLE_NAME = "person";
    static final String COLUMN_PKEY = "uid";
    static final String COLUMN_NAME = "name";

    public SimpleSQLiteOpenHelper(Context context) {
        super(context, DB_NAME, null, DB_VERSION); // create SQLite database
    }

    @Override
    public void onCreate(SQLiteDatabase db) { // create table(s)
        String sql = String.format(
            "create table %s (%s INTEGER PRIMARY KEY, %s TEXT);", TABLE_NAME,
                COLUMN_PKEY, COLUMN_NAME);
        db.execSQL(sql);
    }

    @Override
    public void onUpgrade(SQLiteDatabase db,int oldVersion,int newVersion){
        // For table schema changes.

        // drop old table if you don't need to preserve old data
        String sql = "DROP TABLE IF EXISTS " + TABLE_NAME;
        db.execSQL(sql);
        onCreate(db);

        // Or, those typical data migration code ...
    }
}
```

2. To insert a new row in the SQLite table, create a convenient method named
    createRecord(...) in the SimpleSQLiteOpenHelper class, as shown in
    Listing 4-81. Always get an instance of SQLiteDatabase.

Listing 4-81. Insert Record

```java
public class SimpleSQLiteOpenHelper extends SQLiteOpenHelper {
  ...
  public void createRecord(String data) {
    SQLiteDatabase db = this.getWritableDatabase();

    // Create a new map of values, where column names are the keys
    ContentValues values = new ContentValues();
    values.put(SimpleSQLiteOpenHelper.COLUMN_NAME, data);

    // Insert the new row, returning the primary key value of the new row
    long rowId = db.insert(SimpleSQLiteOpenHelper.TABLE_NAME, "N/A", values);
    Log.d("rowId: ", "" + rowId);
  }
  ...
}
```

3. To get the Name column of the last row, create a convenient method named retrieveMostRecentNameColumn(...) in the SimpleSQLiteOpenHelper class, as shown in Listing 4-82.

   a. Just like in the SQL language, whereClause is in the format of "column=value". Alternatively, you can construct whereClause in the format of "column=?" and supply whereArgs that contain the value to replace the "?" in whereClause.

   b. If you don't need to specify any of these parameters, simply supply null.

Listing 4-82. retrieveMostRecentNameColumn

```java
public class SimpleSQLiteOpenHelper extends SQLiteOpenHelper {
  ...
  public String retrieveMostRecentNameColumn() {
    SQLiteDatabase db = this.getWritableDatabase();

    String[] columns = null; // all columns, same as {"*"}
    String whereClause = null; // for all records
    String[] whereArgs = null; // to replace any ? in whereClause
    String groupBy = null, having = null, orderBy = null;

    Cursor cursor = db.query(TABLE_NAME, columns, whereClause, whereArgs,
        groupBy, having, orderBy);

    boolean notEmpty = cursor.moveToLast();
    String result = null;
    if(notEmpty == true) {
      int columnIndex =
        cursor.getColumnIndex(SimpleSQLiteOpenHelper.COLUMN_NAME);
      result = cursor.getString(columnIndex);
    }

    return result;
  }
  ...
}
```

4. To delete a row, create a convenient method named deleteRecord(...) in the SimpleSQLiteOpenHelper class, as shown in Listing 4-83.

Listing 4-83. deleteRecord from Table

```java
public class SimpleSQLiteOpenHelper extends SQLiteOpenHelper {
  ...
  public void deleteRecord(String name) {

    SQLiteDatabase db = this.getWritableDatabase();
    db.delete(SimpleSQLiteOpenHelper.TABLE_NAME,
              SimpleSQLiteOpenHelper.COLUMN_NAME + "=?",
              new String[] { name });
  }
  ...
}
```

5. To use the SQLite database via the convenient methods, do as shown in
    Listing 4-84 in ScreenOneFragment.java.

    Listing 4-84. Invoke Retrieve and Create from Table

```java
public class ScreenOneFragment extends Fragment {
    ...
    @Override
    public View onCreateView(LayoutInflater inflater, ViewGroup container, Bundle
savedInstanceState) {
        ...
        SimpleSQLiteOpenHelper sqlHelper =
            new SimpleSQLiteOpenHelper(getActivity());
        data = sqlHelper.retrieveMostRecentNameColumn();
        ...
    }

    @Override
    public void onStop() {
        ...
        SimpleSQLiteOpenHelper sqlHelper =
            new SimpleSQLiteOpenHelper(getActivity());
        sqlHelper.createRecord(data);
        ...
    }

    @Override
    public boolean onOptionsItemSelected(MenuItem item) {
        ...
        SimpleSQLiteOpenHelper sqlHelper =
            new SimpleSQLiteOpenHelper(getActivity());
        sqlHelper.deleteRecord(KEY_NAME);
        ...
    }
    ...
}
```

6. Retest the SaveData project. It should work the same as previous solutions.

By no means does the simple SQLite usage shown in Listing 4-84 show enough Android SQLite
Framework API details. There are also important SQL database topics not covered here. Most of the
database operations are encapsulated in the SQLiteDatabase class. See the Android Developers site
at http://developer.android.com/reference/android/database/sqlite/SQLiteDatabase.html for
more information.

Networking and Using Remote Service

A typical client-server solution hosts information on the server side, while client apps collect data from the user to submit to the server, or fetch data and present to users in meaningful ways. You probably hear the buzzwords "mobile commerce" or "m-commerce" a lot nowadays. To describe it in simple terms, mobile apps fetch product items from a server and then submit the purchase orders to the server via the Internet. From a mobile apps programming perspective, this is really not new at all. It is still a client-server programming topic using HTTP GET/POST, which is what most of the e-commerce web sites do.

We will talk about JSON messages and RESTFul services for mobile apps because of its popularity over traditional SOAP-based web services.

Perform Network Operations in Background

For apps with a user interface, you want to perform I/O tasks or network-related code in the background, and do UI updates in the UI main thread. Otherwise, the app appears to lag to the user because the UI thread is blocked, waiting for the task to finish. This principle applies to iOS and probably any UI platforms. The Android SDK provides the convenient android.os.AsyncTask class to perform tasks in a background thread and hook back to the UI main thread when the background task is completed. Generally, when interfacing with a remote server, you want to fetch data from it in the background. When the remote data is received, your UI code presents the data on the screen.

Let's port the iOS app shown in Figure 4-12 to Android to demonstrate this generic paradigm. When the GET or POST button is selected, the app sends HTTP GET or POST to the server in a background thread. When the HTTP response is received, the app renders the data on the user interface.

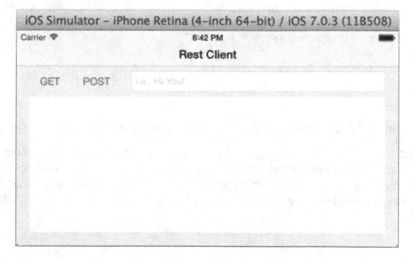

Figure 4-12. iOS RestClient app

ADT PROJECT PREPARATIONS

Use the MvcTemplate project to create this ADT project.

1. Copy the MvcTemplate ADT project and paste it to a new project (⌘c, ⌘v) named **RestClient**.

2. Rename the Android application package. From the newly created RestClient project context menu, select the **Android Tools ➤ Rename Application Package**. Enter a new package name: **com.pdachoice.restclient**.

3. Rename the RestClient/src/com.pdachoice.renameme Java package. From the package context menu, select **Refactor ➤ Rename...** (Alt+(⌘r) and do the following:

   a. Enter a new name: **com.pdachoice.restclient**.

   b. Select **Update references**.

4. You only need one fragment: keep ScreenOneFragment and delete the other two.

   a. Delete the src/ScreenTwoFragment.java and src/ScreenThreeFragment.java classes (multiselect and fn+Delete).

   b. Delete the res/layout/screentwo_fragment.xml and res/layout/screenthree_fragment.xml files (multiselect and fn+Delete).

5. Modify res/layout/screenone_fragment.xml. You need some UI widgets to take user input and to show the data from server (see Listing 4-85).

Listing 4-85. RestClient screenone_fragment.xml

```xml
<RelativeLayout xmlns:android="http://schemas.android.com/apk/res/android"
    xmlns:tools="http://schemas.android.com/tools"
    android:layout_width="match_parent"
    android:layout_height="match_parent"
    android:paddingBottom="@dimen/activity_vertical_margin"
    android:paddingLeft="@dimen/activity_horizontal_margin"
    android:paddingRight="@dimen/activity_horizontal_margin"
    android:paddingTop="@dimen/activity_vertical_margin" >

    <Button
        android:id="@+id/buttonGet"
        android:layout_width="wrap_content"
        android:layout_height="wrap_content"
        android:layout_alignParentLeft="true"
        android:layout_alignParentTop="true"
        android:text="@string/label_get" />
```

```xml
<EditText
    android:id="@+id/editTextEcho"
    android:layout_width="wrap_content"
    android:layout_height="wrap_content"
    android:layout_alignParentRight="true"
    android:layout_alignParentTop="true"
    android:hint="@string/label_hint" >
</EditText>

<WebView
    android:id="@+id/webViewResponse"
    android:layout_width="match_parent"
    android:layout_height="match_parent"
    android:layout_below="@id/buttonGet" />

<Button
    android:id="@+id/buttonPost"
    android:layout_width="wrap_content"
    android:layout_height="wrap_content"
    android:layout_above="@id/webViewResponse"
    android:layout_marginLeft="20dp"
    android:layout_toRightOf="@id/buttonGet"
    android:text="@string/label_post" />

</RelativeLayout>
```

6. Modify res/values/strings.xml, as shown in Listing 4-86.

    Listing 4-86. RestClient String Resources

```xml
<?xml version="1.0" encoding="utf-8"?>
<resources>

    <string name="app_name">Rest Client</string>
    <string name="label_get">GET</string>
    <string name="label_post">POST</string>
    <string name="label_hint">i.e., Hi, you.</string>

</resources>
```

7. Modify res/menu/main.xml. You don't need any action items (see Listing 4-87).

Listing 4-87. Options Menu

```
<menu xmlns:android="http://schemas.android.com/apk/res/android"
    xmlns:app="http://schemas.android.com/apk/res-auto" >

</menu>
```

8. Modify src/ScreenOneFragment.java. Get the UI code in place first, as shown in Listing 4-88.

Listing 4-88. RestClient screen one Fragment

```java
public class ScreenOneFragment extends Fragment implements OnClickListener {

    private View contentView;
    private Button buttonGet;
    private Button buttonPost;
    private EditText editText;
    private WebView webView;

    @Override
    public View onCreateView(LayoutInflater inflater, ViewGroup container, Bundle
savedInstanceState) {
        contentView = inflater.inflate(R.layout.screenone_fragment, container, false);
        buttonGet = (Button) contentView.findViewById(R.id.buttonGet);
        buttonGet.setOnClickListener(this);
        buttonPost = (Button) contentView.findViewById(R.id.buttonPost);
        buttonPost.setOnClickListener(this);
        editText = (EditText) contentView.findViewById(R.id.editTextEcho);
        webView = (WebView) contentView.findViewById(R.id.webViewResponse);
        return contentView;
    }

    public void onClick(View v) {
        // TODO
    }
}
```

9. Build and run the app to make sure the prep is good to go. You should see your UI code, as shown Figure 4-13.

Figure 4-13. ADT RestClient prep work

AsyncTask

IOS ANALOGY

```
dispatch_async(dispatch_get_global_queue(DISPATCH_QUEUE_PRIORITY_DEFAULT, 0), ^{
    // Add code here to do background processing
    dispatch_async( dispatch_get_main_queue(), ^{
        // Update the UI based on the results of the background processing
    });
});
```

You want to perform heavy-lifting tasks like network operations or disk I/O in the background worker threads, and then notify the UI main thread when the tasks are completed. This programming task has been around for a long time in many programming platforms. Do you remember those days when you used wait-and-notify plus semaphore? The interprocess communication (IPC) code to update the UI widgets from a worker thread was not a simple task in the old days. Just like iOS, the Android SDK makes this common task easy by providing several thread wrappers and convenient methods to simplify this programming task. AsyncTask is the one I use most often in Android. It manages the interprocess communication between the UI main thread and the worker thread.

AsyncTask is really a very handy framework class. You will use it very frequently, and not only for networking topics. If you know Java already, it is also very easy to understand and easy to use. However, if you are picking up Java along your Android journey, I think you need two Java lessons—*Anonymous* and *generic type*—because the Java syntax could be too much to start with.

AsyncTask: Anonymous Class

When previously handling widget events, you performed the following three steps to allow the designated delegate object, a.k.a. event handler, to respond to the widgets events:

1. Declare a designated delegate to implement the event-handler interface.

2. Provide an event-handler interface implementation in the delegate class.

3. Register the delegate object to handle the events from the event source, such as a button.

This concept is simple and has been around for a long time, but you need to have a designated "class" so that you can declare and implement the interface. Furthermore, the implementation logics could be in a different class file than where you register the event listener, which makes the code less readable.

The Java Anonymous class offers syntactical sugar that allows you to create an unnamed class on the fly—called the Anonymous class. Using the Anonymous class simplifies those three steps. Let's do a quick exercise.

In Listing 4-88, you implemented the GET and POST buttons handling code using the three-step event-handling protocol. Let's change the coding style by using the Anonymous class, as shown in Listing 4-89.

Listing 4-89. Using Anonymous Class

```java
public class ScreenOneFragment extends Fragment /*implements OnClickListener*/ {
  ...
  @Override
  public View onCreateView(LayoutInflater inflater, ViewGroup container, Bundle savedInstanceState)
{
    ...
//  buttonGet.setOnClickListener(this);
    buttonGet.setOnClickListener(new OnClickListener() {
      @Override
      public void onClick(View v) {
        performGet();
      }
    });
    ...
//  buttonPost.setOnClickListener(this);
    buttonPost.setOnClickListener(new OnClickListener() {
      @Override
      public void onClick(View v) {
        // TODO
      }
    });
    ...
  }

  private void performGet() {
    // TODO
  }
  ...
```

As you can see from Listing 4-89, you don't need to find a class to implement the listener interface anymore. It actually still implements the three-step event-handling pattern with a delegate object created inline using the new `OnClickListener() { ... }`. This also applies to the Java `Abstract` class. The key is to instantiate an instance of an Anonymous class inline without a class file by directly creating an instance of the `Interface` or `Abstract` class. Listing 4-90 shows another example of how to create an Anonymous class with the `Abstract` class.

Listing 4-90. Anonymous Class with Abstract Class

```
AnInterfaceOrAbstractClass myVar = new AnInterfaceOrAbstractClass() {
  @Override
  public void interfaceMethod (...) {
    // ...
  }
};
myVar.doSomething(); // or pass as a parm to anther method
```

Although the Anonymous class doesn't have an explicit class name in your code, the Java compiler does create a Java inner class under the hood. It offers the following syntactic conveniences (Objective-C block code offers similar benefits as well):

- The Java Anonymous class has access to parent properties, methods, or final local variables.

- The implementation is inline in calling a function. In general, it is easier to read the programming flow.

`AsyncTask` is an abstract class in which you can create a Java class that is subclassed from `AsyncTask` in a separated class file. Or, applying the Anonymous class coding technique, you can create an anonymous class using `AsyncTask`.

> **Tip**   The Eclipse autocompletion code-assistant feature, Ctrl+<space>, works very well with anonymous expressions. It is very fun, too. To write anonymous Java code (Listing 4-89), type the following:
>
> buttonGet.setOn<Ctrl+space>Cl<Enter>new OnCl<Ctrl+space><Enter>
>
> Type as many as you know. Press Ctrl+<space> whenever you need the code assistant. Use the <Enter> key to make a selection.

AsyncTask: Generic Type

The Java generic type is a generic class or interface that is parameterized over types, such as `AsyncTask`. To use the generic type to declare a Java class, you specify the *type parameters*. It serves the same purpose as the C++ or C# template class, in case you know C++ or C#. The language syntax might look strange to Objective-C, but all you need to do is choose the type of parameter that makes sense for your purposes. For more information, see `http://docs.oracle.com/javase/tutorial/java/generics/types.html`.

For example, AsyncTask is a generic type that needs to be parameterized. AsyncTask<Params, Progress, Result> has three parameterized types:

- **Params** are the type of parameters sent to the task upon execution. For example, task.execute(button) will pass the button to doInBackground(Params... parms) as a method argument.

- **Progress** is the type of progress unit published during the background computation. For example, publishProgress(downloadedSize, expectedSize) in doInBackground(...) will pass two floats to onProgressUpdate(Progress... progress) as method arguments. To pass a download progress float value, use Float as the parameterized type.

- **Result** is the type of result from the background computation. For example, after getting HTTP GET data, the return string of doInBackground(...) will be passed to onPostExecute(Result result). To pass HTTP GET or POST data as string text, use String as the parameterized type.

Before we get to the network operation code, let's get the IPC code in place using the AsyncTask class. You need to apply the Java Anonymous class and generic type (see Listing 4-92). Continue with the RestClient app using the AsyncTask class.

1. Create a method, performGet(), to do the HTTP GET task (see Listing 4-91):

   a. Create a Java Anonymous class that extends the AsyncTask<View, Float, String> class.

   b. The code in doInBackground(...) is executed in a background worker thread.

   c. The other three methods are executed in the UI main thread.

   d. The return value from the doInBackground(...) is passed to onPostExecute(...) when the work thread is completed.

Listing 4-91. Implement AsyncTask

```
public class ScreenOneFragment extends Fragment {
  ...
  private void performGet() {
    AsyncTask<View, Float, String> task = new AsyncTask< View, Float, String>(){
      @Override
      protected void onPreExecute() {
        // do something in the UI thread before starting doInBackground,
        // For example, show wait cursor, dismiss keyboard, etc
        Log.d("AsyncTask", ">>>onPreExecute");
      }

      @Override
      protected String doInBackground(View... parms) {
        Log.d("AsyncTask", ">>>doInBackground");
        // TODO: fetch data from remote server in the worker thread
```

```
            float expectedSize = 100.0f;
            float downloadedSize = 50.0f;
            publishProgress(downloadedSize, expectedSize);
            return "TODO: aResult";
        }

        @Override
        protected void onProgressUpdate(Float... progress) {
            Log.d("AsyncTask", ">>>onProgressUpdate");
            // do something in the UI thread during doInBackground,
            // For example, update progress bar
            float downloadedSize = progress[0];
            float expectedSize = progress[1];
        }

        @Override
        protected void onPostExecute(String result) {
            Log.d("AsyncTask", ">>>onPostExecute: " + result);
            // do something with the result in UI thread after doInBackground,
            // For example, show result and dismiss wait cursor.
        }
    };
    task.execute(buttonGet);
    }
}
```

2. Build and run the project. The AsnycTask IPC coding block is ready for you.
   You won't see any visual difference yet since either the work thread or the UI
   thread code doesn't do anything except produce some LogCat output. You
   will fill in the blanks.

Getting Data from the Server

So far, we only set up the coding block that handles the button clicks in the background worker
thread. We still need to get data from the server. We are going to use HTTP GET to retrieve data from
a web server, just like a browser does. Browsers use HTTP GET to retrieve an HTML file from an
HTTP server. From mobile apps, you can use HTTP GET to fetch an HTML doc, too—or it can be any
data, such as raw bytes, an XML document, a JSON document, and so forth. The key is to design
the data that both your mobile clients and the server can understand.

HttpURLConnection: HTTP GET

IOS ANALOGY

NSURLConnection

Continue evolving the RestClient project by invoking HTTP GET.

1. To allow Internet access, declare `uses-permission` for Internet usage in
    `AndroidManifest.xml` (see Listing 4-92).

    Listing 4-92. Declare INTERNET uses-permission

    ```xml
    <?xml version="1.0" encoding="utf-8"?>
    <manifest ... >
        ...
        <uses-permission android:name="android.permission.INTERNET"/>
        ...
    ```

2. Create a method that uses the `HttpURLConnection` class to invoke HTTP GET
    to get data from the server (see Listing 4-93):

    a. This is a synchronized operation similar to `NSURLConnection`
        `sendSynchronousRequest`.

    b. You can also use the `AndroidHttpClient` class, which is an
        implementation of Apache `HttpClient` since API Level 8+. It might look
        more familiar to JavaEE developers.

    c. The custom `readStream(InputStream stream)` method converts a bytes
        stream to a Java string. The trick is the regular expression `"\\A"`, which
        matches the beginning of the input stream. Don't you love one-liner code?

    Listing 4-93. HTTP GET

    ```java
    public class ScreenOneFragment extends Fragment {
        ...
        // GET data from url
        private String httpGet(String myurl) {
            InputStream in = null;
            HttpURLConnection conn = null;

            String httpBody = null;
            try {
                URL url = new URL(myurl);

                // create an HttpURLConnection by openConnection
                conn = (HttpURLConnection) url.openConnection();
                conn.setRequestMethod("GET");

                int rc = conn.getResponseCode(); // HTTP status code
                String rm = conn.getResponseMessage(); // HTTP response message.
                Log.d("d", String.format("HTTP GET: %d %s", rc, rm));

                // read message body from connection InputStream
                in = conn.getInputStream(); // get inputStream to read data.
                httpBody = readStream(in);
                in.close();
    ```

```java
    } catch (IOException e) {
      e.printStackTrace();
    } finally {
      conn.disconnect();
    }

    return httpBody;
  }

  // a simple util method that converts InputStream to a String.
  String readStream(InputStream stream) {
    java.util.Scanner s = new java.util.Scanner(stream).useDelimiter("\\A");
    return s.hasNext() ? s.next() : "";
  }
  ...
}
```

3. In performGet(), call the httpGet(...) method to get data from the server
    and display the HTTP message body in the WebView widget (see Listing 4-94):

    a. Repeat: doInBackground(...) is executed in a background thread.

    b. After doInBackground(...) completes, under the hook, AsyncTask
        invokes onPostExecute(String result) in the UI main thread with the
        return data from doInBackground(...).

    c. processResultData(...) simply displays the string result on a WebView
        UI widget.

Note   WebView widget is just like iOS UIWebView. We will talk about it in greater detail in Chapter 7.

---

    d. Path parameters or query string are part of the URL that cannot contain
        special characters, such as a space. Use URLEncoder to encode them.

Listing 4-94. httpGet in Background

```java
public class ScreenOneFragment extends Fragment implements OnClickListener {
  ...
  private static String SERVER_URL = "http://pdachoice.com/ras/service/echo";
  private void performGet() {
    AsyncTask<View, Float, String> task = new AsyncTask<View, Float, String>() {
      @Override
      protected void onPreExecute() {
        // do something in the UI thread before starting doInBackground,
        // For example, show wait cursor or dismiss keyboard.
        dismissKeyboard();
      }
```

```java
    @Override
    protected String doInBackground(View... parms) {
      Log.d("AsyncTask", ">>>doInBackground");
      String resp = null;
      try {
        String pathParm = editText.getText().toString();
        pathParm = URLEncoder.encode(pathParm, "UTF-8");
        resp = httpGet(SERVER_URL + "/" + pathParm);
      } catch (UnsupportedEncodingException e) {
        e.printStackTrace();
      }
      Log.d("", resp);
      return resp;
    }

    @Override
    protected void onProgressUpdate(Float... progress) {
      Log.d("AsyncTask", ">>>onProgressUpdate");
      // do something in the UI thread during doInBackground,
      // For example, update progress bar
    }

    @Override
    protected void onPostExecute(String result) {
      processResultData(result);
    }
  };
  task.execute(buttonGet);
}
private void dismissKeyboard() {
  Log.d("AsyncTask", ">>>onPreExecute");
  InputMethodManager imm = (InputMethodManager) getActivity()
      .getSystemService(Context.INPUT_METHOD_SERVICE);
  imm.hideSoftInputFromWindow(getView().getWindowToken(), 0);
}

private void processResultData(String result) {
  Log.d("AsyncTask", ">>>onPostExecute: " + result);
  try {
    result = URLDecoder.decode(result, "UTF-8");
  } catch (UnsupportedEncodingException e) {
    e.printStackTrace();
  }
  webView.loadData(result, "text/html", null);
}
...
}
```

> **Note** SERVER_URL = "http://pdachoice.com/ras/service/echo" is a simple web service that echoes back the path parameter. Desktop browsers are fully capable of rendering plain text as well as HTML documents. You can use a desktop browser to verify the data from the server.

4. Build and run the RestClient project and enter **"Hi, you!"** to see the live app in action, as shown in Figure 4-14.

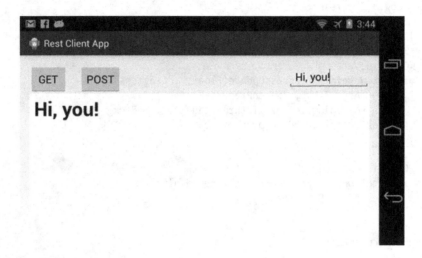

Figure 4-14. doGet in RestClient app

Send Data to Server

To submit user input to the server from an HTML web page, it is very common to use HTML Form to submit *form data* to HTTP server. The form data is transmitted using the HTTP POST method. This is very common in iOS and Android apps as well.

Technically speaking, you can also send a *query string* to an HTTP server using the HTTP GET method, just like many web pages do. In this case, you can simply build the URL with query strings and use the previous httpGet(...) method to send data over to your server. It is a design decision to make by understanding GET vs. POST usages and conventions.

The key is to design the form data or query string that your mobile clients and server both understand.

HttpURLConnection: HTTP POST

The following demonstrates Android HTTP POST usage.

1. Similar to HTTP GET, use the HttpURLConnection class to send data to the server. Add the following method (see Listing 4-95):

   a. To send data to the server, open an OutputStream from HttpURLConnection to write data to it.

   b. Just like most of the programming platforms, close IntputStream and OutputStream, and then disconnect the connection after using them.

Listing 4-95. HTTP POST

```java
public class ScreenOneFragment extends Fragment implements OnClickListener {
  ...
  // Send POST data to server
  String httpPost(String myurl, String formData) {
    HttpURLConnection conn = null;
    String httpBody = null;
    try {
      URL url = new URL(myurl);
      conn = (HttpURLConnection) url.openConnection();
      conn.setRequestMethod("POST");

      OutputStream out = new BufferedOutputStream(conn.getOutputStream());
      out.write(formData.getBytes());
      out.close();

      // To handle HTTP response. Same as HTTP GET
      int rc = conn.getResponseCode(); // HTTP status code
      String rm = conn.getResponseMessage(); // HTTP response message
      Log.d("d", String.format("HTTP GET: %d %s", rc, rm));

      // read message body from connection InputStream
      InputStream in = new BufferedInputStream(conn.getInputStream());
      httpBody = readStream(in);
      in.close();
    } catch (IOException e) {
      e.printStackTrace();
    } finally {
      conn.disconnect();
    }
    return httpBody;
  }
  ...
}
```

> **Note**   Our web server, SERVER_URL = "http://pdachoice.com/ras/service/echo", also accepts
> HTTP POST data and echoes the data back.

2. Modify the performPost(...) to trigger HTTP POST (see Listing 4-96).

    a. Same as performGet(...), you use AsyncTask to perform remote access
        API in the background and process the result in a UI thread.

    b. HTTP form data is in the format of key1=value1&..., the same as an
        HTTP query.

    c. HTTP form data, path parameters, and query strings cannot contain
        special characters that need to be URL encoded. Simply use
        URLEncoder.encode(...).

    d. Call the performPost(...) on a POST button click.

Listing 4-96. Invoke httpPost in Background

```
public class ScreenOneFragment extends Fragment {

  @Override
  public View onCreateView(LayoutInflater inflater, ViewGroup container, Bundle
savedInstanceState) {
    ...
    buttonPost.setOnClickListener(new OnClickListener() {
      @Override
      public void onClick(View v) {
        performPost();
      }
    });
    ...
  }


  ...
  private void performPost() {
    AsyncTask<View,Float,String> task = new AsyncTask<View,Float,String>(){
      @Override
      protected void onPreExecute() {
        // do something in the UI thread before starting doInBackground,
        // For example, show wait cursor or dismiss keyboard.
        dismissKeyboard();
      }
      @Override
      protected String doInBackground(View... parms) {
        String resp = null;
        try {
```

```
            // form data: key=value&...
            String data = editText.getText().toString();
            data = URLEncoder.encode(data, "UTF-8");
            String formData = "echo=" + data;
            resp = httpPost(SERVER_URL, formData);
        } catch (UnsupportedEncodingException e) {
            e.printStackTrace();
        }
        Log.d("", resp);
        return resp;
    }
    @Override
    protected void onPostExecute(String result) {
        processResultData(result);
    }
};
task.execute(buttonPost);
  }
  ...
}
```

3. To test the POST button in Listing 4-96, run the RestClient project and enter **"Hi, you"** to see the live app in action, as shown in Figure 4-15.

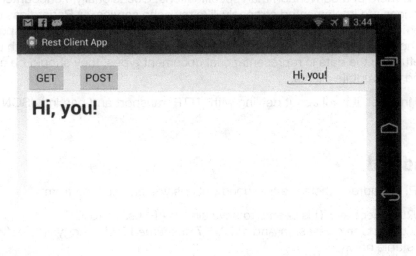

Figure 4-15. RestClient app do POST

The echo server actually responded in HTML format: <HTML><BODY><H1>Hi, you!</H1></BODY></HTML>. Android WebView widgets are capable of rendering the HTML <H1> tag. We will talk about the response data format later.

Consume RESTFul Web Services

REST (REpresentational State Transfer) defines a set of architectural principles by which you can design web services that focus on a system's resources, including how the resource states are addressed and transferred over HTTP by a wide range of clients written in different languages. If measured by the number of web services that use it, REST has emerged in the last few years alone as a dominant web service design model. In fact, REST has had such a large impact on the Web that it has mostly displaced SOAP- (Simple Object Access Protocol) and WSDL- (Web Services Description Language) based interface design, because it's a considerably simpler style to use.

RESTFul services are implemented as server apps/services. Most of the heavy-duty parts belong to server/service developers. Typically, most of the RESTFul service implementations follow some of these design principles:

- Use HTTP methods explicitly.

- Be stateless.

- Expose directory structure–like URIs.

- Transfer XML or JavaScript Object Notation (JSON), or both.

On the mobile client side, in a nutshell, it is all about how to consume the service by sending appropriate requests and interpreting the responses correctly.

Note that REST is more of a convention than specifications. Occasionally, I encounter some so-called REST services are implemented strangely, like my echo service. ☺ Regardless of how they should be implemented on the server side, you just need to follow the service API specs precisely because that is how software programming works. As long as the services stick with using HTTP transport and returning the data in representational document types, they should be easy enough for both Android and iOS mobile clients.

In this case and in most, it is all about dealing with HTTP transport and parsing JSON messages in mobile clients.

HTTP in Android

For the HTTP API in Android, there are two good options you can choose from:

- `HttpURLConnection`: This seems to have similar API usage to iOS `NSURLConnection` classes. In Android API 7, it seemed fairly buggy. It is definitely quite stable now.

- `AndroidHttpClient`: This was ported from the JavaEE Apache framework. It offers higher-level API usages and has been in the Java community for a long time. JavaEE developers might find it more appealing.

I am using `HttpURLConnection` in this book because the API usage seems closer to the way that iOS `NSURLConnection` works.

HTTP Method

```
IOS ANALOGY
```

NSMutableURLRequest: (void)setHTTPMethod:(NSString *)method;

Let's cut to the chase: specify the HTTP method using the `HttpURLConnection` class.

`HttpURLConnection:setRequestMethod("POST"). // or GET, PUT, DELETE etc.`

> **Note**   An HTTP method is case-sensitive according to HTTP protocol specs.

REST suggests using HTTP methods explicitly in a way that's consistent with the protocol definition. This basic REST design principle establishes a one-to-one mapping among create, read, update, and delete (CRUD) operations and HTTP methods, as follows:

- To create a resource on the server, use `POST`.
- To retrieve a resource, use `GET`.
- To change the state of a resource or to update it, use `PUT`.
- To remove or delete a resource, use `DELETE`.

The most common ones are `GET` and `POST` for sure. Many services are even deployed with simpler conventions: `GET` for retrieving ready-only resources, and `POST` for anything else that modifies the resources. To the extreme, some exclusively use `POST`. The RESTful architectural style is beyond the scope of our current topic. In practice, you just need to use the right HTTP method dictated by the services API specs.

> **Note**   For client apps to consume certain remote services, the server implementations dictate how clients consume the service. For porting from an iOS app, your Android app should consume the same service as your iOS app. You should just choose the same HTTP method your iOS app currently uses, because that is what the server expects.

HTTP Headers

```
IOS ANALOGY
```

NSMutableURLRequest: (void)setValue:(NSString *)value forHTTPHeaderField:(NSString *)field;

To specify HTTP headers using the `HttpURLConnection` class, use the one-liner shown in Listing 4-97.

Listing 4-97. HTTP Headers

```
HttpURLConnection: setRequestProperty("accept", "application/json").
```

> **Note**   HTTP header names are not case-sensitive according to HTTP protocol specs.

You use this method to set either the well-known headers or any custom headers that the server defines. As an example, the `accept` header is commonly used in many services. Services are commonly implemented to support various clients and allow their client apps to choose which data format is right for them. This is known as *content negotiation*. Client apps use the preceding API to specify the HTTP accept header with MIME type values.

To specify the response content type in our RestClient project, modify the `httpGet(...)` and `httpPost(...)` in `ScreenOneFragment.java` (see Listing 4-98).

Listing 4-98. Set Accept Header

```java
public class ScreenOneFragment extends Fragment implements OnClickListener {
    ...
    // GET data from url
    private String httpGet(String myurl) {
        ...
        URL url = new URL(myurl);
        // create an HttpURLConnection by openConnection
        conn = (HttpURLConnection) url.openConnection();
        conn.setRequestMethod("GET");
        conn.setRequestProperty("accept", "text/html");
        ...
    }

    // Send POST data to server
    String httpPost(String myurl, String formData) {
        ...
        URL url = new URL(myurl);
        // create an HttpURLConnection by openConnection
        conn = (HttpURLConnection) url.openConnection();
        conn.setRequestMethod("POST");
        conn.setRequestProperty("accept", "text/html");
        ...
    }
    ...
}
```

> **Note**   Our sample echo service supports "text/html", "text/plain", and "application/json" content types. To demonstrate the content negotiation visually, I choose to use a WebView widget to render the server response and specify the "text/html". In general, "application/json" is more suitable for data exchange.

JSON

For web services, you frequently deal with a structured representational resource like XML and JSON documents. The Android SDK includes parsers for both.

Previously, we specified "text/html" as the accept header (see Listing 4-98) and let WebView render the HTML document in our RestClient app. RESTful client apps normally don't request text/HTML content types. The same echo service also supports the "application/json" content type.

To change our RestClient app to use a JSON document, do the following:

1.   In our httpGet(...) and httpGet(...) methods, request a JSON content response, as shown in Listing 4-99.

   Listing 4-99. Set Application/JSON Accept Header

   ```
   public class ScreenOneFragment extends Fragment {
     ...
     // GET data from url
     private String httpGet(String myurl) {
       ...
       conn.setRequestProperty("accept", "application/json");
       ...
     }

     // Send POST data to server
     String httpPost(String myurl, String formData) {
       ...
       conn.setRequestProperty("accept", "application/json");
       ...
     }
     ...
   }
   ```

2.   Modify the processResultData(...) method to use the JSONObject. The code in Listing 4-100 creates a JSONObject from a response string. Add the HTML presentational <H1> tag for the WebView widget to render the result, as follows:

   a.   To convert a JSON string to JSONObject: new JSONObject(jsonString).

   b.   To convert JSONObject to JSON string: JSONObject.toString().

c. To get value by key: JSONObject.getString(key) // get(...), getXXX, and so forth.

d. After parsing the JSON string, wrap the data with an HTML <H1> tag and render the whole string in WebView.

> **Note** In the JSON and Saving a JSON Document section, you used the JSONObject for persistent storage purposes. This is the same class we will use to handle the "application/json" data from remote services.

Listing 4-100. Receive JSON Doc

```java
public class ScreenOneFragment extends Fragment implements OnClickListener {
  ...
  private void processResultData(String result) {
    String htmlString = "";
    try {
      result = URLDecoder.decode(result, "UTF-8");
      JSONObject jo = new JSONObject(result); // String to JSONObject
      Iterator<String> keys = jo.keys();
      String key, value;
      while (keys.hasNext()) {
        key = keys.next();
        value = jo.getString(key); // get(...), getXXX, etc.
        htmlString += key + " - " + value;
      }
    } catch (UnsupportedEncodingException e) {
      e.printStackTrace();
    } catch (JSONException e) {
      e.printStackTrace();
    }

    htmlString = String.format("<H1>%s</H1>", htmlString);
    webView.loadData(htmlString, "text/html", "UTF-8");
  }
  ...
```

There is nothing new in this code. I just wanted to emphasize the common RESTFul web services with JSON usage. The JSONObject class offers a simple API usage. I like to use it for keeping my code simple and clean, and it works very well for smaller data. Since API Level 11+, you can also use android.util.JsonReader to parse InputStream directly. Which one to pick? It seems to come down to the same old topic of an XML DOM (document object model) parser vs. a SAX (Simple API for XML) parser. I just wanted to point out the alternative when your JSON document is fairly big and you are only interested in certain key-value pairs. If you can influence the service implementations, it is even better to have optimized mobile web services so that you don't get into the parser performance topics.

There are also other open source parser libraries to parse JSON; some are capable of object mappings, some are capable of parsing input stream. For example, JavaEE developers are probably familiar with *GSON* or *Jackson*. I have good experiences using both.

3. Build and run the RestClient to see the RESTFul service with JSON in action, as shown in Figure 4-16.

Figure 4-16. RestClient consume JSON data

Summary

This chapter introduced the most common programming component mappings from iOS to Android:

- User interface and UI widgets
- Persistent storage options
- Network and remote services with JSON

These components are presented in almost any app. Many meaningful apps actually only deal with the components we discussed. This chapter listed all the viable options in detail, with step-by-step instructions on how to translate the iOS components into counterpart Android components.

Although this chapter takes up numerous pages, most of the mapping guidelines in it are easy to follow, simply because the mappings are straightforward. All you need are the guided instructions for the mapped class or methods.

CHECKPOINT

This was a long chapter that covered a lot of smaller portable pieces. Do you remember the following?

1. iOS UI widgets map very well to Android UI widgets, but there are more widgets in Android.

2. iOS AutoLayout best matches Android RelativeLayout, but there are more Android layout mangers.

3. Both UIViewController and Fragment have lifecycle callbacks (view states vs. controller states).

4. iOS NSUserDefaults vs. Android SharedPreferences.

5. NSFileManager vs. the Java File API.

6. iOS Core Data Framework vs. Android SQLite database API.

7. Use JSON docs to encapsulate data.

8. iOS NSURLConnection vs. Android HttpUrlConnection.

9. Performing I/O or networking code in a background worker thread using the AsyncTask in Android.

More was covered than this. You don't have to remember it all. When you encounter anything you can't recall, use this book's table of contents to look up the mapping guidelines and the sample code in the ADT projects.

Part 3

One Step Further

Previously, you focused on the direct mapping techniques from iOS to Android. The results are a set of instructions and guidelines that you can follow to port iOS apps with a user interface to the Android platform. However, you can create more than user interface applications and you actually have more freedom in Android. You will discover more of the uniqueness of the Android Application Framework, including application resources and the other application components.

You will be introduced to porting the common mobile use cases from iOS to Android as a whole, instead of lower-level SDK class-to-class mappings. These individual topics are introduced in no particular order. They are all commonly used in iOS apps as well.

Chapter 5

More About Android Application Components

We have used activity to create ADT projects with a user interface. To launch these apps, users simply go to the application launcher, find the app icon, and tap the icon to start the app. The *application launcher* is actually a system built-in app with a user interface that allows users to select the app by tapping the launch icons to start the app. (In iOS, it is called the *Home screen* or the *Springboard*.) Technically speaking, in Android, you don't say, "Launch an application from the system application launcher." Instead, you should say, "Activate an application component."

How does it work? The application launcher app simply sends a special object—called `Intent` (see Listing 5-6)—to the Android system to start an application component.

You can launch your Android app in the same way the Android system launches an app—activating and communicating with other application components, including background services. This opens a lot of possibilities that are probably not easy to achieve in iOS apps, like creating or using background services, or those traditional interprocess communication (IPC) use cases, and so forth.

In Chapter 2, I gave high-level introductions about four types of application components, and focused on activity and fragment code for Android graphical user interface (GUI) app–related aspects. In this chapter, you will learn more about the other three application components: *service*, *broadcast receiver*, and *content provider*. They are Android-specific: you won't find equivalent topics in iOS. And for porting iOS apps to Android, you probably will use them less frequently than activity or fragment topics. However, you already know activity, and there are fewer SDK classes to learn. Actually, they are handy for many practical use cases. A small effort goes a long way.

Before we go over the application components, let's discuss the intent and intent-filter rules, because they are the linkage that activates the application components.

Intent and Intent Filter

IOS ANALOGY

[[UIApplication sharedApplication] openURL:myURL];

Not exactly the same, but it is portable to Android.

You send Intent objects to activate three out of four application components: activity, service, and broadcast receiver. You send appropriate Intent objects to the system and let the system deliver them to the appropriate application components. Application components are described with <intent-filter> attributes in an application's AndroidManifest.xml file. The Intent object carries the target component information so that the system can match the qualified components for you. The Intent object must match the <intent-filter> described in the receiving component's manifest file.

An Intent object contains information of interest to the application component that receives the intent (such as the action to be taken and the data to act on), plus information of interest to the Android system (such as the category of the component that should handle the intent, and instructions on how to launch a target activity). You can also bundle extra key-value paired information to be delivered to the application components.

Let's first get the ADT prep project in place so that we can immediately experience the common intent-related programming tasks along the way.

ADT PROJECT PREPARATIONS

Same as usual, let's use our MvcTemplate project to create the ADT project, which is named AppComponents.

1. Copy the MvcTemplate ADT project and paste it to a new project (⌘c, ⌘v). The project name is **AppComponents**.

2. Rename the Android application package. From the newly created AppComponents project context menu, select **Android Tools ➤ Rename Application Package**. Enter the new package name: **com.pdachoice.appcomponents**.

3. Rename the AppComponents/src/com.pdachoice.renameme Java package. From the package context menu, select **Refactor ➤ Rename...** (Alt+⌘r). Enter the new name: **com.pdachoice.appcomponent**. Select the **Update references** check box.

4. You only need one fragment: keep ScreenOneFragment and delete the other two:

   a. Delete src/ScreenTwoFragment.java and src/ScreenThreeFragment.java classes (multiselect and fn+Delete).

   b. Delete res/layout/screentwo_fragment.xml and res/layout/screenthree_fragment.xml files (multiselect and fn+Delete).

5. Modify res/layout/screenone_fragment.xml. Prepare three action buttons in it, as shown in Listing 5-1.

Listing 5-1. screenone_fragment.xml with Three Buttons

```xml
<?xml version="1.0" encoding="utf-8"?>
<RelativeLayout xmlns:android="http://schemas.android.com/apk/res/android"
    android:layout_width="match_parent"
    android:layout_height="match_parent" >

    <Button
        android:id="@+id/btnImplicit"
        android:layout_width="wrap_content"
        android:layout_height="wrap_content"
        android:layout_centerHorizontal="true"
        android:layout_centerVertical="true"
        android:text="@string/actionImplicit" />

    <Button
        android:id="@+id/btnExplicit"
        android:layout_width="wrap_content"
        android:layout_height="wrap_content"
        android:layout_above="@+id/btnImplicit"
        android:layout_alignRight="@+id/btnImplicit"
        android:layout_marginBottom="50dp"
        android:text="@string/actionExplicit" />

    <Button
        android:id="@+id/btnUseService"
        android:layout_width="wrap_content"
        android:layout_height="wrap_content"
        android:layout_below="@+id/btnImplicit"
        android:layout_centerHorizontal="true"
        android:layout_marginTop="50dp"
        android:text="@string/actionComp" />
</RelativeLayout>
```

6. Modify res/values/strings.xml to change the app name and to add some text that we will need later, as shown in Listing 5-2.

Listing 5-2. strings.xml

```xml
<?xml version="1.0" encoding="utf-8"?>
<resources>

    <string name="app_name">Application Components</string>
    <string name="actionExplicit">useExplicitIntent()</string>
    <string name="actionImplicit">useImplicitIntent()</string>
```

```
<string name="actionComp">useHelloService()</string>
<string name="permission">BroadcastReceiver: Just want to say Hi</string>

</resources>
```

7. Modify src/ScreenOneFragment.java to handle the buttons' onClick events, as shown in Listing 5-3.

    Listing 5-3. ScreenOneFragment.java

```java
public class ScreenOneFragment extends Fragment implements OnClickListener {
  private View contentView;
  private Button btnExplicit;
  private Button btnImplicit;
  private Button btnUseService;
  @Override
  public View onCreateView(LayoutInflater inflater, ViewGroup container,
      Bundle savedInstanceState) {
    contentView = inflater.inflate(R.layout.screenone_fragment, container,false);

    btnExplicit = (Button) contentView.findViewById(R.id.btnExplicit);
    btnImplicit = (Button) contentView.findViewById(R.id.btnImplicit);
    btnUseService = (Button) contentView.findViewById(R.id.btnUseService);

    btnExplicit.setOnClickListener(this);
    btnImplicit.setOnClickListener(this);
    btnUseService.setOnClickListener(this);

    return contentView;
  }

  @Override
  public void onClick(View v) {
    if(v == btnExplicit) {
      // TODO useExplicitIntent();
    } else if (v == btnImplicit) {
      // TODO useImplicitIntent();
    } else if (v == btnUseService) {
      // TODO useHelloService();
    }
  }
}
```

8. Build and run the app to make sure the prep is good. Figure 5-1 is an example of the app and shows how it should look.

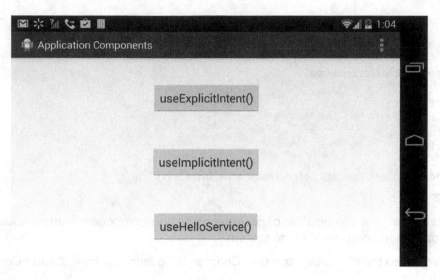

Figure 5-1. AppComponents prep

There are three action buttons that will be used to demonstrate the topics in this subject.

Depending on how the Intent objects are created, it can be grouped into two types: *explicit intents* and *implicit intents*.

Explicit Intents

Explicit intents designate the target component by its name. Since component names are generally not known to other developers, explicit intents are typically used for application-internal messages, such as an activity starting a service or launching another activity in the same manifest file.

To target a particular application component, you need the manifest package name and the component class name that system can use to identify the target application component.

> **Note**   You can also use explicit intent to invoke the application components defined in other apps, but you need to take into consideration that the app might not be installed yet.

Listing 5-4 is an example of how you can precisely find the package name and the component name in your manifest file.

Listing 5-4. Explicit Intent

```
<manifest
    ...
    package="com.pdachoice.renameme"
    ... >

    ...
    <application ... >
        <activity
            ...
            android:name="com.pdachoice.renameme.MainActivity"
            ...
```

Explicit intent is trivial. The combination of package name and component name uniquely identify the Android application component in the system.

Previously, we created the RestClient app (see Chapter 4). To launch it from the AppComponents app, do the following:

1. Find out the application package name and the component name. They are given to you by the developer or, in our case, RestClient, you can easily find it in the AndroidManifest.xml file (see Listing 5-5). The package name is com.pdachoice.restclient and the component name is com.pdachoice.restclient.MainActivity.

    Listing 5-5. RestClient AndroidManifest.xml

    ```
    <?xml version="1.0" encoding="utf-8"?>
    <manifest xmlns:android="http://schemas.android.com/apk/res/android"
        package="com.pdachoice.restclient"
        ... >

        ...
        <application
            ... >
            <activity
                ...
                android:name="com.pdachoice.restclient.MainActivity"
                ... >

                ...
            </activity>
        </application>

    </manifest>
    ```

2. Create and invoke the useExplicitIntent() method in ScreenOneFragment.java, as shown in Listing 5-6.

Listing 5-6. Send Explicit Intent

```java
public class ScreenOneFragment extends Fragment implements OnClickListener {
  ...
  @Override
  public void onClick(View v) {
    Log.v("SceenOneFragment", "onClick");
    if(v == btnExplicit) {
      useExplicitIntent();
    } else if (v == btnImplicit) {
      // TODO useImplicitIntent();
    } else if (v == btnUseService) {
      // TODO useHelloService();
    }
  }

  private void useExplicitIntent() {
    String pkg = "com.pdachoice.restclient";
    String cls = "com.pdachoice.restclient.MainActivity";
    ComponentName component = new ComponentName(pkg, cls);
    Intent intent = new Intent();
    intent.setComponent(component);

    try {
      getActivity().startActivity(intent);
    } catch (ActivityNotFoundException e) {
      // TODO: you may direct to Google Play to install the app
      Log.d("", e.getLocalizedMessage());
    }
  }
}
```

Note   You should expect errors with the try-catch block. You cannot assume that the presented app or activity is already installed.

3.   Build and run the AppComponents app to see the code in action (see Figure 5-2).

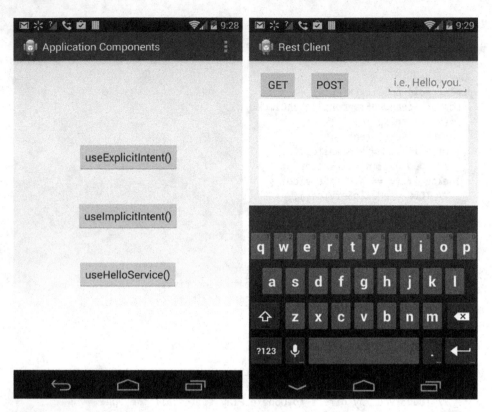

Figure 5-2. AppComponents launch RestClient

You might need to install the RestClient app first; otherwise, you will encounter an error because your app would try to activate something that does not exist. For a serious production app, you'll want to write some code to give users a better experience: I normally direct them to the App Store for my iOS apps. You can do the same thing in Android.

Implicit Intents

In contrast to explicit intents, *implicit intents* do not explicitly name a target component. Implicit intents are often used to activate components from other applications that you don't know the exact name of, or when you only need *any* application component that can fulfill the purpose. The implicit intents must include enough information for the system to determine which of the available components is best to run for that intent. It may contain the following attributes:

- **Action:** The general action to be performed by the receiving application component. Together with the Action object, the intent normally contains other pieces of information—data and extra (described next)—for the receiving application component to operate on. On the other hand, if you are defining the intent filter for your application component to receive an Intent object, define it as an entire protocol for the Intent objects your components can handle.

- **Data and Type:** The data to operate on by the receiving application component. It should be a URI that references to the data and the MIME type of that data. For example, a person's record in a contacts database, or a reference to a remote video, expressed as a URI. Normally, the type is inferred from the URI to the data itself. You can also explicitly set the Type attribute and ignore the reference to any particular resource.

- **Extra:** The Intent object can contain a bundle of any additional information that gets sent into the receiving application components. Android Bundle normally contains smaller key-value paired messages—such as primitive data, a string, and so forth—that the receiving application component can directly extract from the Bundle object, as opposed to the URI to the resource mentioned earlier. For example, if we have an action to send an e-mail message, you could also include extra pieces of data in the Extra object to supply a subject, body, and so forth.

- **Category:** This additional information is used to describe the type of application component that should handle this action. For example, the system launcher sends intents with this attribute, and you define this attribute in your activity <intent-filter> to be activated by the launcher.

- **Flags:** Flags of various sorts. Many flags instruct the Android system on how to launch an activity and how to treat it after it has launched.

The Android system uses these Intent attributes to match the <intent-filter> elements defined in AndroidManifest.xml.

Although it's kind of wordy, it is actually easier to understand this with sample code. Try the following:

1. To reuse an existing application component, all that is required is to find out the intent filter defined for the application component. Most likely, this is given to you by the developer. On the other hand, to design a reusable component that allows others to activate it, consider defining the whole intent as a protocol. Let's create an intent filter in RestClient AndroidManifest.xml (see Listing 5-7). The action is com.pdachoice. restclient.SOME_NAME and the category is android.intent.category. DEFAULT.

Listing 5-7. RestClient AndroidManifest.xml

```
<?xml version="1.0" encoding="utf-8"?>
<manifest xmlns:android="http://schemas.android.com/apk/res/android"
    package="com.pdachoice.restclient"
    ... >

    ...
    <application
        ... >
        <activity
            ...
```

```
                android:name="com.pdachoice.restclient.MainActivity"
            ... >

            ...
            <intent-filter>
                <action android:name="android.intent.action.MAIN"/>
                <category android:name="android.intent.category.LAUNCHER" />
            </intent-filter>

            <intent-filter>
                <action android:name="com.pdachoice.restclient.SOME_NAME"/>
                <category android:name="android.intent.category.DEFAULT" />
            </intent-filter>
            ...

        </activity>
    </application>

</manifest>
```

> **Note**   Android automatically applies the CATEGORY_DEFAULT category to all implicit intents passed to
> startActivity() and startActivityForResult(). So if you want your activity to receive implicit intents, it must
> include a category for "android.intent.category.DEFAULT" in its intent filters.

2. After you have updated the RestClient manifest file, build and run the app to
   reinstall it.

3. Create and invoke the useImplicitIntent() method (see Listing 5-8) in
   ScreenOneFragment.java.

Listing 5-8. Send Implicit Intent

```java
public class ScreenOneFragment extends Fragment implements OnClickListener {

  ...
  @Override
  public void onClick(View v) {
    if (v == btnExplicit) {
      useExplicitIntent();
    } else if (v == btnImplicit) {
      useImplicitIntent();
    } else if (v == btnUseService) {
      // TODO useHelloService();
    }
  }
}
```

```
        private void useImplicitIntent() {
          String action ="com.pdachoice.restclient.SOME_NAME";
          String category = "android.intent.category.DEFAULT";

          Intent intent = new Intent(action);
          intent.addCategory(category);

          try {
            getActivity().startActivity(intent);
          } catch (ActivityNotFoundException e) {
            // TODO: you may direct to Google Play to install the app
            Log.d("", e.getLocalizedMessage());
          }
        }
        ...
      }
```

4. Build and run the AppComponents app to see the code in action. When you
    tap the **UseImplicitIntent()** button, the implicit intent activates the RestClient
    the same way that it is activated by explicit intent (see Figure 5-2).

Services

<table>
<tr><td align="center">IOS ANALOGY</td></tr>
</table>

None. iOS background modes are not real services, but they probably can be ported to an Android service.

To create a service, you declare the service component in the manifest file and provide the
implementation by creating a Java subclass of Service that handles the service lifecycle callback,
just like Activity. Traditionally, there are two Service classes you can extend:

- Service: This is the base class for all services. When you extend this class, it
  is important that you create a new thread in which to do all the service's work
  because the service uses your application's main thread by default, which could
  slow the performance of any activity your application is running.

- IntentService: This is a subclass of Service that contains a worker thread to
  handle all start requests, one at a time. This is the best option if it is not required
  for your service to handle multiple requests simultaneously. All you need to do
  is implement onHandleIntent(), which executes your code in the background
  thread.

IntentService

IntentService is designed to queue the client requests and process the requests sequentially in a
background thread. If your services do not have to process multiple client requests simultaneously,
or respond to the request in real time, extend your service from IntentService and override one
method, onHandleIntent(), to provide the worker code.

It works for the majority of the practical usages, except real-time service. You can create a thread or AsyncTask in the handling method to improve timing, but I would not say that this makes your service a real-time service. Your best choice is to use a service and create a worker thread for each request for a real-time service.

The steps to take for creating services are basically the same as creating activities: declare the component in the manifest and provide Java class implementation. Do the following to create a HelloService service in the AppComponents project:

1. Declare a HelloService service component in AndroidManifest.xml, as shown in in Listing 5-9. Just like activity, declare services within <application></application>.

Listing 5-9. Service

```
<manifest ...
    package="com.pdachoice.appcomponents"
    ... >

    ...
    <application ... >

        <service android:name="com.pdachoice.appcomponents.HelloService" />
        <activity ...
        ...
```

Note   Table A-1 in the Appendix lists the service attributes definitions. Most of them are optional attributes that you can either define in the manifest file or in your Java code.

2. Create the HelloService.java class (see Listing 5-10). Extend the IntentService class. You only need to put the worker code inside the onHandleIntent(...) method. The runtime requests are queued sequentially and executed in a background work thread.

Listing 5-10. HelloService.java

```
public class HelloService extends IntentService {
    private static final String tag = "HelloService";

    public HelloService() {
        super("HelloService");
    }

    @Override
    protected void onHandleIntent(Intent intent) {
        Log.i("HelloService", " onHandleIntent ");
        // executed in background thread, not UI thread
```

```
    String fname = intent.getExtras().getString("fname");
    String lname = intent.getExtras().getString("lname");

    Log.w(tag, String.format("TODO: %s %s ...", fname, lname));
  }
}
```

> **Note**   You need to explicitly provide a constructor to match the superclass. This is just a Java language rule.
> You will not miss this rule because the Java compiler will tell you to do it.
>
> The AppComponents app has two components now: MainActivity and the new HelloService both live in the
> same app. Both can be activated by the appropriate intent.

3. Create the useHelloService() method to activate the HelloService,
   as shown in Listing 5-11.

   a. Create an explicit intent with a package name and class name strings.
      You can get the exact strings from the AndroidManifest.xml file or from
      the developer.

   b. To send key-value pairs to the target application component, use
      intent.putExtra(...).

Listing 5-11. Use HelloService

```
public class ScreenOneFragment extends Fragment {

  ...
  @Override
  public void onClick(View v) {
    if (v == btnExplicit) {
      useExplicitIntent();
    } else if (v == btnImplicit) {
      useImplicitIntent();
    } else if (v == btnUseService) {
      useHelloService();
    }
  }
  void useHelloService() {
    ComponentName component = new ComponentName(
          "com.pdachoice.appcomponents",
          "com.pdachoice.appcomponents.HelloService");

    Intent intent = new Intent();
    intent.setComponent(component);

    intent.putExtra("fname", "Mobile");
    intent.putExtra("lname", "Developer");
```

```
        getActivity().startService(intent);
    }
    ...
}
```

> **Note** If the target application component is in the same app, that target must be declared in the same AndroidManifest.xml as the sending application component, you can simply use the following one-liner:
>
> Intent intent = new Intent(getActivity(), HelloService.class)

4.　Build and run the AppComponents project to visualize the code in action. Our HelloService component doesn't do much yet, but you should be able to see the output in ADT LogCat view, as shown in Figure 5-3.

Figure 5-3. HelloService LogCat output

PendingIntent

When an application component is activated by an Intent object, the receiving application component is running within the application that originally declares the component in the receiving application's AndroidManifest.xml file. PendingIntent works differently in terms of the application context: the receiving application component will be executed in the same application context that the intent is coming from. Consequently, you are granting the receiving component the same right to perform the operations you have declared in your manifest, as if it were you (with the same permissions and identity). As such, you should be careful about how you build the pending intent; almost always, the base intent you supply should have the component name explicitly set to one of your own components to ensure that it is ultimately sent there and nowhere else.

To activate your HelloService using PendingIntent instead of the regular intent that was used previously, do the following (and see Listing 5-12):

1.　Create the Intent object exactly the same way as before.

2.　Use PendingIntent.getService(...) or PendingIntent.getActivity(...), respectfully, to create a PendingIntent object that wraps the original Intent object and the current context.

Listing 5-12. PendingIntent

```java
public class ScreenOneFragment extends Fragment {

  ...
  void useHelloService() {
    ComponentName component = new ComponentName("com.pdachoice.appcomponents",
        "com.pdachoice.appcomponents.HelloService");

    Intent intent = new Intent();
    intent.setComponent(component);

    intent.putExtra("fname", "Mobile");
    intent.putExtra("lname", "Developer");

    // getActivity().startService(intent);
    // Create PendingIntent to wrap the original intent with extra parms
    try {
      PendingIntent pendingIntent = PendingIntent.getService(getActivity(), 0,
          intent, PendingIntent.FLAG_UPDATE_CURRENT);

      pendingIntent.send();
    } catch (CanceledException e) {
      e.printStackTrace();
    }
  }
  ...
}
```

Listing 5-12 does exactly the same thing as Listing 5-11—it activates `HelloService`. Many built-in system services are activated by `PendingIntent`, so you can treat those services as if they were your own services. You will use them—and I wanted to give you a heads-up.

Broadcast Receivers

As the name implies, a *broadcast receiver* receives messages from other application components. You can use it to implement the well-known GoF publisher-subscriber design patterns for communications within the same app locally, or among application components across apps in the system globally. Creating a broadcast receiver is basically the same as creating an activity or service.

You declare the `<Receiver>` application component in the `AndroidManifest.xml` file and provide a Java class by subclassing from the `BroadcastReceiver` class. To send broadcast messages, there are two types of intent messages that can be received by broadcast receivers:

- *Normal broadcasts* (sent with `Context.sendBroadcast`): These are completely asynchronous—fire and forget.

- *Ordered broadcasts* (sent with `Context.sendOrderedBroadcast`): These are delivered to one receiver at a time in the order defined by the `android:priority` attribute of the matching intent filter. Honestly, I have never used this type. I think it is a handy option, but I will not go over this type in this book.

Do the following to create your `HelloBroadcastReceiver` in the AppComponents project:

1. Declare a `HelloBroadcastReceiver` component in `AndroidManifest.xml` (see Listing 5-13), as follows:

   a. Declare the receiver component inside `<application></application>`, just like declaring activity or service.

   b. Define the intent filter for how to receive implicit intents. For simplicity, our `HelloBroadcastReceiver` only specifies a simple action attribute.

   c. Optionally, you may make your application component unavailable to any other apps by specifying `android:exported="false"`. This makes the broadcast receiver private to your own app. The default is `true`.

   Listing 5-13. Declare Broadcast Receiver

```
<manifest ... >
    ...
    <application ... >
        ...
        <receiver
            android:name="com.pdachoice.appcomponents.HelloBroadcastReceiver"
            android:exported="true" >
            <intent-filter>
                <action android:name="com.pdachoice.appcomponents.Hello" />
            </intent-filter>
        </receiver>
        ...
    </application>

</manifest>
```

2. This is an optional step, but it is important for security reasons: your `BroadcastReceiver` code can be activated by other apps that send matching intents. To prevent other apps from using your code without user permission, define your own permission and declare `android:permission` on your receiver; this forces senders to declare the `uses-permission` in order to make users aware of any security concerns as shown in Listing 5-14.

> **Note** Recall that you declared INTERNET uses-permission in the RestClient manifest file in Chapter 4. When using sensitive features or API, it is the developer's responsibility to make users aware of it. By declaring <uses-permission />, users can decide whether they want to opt-in the permission to install the app.

Listing 5-14. Declare Broadcast Receiver Permission

```
<manifest ... >
    ...
    <permission
        android:name="com.pdachoice.appcomponents.HELLO_PERMISSION"
        android:description="@string/permission"
        android:label="@string/app_name" />

    <application ... >
        ...
        <receiver ...
            android:permission="com.pdachoice.appcomponents.HELLO_PERMISSION" >
            ...
        </receiver>
        ...
    </application>
</manifest>
```

3. Implement the HelloBroadcastReceiver.java class, as shown in Listing 5-15:

    a. Broadcast receivers must extend the BroadcastReceiver class.

    b. Override the onReceive(...) method that is the only lifecycle callback: the BroadcastReceiver code entry point.

    c. The onReceive(...) method is considered to be executed in the foreground process. This has a negative implication to the UI thread. If the broadcast receiver activates with the UI thread running, make sure that the onReceive(...) method is responsive, because it could block the UI thread and impose bad user experiences.

Listing 5-15. Broadcast Receiver Entry Method: onReceive(...)

```
// extends BroadcastReceiver
public class HelloBroadcastReceiver extends BroadcastReceiver {

    private static final String tag = "HelloReceiver";

    @Override // BroadcastReceiver lifecycle entry point
    public void onReceive(Context context, Intent intent) {
        String hello = intent.getExtras().getString("name");
        Log.w(tag, "onReceive: " + hello);
    }
}
```

> **Note**   Once returning from onReceive(...), the BroadcastReceiver is no longer active. If the application that hosts the receiver doesn't have any active component, then upon returning from onReceive(...), the Android system considers the application process to be empty and can aggressively terminate the application process to release all the resources. To keep your broadcast receivers ready at all times, even when no UI activity is active, a service is often used in conjunction with a broadcast receiver to keep the containing process active for the entire operation.
>
> Also, the onReceive(...) method is considered to be executed in the foreground process and could affect the responsiveness of your app. Particularly, when the broadcast receivers are activated with the UI thread running, make sure that the onReceive(...) method is responsive without blocking the UI thread.

4. To activate the HelloBroadcastReceiver (see Listing 5-16), create a matching intent and send it. You can do it from other apps. For simplicity, you can do it from the previous HelloService.java. Since the HelloBroadcastReceiver intent filter only specifies an action attribute, we only need to create the Intent object with the matching action.

Listing 5-16. sendBroadcast

```java
public class HelloService extends IntentService {

    @Override
    protected void onHandleIntent(Intent intent) {

        ...
        sendGlobalBroadcast(fname, lname);
    }

    private void sendGlobalBroadcast(String fname, String lname) {
        // create a new Implicit Intent and set the action intent-filter
        Intent broadcastIntent = new Intent();
        broadcastIntent.setAction("com.pdachoice.appcomponents.Hello");

        // bundle "Extra" data to send to broadcast receivers
        broadcastIntent.putExtra("name", String.format("Hi, %s %s!", fname, lname));
        sendBroadcast(broadcastIntent);
    }
}
```

5. In Java code, call sendBroadcast(...) with a permission string, as shown in Listing 5-17. This in an optional step, but it is important for security reasons. The Android system simply delivers the intent to any BroadcastReceiver component that matches the intent filter <action> attribute, including any BroadcastReceiver in other apps. To avoid other apps, receive your data in the Intent object sent from your code. You may bundle a permission parameter in your Intent object. This forces the receivers to declare the uses-permission to make users aware of any security concerns.

Listing 5-17. sendBroadcast with Permission

```java
public class HelloService extends IntentService {

  private void sendGlobalBroadcast(String fname, String lname) {
    ...
    //    this.sendBroadcast(broadcastIntent);
    // specify permission
    String permission = "com.pdachoice.appcomponents.HELLO_PERMISSION";
    sendBroadcast(broadcastIntent, permission);
  }
}
```

6. For receiving the broadcast message, you need to declare uses-permisson in AndroidManifest.xml, as shown in Listing 5-18.

Listing 5-18. Declare uses-permission

```xml
<manifest ... >
  ...
  <uses-permission android:name="com.pdachoice.appcomponents.HELLO_PERMISSION" />
  ...
```

7. Build and run the AppComponents project to visualize the code in action. When the **useHelloService()** button is selected, an intent is created and sent to start our HelloService. Upon HelloService receiving the intent, it processes the intent by broadcasting an implicit intent. Your HelloBroadcastReceiver intent filter matches the action criteria and receives the broadcast Intent object. Our HelloBroadcastReceiver doesn't do much, but you should be able to see the output in ADT LogCat view as shown in Figure 5-4.

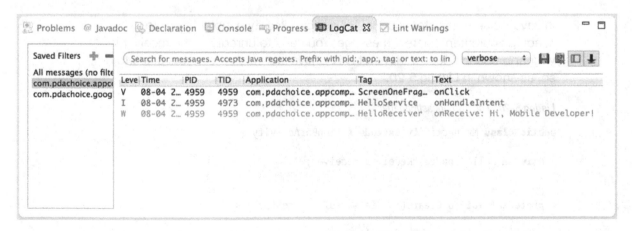

Figure 5-4. HelloReceiver LogCat output

Table A-2 in the Appendix lists the <receiver> attributes. Most of them are optional.

LocalBroadcastManager

NSNotificationCenter is the iOS equivalent of LocalBroadcastManager.

It is not a good idea to broadcast sensitive data to the whole system. You may want to make sure certain message communications only happen within your app. Android provides *LocalBroadcastManager*, which you use to register receivers and send intents—all within the same app. For example, to prevent your intent from being listened to by receivers other than those declared internally in the AppComponents app, do the following:

1. This is a pure Java code solution. Do *not* declare the `<receiver>` element in the manifest file. Remove it from `AndroidManifest.xml`, as shown in Listing 5-19.

   Listing 5-19. Remove the Broadcast Receiver Element

   ```
   <manifest ... >
       ...
       <application ... >
           ...
   <!--
           <receiver
               android:name="com.pdachoice.appcomponents.HelloBroadcastReceiver"
               ...
           </receiver>
   -->
       </application>
   </manifest>
   ```

2. In Java runtime, register your `HelloBroadcastReceiver` object prior to sending your internal intent message. You need to unregister the receiver if your app doesn't need it. `MainActivity.java` is a very reasonable place to do so, as shown in Listing 5-20.

   Listing 5-20. LocalBroadcastManager

   ```
   public class MainActivity extends ActionBarActivity {

     private HelloBroadcastReceiver receiver;

     @Override
     protected void onCreate(Bundle savedInstanceState) {
       ...
       String action = "com.pdachoice.appcomponents.Hello";
       IntentFilter filter = new IntentFilter(action);
       receiver = new HelloBroadcastReceiver();
       LocalBroadcastManager.getInstance(this).registerReceiver(receiver, filter);
     }
   ```

```
    @Override
    protected void onStop() {
        super.onStop();
        LocalBroadcastManager.getInstance(this).unregisterReceiver(receiver);
    }
}
```

3. Instead of sending a broadcast Intent object, use the following method for broadcasting local Intent objects, as shown in Listing 5-21.

Listing 5-21. Broadcast Intent Locally

```
public class HelloService extends IntentService {
    ...
    private void sendLocalBroadcast(String fname, String lname) {
        Intent broadcastIntent = new Intent();
        broadcastIntent.setAction("com.pdachoice.appcomponents.Hello");

        // bundle "Extra" data to send to broadcast receivers
        broadcastIntent.putExtra("name", String.format("Hi, %s %s!", fname, lname));

        LocalBroadcastManager manager = LocalBroadcastManager.getInstance(this);
        manager.sendBroadcast(broadcastIntent);
    }
    ...
}
```

A local broadcast is also more efficient than sending a global broadcast. I've found that many Android programmers often overlook this class because most use cases don't actually require global broadcasting.

Note   In real life, you probably don't broadcast your personal or sensitive data either.

Content Providers

IOS ANALOGY

None.

A *content provider* encapsulates persistent storage and manages data access by providing the common database CRUD (create, delete, update, delete) pattern. It presents data similar to the tables in a relational database. If you want to share your data with other apps, you develop your own content provider. The Android framework also includes system content providers that manage certain data, such as audio, video, pictures, contact information, and so forth. These system content providers are accessible to any Android app.

When you want to access data managed by a content provider, you use a `ContentResolver` object that communicates with the provider for you.

> **Note**   Sharing data across apps are typically advanced tasks in iOS apps. You would probably rarely need to use this Android technique to translate your iOS apps. However, there are useful services/apps that require using this technique to interface with them. We will focus more on how to *use* this technique, rather than how to create it.

ContentProvider

`ContentProvider` is also a type of Android application component. The steps for creating your own content provider are similar to creating activities or any application components: declare the component in application manifest and provide Java class implementation that extends the `ContentProvider` framework class.

Do the following to create a `HelloContentProvider` in your AppComponents project:

1. Declare a provider component, `HelloContentProvider`, in `AndroidManifest.xml` (see Listing 5-22).

    a. Just like the other three application components, declare a provider within `<application></application>`. As usual, the android:name is mandatory.

    b. `android:authorities` should uniquely reference to the content provider. The Android package name with an implementation class name is a good choice.

    c. Optionally, you can make your provider component private to your own app by specifying exported="false".

Listing 5-22. Declare Content Provider

```
<manifest ...
    package="com.pdachoice.appcomponents"
    ... >

    ...
    <application ... >
        ...
```

```
<provider
    android:name="com.pdachoice.appcomponents.HelloContentProvider"
    android:authorities="com.pdachoice.appcomponents.HelloContentProvider"
    android:exported="true" >
</provider>
...
```

2. Our HelloContentProvider manages a dummy SQLite database. Create a
   dummy database helper for our provider data source, as shown in
   Listing 5-23 (see Chapter 4 for detailed SQLite tasks.)

Listing 5-23. Create DummyDbHelper

```java
public class DummyDbHelper extends SQLiteOpenHelper {

    private static final String DB_NAME = "DummyDbHelper.db";
    private static final int DB_VERSION = 1;

    static final String TABLE_NAME = "DummyDbHelper";
    static final String COLUMN_PKEY = "uid";
    static final String COLUMN_NAME = "name";

    public DummyDbHelper(Context context) {
        super(context, DB_NAME, null, DB_VERSION);
    }

    @Override
    public void onCreate(SQLiteDatabase db) {
        String sql = String.format(
            "create table %s (%s INTEGER PRIMARY KEY, %s TEXT);", TABLE_NAME,
            COLUMN_PKEY, COLUMN_NAME);
        db.execSQL(sql);
    }

    @Override
    public void onUpgrade(SQLiteDatabase db,int oldVersion,int newVersion){
        // For table schema changes.
        // drop old table if you don't need to preserve old data
        String sql = "DROP TABLE IF EXISTS " + TABLE_NAME;
        db.execSQL(sql);
        onCreate(db);

        // Or, those typical data migration code ...
    }
}
```

3. Create the HelloContentProvider.java class that manages content using the preceding database, as shown in Listing 5-24. Note the following:

    a. The custom content provider class must extend from ContentProvider.

    b. onCreate() is the content provider application component lifecycle callback.

    c. getType(uri) describes the MIME type of the resource. It is handy for content negotiation.

    d. Provide the data access API. The method signatures of these methods closely reflect SQLite database CRUD method definitions.

Listing 5-24. HelloContentProvider

```java
public class HelloContentProvider extends ContentProvider {
  private DummyDbHelper dbHelper;

  @Override
  public boolean onCreate() {
    dbHelper = new DummyDbHelper(getContext());
    return true;
  }
  @Override
  public String getType(Uri uri) {
    return ContentResolver.CURSOR_ITEM_BASE_TYPE; // MIME type for row
  }
  @Override
  public Cursor query(Uri uri, String[] columns, String selection,
      String[] selectionArgs, String sortOrder) {
    return dbHelper.getReadableDatabase().query(DummyDbHelper.TABLE_NAME,
        columns, selection, selectionArgs, null, null, null);
  }
  @Override
  public Uri insert(Uri uri, ContentValues values) {
    long rowid = dbHelper.getWritableDatabase().insert(
        DummyDbHelper.TABLE_NAME, null, values);

    String rowUri = String.format("content://%s/%s/%d",
        "com.pdachoice.appcomponents.HelloContentProvider",
        DummyDbHelper.TABLE_NAME, rowid);
    return Uri.parse(rowUri);
  }
  @Override
  public int delete(Uri uri, String selection, String[] selectionArgs) {
    return dbHelper.getWritableDatabase().delete(DummyDbHelper.TABLE_NAME,
        selection, selectionArgs);
  }
  @Override
  public int update(Uri uri, ContentValues values, String selection,
      String[] selectionArgs) {
```

```
        return dbHelper.getWritableDatabase().update(DummyDbHelper.TABLE_NAME,
            values, selection, selectionArgs);
    }
}
```

Table A-3 in the Appendix lists the provider XML attributes. Most of them are optional.

ContentResolver

You use ContentProvider via a framework client object called ContentResolver. This object has the same data access API that calls the identically named methods defined in the content provider. The client apps could be running in different process from the content providers. The ContentResolver object handles the IPC for you. As a side note, you need to be mindful when considering concurrent access to content provider code.

> **Note**   In iOS, you cannot create the Android-like ContentProvider to export your application data. You probably won't need to create your own ContentProvider to port your iOS apps to Android. However, you will need to use ContentResolver in several situations, because all the system apps export their data via ContentProvider, and you need to use the corresponding ContentResolver to read or write data to these external data sources; for example, to read and write contacts, and to read and create calendar events.

Recall that when the useHelloService() action button is selected in the AppComponents app, it invokes our HelloService. In turn, HelloService broadcasts a simple intent. Our HelloBroadcastReceiver receives the intent and outputs a simple message in LogCat view (see Figure 5-4). Let's modify our HelloBroadcastReceiver to demonstrate usage of the preceding content provider:

1. Create a matching ContentResolver instance to insert and retrieve data, as shown in Listing 5-25:

    a. Content URI includes the name of the entire provider (its authority) and a path that points to a table. Make sure that the URI authority matches the android:authorities defined in the AndroidManifest.xml file. The path is optional; however, a path is frequently used to identify a table or a record in a table.

    b. Make sure that ContentResolver has the same method signatures as the data access API in ContentProvider.

Listing 5-25. DummyProvider Insert and Retrieve

```
public class HelloBroadcastReceiver extends BroadcastReceiver {

    private static final String tag = "HelloReceiver";
    static String AUTHORITY = "com.pdachoice.appcomponents.HelloContentProvider";
    static String PATH = "DummyDbHelper"; // optional
```

```java
    @Override
    // BroadcastReceiver lifecycle entry point
    public void onReceive(Context context, Intent intent) {
        String hello = intent.getExtras().getString("name");
        Log.e(tag, "onReceive: " + hello);

        insertIntoDummyProvider(context);
        retrieveFromDummyProvider(context);
    }

    private void insertIntoDummyProvider(Context context) {
        ContentResolver resolver = context.getContentResolver();

        String s = String.format("content://%s/%s", AUTHORITY, PATH);
        Uri uri = Uri.parse(s);

        ContentValues values = new ContentValues();
        values.put(DummyDbHelper.COLUMN_NAME, "dummy test data");
        resolver.insert(uri, values);
    }

    private void retrieveFromDummyProvider(Context context) {
        ContentResolver resolver = context.getContentResolver();

        String s = String.format("content://%s", AUTHORITY);
        Uri uri = Uri.parse(s);
        Cursor cursor = resolver.query(uri, null, null, null, null);

        // TODO do something more meaningful
        cursor.moveToLast();
        String key = cursor.getString(0);
        String value = cursor.getString(1);
        String mimeType = resolver.getType(uri);
        String txt = String.format("%s-%s \n(MIME: %s)", key, value, mimeType);

        Toast.makeText(context, txt, Toast.LENGTH_LONG).show();
    }
}
```

2. Build and run the AppComponents project to see the code in action.
   Figure 5-5 shows the content inserted and the data retrieved via our content provider.

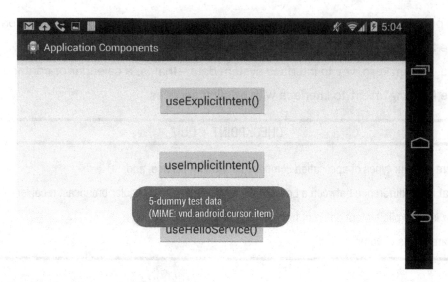

Figure 5-5. HelloBroadcastReceiver use ContentProvider

Both `HelloContentProvider` and the calling client code all run in the same app/process, simply for convenience purposes. `HelloContentProvider` can be accessed the same way from any external app.

> **Note**   To interface with the content provider from system or third parties, get the URI and authorities from the developer. You just need to know the access protocol from the provider.

Summary

I consider the topics in this chapter to be relatively advanced for iOS developers because the vocabularies and concepts do not exist in the iOS development environment. Almost always, your iOS apps are GUI apps that naturally get translated to Android activity and fragments that are not the focus of this chapter. The other three application components and intent matching rules are fairly new. You may be able to relate an iOS concept, but the XML attributes and the programming syntax are just different.

You probably don't need to create your own service or content provider for porting your iOS apps. I was able to work without them to port my iOS GUI apps for a long time. This is very different from previous chapters, in which you found good mappings between iOS and Android.

But the time will come to appreciate these unique Android features; the topics in this chapter naturally came to me eventually. A big thumbs-up to you for getting here. I have to say you are in a better position than I was because you know these unique Android components now, and when these Android components come to you later, you naturally will have a better grip.

Let me single out some topics on porting iOS apps that I think you might encounter more frequently:

- Use `LocalBroadcastManager` in the same way as iOS `NSNotificationCenter`.
- Use `ContentResolver` to interface system data—that is, a calendar or contacts.
- Use `PendingIntent` to interface with existing services.

CHECKPOINT + QUIZ

1. There are four types of application components: activity, service, and ...?
2. What is the difference between a LocalBroadcastManager and a regular broadcast receiver?
3. How is an explicit intent different from an implicit intent?

All the answers are in this chapter.

Chapter 6

Android Application Resources

In Chapter 2, we briefly mentioned *application resources* without getting into implementation details. This is actually a very important topic because it is how Android addresses a well-known mobile issue: *device fragmentation*. Comparing this to the iOS platform, the magnitude of the issue is larger because there are more manufacturers that produce different devices with various configurations in terms of form factors, capacities, and so forth. To reach most users and make sure your apps still look right on the various devices, you provide *alternative application resources* for the supported device configurations. By providing alternative application resources, the Android resource framework chooses the best fit based on the device configuration during application launch.

We are going to talk about all the application *resource types* first, followed by how to provide alternative application resources.

Resource Types

All the application resources should be located in $PROJ/res/ subfolders and separated by subfolder depending on the type. The ADT project templates create the resource subfolders for the most common application resources. Figure 6-1 shows them in the $PROJ/res/ subfolders.

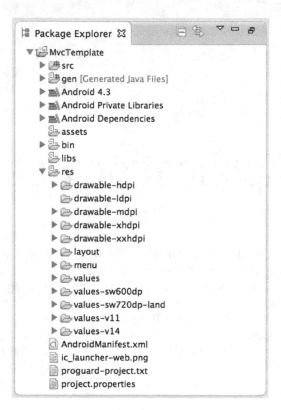

Figure 6-1. *Application resource folders*

Some application resources might not exist yet. These are optional ones for which you need to create a folder manually—with the right name.

You may need to create a resource folder yourself if it is not present. Different types of application resources have different syntactical rules that clearly define individual purposes and usages. They are all stored in the $PROJ/res folder but are separated by subfolders. The subfolders need to exactly match the names that are defined. As mentioned earlier, the ADT project creation template creates the folders for the common resource types. When you need to create a resource subfolder, you have to name it the right way.

The following subsections describe all the types of application resources. You have already been using some of them, such as view layout files and strings. Occasionally, you used drawables (images and video), animation resources, measurements, and so forth. Some of the following application resources might be new to an iOS developer, but it is worth your time to read them all.

String Resources

You have been creating and using *strings* in $PROJ/res/values/strings.xml. You actually also used a *string array* once. Just to refresh your memory, take a quick look at Listing 6-1, strings.xml, in your CommonWidgets project.

Listing 6-1. *string-array*

```
<?xml version="1.0" encoding="utf-8"?>
<resources>

    <string name="app_name">Common Widgets</string>
    <string name="action_settings">Settings</string>
    <string name="labelText">Simple text Label</string>

    ...
    <string-array name="spinnerItems">
        <item>Item 0</item>
        <item>Item 1</item>
        <item>Item 2</item>
        <item>Item 3</item>
        <item>Item 4</item>
    </string-array>
    ...
</resources>
```

In the Java code, you used getStringArray(R.array.spinnerItems) to get the string[] to use that string-array resource, as shown in Listing 6-2.

Listing 6-2. *getStringArray*

```
...
public View onCreateView(LayoutInflater inflater, ViewGroup container,
    Bundle savedInstanceState) {

    ...

    // datasource Adapter
    String[] datasource = getResources().getStringArray(R.array.spinnerItems);
```

The third type of string resource, called *quantity strings (plurals)*, is relatively less common. This one is used primarily for language translations. Words that are plural or express a quantity could have a different meaning when translated into a different language. For example, a *car* vs. *cars*, or *match* vs. *matches* in English. Some languages simply don't note the differences, whereas in other languages the differences are more complex. There are simple programmatical efforts you can take to work around this; Listing 6-3 offers a quick example. We will not use the quantity strings resource in this book.

Listing 6-3. *Plurals String Resource*

```
<?xml version="1.0" encoding="utf-8"?>
<resources>

    ...
    <plurals name="numOfPen">
        <item quantity="one">One pen is one dollar</item>
        <item quantity="other">%d pens are %d dollars</item>
    </plurals>
    ...

</resources>
```

In your Java code, you used getQuantityString(R.plurals.numOfPen, 2, 2, 2) to get the string based on the quantity: String numOfPen = getResources().getQuantityString(R.plurals.numOfPen, 2, 2, 2);

This could be a handy tool when you need to build a dynamic UI based on user input, such as a multilanguage shopping cart, although I rarely use this technique.

Drawable Resources

The most obvious type of Android *drawable resource* is the 2D graphic image, but an Android drawable resource is more than an image asset. It covers almost everything that can be drawn on screens or affects the drawing. Drawable resources should be saved in $PROJ/res/drawable/ folders. Just to name a few, the following are relatively commonplace to the beginner:

■ **Bitmap file**: This is the graphic image file. JPEG, GIF, PNG, and BMP formats are generally supported in most of the devices. The WebP format was introduced after Android 4.0.

■ **State list:** This is an XML file containing multiple state-related graphic images. It is very handy to highlight a widget in various states; for example, to show a button with a different background image when it is selected or in a different state, you define a *state list* that contains images for the states. The drawable_ withstates.xml file as shown in Listing 6-4 provides an example.

Listing 6-4. State List

```xml
<?xml version="1.0" encoding="utf-8"?>
<selector xmlns:android="http://schemas.android.com/apk/res/android">

  <item android:state_pressed="true" android:drawable="@drawable/pressed" />
  <item android:state_focused="true" android:drawable="@drawable/focused" />
  <item android:state_hovered="true" android:drawable="@drawable hovered" />
  <item android:state_selected="true" android:drawable="@drawable/selected" />
  <item android:state_checkable="true" android:drawable="@drawable/checkable" />
  <item android:state_checked="true" android:drawable="@drawable/checked" />
  <item android:state_enabled="true" android:drawable="@drawable/enabled" />
  <item android:state_activated="true" android:drawable="@drawable/activated" />
  <item android:drawable="@drawable/button_normal" /> <!-- default -->
</selector>
```

■ The XML file shown in Listing 6-4 creates a state list drawable that you can apply to a UI widget the same way that you use a regular bitmap drawable, as shown in Listing 6-5.

Listing 6-5. Use State List Drawable

```xml
<Button
    android:layout_height="wrap_content"
    android:layout_width="wrap_content"
    android:background="@drawable/drawable_withstates" />
```

> **Note**   Android simply chooses the first matched state from the XML file. You normally put the default at the end.

There are other types of drawable resources that aren't covered in this book. For your convenience, Table 6-1 lists all the types of drawable resources and includes a short description.

Table 6-1. *Drawable Resources*

Attribute	Description
Bitmap file	A bitmap graphic file (`.png`, `.jpg`, or `.gif`).
Nine-Patch file	A PNG file with stretchable regions to allow image resizing based on content (`.9.png`).
Layer list	A drawable that manages an array of other drawables. These are drawn in array order, so the element with the largest index is drawn on top.
State list	An XML file that references different bitmap graphics for different states (for example, to use a different image when a button is pressed).
Level list	An XML file that defines a drawable that manages a number of alternate drawables, each assigned a maximum numerical value.
Transition drawable	An XML file that defines a drawable that can cross-fade between two drawable resources.
Inset drawable	An XML file that defines a drawable that insets another drawable by a specified distance. This is useful when a view needs a background drawable that is smaller than the view's actual bounds.
Clip drawable	An XML file that defines a drawable that clips another drawable based on this drawable's current level value.
Scale drawable	An XML file that defines a drawable that changes the size of another drawable based on its current level value. Creates a `ScaleDrawable`.
Shape drawable	An XML file that defines a drawable that changes the shape of another drawable based on its current level value.
Color	A color resource can also be used as a drawable.

Layout and Menu Resources

You should be fairly familiar with the layout and menu resources by now: screens and menus are defined in XML files for Android GUI apps. A screen layout file is an application resource called a *layout resource*, and the files need to be saved in `$PRPJ/res/layout/` folders. To reference to the layout resources, you have used `R.layout.screenone_fragment` in your `ScreenOneFragment.java`; for example, in our MvcTemplate project (see Chapter 3).

Menu resources are similar to the layout resources that you have used many times, such as the CommonWidgets project for the menu system in Chapter 4. Menu layout files need to be saved in the `$PRPJ/res/menu/` folder.

Value Resource Types

In addition to those string texts, there are also *value types* that are used in layout files. They should also be defined as externalized application resources. For example, instead of hard-coding the padding, margins, or font size, you should externalize these values as appropriate application resources.

Bool and Integer Resources

A *boolean resource* defines `true` or `false` booleans. An *integer resource* defines integer values. They need to be saved in the `res/values/` folder. The name of the file is arbitrary. The usages are very similar to the string resource that you have been using many times. For example, in `CommonWidgets/res/layout/screenone_fragment.xml`, you could hard-code `android:checked="true"` for the `RadioButton` widget and `android:max="100"` for `ProgressBar`. A better way would be to define an external resource in the `res/values/` folder, as shown in Listing 6-6.

Listing 6-6. Boolean Resource

```
<?xml version="1.0" encoding="utf-8"?>
<resources>
    ...
    <bool name="radioBtnChecked">true</bool>
    <bool name="maxProgress">100</bool>
    ...
</resources>
```

> **Note** You actually can define the boolean resources or any value resources in the existing string.xml, although this doesn't sound right. You can create a specific file name for all the booleans, or maybe a generic file name for all the value types resources, such as res/values/booleans.xml or res/values/values.xml, as long as the file is in the res/values folder. Both are legitimate and the choice is yours.

Then, you can use that bool resource in `CommonWidgets/res/layout/screenone_fragment.xml`, as shown in Listing 6-7.

Listing 6-7. Use Boolean Resource

```
...
<RadioButton
  android:id="@+id/radio0"
  ...
  android:checked="@bool/radioBtnChecked" />
...
<ProgressBar
  android:id="@+id/progressBar2"
  ...
  android:max="@integer/maxProgress" />
```

To use the boolean or integer resources in your Java code, use the Java code as shown in Listing 6-8.

Listing 6-8. getInteger(…) and getBoolean(…)

```
// getResources is available in Fragment or Activity context
boolean b = getResources().getBoolean(R.bool.radioBtnChecked);
int i = getResources().getInteger(R.integer.maxProgress);
```

Color Resource

Colors are generally specified by RGB values with an alpha channel. In Android, you define color values in hex color codes in the following formats: #RGB, #ARGB, #RRGGBB, or #AARRGGBB (start with the pound (#) sign). Other than the resource identifier and the value format, most of the value type resources usages are similar. Listing 6-9 is an example of what you actually defined in the CommonWidget/res/values/strings.xml project file.

Listing 6-9. Color Resource

```
<?xml version="1.0" encoding="utf-8"?>
<resources>
    ...
    <color name="bgcolor">#33808080</color>
    ...
</resources>
```

In CommonWidgets/res/layout/screenone_fragment.xml, you used this color resource to assign the background of the whole screen, as shown in Listing 6-10.

Listing 6-10. Use Color Resource

```
<ScrollView xmlns:android="http://schemas.android.com/apk/res/android"
    android:layout_width="match_parent"
    android:layout_height="wrap_content" >

    <RelativeLayout
        android:id="@+id/layoutContainer"
        ...
        android:background="@color/bgcolor"
        ...
```

You can use Java code to get the color resource, as shown in Listing 6-11.

Listing 6-11. getColor(…)

```
// getResources is available in Fragment or Context
int color = getResources().getColor(R.color.bgcolor);
```

Dimension Resource

In layout files, as well as many other resources defined in XML files, many attributes are specified by a number and a unit, such 25dp. These values are called *dimension resources* and should be externalized in a resource file. Again, the usages are similar to other value types of resources, except the resource name identifier is <dimen>. They should be saved in the res/values/ folder, and the file name is arbitrary.

ADT project templates automatically create the res/values/dimens.xml file. That should be a strong hint that dimension resources are commonly used. Let's take a look at Listing 6-12, which shows how you defined them in CommonWidgets/res/values/dimens.xml.

Listing 6-12. *Dimension Resource*

```
<resources>

    <!-- Default screen margins, per the Android Design guidelines. -->
    <dimen name="activity_horizontal_margin">16dp</dimen>
    <dimen name="activity_vertical_margin">16dp</dimen>
    <dimen name="label_textsize">36dp</dimen>
    <dimen name="label_marginTop">90dp</dimen>
    <dimen name="button_marginEnd">20dp</dimen>
    <dimen name="borderPadding">3dp</dimen>

</resources>
```

Listing 6-13 shows how they are used in Common/res/layout/screenone_fragment.xml.

Listing 6-13. *Use Dimension Resource*

```
<?xml version="1.0" encoding="utf-8"?>
<ScrollView xmlns:android="http://schemas.android.com/apk/res/android"
    android:layout_width="match_parent"
    android:layout_height="wrap_content" >

    <RelativeLayout
        android:id="@+id/layoutContainer"
        ...
        android:padding="@dimen/borderPadding" >

        <!-- a very long content view -->

        <TextView
            android:id="@+id/textViewLabel"
            ...
            android:layout_marginBottom="@dimen/borderPadding"
            ... />
        ...
```

You can use Java code to get the dimension resource, as shown in Listing 6-14.

Listing 6- 14. Dimension Resource

```
// getResources is available in Fragment or Context
float dimen = getResources().getDimension(R.dimen.borderPadding);
```

Integer Array Resource

Similar to string-array (introduced in Listing 6-1), you define an integer array in a resource file that should be saved in the res/values/ folder. The file name is arbitrary, just like all other value types of app resources. The usages for all the value type app resources are similar. The resource type identifier name is <integer-array>.

Listing 6-15 shows an integer-array resource named luckNumbers.

Listing 6-15. integer-array Resource

```
<?xml version="1.0" encoding="utf-8"?>
<resources>

    ...

    <integer-array name="luckNumbers">
        <item>2</item>
        <item>5</item>
        <item>8</item>
    </integer-array>

</resources>
```

You can get the luckNumbers integer-array in your Java code, as shown in Listing 6-16.

Listing 6-16. getIntArray(...)

```
// getResources is available in Fragment or Context
int[] luckerNumbers = getResources().getIntArray(R.array.luckNumbers);
```

Color State List Resource

Syntactically and usage-wise, a *color state list resource* looks almost the same as a *drawable state list* resource. To understand the color usages, you can think of color as a color-only image resource in Android. In fact, almost all the UI widget attributes that you can specify as a bitmap resource also take a color resource. However, color and color state list resources need to be saved in the res/color/ folder. You may compare the following sample color list resource, res/color/color_ withstates.xml (see Listing 6-17), with the drawable state list resource (see Listing 6-4).

Listing 6-17. Color List Resource

```xml
<?xml version="1.0" encoding="utf-8"?>
<selector xmlns:android="http://schemas.android.com/apk/res/android">

  <item android:state_pressed="true" android:drawable="#ffff0000" />
  <item android:state_focused="true" android:drawable="#ffff1100" />
  <item android:state_hovered="true" android:drawable="#ffff2200" />
  <item android:state_selected="true" android:drawable="#ffff3300" />
  <item android:state_checkable="true" android:drawable="#ffff4400" />
  <item android:state_checked="true" android:drawable="#ffff5500" />
  <item android:state_enabled="true" android:drawable="#ffff6600" />
  <item android:state_activated="true" android:drawable="#ffff7700" />

  <item android:drawable="#ffff8800" /> <!-- default -->

</selector>
```

> **Note**   Do you see any difference? The only difference is using color code in the form of #AARRGGBB instead of a reference to bitmap resources. The matching rule is the same, too. Android chose the first matched item, which means that you almost always want to put the default color last in the list.

To use the preceding color state list resource, you can use the same sample code shown in Listing 6-18.

Listing 6-18. Use Color List Resource

```xml
<Button
    android:layout_height="wrap_content"
    android:layout_width="wrap_content"
    android:background="@drawable/color_withstates" />
```

Animation Resources

In Chapter 4 you used animation resources to create

- *Property animations*, which are saved in the $PROJ/res/animator/ folder.
- *View animations*, which are saved in the $PROJ/res/anim/ folder.

The *view animations* actually have two types. The one you used to create a screen animation effect is called a *tween animation*. A *frame animation* is the other type of view animation. You define the images in order in an XML file called an *animation drawable*. For example, you can create a frame animation resource in $PROJ/res/drawable/sample_frames.xml, as shown in Listing 6-19.

Listing 6-19. *Frame Animation Resource*

```
<animation-list xmlns:android="http://schemas.android.com/apk/res/android"
    android:oneshot="false">

  <item android:drawable="@drawable/ani00342" android:duration="100" />
  <item android:drawable="@drawable/ani00343" android:duration="100" />
  <item android:drawable="@drawable/ani00344" android:duration="100" />
  <item android:drawable="@drawable/ani00345" android:duration="100" />
  <item android:drawable="@drawable/ani00346" android:duration="100" />
  <item android:drawable="@drawable/ani00347" android:duration="100" />
  <item android:drawable="@drawable/ani00348" android:duration="100" />
  <item android:drawable="@drawable/ani00349" android:duration="100" />
  <item android:drawable="@drawable/ani00350" android:duration="100" />

</animation-list>
```

You use the frame animation resource just like the tween animation (see Listing 6-20).

Listing 6-20. *Use Frame Animation Resource*

```
ImageView ivSample = (ImageView) contentView.findViewById(R.id.ivSample);
ivSample.setImageResource(R.drawable.sample_frames);

AnimationDrawable sampleAnim = (AnimationDrawable) ivSample.getBackground();
sampleAnim.start();
```

> **Animated GIF Tip**   Both iOS and Android do not support animated GIFs. The frame animation is an easy choice for short animations that behave like animated GIFs. You do want to watch out for memory usage, though.

Style Resource

As you have been specifying the UI attributes defined in the layout files, you may have noticed that many attributes are interrelated and used consistently. This happens for a good reason; for example, when you want to use the same set of colors consistently across the app. If one color changes, you might want to change another color consistently. It is also preferable that you make the changes in one place, instead of changing all the attributes in different layout files.

This is when the *style resource* comes to the rescue. Instead of specifying the values in every individual UI widget attribute in every layout file, you specify the values of the widget attributes in style resource files. Consequently, you don't need to specify the widget attributes on the individual widget anymore, and the layout files become more compact with fewer attributes explicitly defined.

> **Note**   The best analogy is probably the HTML CSS file.

You can define a style resource for only one UI widget or for all the widgets in your app. All you do is specify the style resource on the widget android:style attribute, or specify the style resource on the application or activity android:theme attribute.

Style resources are saved in the res/values/ folder. The file name is arbitrary but it is conventionally named styles.xml. Before we create our custom style resource, let's look at how you have been using the system style. Recall all the buttons you have created; you did not specify any color, but they all rendered in a grayish color (for example, see Figure 5-5). Where is the gray color coming from? Apparently, the ADT project creation Blank Activity template defines a style resource named AppTheme in the res/values/styles.xml file. AppBaseTheme is the parent of AppTheme, which is inherited from a system theme called Theme.AppCompat.Light, as shown in Listing 6-21.

Listing 6-21. styles.xml

```
<resources>

    <!--
        Base application theme, dependent on API level. This theme is replaced
        by AppBaseTheme from res/values-vXX/styles.xml on newer devices.
    -->
    <style name="AppBaseTheme" parent="Theme.AppCompat.Light">
        <!--
            Theme customizations available in newer API levels can go in
            res/values-vXX/styles.xml, while customizations related to
            backward-compatibility can go here.
        -->
    </style>

    <!-- Application theme. -->
    <style name="AppTheme" parent="AppBaseTheme">
        <!-- All customizations that are NOT specific to a particular API-level can go here. -->
    </style>

</resources>
```

Furthermore, the application AndroidManifest.xml file specifies android:theme="@style/AppTheme", which defines the default attributes for the whole app (see Listing 6-22).

Listing 6-22. Application android:theme

```
<?xml version="1.0" encoding="utf-8"?>
<manifest ... >
    ...
    <application
        ...
        android:theme="@style/AppTheme" >

        ...
    </application>
</manifest>
```

The manifest application android:theme attribute is mandatory and serves the default values of all the attributes for all the widgets. This is why your widgets have certain attributes specified, even if you did not specify them. This is an important topic. Let's do some hands-on exercises.

ADT PROJECT PREPARATIONS

Let's just reuse the existing CommonWidgets project.

---

1. Modify the res/values/styles.xml file, as shown in Listing 6-23, to create your own custom style just for Button widgets. Although it only affects Button widgets in the app, the principles of how to create style are the same:

    a. You can specify the new style for all the buttons in the theme.

    b. You can also specify the new style for a given button; for example: <Button android:style="@style/myButton"...>

Listing 6-23. Custom Button Style

```
<resources>

    ...
    <!-- Application theme. -->
    <style name="AppTheme" parent="AppBaseTheme">
        <!-- All customizations that are NOT specific to a particular API-level can go here. -->
        <item name="android:buttonStyle">@style/myButton</item>
    </style>

    <style name="myButton">
        <item name="android:textSize">50sp</item>
        <item name="android:textColor">@android:color/white</item>
        <item name="android:background">#008</item>
    </style>

</resources>
```

You may build and run the app to see the new look of your custom buttons.

We have already talked about all the Android resource types. Again, they need to reside in a specific folder, as shown in Table 6-2.

Table 6-2. Resource Type Folders

Resource Type	Folder and Resource ID
Property animation	res/animator/filename.xml The file name will be used as the resource ID.
Tween animation	res/anim/filename.xml The file name will be used as the resource ID.
Frame animation	res/drawable/filename.xml The file name will be used as the resource ID.
Color state list	res/color/filename.xml The file name will be used as the resource ID.
Drawable: Bitmap, state list, etc.	res/drawable/filename The file name is used as the resource ID.
Layout	res/layout/filename.xml The file name will be used as the resource ID.
Menu	res/menu/filename.xml The file name will be used as the resource ID.
String: simple string, string array, or quantity strings	res/values/filename.xml The file name is arbitrary (strings.xml, conventionally). The element's name will be used as the resource ID.
Style	res/values/filename.xml The file name is arbitrary (styles.xml conventionally). The element's name will be used as the resource ID.
Miscellaneous value types: Bool, integer, dimension, color, integer, integer array, etc.	res/values/filename.xml The file name is arbitrary. The element's name will be used as the resource ID.

Some specific subtopics might seem off the porting topic. Particularly, the style resource wasn't easy for me to learn because I wasn't familiar with HTML CSS. However, I never had any problem with porting the iOS widgets to Android. Looking at that old code, I think it could have been implemented in a more efficient fashion if I had known how to create and apply style resources. As long as you know the concept now, I am sure this won't stop you from writing working Android code.

Configuration Qualifiers

IOS ANALOGY

iPad storyboard vs. iPhone storyboard file for iOS universal apps.

_2x assets files for Retina display.

In iOS, you need to create an iPad-specific storyboard for iPad, primarily due to the larger screen size. In Android, layout files are equivalent to the iOS storyboard, and you do the same: create a set of layout files for the Android tablet screen. The concept of supporting different device configurations is actually the same as iOS, just with different terminologies. The different set of layout files for Android are called *alternative resources*. You also provide higher resolution images for the tablet version. The image assets are also a common type of Android application resource.

Thinking more broadly, you provide alternative resources not only for screen size or pixel density in Android, you do so for any specific device configuration as well. The Android device configurations are identified by configuration qualifiers. Please glance through the list of Android configuration qualifiers listed in Table A-4 (in the Appendix of this book) to get a feel for the Android device configurations that I am talking about here. Some are typical, like screen size and screen density, which you can immediately relate to your iOS experience. Some just make sense, like language. Some of them are fairly interesting and I really want to try them out some day, like night mode.

> **Note**   There are many Android configuration qualifiers. The possible device configuration combinations are mathematically huge. Do you realize the possible magnitude of device fragmentation issues in Android programming? There is no practical way to supply all the alternative resources. You just need to be smart about choosing the configuration qualifiers you want to support to have the best agnostic UX for your target users.

The concept is actually very simple. Create alternative resources and save them in appropriate *alternative resource folders* that can be identified by a configuration qualifier. This is achieved through the following naming rules:

```
$PROJ/res/<resource type folder>-<configuration_qualifier>/same_filename
```

- `<resource type folder>`: Recall that resources need to be saved in the appropriate folder (see Table 6-2).

- `<configuration_qualifier>`: You need to use the values of the configuration qualifiers listed in Table A-4 (in the Appendix).

It is even easier to show you through a practical example, that is the well-known I18N topic. In the next section, let's go through the steps that you normally follow.

Internationalization

In Android, Language and Region is a type of device configuration that can be identified by appropriate *configuration identifiers*. A quick look at configuration qualifiers (Table A-4) in this book's Appendix shows that the language is defined by a two-letter ISO 639-1 language code, optionally followed by a two-letter country code preceded by a lowercase "r", such as en-rUS.

ADT PROJECT PREPARATIONS

Same as usual, use the MvcTemplate project to create a new ADT project.

1. Copy MvcTemplate ADT project and paste it to a new project (⌘c, ⌘v) named **I18N**.

2. Rename the Android application package. From the newly created I18N project context menu, select **Android Tools ➤ Rename Application Package**: Enter a new package name: **com.pdachoice.i18n**.

3. Rename the I18N/src/com.pdachoice.renameme Java package. From the package context menu, select **Refactor ➤ Rename...** (Alt+⌘r) and do the following:

   a. Enter a new name: **com.pdachoice.i18n**.

   b. Select **Update references**.

The brand-new ADT project should give you a clean start.

Continue the following steps to internationalize the ADT project in Spanish, French, and Chinese by providing alternative resources for each language, respectively.

1. This first step should have been done already. I just want to emphasize that you need to externalize the string texts as string resources. Meaning, instead of hard-coding the strings in Java source code or other application resource files, you define all the strings text as string resources in the `$PROJ/res/values/strings.xml` file.

2. Copy and paste the whole `$PROJ/res/values/` folder to create a `$PROJ/res/values-es/` folder for Spanish, a `$PROJ/res/values-fr/` folder for French, and a `$PROJ/res/values-zh/` folder for Chinese. The `es`, `fr`, and `zh` are the configuration qualifiers for languages. The three new folders and the `res/values` folder should contain the same files as those shown in Figure 6-2.

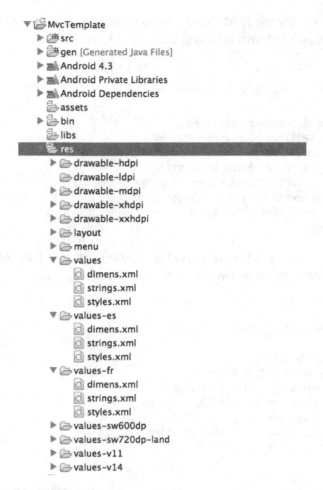

Figure 6-2. *Language configuration qualifiers*

3. Translate and modify the $PROJ/res/values-es/strings.xml file for the Spanish language, as shown in Listing 6-24.

Listing 6- 24. *Spanish Texts*

```xml
<?xml version="1.0" encoding="utf-8"?>
<resources>
    <string name="app_name">Renombrar</string>
    <string name="action_settings">Configuración</string>
    <string name="hello_world">¡Hola, mundo!</string>
    <string name="label_screenone">Página uno</string>
    <string name="label_screentwo">Página dos</string>
    <string name="label_screenthree">Página tres</string>
    <string name="button_next">próximo</string>
</resources>
```

4. Translate and modify the `$PROJ/res/values-fr/strings.xml` file for the French language, as shown in Listing 6-25.

Listing 6-25. *French Texts*

```xml
<?xml version="1.0" encoding="utf-8"?>
<resources>
    <string name="app_name">renommez</string>
    <string name="action_settings">réglages</string>
    <string name="hello_world">Bonjour tout le monde!</string>
    <string name="label_screenone">écran une</string>
    <string name="label_screentwo">deux écrans</string>
    <string name="label_screenthree">trois écrans</string>
    <string name="button_next">Ensuite</string>
</resources>
```

5. Translate and modify the `$PROJ/res/values-zh/strings.xml` file for the Chinese language, as shown in Listing 6-26.

Listing 6-26. *Chinese Texts*

```xml
<?xml version="1.0" encoding="utf-8"?>
<resources>
    <string name="app_name">重命名</string>
    <string name="action_settings">設置</string>
    <string name="hello_world">世界,你好!</string>
    <string name="label_screenone">第一個屏幕</string>
    <string name="label_screentwo">第二個屏幕</string>
    <string name="label_screenthree">最後屏幕</string>
    <string name="button_next">下一個</string>
</resources>
```

6. Optionally, you can safely delete the `dimens.xml` and `styles.xml` from the language-specific alternative resource folders since you are not going to provide alternative measurements or styles. You should when you need to, however. You simply give alternative values in these files for language- or locale-specific qualifiers, respectively, just like you did for string texts.

Note   Android applies the best-match policy to choose an appropriate resource, which means that as long as it is in the res/values/ folder, the resources will be used. Or, you can say the original resources will be inherited if not overridden.

7. Create a `$PROJ/res/drawable-es/` folder for Spanish, a `$PROJ/res/drawable-fr/` folder for French, and a `$PROJ/res/drawable-zh/` folder for Chinese-specific images or drawables.

8. `ic_launcher.png` is the launch icon. It also appears as the app icon on the action bar. Create and put the languages-specific `ic_launcher.png` image files into the folders mentioned in step 7, respectively.

Note   You can download the aforementioned icons (see Figure 6-3) from the following links. Make sure to rename them as ic_launcher.png exactly where they are located in the correct folders and with appropriate configuration qualifiers.

http://pdachoice.com/me/res/ic_launcher_fr.png

http://pdachoice.com/me/res/ic_launcher_fr.png

http://pdachoice.com/me/res/ic_launcher_zh.png

Figure 6-3. Launch icons

Let's run the app now. It should look exactly the same as it was before, unless your Android device language is already set to Español, Français, or Chinese. To see the app in these languages, change the language in the system Settings app, as follows:

- On a newer device, select **Languages & input ➤ Language ➤ Español**.
- On an older device, select **Language & Keyboard ➤ Select locale ➤ Español**.

Caution   Your entire phone, including the Settings app, will appear in Español. To find your way back to English, remember what the language icon in the Settings app looks like, in case you cannot read Español.

Relaunch the app. You should see it showing language-specific strings and icons (see Figure 6-4).

Figure 6-4. *Internationalized I18N app*

In general, texts, images with texts, sounds, and videos are common targets for I18N. Some UI widgets or layouts might also need to be adjusted. You want to externalize the measurements and provide alternative values in alternative application resource files when needed. You can also choose to provide alternative layout files when it makes sense. Layout is a type of application resource as well.

MULTIPLE SCREEN SUPPORT

Multiple screen support is another common task that requires alternative application resources. There are three types of screen configurations: *screen size*, *orientation,* and *screen density*, with priority in the listed order. You can compound multiple qualifiers together in one directory name by separating each qualifier with a dash and listed in order of precedence (see Table A-4 in the Appendix). For example, the `res/drawable-large-land-mdpi/` folder would provide the image assets for devices with a large screen, in landscape mode, and with MDPI screen resolution. It is also possible that multiple alternative application resources match the device configuration. Although Android makes the best match based on the same precedence, design your alternative application resource wisely to avoid confusion.

The following link from the official Android Developers site provides general guidelines to support multiple screens:

`http://developer.android.com/guide/practices/screens_support.html`

In my opinion, supporting multiple screens is probably one of the most practical and important usages of alternative application resources, other than I18N. If you don't read it now, you might want to bookmark it for future reference because you will want to reach the most users.

Summary

Conceptually, Android and iOS both use naming rules to manage different sets of assets used by apps with different device configurations. However, I think the rules defined in the Android SDK are more complete than iOS; I think it is this way because the possible Android device configurations are much greater than the current iOS device configurations.

Please allow me to repeat the following to close this chapter.

The concept is actually very simple. Create alternative resources and save them in appropriate alternative resource folders that can be identified by configuration qualifiers. This is achieved by the following naming rules:

`$PROJ/res/`**`<resource type folder>`**`-`**`<configuration_qualifier>`**`/same_filename`

- `<resource type folder>`: Recall that resources need to be saved in the appropriate folder (see Table 6-2).
- `<configuration_qualifier>`: You need to use the specific values of the configuration qualifiers listed in Table A-4 (located in this book's Appendix).

Lastly and practically, always consider agnostic UX designs and evaluate the level of effort needed to create all possible alternative application resources.

CHECKPOINT + QUIZ

1. The types of resources are layout, strings, drawables, value types, and ???

2. The alternative resource folder naming rule is `res/<resource type folder>-<????>`

3. How do you implement I18N?

You should remember I18N implementation because you did the hands-on exercise.

Chapter 7

Common Mobile Use Cases

If you have been creating apps for a while, you naturally find many repeatable patterns or use cases. This is no exception on mobile platforms. In this chapter, we will cover the following common use cases in the Android platform:

- Hybrid apps
- Use system apps
- Mobile search
- Map and location awareness
- Mobile analytics

These are all independent topics that have no dependencies to each other. I find them popular and widely used in many mobile apps nowadays.

Hybrid Apps: Embedded Browsers

You can display rich HTML content in your mobile apps on almost all the popular mobile platforms, including iOS, Android, Blackberry, and Windows Phones. This enables you to deliver web content as part of your mobile apps. A common usage scenario is when you want to provide information in your app that needs to be updated frequently, and you want to host the content online as a web page. To take it one step further, the web content does not have to be remote. You can bundle the web page content with the native app. This enables web developers to leverage their web development skills and create so-called *hybrid apps*.

With new features from HTML5 and CSS3, many web developers are creating many meaningful and interactive web apps that are shortening the gaps between native apps and mobile web apps. There are many so-called cross-platform compilers that convert web pages into native apps. Most of these tools are leveraging the platform-specific *embedded browser* in SDK to interpret HTML pages and JavaScript code, for example, the popular PhoneGap or the Apache Cordova platform. Thus far, I still think it is generally better to let mobile web pages live in system browsers. Web developers probably don't agree with my opinion. ☺ One thing is for sure, however, the embedded browser is still a very useful element for both iOS and Android, and it continues to evolve in better ways. You do want to keep your eyes on it.

The iOS app at `http://pdachoice.com/me/webview/` uses a `UIWebView` to load a URL.

It has a `UIToolbar` that contains four buttons: *Back*, *Forward*, *Home*, and *About Me*. You are going to create an ADT project that has the same basic browser features. The Android embedded browser widget is more open than the iOS `UIWebView` and you can actually do more interesting stuff with it, as shown in Figure 7-1.

Figure 7-1. iOS HybridApp

```
┌──────────────────────────────────────────────────────────────┐
│                    ADT PROJECT PREPARATIONS                    │
└──────────────────────────────────────────────────────────────┘
```

As usual, let's prepare an ADT project using our MvcTemplate project for the Android version of the HybridApp application.

1. Copy the MvcTemplate ADT project and paste it into a new project (⌘c, ⌘v) named **HybridApp**.

2. Rename the Android application package. From the newly created HybridApp project context menu, select **Android Tools ➤ Rename Application Package**. Enter a new package name: **com.pdachoice.hybridapp**.

3. Rename the Hybrid/src/com.pdachoice.renameme Java package. From the package context menu, select **Refactor ➤ Rename ...** (Alt+⌘r) and do the following:

    a. Enter a new name: **com.pdachoice.hybridapp**.

    b. Select **Update references**.

4. Modify res/values/strings.xml, as shown in Listing 7-1. You will need to add some text, as shown in the iOS app screenshots in Figure 7-1.

    Listing 7-1. *Hybrid App Strings*

    ```xml
    <?xml version="1.0" encoding="utf-8"?>
    <resources>

        <string name="app_name">Hybrid App</string>
        <string name="optionMenuBack">Back</string>
        <string name="optionMenuForward">Forward</string>
        <string name="optionMenuHome">Home</string>
        <string name="optionMenuMe">Me</string>

    </resources>
    ```

5. We only need one fragment: keep ScreenOneFragment and delete the other two.

    a. Delete the src/ScreenTwoFragment.java and src/ScreenThreeFragment.java classes (multiselect and fn+Delete).

    b. Delete the res/layout/screentwo_fragment.xml and res/layout/screenthree_fragment.xml files (fn+Delete).

6. Modify res/layout/screenone_fragment.xml (see Listing 7-2). You don't need anything in it yet.

    Listing 7-2. *screenone Layout File*

    ```xml
    <?xml version="1.0" encoding="utf-8"?>
    <RelativeLayout xmlns:android="http://schemas.android.com/apk/res/android"
        android:layout_width="match_parent"
        android:layout_height="match_parent" >

    </RelativeLayout>
    ```

7. Delete the code related to the nextButton from src/ScreenOneFragment.java (see Listing 7-3).
    It was deleted from the layout file already.

Listing 7-3. *ScreenOneFragment.java*

```java
public class ScreenOneFragment extends Fragment {
  private View contentView;

  @Override
  public View onCreateView(LayoutInflater inflater, ViewGroup container,
      Bundle savedInstanceState) {
    contentView = inflater.inflate(R.layout.screenone_fragment, container,
        false);

    return contentView;
  }
}
```

8. To translate the four UIBarButtonItem buttons, use action items in the action bar.

    a. You need to drag two image files, home.png and home.png, into the res/drawable-mdpi/folder
        for the **Home** button and the **Me** button. You can download the images from
        http://pdachoice.com/me/res/32/home.png and http://pdachoice.com/me/res/32/me.png.

    b. Modify the res/menu/main.xml (see Listing 7-4) to provide the menu resource.

Listing 7-4. *Hybrid App Action Items*

```xml
<menu xmlns:android="http://schemas.android.com/apk/res/android"
    xmlns:app="http://schemas.android.com/apk/res-auto" >

    <item
        android:id="@+id/actionBack"
        android:icon="@android:drawable/ic_media_previous"
        app:showAsAction="always"
        android:title="@string/optionMenuBack"/>
    <item
        android:id="@+id/actionMe"
        android:icon="@drawable/me"
        app:showAsAction="always"
        android:title="@string/optionMenuMe"/>
    <item
        android:id="@+id/actionHome"
        android:icon="@drawable/home"
        app:showAsAction="always"
        android:title="@string/optionMenuHome"/>
    <item
```

```
            android:id="@+id/actionFwd"
            android:icon="@android:drawable/ic_media_next"
            app:showAsAction="always"
            android:title="@string/optionMenuForward"/>
</menu>
```

9. Enable the fragment options menu, load the menu resource, and handle the options menu items events in the appropriate fragment lifecycle callbacks (see Listing 7-5).

Listing 7-5. Inflate Options Menu

```java
public class ScreenOneFragment extends Fragment implements  {
    ...
    @Override
    public View onCreateView(LayoutInflater inflater, ViewGroup container,
        Bundle savedInstanceState) {
      ...
      // Options Menu
      setHasOptionsMenu(true); // need to enable it explicitly
      ...
    }

    @Override
    public void onCreateOptionsMenu(Menu menu, MenuInflater inflater) {
        super.onCreateOptionsMenu(menu, inflater);
        inflater.inflate(R.menu.main, menu);
    }

    @Override
    public boolean onOptionsItemSelected(MenuItem item) {
      Log.d("MainActivity", "onOptionsItemSelected: " + item.getItemId());
      // TODO
      return super.onOptionsItemSelected(item);
    }
    ...
}
```

10. Unless you are using WebView to load pages from local files, most likely your WebView element needs to access the Internet. You need to let users know by declaring the uses-permission in the manifest file. Modify the AndroidManifest.xml file to add the uses-permission (see Listing 7-6). Users will see the requests when installing the app from the Google Play Store.

Listing 7-6. *Declare INTERNET uses-permission*

```
<manifest ... >
    ...
    <uses-permission android:name="android.permission.INTERNET" />
    ...
</manifest>
```

> **Note**   By default, a basic Android application has no permissions associated with it. To allow app use on the
> Internet, declare "android.permission.INTERNET" permission in the manifest file. When users download the
> app from Google Play Store, they will see the list of permissions required by the app. Users need to accept
> the permission request to install the app.

11. Build and run the ADT project, just to make sure it is good. The Android app should display a screen
     with options menu only. This gives us a clean start.

WebView

IOS ANALOGY

UIWebView

The embedded browser in Android SDK is called WebView. We will use it to load a web page, just like
you use UIWebView to load a URL in an iOS app. To show and to learn by example, continue with the
ADT HybridApp project, doing the following:

1. Add the WebView widget to res/layout/screenone_fragment.xml (see Listing 7-7).

Listing 7-7. *WebView Widget*

```
<?xml version="1.0" encoding="utf-8"?>
<RelativeLayout xmlns:android="http://schemas.android.com/apk/res/android"
    android:layout_width="match_parent"
    android:layout_height="match_parent" >

    <WebView
        android:id="@+id/webView"
        android:layout_width="match_parent"
        android:layout_height="match_parent" />

</RelativeLayout>
```

2. Call `WebView.loadUrl(...)` to load a page (see Listing 7-8).

Listing 7-8. loadUrl

```java
public class ScreenOneFragment extends Fragment {
  private View contentView;
  private WebView mWebView;

  @Override
  public View onCreateView(LayoutInflater inflater, ViewGroup container,
      Bundle savedInstanceState) {
    ...
    // WebView ...
    mWebView = (WebView) contentView.findViewById(R.id.webView);
    mWebView.loadUrl("http://pdachoice.com/me/webview/index.html");

    return contentView;
  }
  ...
}
```

> **Note** WebView can load contents from a remote or local file using URL notations. You can also load from an HTML string using loadData(...), for example:
>
> webView.loadUrl("http://pdachoice.com/me/");
>
> webView.loadUrl("file:///android_res/drawable/pdachoice.html");
>
> webView.loadData("<html>Hello Android</html>", "text/html", null);

3. By default, a `WebView` provides no browser-like widgets. It does not enable JavaScript and web page errors are ignored. If your goal is only to display static HTML as a part of your UI, Listing 7-8 would be just fine. However, due to the popularity of JavaScript in mobile web development, most likely you want to enable the JavaScript via the `WebSettings` object (see Listing 7-9). The sample page contains JavaScript in it.

Listing 7-9. WebView WebSettings

```java
public class ScreenOneFragment extends Fragment {
  ...
  @Override
  public View onCreateView(LayoutInflater inflater, ViewGroup container,
      Bundle savedInstanceState) {
    ...

    // WebView ...
```

```
    ...
    WebSettings webSettings = mWebView.getSettings();
    webSettings.setJavaScriptEnabled(true);

    return contentView;
  }
  ...
}
```

4. Create and set a `WebChromeClient` subclass. This class is called when something that might impact a browser UI happens; for instance, progress updates and JavaScript alerts are sent here. Set up the `WebChromeClient` and override the `onProgressChanged(...)` to receive `WebView` rendering progress callbacks (see Listing 7-10).

Listing 7-10. WebChromeClient

```
public class ScreenOneFragment extends Fragment {
  private View contentView;
  private WebView mWebView;

  @Override
  public View onCreateView(LayoutInflater inflater, ViewGroup container,
      Bundle savedInstanceState) {
    ...
    // WebView ...
    ...
    WebChromeClient webChromeClient = new WebChromeClient() {
      @Override
      public void onProgressChanged(WebView view, int progress) {
        // TODO: show page loading progress
      }
    };

    mWebView.setWebChromeClient(webChromeClient);

    return contentView;
  }
  ...
}
```

5. Create and set a `WebViewClient` subclass (see Listing 7-11). The `WebView` page load lifecycle events are called when something impacts the rendering of the content, such as errors or form submissions.

Listing 7-11. WebViewClient

```
public class ScreenOneFragment extends Fragment {
  private View contentView;
  private WebView mWebView;

  @Override
```

```
public View onCreateView(LayoutInflater inflater, ViewGroup container,
    Bundle savedInstanceState) {
  ...
  // WebView ...
  ...
  WebViewClient webViewClient = new WebViewClient() {
    @Override
    public void onReceivedError(WebView view, int errorCode,
        String description, String failingUrl) {
      Toast.makeText(getActivity(), "Error!" + description,
        Toast.LENGTH_SHORT).show();
    }
  };
  mWebView.setWebViewClient(webViewClient);

  return contentView;
}
...
}
```

6. Figure 7-2 shows the basic WebView usage. You may build and run the app to
    visualize how the app looks now.

Figure 7-2. Android WebView

Activity Progress Indicator

IOS ANALOGY

[UIApplication sharedApplication].networkActivityIndicator

When loading content or web pages from a remote server, you want to show users some visual indicator. Both the iOS and the Android platforms provide a system visual indicator for this purpose. In Android, you can use the *activity progress indicator* system feature, which is a horizontal progress bar on top of the activity title bar.

To show the WebView page-loading progress using this system feature, do the following:

1. This system feature must be enabled before setting the activity content view. You can do it in the activity onCreate(...) callback before setContentView(...), as shown in Listing 7-12.

    Listing 7-12. requestWindowFeature

    ```java
    public class MainActivity extends ActionBarActivity {

        @Override
        protected void onCreate(Bundle savedInstanceState) {
            super.onCreate(savedInstanceState);
            requestWindowFeature(Window.FEATURE_PROGRESS);

            // setup the content view.
            setContentView(R.layout.activity_main);
            ...
        }
        ...
    }
    ```

2. After the feature is enabled, call Activity.setProgress(...) to show the progress. To show the WebView loading progress, you can call it in the WebChromeClient.OnProgressChanged(...) callback (see Listing 7-13).

    Listing 7-13. Activity.setProgress(...)

    ```java
    public class ScreenOneFragment extends Fragment {
        ...
        @Override
        public View onCreateView(LayoutInflater inflater, ViewGroup container,
            Bundle savedInstanceState) {
            ...
            // WebView ...

            ...
            WebChromeClient webChromeClient = new WebChromeClient() {
    ```

```
        @Override
        public void onProgressChanged(WebView view, int progress) {
          getActivity().setProgress(progress * 100);
        }
      };
      ...
    }
    ...
  }
```

While the progress value from the callback ranges from 0 to 100, the valid ranges of the system progress bar are from 0 to 10,000. If 10,000 is reached, the progress bar is completely filled and fades out.

You may build and run the app to visualize your hard work.

WebView Page Navigation

When an HTTP link in your WebView is clicked, the system default web browser opens and loads the destination URL. The external web browser becomes the active app. Quite frequently, you want to keep your users in your app by loading the selected HTTP links in your WebView. This is another reason you want to setWebViewClient(...) with your own WebViewClient instance.

1. Provide a WebViewClient object for your WebView. Previously, you did so to receive the onReceivedError(...) callback (see Listing 7-11).

Note   We only override the WebViewClient.onReceivedError(...) callback method. There are more things you can achieve by overriding others. For more details, see Javadoc at

http://developer.android.com/reference/android/webkit/WebViewClient.html.

---

2. The WebView widget doesn't have those standard browser UI controls. It is the developer's responsibility to provide any UI controls. After you hook with your UI controls, you can simply call the WebView methods to complete those common browser behaviors. The code in Listing 7-14 simply implements these controls in the options menu.

    a. To go back to the previous page, use WebView.goBack().

    b. To go forward, use WebView.goForward().

    c. To reload the current page, use WebView.reload().

Listing 7-14. WebView Navigation API

```java
public class ScreenOneFragment extends Fragment {
  ...
  @Override
  public boolean onOptionsItemSelected(MenuItem item) {
    Log.d("MainActivity", "onOptionsItemSelected: " + item.getItemId());

    switch (item.getItemId()) {
    case R.id.actionBack:
      doGoBack();
      break;
    case R.id.actionFwd:
      doGoForward();
      break;
    case R.id.actionHome:
      // TODO
      break;
    case R.id.actionMe:
      // TODO
      break;
    default:
      break;
    }

    return super.onOptionsItemSelected(item);
  }

  // Go Back to previous page or reload
  private void doGoBack() {
    if (mWebView.canGoBack()) {
      mWebView.goBack();
    } else {
      mWebView.reload();
    }
  }

  // Go Forward or reload
  private void doGoForward() {
    if (mWebView.canGoForward()) {

      mWebView.goForward();
    } else {
      mWebView.reload();
    }
  }
}
```

3.   You may build and run the app to see your code in action.

Interface with JavaScript

For serious web developers using JavaScript to create interactive web apps, `WebView` provides a toll-free bridge to create mobile apps. `WebView` also allows native code to interface with JavaScript loaded with the web page. Both iOS and Android inject JavaScript code from the native code into the embedded browser. On the Android platform, you can also call native code from JavaScript code. Web developers normally feel it is easier to use their familiar development skills to create their web apps. Using this hybrid approach opens a different way to create mobile apps.

In general, I choose to design mobile web apps for a mobile browser, and I let native apps stay as native as possible—mainly for managing user expectations. There are definitely use cases and practical reasons for using the hybrid approach. As a real-life example, I had an iOS app that needed to display some charts. I did not have a reliable Objective-C library to draw these charts. Instead of implementing an Objective-C charting library myself, I chose to use `UIWebView` to render a web page using a JavaScript charting library. Best of all, I had a JavaScript guru help me out, and the solution works on both Android and iOS. I knew the performance would be slower, but overall, it worked just fine.

The so-called hybrid approach has gained a bit of attraction in recent years, but more on this is beyond the scope of this book. If you don't write JavaScript code, you may skip the rest of the hybrid app topics. JavaScript web developers will be naturally more excited about this topic. It is certainly a powerful tool with a lot of interesting potential. You should know the existence of this feature at the very least.

Let's continue the ADT HybridApp project with code for interfacing with JavaScript.

JavaScript Injection

```
                                IOS ANALOGY
```

UIWebView stringByEvaluatingJavascriptFromString

To call JavaScript functions from Android Java code, you simply inject JavaScript code into `WebView`. The following code shows a typical usage that invokes a JavaScript function from Android Java code:

1. Create a JavaScript function to be loaded with the web page. The sample URL, `http://pdachoice.com/me/webview/`, loads a JavaScript file, `myjs.js`, which has the JavaScript function, `showPage(...)` (see Listing 7-15).

   Listing 7-15. JavaScript showPage(...)

```
function showPage(arg) {
        var toPage, fromPage;

        if (arg == "pgme") {
                toPage = $("#pgme");
                fromPage = $("#pgHome");
```

```
        } else {
                fromPage = $("#pgme");
                toPage = $("#pgHome");
        }

        fromPage.fadeOut(0, function(e) {
                toPage.fadeIn();
        });
    }
```

2. To inject any JavaScript code, prefix the code with "javascript:". For example, when the native Home or Me action item is selected, use the injectJsCode(...) method to call the JavaScript function in Listing 7-15 to show a new page (see Listing 7-16).

Listing 7-16. *Inject JavaScript from Java*

```java
public class ScreenOneFragment extends Fragment {
  ...
  @Override
  public boolean onOptionsItemSelected(MenuItem item) {
    ...
    case R.id.actionHome:
      injectJsCode("showPage('pgHome')");
      break;
    case R.id.actionMe:
      injectJsCode("showPage('pgme')");
      break;
    ...
  }

  private void injectJsCode(String jsCode) {
    mWebView.loadUrl("Javascript:" + jsCode);
  }
  ...
}
```

The following is the only trick:

```
loadUrl("javascript:" + "<any Javascript code literally>").
```

WebView JavaScript Interface

IOS ANALOGY

Note It's not trivial in iOS, but it is still can be done in iOS. I will discuss it in my next iOS book. ☺

In WebView, you can also call your Android native Java code from your JavaScript code. The following code echoes the Android Toast when the $("#pgme") or $("#pgHome") web page is rendered:

1. Enable the WebView JavaScript interface support by adding your JavascriptInterface callback object (see Listing 7-17).

   Listing 7-17. Add JavascriptInterface Callback Object

   ```java
   public class ScreenOneFragment extends Fragment {
     ...
     @Override
     public View onCreateView(LayoutInflater inflater, ViewGroup container,
         Bundle savedInstanceState) {
       ...
       // WebView ...

       ...
       mWebView.addJavascriptInterface(new Object() {
         @JavascriptInterface
         public void showToast(String msg) {
           Toast.makeText(getActivity(), msg, Toast.LENGTH_SHORT).show();
         }
       }, "HybridApp");
       ...
     }
     ...
   }
   ```

Note The code in Listing 7-17 registers a Java callback object and injects a *JavaScript global variable* named HybridApp into WebView. This allows the Java object's methods to be accessible from JavaScript code via the JavaScript global variable, HybridApp.

---

2. From JavaScript code, you can invoke the Java native methods defined in the Java JavascriptInterface. Modify the JavaScript showPage(arg) function to call the native Java showToast(...) method in the preceding's Anonymous class (see Listing 7-18).

   Listing 7-18. Calling a Java Method from JavaScript

   ```javascript
   function showPage(arg) {
       var toPage, fromPage;

       if (arg == "pgme") {
           toPage = $("#pgme");
           fromPage = $("#pgHome");
       } else {
           fromPage = $("#pgme");
           toPage = $("#pgHome");
       }
   ```

```
        fromPage.fadeOut(0, function(e) {
            toPage.fadeIn();
        });

        HybridApp.showToast(arg);
    }
```

3. After setting up the WebView JavaScript interface, you simply use the named JavaScript global variable, HybridApp, to access your native Java methods.

4. You may build and run the app to see how it works.

FINAL TOUCH

You have completed the main topics in this ADT project, comparing the Android app with the iOS app look and feel. Optionally, you can tighten some minor cosmetic loose ends. The Android app has an app icon on the action bar, which you don't have on the iOS app. You may choose to disable the action bar app icon in the MainActivity OnCreate(...) (see Listing 7-19).

Listing 7-19. Disable Action Bar App Icon

```java
public class MainActivity extends ActionBarActivity {

    @Override
    protected void onCreate(Bundle savedInstanceState) {
        super.onCreate(savedInstanceState);
        setContentView(R.layout.activity_main);
        ...
        ActionBar actionBar = getSupportActionBar();
        actionBar.setDisplayShowTitleEnabled(false);
        actionBar.setDisplayShowHomeEnabled(false);
        ...
    }
    ...
}
```

Take a look at Figure 7-3, which is from my Nexus 4 device.

Figure 7-3. Android HybridApp

Use System Apps

The preloaded system apps are most likely well designed to allow external apps to use them. For example, you can make phone calls, send SMS, or send e-mails from your apps by using the *preloaded apps* and integrating their user interfaces into yours. Recall the "Intent and Intent Filter" section in Chapter 5; you launched other application components with an appropriate Intent object. You do the same with system apps.

There is really nothing new in this chapter. The key is to find out how to create appropriate intents that match the intent-filter rules to activate these system application components, or any application components. The following subchapters show how to create the Intent objects, primarily implicit intent (see the "Implicit Intents" section in Chapter 5) to use the activities from the system apps. You will see that among all Intent attributes, the following are our primary interests:

- **Action**: The general action to be performed, such as ACTION_VIEW, ACTION_EDIT, ACTION_MAIN, and so forth.

- **Data**: The data to operate on, such as a person's record in a contacts database, expressed as a URI.

- **Type**: The MIME type of the intent data. Normally, the type is inferred from the intent data, but you can specify it.

- **Extra**: The extra parameters to send to the receiving component. This is not new, actually. We have been using Bundle to pass extra parameters between activities or fragments.

ADT PROJECT PREPARATIONS

As usual, let's prepare an ADT project using our MvcTemplate project for interfacing with systems apps.

1. Copy the MvcTemplate ADT project and paste it to a new project (⌘c, ⌘v) named **UseSystemApps**.

2. Rename the Android application package. From the newly created UseSystemApps project context menu, select **Android Tools ➤ Rename Application Package**. Enter a new package name: **com.pdachoice.usesystemapps**.

3. Rename the UseSystemApps/src/com.pdachoice.renameme Java package. From the package context menu, select **Refactor ➤ Rename ...** (Alt+⌘r) and do the following:

   a. Enter a new name: **com.pdachoice.usesystemapps**.

   b. Select **Update references**.

4. You only need one fragment: keep the ScreenOneFragment and delete the other two, as follows:

   a. Delete the src/ScreenTwoFragment.java and src/ScreenThreeFragment.java classes (multiselect and fn+Delete).

   b. Delete the res/layout/screentwo_fragment.xml and res/layout/screenthree_fragment.xml files (multiselect and fn+Delete).

5. Modify res/layout/screenone_fragment.xml (see Listing 7-20). To keep it simple, you don't need anything in the layout.

Listing 7-20. *Screen One Layout File*

```xml
<?xml version="1.0" encoding="utf-8"?>
<RelativeLayout xmlns:android="http://schemas.android.com/apk/res/android"
    android:layout_width="match_parent"
    android:layout_height="match_parent" >

</RelativeLayout>
```

6. Modify the app name in res/values/strings.xml and add some text (see Listing 7-21).

Listing 7-21. *UseSystemApps Text*

```xml
<?xml version="1.0" encoding="utf-8"?>
<resources>
    <string name="app_name">Use System Apps</string>
    <string name="actionPhone">usePhone()</string>
    <string name="actionSms">useSms()</string>
    <string name="actionEmail">useEmail()</string>
    <string name="actionMedia">useMediaPlayer()</string>
</resources>
```

7. Modify res/menu/main.xml by adding some action items (see Listing 7-22). You will use them to trigger demo code, using system application components.

Listing 7-22. *UseSystemApps Options Menu Layout*

```xml
<menu xmlns:android="http://schemas.android.com/apk/res/android"
    xmlns:app="http://schemas.android.com/apk/res-auto" >

    <item
        android:id="@+id/actionPhone"
        android:title="@string/actionPhone"
        app:showAsAction="never"/>
    <item
        android:id="@+id/actionSms"
        android:title="@string/actionSms"
        app:showAsAction="never"/>
    <item
        android:id="@+id/actionEmail"
        android:title="@string/actionEmail"
        app:showAsAction="never"/>
    <item
        android:id="@+id/actionMedia"
        android:title="@string/actionMedia"
        app:showAsAction="never"/>

</menu>
```

8. Modify src/ScreenOneFragment.java by removing unnecessary code. Enable the options menu (see Listing 7-23).

    Listing 7-23. UseSystemApps Inflate Options Menu

```java
public class ScreenOneFragment extends Fragment {
  private View contentView;

  @Override
  public View onCreateView(LayoutInflater inflater, ViewGroup container,
      Bundle savedInstanceState) {
    contentView = inflater.inflate(R.layout.screenone_fragment, container,
        false);

    setHasOptionsMenu(true);

    return contentView;
  }

  @Override
  public void onCreateOptionsMenu(Menu menu, MenuInflater inflater) {
    super.onCreateOptionsMenu(menu, inflater);
    inflater.inflate(R.menu.main, menu);
  }

  @Override
  public boolean onOptionsItemSelected(MenuItem item) {
    Log.d(">>>onOptionsItemSelected", item.getTitle().toString());

    return super.onOptionsItemSelected(item);
  }
}
```

9. Build and run the app to make sure the prep project is good to go (see Figure 7-4).

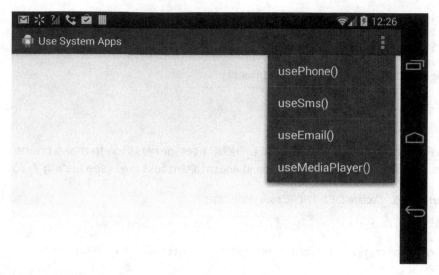

Figure 7-4. UseSystemApps prep

The app should have nothing on the main screen except the options menu.

Phone Dialer

To make a phone call from your app, you can use the usePhone() method shown in Listing 7-24 to send an appropriate intent to launch the preloaded phone dialer.

1. Specify the following intents:

   a. **Action**: ACTION_DIAL

   b. **Data**: tel:12345

Listing 7-24. Phone Dialer Intent

```java
public class ScreenOneFragment extends Fragment {
  ...
  @Override
  public boolean onOptionsItemSelected(MenuItem item) {
    Log.d(">>>onOptionsItemSelected", item.getTitle().toString());
    switch (item.getItemId()) {
    case R.id.actionPhone:
      usePhone();
      break;

    default:
      break;
    }

    return super.onOptionsItemSelected(item);
  }
```

```
private void usePhone() {
    Intent intent = new Intent(Intent.ACTION_DIAL); // or, try ACTION_CALL
    String uri = "tel:12345";
    intent.setData(Uri.parse(uri));
    getActivity().startActivity(intent);
}
...
}
```

2. The Phone Dialer app requires CALL_PHONE uses-permission to make phone
    calls. Declare the uses-permission in AndroidManifest.xml (see Listing 7-25).

    Listing 7-25. *Declare CALL_PHONE uses-permission*

```
<manifest ... >
    ...
    <uses-permission android:name="android.permission.CALL_PHONE" />
    ...
```

3. Build and run the UseSystemApps. Select **usePhone()** from the options
    menu to see the phone dialer activity launched from the UseSystemApps
    app (see Figure 7-5).

Figure 7-5. *Nexus 4 phone dialer*

SMS Messaging

To send SMS messages, you can use the useSms() method (see Listing 7-26), which brings up the SMS messaging app/screen.

1. Specify the following intents:

    a. **Action**: ACTION_VIEW

    b. **Type**: "vnd.android-dir/mms-sms"

    c. **Extras**: Sms_body, address, and so forth

    Listing 7-26. SMS Messaging Intent

    ```java
    public class ScreenOneFragment extends Fragment {
      ...
      @Override
      public boolean onOptionsItemSelected(MenuItem item) {
        ...
        case R.id.actionSms:
          useSms();
          break;
        ...
      }

      private void useSms() {
        try {
          Intent intent = new Intent(Intent.ACTION_VIEW);
          intent.setType("vnd.android-dir/mms-sms");
          intent.putExtra("sms_body", "Hello World!");
          intent.putExtra("address", "0123456789");
          startActivity(intent);
        } catch (ActivityNotFoundException e) {
          // some KitKat devices only have Google Hangouts without the
          // SMS messaging app. The following intent is more generic.

          Intent intent = new Intent(Intent.ACTION_SEND);
          intent.setType("text/plain");
          intent.putExtra(Intent.EXTRA_TEXT, "Hello World!");
          startActivity(intent);
        }
      }
      ...
    }
    ```

2. Build and run the UseSystemApps. Select **useSms()** from the options menu to see the preloaded system messaging activity launched from your app (see Figure 7-6).

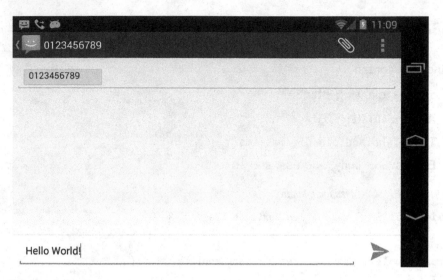

Figure 7-6. Nexus 4 messaging app

E-mail

To send e-mail, you can use the useEmail() method (see Listing 7-27), which launches a preloaded e-mail client.

1. Specify the following intents:

    a. **Action**: ACTION_SENDTO

    b. **Data**: "mailto:someone@gmail.com"

    c. **Extras**: Subject, text, and so forth

Listing 7-27. E-mail Intent

```java
public class ScreenOneFragment extends Fragment {
  ...
  @Override
  public boolean onOptionsItemSelected(MenuItem item) {
    ...
    case R.id.actionEmail:
      useEmail ();
      break;
    ...
}

  private void useEmail() {
    Intent intent = new Intent(Intent.ACTION_SENDTO);
    Uri uri = Uri.parse("mailto: someone@gmail.com");
    intent.setData(uri);
    intent.putExtra(Intent.EXTRA_SUBJECT, "Subject of email");
```

```
        intent.putExtra(Intent.EXTRA_TEXT, "Body of email");
        startActivity(Intent.createChooser(intent, "Choose a Mail client:"));
    }
    ...
}
```

> **Note**   It is always possible that zero or more than one application component matches your implicit intent object. Many third-party apps declare the same intent matching rules as those system apps because they want people to use their apps. You can use Intent.createChooser(...) to supply a custom chooser title. In case of no matching, you still get a chooser dialog instead of a runtime error. Or, you may catch an exception and redirect to the Play Store to download a particular app, such as one of your own.

2. Build and run the UseSystemApps. Select **useEmail()** from the options menu to see an e-mail activity launched from your app (see Figure 7-7).

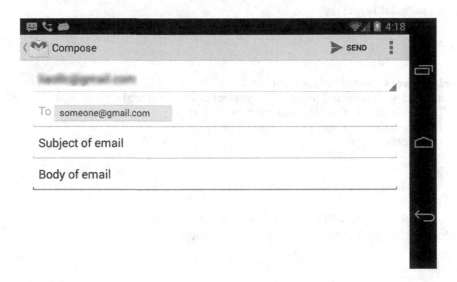

Figure 7-7. Nexus 4 Gmail app

Media Player

Most of the Android phones come with a preloaded media player. To play video, you can use the useMediaPlayer() method shown in Listing 7-28, which brings up the video player app/screen.

1. Specify the following intents:

    a. **Action**: ACTION_VIEW

    b. **Data**: "http://www.pdachoice.com/me/sample_mpeg4.mp4"

    c. **Type**: "video/mp4"

Listing 7-28. Media Player Intent

```
public class ScreenOneFragment extends Fragment {
  ...
  @Override
  public boolean onOptionsItemSelected(MenuItem item) {
    ...
    case R.id.actionMedia:
      useMediaPlayer();
      break;
    ...
  }

  private void useMediaPlayer() {
    Uri uri = Uri.parse("http://www.pdachoice.com/me/sample_mpeg4.mp4");
    Intent intent = new Intent(Intent.ACTION_VIEW);
    intent.setDataAndType(uri, "video/mp4");
    startActivity(intent);
  }
  ...
}
```

2. Build and run the app to see how it works. Figure 7-8 shows the app matching the implicit intent on my Nexus 4 device.

Figure 7-8. Choose a media player

It takes only a couple of lines to reuse these preloaded apps, which is better than reinventing the wheel. By integrating these system apps, the features and screens appear as if they are part of your own app.

You might be wondering how you can find the required matching `Intent` attributes. You just have to get them from developers. For preloaded system apps, you can get them from Internet search results very quickly.

Mobile Search Framework

In general, it is less desirable to design deep hierarchical screen navigations on small screens. In my opinion, a one-level drilldown list is very friendly. A two-level drilldown seems acceptable, in general. I start to frown when I see three-level drilldown screens. Still, the data hierarchy could be even deeper than three levels. In order to present a deep information hierarchy, a *mobile search UX design pattern*, embraced by both iOS and Android platforms, comes to the rescue. Both iOS and Android platforms provide framework classes and API for mobile developers to achieve a consistent search UX with those in system apps.

Let's create an ADT project to visualize this common search framework. The iOS app in Figure 7-9 shows this common UX pattern, which is also used in many iOS system apps.

Figure 7-9. iOS SearchDisplayController

ADT PROJECT PREPARATIONS

In Chapter 3, you created an ADT project called MasterDetail. It already looks very close to what we are trying to achieve here, except it doesn't have a search bar. Let's prepare a new ADT project using the MasterDetail project for our purpose and by doing the following:

1. Copy the MasterDetail ADT project and paste it to a new project (⌘c, ⌘v) named **MobileSearch**.

2. Rename the Android application package. From the newly created MobileSearch project context menu, select **Android Tools ➤ Rename Application Package**. Enter a new package name: **com.pdachoice.mobilesearch**.

3. Rename the MobileSearch/src/com.pdachoice.masterdetail Java package. From the package context menu, select **Refactor ➤ Rename...** (Alt+⌘r) and do the following:

   a. Enter a new name: **com.pdachoice.mobilesearch**.

   b. Select **Update references**.

4. Modify res/values/strings.xml (see Listing 7-29) to modify the app name and add some text.

Listing 7-29. *MobileSearch App Strings*

```xml
<?xml version="1.0" encoding="utf-8"?>
<resources>

    <string name="app_name">Mobile Search</string>
    <string name="action_settings">Settings</string>
    <string name="hello_world">Hello world!</string>
    <string name="menu_search">Search</string>
    <string name="search_hint">search</string>
    <string name="delete_history">Clear Search History</string>

</resources>
```

5. To make the mobile search code obvious and simple, modify MasterListFragment.java (see Listing 7-30) as follows:

   a. Initialize the ListView with hard-coded items instead of inserting a timestamp.

   b. Remove the code that adds a timestamp in onOptionsItemSelected(...).

   c. Fix a trivial error in onListItemClick(...).

Listing 7-30. *MasterListFragment.java*

```java
public class MasterListFragment extends ListFragment {

    private static final String[] items = {"a","ab","abc", "abcd", "abcde","abcdef",
"abcdefg" };
```

```java
    ArrayAdapter<String> myListAdapter;
    @Override
    public void onCreate(Bundle savedInstanceState) {
        super.onCreate(savedInstanceState);

        myListAdapter = new ArrayAdapter<String>(getActivity(),
                android.R.layout.simple_list_item_1, Arrays.asList(items));
        this.setListAdapter(myListAdapter);

        setHasOptionsMenu(true);
    }
    ...

    // callback method when menu items are selected.
    @Override
    public boolean onOptionsItemSelected(MenuItem item) {
      // TODO
      return true;
    }
    ...

    // callback method when list item is selected.
    @Override
    public void onListItemClick(ListView l, View v, int pos, long id){
      Fragment frag = new DetailFragment();

      Bundle parms = new Bundle();
      parms.putString("ts", items[pos]);
      frag.setArguments(parms); // pass data to other Fragment

      ((MainActivity) getActivity()).pushViewController(frag, true);
    }
```

6. Modify $PROJ/res/menu/main.xml (see Listing 7-31).

Listing 7-31. Options Menu Layout

```xml
<menu xmlns:android="http://schemas.android.com/apk/res/android"
    xmlns:app="http://schemas.android.com/apk/res-auto" >
    <!-- empty for now -->
</menu>
```

7. Build and run the Android MobileSearch project. You should see an Android app that looks like the iOS app shown in Figure 7-9, but without the UISearchBar.

SearchView

If you're developing your application for Android 3.0, you should insert the SearchView widget as an *action view* in the action bar. Action view is an action item in which you specify a view widget as a replacement for an action button.

Although there is a search dialog method that is available since API Level 1, the SearchView widget is also available from the v7 Support Library. Using the SearchView widget is practically the only choice you need to know. We will only focus on SearchView for our porting topic.

To use the SearchView widget in the MobileSearch app, do the following:

1. Conventionally, you want to put the SearchView widget in ActionBar. Create an action item with ActionView in $PROJ/res/menu/main.xml (see Listing 7-32).

    Listing 7-32. SearchView Widget in Options Menu

    ```xml
    <menu xmlns:android="http://schemas.android.com/apk/res/android"
        xmlns:app="http://schemas.android.com/apk/res-auto" >

        <item
            android:id="@+id/menuAction"
            android:icon="@android:drawable/ic_menu_search"
            android:title="@string/menu_search"
            app:actionViewClass="android.support.v7.widget.SearchView"
            app:showAsAction="ifRoom|collapseActionView"/>

    </menu>
    ```

2. Keep a reference to the SearchView widget (see Listing 7-33).

    Listing 7-33. Inflate Options Menu and getActionView

    ```java
    public class MasterListFragment extends ListFragment {

      private SearchView searchView;
      ...
      // render option menu from resource file, menu.xml
      @Override
      public void onCreateOptionsMenu(Menu menu, MenuInflater inflater) {
        inflater.inflate(R.menu.main, menu);

        MenuItem searchItem = menu.findItem(R.id.menuAction);
        searchView = (SearchView) MenuItemCompat.getActionView(searchItem);
      }
      ...
    }
    ```

3. Register an OnQueryTextListener and implement OnQueryTextListener event listeners for SearchView (see Listing 7-34). Use onQueryTextChange(query) to perform a live search on the local cache with each keystroke. This gives users immediate feedback as they type.

Note   In addition to performing a live search on the local cache, you might want to perform a remote query onQueryTextSubmit(query), which is not demonstrated here.

Listing 7-34. *onQueryTextChange(query)*

```java
public class MasterListFragment extends ListFragment
                    implements OnQueryTextListener {
  ...
  // render option menu from resource file, menu.xml
  @Override
  public void onCreateOptionsMenu(Menu menu, MenuInflater inflater) {
    ...
    searchView.setOnQueryTextListener(this);
    ...
  }

  @Override
  public boolean onQueryTextSubmit(String query) {
    Log.d("MasterListFragment", "onQueryTextSubmit: " + query);
    searchView.setQuery(query, false); // leave query text in SearchView

    InputMethodManager imm = (InputMethodManager) getActivity()
                        .getSystemService(Context.INPUT_METHOD_SERVICE);
    // dismiss keyboard
    imm.hideSoftInputFromWindow(getView().getWindowToken(), 0);

    doSearch(query);

    // true if the query has been handled by the listener,
    // false to let the SearchView perform the default action.
    return false;
  }

  @Override
  public boolean onQueryTextChange(String query) {
    Log.d("MasterListFragment", "onQueryTextChange: " + query);
    doSearch(query);

    // true if the action was handled by the listener
    // false if the SearchView should perform the default action of showing
    // any suggestions if available,
    return false;
  }
```

```
    private void doSearch(String query) {
      // TODO Auto-generated method stub
    }
    ...
}
```

4. Implement OnCloseListener event listeners for SearchView (see Listing 7-35). Clear the search result by resetting it to the original list.

Listing 7-35. Clear Search Result

```
public class MasterListFragment extends ListFragment implements
                        OnQueryTextListener, OnCloseListener {
  private SearchView searchView;
  ...
  // render option menu from resource file, menu.xml
  @Override
  public void onCreateOptionsMenu(Menu menu, MenuInflater inflater) {
    ...
    searchView.setOnCloseListener(this);
    ...
  }

  @Override
  public boolean onClose() {
    Log.w("MasterListFragment", "onClose");

    myListAdapter = new ArrayAdapter<String>(
        getActivity(),
        android.R.layout.simple_list_item_1,
        Arrays.asList(items));
    setListAdapter(myListAdapter);
    return false;
  }
  ...
}
```

5. Some of the SearchView widget's look and feel can also be changed in Java code (see Listing 7-36).

Listing 7-36. SearchView Look-and-Feel Options

```
public class MasterListFragment extends ... {

  private SearchView searchView;
  ...
  // render option menu from resource file, menu.xml
  @Override
  public void onCreateOptionsMenu(Menu menu, MenuInflater inflater) {
    ...
    searchView.setIconifiedByDefault(true); // default to true.
    searchView.setQueryHint(getActivity().getResources().getText(
```

```
            R.string.search_hint));

    // searchView.setImeOptions(EditorInfo.IME_ACTION_SEARCH); // for API 14+
    // searchView.setInputType(InputType.TYPE_CLASS_TEXT); // for API 14+
}
...
}
```

6. The `MasterListFragment.doSearch(String query)` method in Listing 7-37 simply tests whether any item in the query string is case-insensitive. This is a very simple test for something very common in a live search.

Listing 7-37. Live Search

```java
public class MasterListFragment extends ... {
    ...
    private void doSearch(String query) {
        Log.w("MasterListFragment", "doSearch: " + query);
        List<String> filteredList = new ArrayList<String>();
        if (query == null || query.length() == 0) {
            filteredList = Arrays.asList(items);
        } else {
            for (int i = 0; i < items.length; i++) {
                if (items[i].toLowerCase().contains(query.toLowerCase())) {
                    filteredList.add(items[i]);
                }
            }
        }

        // reload List view with the filtered results
        myListAdapter = new ArrayAdapter<String>(getActivity(),
                android.R.layout.simple_list_item_1, filteredList);
        this.setListAdapter(myListAdapter);
    }
    ...
}
```

7. Build and run the MobileSearch app to see your search code in action (see Figure 7-10). It offers the same search feature, except it embeds the SearchView widget in the ActionBar as opposed to the iOS UISearchBar below the navigation bar. This Android style actually has been adapted by many iPad apps because the navigation bar has more free space. Although you can put SearchView in any place, it is better to keep the Android standard search UX.

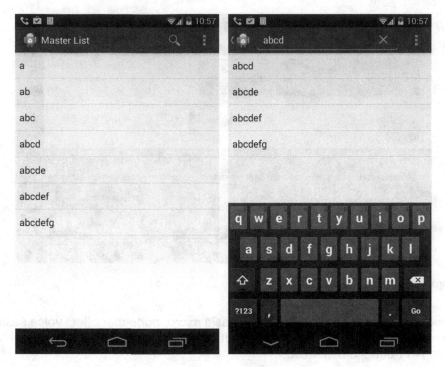

Figure 7-10. MobileSearch app

The current MobileSearch app is not taking full advantage of the Android search framework yet. It only uses a SearchView widget, places it in ActionBar, and implements the common widget handlers. Nothing is really new except the SearchView widget. Simplicity was the objective that is fully achieved.

Voice Search

The current MobileSearch app has pretty much everything the iOS app offers:

- A conventional search UX
- Live search

It still seems to be missing something, however. Let's take a look at the Google Play Store app (see Figure 7-11).

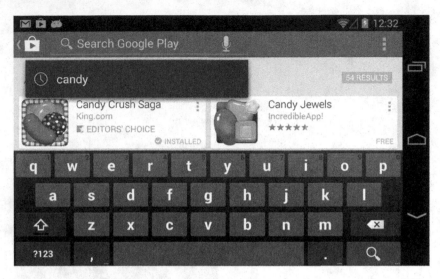

Figure 7-11. *Google Play Store voice search*

The SearchView widget in the Google Play Store has a *microphone* that offers voice search. Although you can bring up the built-in voice input from a soft keyboard, the Android voice search feature shown in Figure 7-11 offers a better UX.

To enable voice search using the Android Search framework, do the following:

1. Create a search configuration file, $PROJ/res/xml/searchable.xml (see Listing 7-38), as follows:

   a. First, create a $PROJ/res/xml/ folder if it does not exist.

   b. Instead of customizing the SearchView in Java code as you did previously, this is the configuration file for using the search framework. You can actually do more with the search configuration file.

Listing 7-38. *searchable.xml*

```xml
<?xml version="1.0" encoding="utf-8"?>
<searchable xmlns:android="http://schemas.android.com/apk/res/android"
    android:hint="@string/search_hint"
    android:label="@string/app_name"
    android:voiceSearchMode="showVoiceSearchButton|launchRecognizer" >

</searchable>
```

> **Note** For more information, see the online reference at:
> http://developer.android.com/guide/topics/search/searchable-config.htm.

2. Modify AndroidManifest.xml (see Listing 7-39), as follows:

    a. Create a new <intent-filter> so that the MainActivity can receive the search intents.

    b. The meta-data needs to match the searchable configuration file path.

    c. When the search result is delivered to your MainActivity, the activity is restarted and reinitialized by default. I use android:launchMode="sin gleInstance" to stay with the current activity and preserve the current states. You will handle the search intent in a new lifecycle callback in the Activity class later.

Listing 7-39. *Declare Activity to Receive Search Results Intent*

```xml
<?xml version="1.0" encoding="utf-8"?>
<manifest ... >
    ...
    <application ... >
        <activity
            ...
            android:launchMode="singleInstance" >
            ...
            <intent-filter>
                <action android:name="android.intent.action.SEARCH" />
            </intent-filter>

            <meta-data
                android:name="android.app.searchable"
                android:resource="@xml/searchable" />

        </activity>
    </application>

</manifest>
```

3. Modify MainActivity.java (see Listing 7-40):

    a. Keep an object reference to MasterListFragment. You need it to deliver the query text.

    b. In singleInstance mode, the existing Activity instance receives an onNewIntent(intent) callback.

    c. The search framework, SearchManager, delivers intents with query text.

Listing 7-40. Activity.onNewIntent(...)

```java
public class MainActivity extends ActionBarActivity {

  private MasterListFragment masterListFragment;

  @Override
  protected void onCreate(Bundle savedInstanceState) {
    super.onCreate(savedInstanceState);

    ...
    masterListFragment = new MasterListFragment();
    pushViewController(masterListFragment, false);
  }

  @Override
  protected void onNewIntent(Intent intent) {
    if (Intent.ACTION_SEARCH.equals(intent.getAction())) {
      String query = intent.getStringExtra(SearchManager.QUERY);
      masterListFragment.onQueryTextSubmit(query);
    }
  }
  ...
```

4. Modify MasterListFragment.onCreateOptionsMenu(...) to tell where to deliver the search information, which is getActivity().getComponentName(), the MainActivity (see Listing 7-41).

Listing 7-41. SearchView.setSearchableInfo(...)

```java
public class MasterListFragment extends ... {
  ...
  // render option menu from resource file, menu.xml
  @Override
  public void onCreateOptionsMenu(Menu menu, MenuInflater inflater) {
    ...
    searchView.setQueryRefinementEnabled(true);
    SearchManager searchManager = (SearchManager)getActivity()
        .getSystemService(Context.SEARCH_SERVICE);
    SearchableInfo info = searchManager.getSearchableInfo(getActivity()
        .getComponentName());
    searchView.setSearchableInfo(info);
  }
  ...
}
```

5. Build and run the app to see the voice search in action (see Figure 7-12).

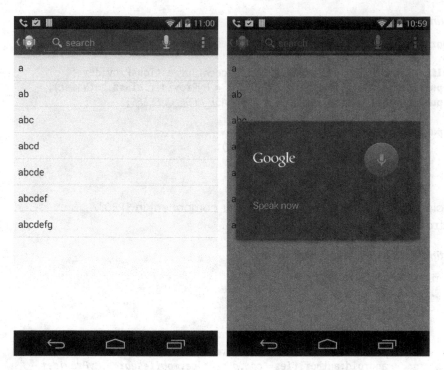

Figure 7-12. Voice search

The search is based on dictation, but spelling doesn't seem to be working too well.

Recent Search Suggestions

Google Play Store apps provide search suggestions based on the most recent search queries (see Figure 7-11), which you can select to search. The Android search framework uses a content provider to persist a user's search suggestions.

To implement the Recent Search Suggestions feature, do the following to create a *content provider* that stores the most recent queries:

1.   Create a content provider Java class that provides the suggestions, such as MyProvider.java (see Listing 7-42). If you want to provide the suggestions based on the recent searches, all you need to do is inherit your class from SearchRecentSuggestionsProvider.

Listing 7-42. *SearchRecentSuggestionsProvider*

```java
import android.content.SearchRecentSuggestionsProvider;

public class MyProvider extends SearchRecentSuggestionsProvider {
    public final static String AUTHORITY = MyProvider.class.getName();
    public final static int MODE = DATABASE_MODE_QUERIES;

    public MyProvider() {
        setupSuggestions(AUTHORITY, MODE);
    }
}
```

2. Declare the MyProvider content provider component in $PROJ/
    AndroidManifest.xml (see Listing 7-43).

Listing 7-43. *MyProvider Content Provider*

```xml
<manifest ... >
    ...
    <application ... >
        ...
        <provider
            android:name="com.pdachoice.mobilesearch.MyProvider"
            android:authorities="com.pdachoice.mobilesearch.MyProvider"
            android:exported="false" />
    </application>

</manifest>
```

3. Specify the MyProvider content provider in the search configuration file,
    $PROJ/res/searchable.xml (see Listing 7-44).

Listing 7-44. *Search Configuration File*

```xml
<?xml version="1.0" encoding="utf-8"?>
<searchable
    ...
    android:searchSuggestAuthority="com.pdachoice.mobilesearch.MyProvider"
    android:searchSuggestSelection=" ?"
    ... >
</searchable>
```

4. Save the query text that the user enters to the MyProvider content provider
    (see Listing 7-45).

Listing 7-45. Save User Query Strings

```java
public class MasterListFragment extends ... {
  ...
  @Override
  public boolean onQueryTextSubmit(String query) {
    ...
    // save the query string
    SearchRecentSuggestions suggestions = new SearchRecentSuggestions(
        getActivity(), MyProvider.AUTHORITY, MyProvider.MODE);
    suggestions.saveRecentQuery(query, null);
    ...
  }
  ...
}
```

5. Take the extra step to respect the user's privacy by providing a Delete option. Do the following to add an action item in `res/menu/main.xml` (see Listing 7-46).

Listing 7-46. An Action Item to Delete Search History

```xml
<menu ... >
    ...
    <item
        android:id="@+id/delete_history"
        app:showAsAction="never"
        android:title="@string/delete_history">
    </item>
</menu>
```

6. Implement the Delete action item selection handler (see Listing 7-47).

Listing 7-47. Clear Search History

```java
public class MasterListFragment extends ... {
  ...
  // callback method when menu items are selected.
  @Override
  public boolean onOptionsItemSelected(MenuItem item) {
    if(item.getItemId() == R.id.delete_history) {
        SearchRecentSuggestions suggestions = new SearchRecentSuggestions(
            getActivity(), MyProvider.AUTHORITY, MyProvider.MODE);
        suggestions.clearHistory();
    }

    return true;
  }
  ...
}
```

7. Build and run the app to see the search history, as shown in Figure 7-13.

Figure 7-13. MobileSearch app

Map and Location Awareness

Location- and maps-based apps offer a compelling experience on mobile devices. Knowing where users are located allows your application to be smarter and deliver better information to them. When developing a location-aware application for Android, you can use the Android platform location API or the *Google Location Services API*, which is part of Google Play services and provides a more powerful framework that automatically handles location providers, user movement, and location accuracy. It also handles location update scheduling based on power consumption parameters that you provide. In most cases, you'll get better battery performance, as well as better accuracy, by using the Google Location Services API.

The *Google Maps Android API* is a superb choice for showing a map. In this chapter, we will use the Google Location Services API and the Google Maps Android API; both are part of the *Google Play services SDK*.

Google Play Services

The Google Play services SDK provides you with easy access to Google services and is tightly integrated with the Android OS. With Google Play services, your app can take advantage of the latest Google-powered features, such as Game, Maps, Location, Google+, In-app Billing, Cloud Messaging, Authorization, and so forth.

This seems like a smart move from Google. Instead of bundling these features in the Android SDK, which relies on device carriers or manufacturers to release new SDK versions and upgrades, devices running Android 2.2 or newer and that have the Google Play Store app automatically receive updates to Google Play services. It enhances your app with the most recent version of Google Play services without worrying about your users' Android version.

We will use Google Maps and the Google Location Services API from Google Play services to implement the subjects in this chapter.

You need to get the SDK for development. The Google Play services are not part of the Android framework. Your ADT probably doesn't have the Google Play services SDK yet, so you need to install it for development. The following procedure downloads the SDK and imports the library into your Eclipse workspace.

1. To launch the Android SDK Manager, in the ADT top menu bar, select **Window ➤ Android SDK Manager**.

2. Scroll to the bottom of the screen. Google Play services is in the `Extras` folder (see Figure 7-14).

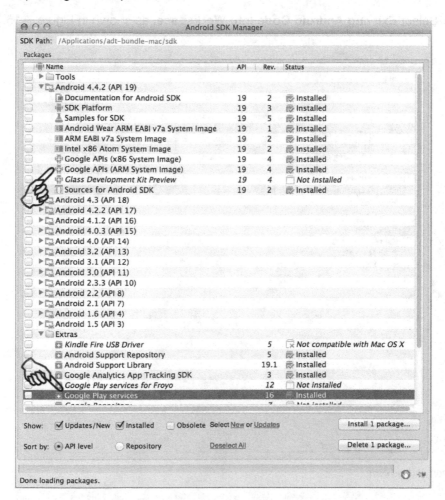

Figure 7-14. Google Play services in Extras folder

a. Select Google Play services if it is showing **Not installed**.

b. Install Google APIs for the emulator. For example, I will be able to create a 4.2.2 emulator capable of running Google Play services.

c. Follow the onscreen instructions to complete the install. Upon completion, the screen is refreshed and shows Google Play services as **Installed**.

3. At the top of the screen shown in Figure 7-14, the **SDK Path** is /Application/adt-bundle-mac/sdk. Note this path because you will need it later.

4. To use Google Play services, import the Google Play services library project into your ADT workspace from the newly installed location, as follows:

a. From the Package Explore context menu, select **Import...**. Alternatively, you can open the Import wizard from the ADT top menu bar at **File ➤ Import...**.

b. Select **Existing Android Code Into Workspace**, as shown in Figure 7-15.

Figure 7-15. Import Android code

5. In the **Import Projects** screen, locate the Google Play services library project. Figure 7-16 shows the projects inside the google_play_services folder:

    a. The **Root Directory** is <android-sdk>/extras/google/google_play_services/ where my **<android-sdk>** is /Applications/adt-bundle-mac/sdk.

    b. For now, we are only interested in the libproject/google-play-service_lib library project and the samples/maps project. Select these two projects.

    c. The sample project name defaults to MainActivity. You can click the text to rename it something like *Map Demo*.

    d. Make sure that the **Copy projects into workspace** check box is selected.

    e. The sample project has a compilation error. You will fix it next.

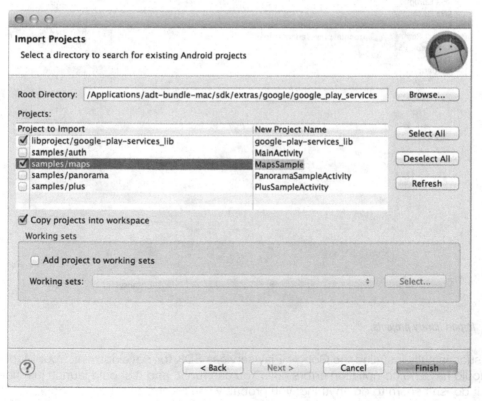

Figure 7-16. Import Google Play services library and samples projects

6. From the newly imported MapDemo project, select **Properties** from the
    context menu (shortcut key: command+I) to open the Project Properties
    screen (see Figure 7-17). Add the following two Android library projects:

    a. **V7 compatibility support library**. As usual, have it backward-
        compatible.

    b. **Google Play Service library**. No surprise, the MapDemo ADT project
        needs the Google Play services Android library.

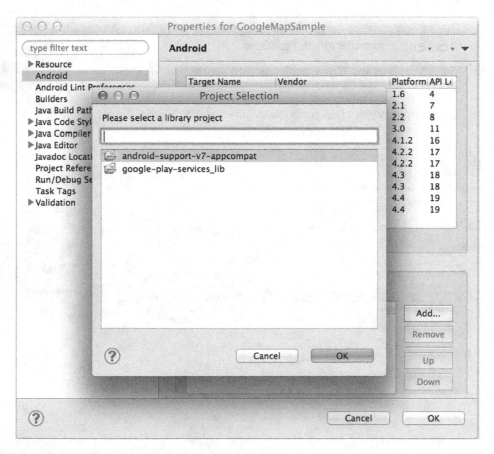

Figure 7-17. Import library projects

You have successfully installed the Google Play services SDK for development. Your MapDemo
project should have no compilation errors now. You can run it, and it should launch just fine.
However, it doesn't seem to do anything: you probably see an empty screen as opposed to a map.
Read the LogCat output and you should see errors from connecting to Google servers. No worry.
The runtime errors come from the Google Maps Android API v2, which requires a *Google API key*.
It is free and you will get one.

Google Maps Android API

With the Google Maps Android API, you can create maps based on Google Maps data. The API automatically handles access to Google Maps servers, loads map data, renders maps, and responds to map gestures. You can also use the API to add graphics to a map to provide additional information, such as the following:

- **Markers**: Icons anchored to specific positions on the map.
- **Polylines**: Sets of line segments.
- **Polygons**: Enclosed segments.
- **Ground overlays**: Bitmap graphics anchored to specific positions on the map.
- **Tile overlays**: Sets of images that are displayed on top of the base map tiles.

It is also easy to change the user's view of a particular map area and allow user interactions with the map.

We will go over the fundamental usage of the Google Maps Android API. You also will have a working sample project from Google. You should be comfortable looking up the API reference document or the MapsSample project.

The Google Maps API Key

To access Google Maps data, you need a Google API key. It is free. Google just wants to know which apps are accessing their servers. Let's do a step-by-step walkthrough of how to obtain your own Google API key:

1. To obtain the free Google Maps Android API key, you need to supply your Android application package name and SHA1 certificate fingerprint. For the MapDemo project, the package name is `package="com.example.mapdemo"` defined in the ADT project `AndroidManifest.xml` file.

2. In ADT, your debug builds are signed with a debug signing certificate. You can find the debug signing certificate and the SHA1 fingerprint in your Eclipse ADT Android settings page (see Figure 7-18).

   a. Open the ADT **Preferences** screen from the ADT top menu bar (shortcut key command+,).

   b. Select **Android ➤ Build** from the left panel. You will find the debug keystore file path and the SHA1 fingerprint.

   c. You can also get the debug SHA1 fingerprint using a shell command in the Terminal program, as shown in Listing 7-48.

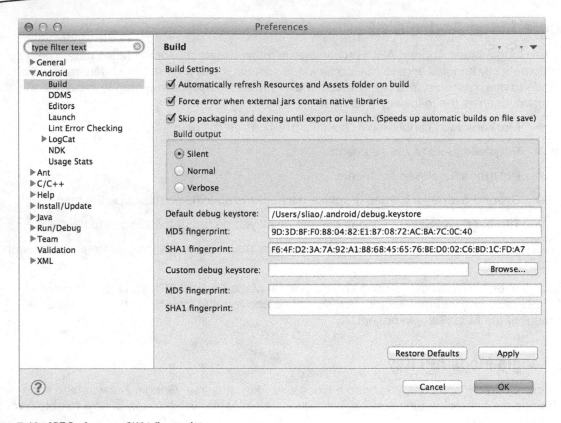

Figure 7-18. ADT Preferences SHA1 fingerprint

Listing 7-48. Keytool

```
[~/.android]$ keytool -list -v -keystore debug.keystore -storepass android -keypass android

Keystore type: JKS
Keystore provider: SUN

Your keystore contains 1 entry

Alias name: androiddebugkey
Creation date: Dec 19, 2012
Entry type: PrivateKeyEntry
Certificate chain length: 1
Certificate[1]:
Owner: CN=Android Debug, O=Android, C=US
Issuer: CN=Android Debug, O=Android, C=US
Serial number: 50d29c3f
Valid from: Wed Dec 19 21:03:59 PST 2012 until: Fri Dec 12 21:03:59 PST 2042
Certificate fingerprints:
        MD5:  9D:3D:BF:F0:B8:04:82:E1:B7:08:72:AC:BA:7C:0C:40
        SHA1: F6:4F:D2:3A:7A:92:A1:B8:68:45:65:76:BE:D0:02:C6:BD:1C:FD:A7
```

```
     Signature algorithm name: SHA1withRSA
     Version: 3


*****************************************
*****************************************
```

[~/.android]$

> **Note** The debug key is in the ~/.android/debug.keystore file by default, which is specified and can be modified in the ADT Android Preference screen, as shown in Figure 7-23.

3. Release apps are signed with a release signing certificate. Thus, you need a different Google Maps API key. Use the keytool (see Listing 7-48) command to get the SHA1 fingerprint from the released keystore. Everything is the same except a different keystore file for the release signing certificate. Note, you can use an ADT tool (see Figure 7-19) to create a new certificate, and then sign it, export it, and release the app. Go to the ADT project context menu and select **Android Tools ➤ Export Signed Application Package....**

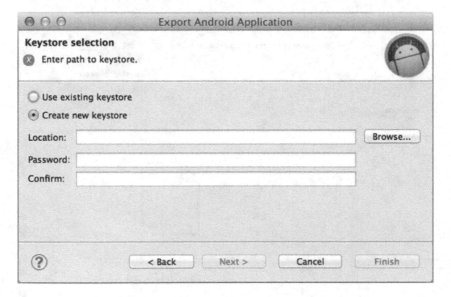

Figure 7-19. Export Android app and create new keystore

Note   To build the Mapdemo app with the release signing certificate, most likely you will encounter an I18N Lint MissingTranslation error. The ADT provides lint tool to check Android specific code issues. You may change the MissingTranslation severity to warning: from the project property context menu ➤ **Android Lint Preferences** ➤ **Correctness: Messages** ➤ **MissingTranslation,** and select Warning from the severity dropdown. You may need to perform clean build after changing the Lint settings.

4.   After you have the application package and the SHA1 fingerprint, you can create a new project for your MapDemo app in the **Google Developers Console** (a.k.a. Google Cloud Platform) at `https://console.developers.google.com`.

Note   You need a Google account. If necessary, apply for one at http://mail.google.com.

5.   If you haven't been to the Google Developers Console before, you're prompted to create a project immediately (see Figure 7-20). You might have already used it, however, and see a screen with existing projects and the red **Create Project** button.

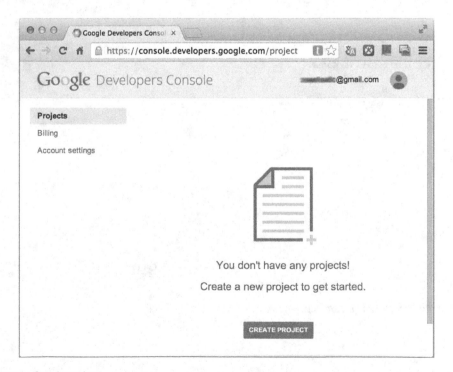

Figure 7-20. *Create a Google project*

6. Select the **Create Project** button to create a new project (see Figure 7-21). Enter `Google Maps Android Project` as the **Project name**.

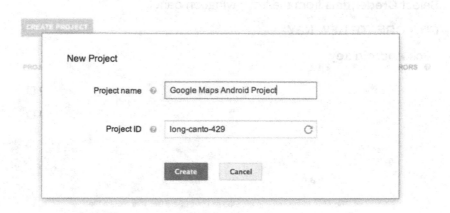

Figure 7-21. Enter project name

7. After the new project is created, select **APIs & auth** from the left navigation panel. Enable **Google Maps Android API v2**. You might need to scroll down a long list to find it. Follow the onscreen instructions to complete this step. After it is enabled, the status should show that it is **ON** (see Figure 7-22).

Figure 7-22. Enable Google Maps Android API v2

8. You need to register your Android apps that use the Google API (see Figure 7-23) by doing the following:

a. Select **Credentials** from the left navigation panel.

b. Click **CREATE NEW KEY**.

c. Click **Android key**.

Figure 7-23. *Create Android key*

d. Enter your SHA1 fingerprint and the Android app package name. The input should be one SHA1 certificate fingerprint and a package name separated by a semicolon, as shown in Figure 7-24. Click the **Create** button when done.

Create an Android key and configure allowed Android applications

This key can be deployed in your Android application.
API requests are sent directly to Google from your client Android device. Google verifies that each request originates from an Android application that matches one of the certificate SHA1 fingerprints and package names listed below. You can discover the SHA1 fingerprint of your developer certificate using the following command:

```
keytool -list -v -keystore mystore.keystore
```
Learn more

Accept requests from an Android application with one of the certificate fingerprints and package names listed below
One SHA1 certificate fingerprint and package name (separated by a semicolon) per line. Example:
45:B5:E4:6F:36:AD:0A:98:94:B4:02:66:2B:12:17:F2:56:26:A0:E0;com.example

```
F6:4F:D2:3A:7A:92:A1:B8:68:45:65:76:BE:D0:02:C6:BD:1C:FD:A7;com.example.mapdemo
```

    Create   Cancel

Figure 7-24. Create Android key

9. Figure 7-25 shows the result with the Android app API key. Jot down the API key. You will need it for the MapDemo Android project.

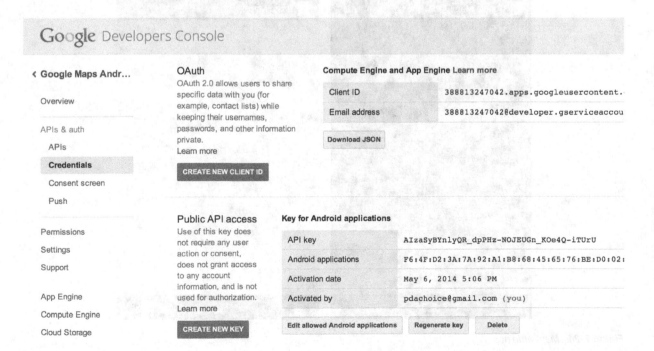

Figure 7-25. API key

10. Let's try the Google Maps Android API key. The MapDemo project runs, but without any maps shown due to failing to connect to Google services. All it needs is a valid API key to unlock the access. Open `$PROJ/AndroidManifest.xml` to enter the `com.google.android.maps.v2.API_KEY` value with your own API key (see Listing 7-49).

Listing 7-49. Enter API Key in AndroidManifest.xml

```xml
<?xml version="1.0" encoding="utf-8"?>
<manifest ... >
  ...
  <application ... >
    <!-- ** You need to replace the key below with your own key. **
    The example key below will not be accepted because it is not linked to
    The certificate which you will use to sign this application.
    See: https://developers.google.com/maps/documentation/android/start
         for instructions on how to get your own key. -->
    <meta-data android:name="com.google.android.maps.v2.API_KEY"
    android:value="AIzaSyDngxdxxxxxxxxxxxxxxxxxxxxxL9zx6G28"/>
    ...
```

11. Build and run the MapDemo project to verify the API key. You should see the maps shown in Figure 7-26. Your own API key is working!

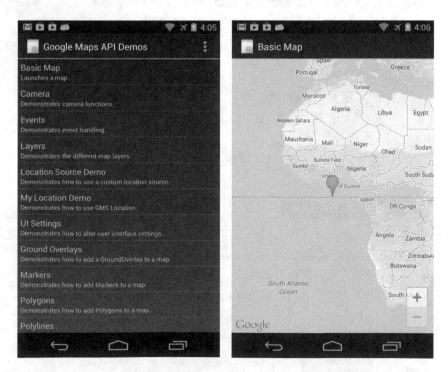

Figure 7-26. MapDemo app

You have completed the one-time setup tasks, including installing the Google Play services SDK and obtaining your own Google API key. Although you haven't written a line of code yet, you are able to see them working in the imported MapDemo sample project.

You are ready for some coding fun!

ADT PROJECT PREPARATIONS

To show and to learn by example, let's prepare an ADT project using our MvcTemplate project.

1. Copy the MvcTemplate ADT project and paste it to a new project (⌘c, ⌘v) named **GoogleMapApp**.

2. Rename the Android application package. From the newly created GoogleMapApp project context menu, select **Android Tools ➤ Rename Application Package**. Enter a new package name: **com.pdachoice.googlemapapp**.

3. Rename the GoogleMapApp/src/com.pdachoice.renameme Java package. From the package context menu, select **Refactor ➤ Rename**... (Alt+⌘r) and do the following:

   a. Enter a new name: **com.pdachoice.googlemapapp**.

   b. Select **Update references**.

4. You only need one fragment: keep ScreenOneFragment and delete the other two.

   - Delete the src/ScreenTwoFragment.java and src/ScreenThreeFragment.java classes (multiselect and fn+Delete).

   - Delete the res/layout/screentwo_fragment.xml and res/layout/screenthree_fragment.xml files (multiselect and fn+Delete).

5. Modify res/layout/screenone_fragment.xml. To keep it simple, you don't need anything in the layout for now (see Listing 7-50).

Listing 7-50. Layout File

```xml
<?xml version="1.0" encoding="utf-8"?>
<RelativeLayout xmlns:android="http://schemas.android.com/apk/res/android"
    android:layout_width="match_parent"
    android:layout_height="match_parent" >

</RelativeLayout>
```

6. Modify res/values/strings.xml to modify the app name and add some text (see Listing 7-51).

Listing 7-51. App Strings

```xml
<?xml version="1.0" encoding="utf-8"?>
<resources>

    <string name="app_name">Google Map App</string>
    <string name="action_location">Set Location</string>
```

```xml
        <string name="action_marker">Set Marker</string>
        <string name="action_circle">Set Circle</string>

    </resources>
```

7. Modify res/menu/main.xml by adding some action items (see Listing 7-52). We will use them to invoke GoogleMap API usage.

Listing 7-52. GoogleMapApp Options Menu Layout

```xml
<menu xmlns:android="http://schemas.android.com/apk/res/android"
    xmlns:app="http://schemas.android.com/apk/res-auto" >

    <item
        android:id="@+id/action_location"
        android:title="@string/action_location"
        app:showAsAction="never"/>

    <item
        android:id="@+id/action_marker"
        android:title="@string/action_marker"
        app:showAsAction="never"/>

    <item
        android:id="@+id/action_circle"
        android:title="@string/action_circle"
        app:showAsAction="never"/>

</menu>
```

8. Modify src/ScreenOneFragment.java by removing unnecessary code (see Listing 7-53).

Listing 7-53. ScreenOneFragment.java

```java
public class ScreenOneFragment extends Fragment {
  private View contentView;

  @Override
  public View onCreateView(LayoutInflater inflater, ViewGroup container,
      Bundle savedInstanceState) {
    contentView = inflater.inflate(R.layout.screenone_fragment, container,
        false);
    this.setHasOptionsMenu(true);

    return contentView;
  }
```

```java
    @Override
    public void onCreateOptionsMenu(Menu menu, MenuInflater inflater) {
        super.onCreateOptionsMenu(menu, inflater);
        inflater.inflate(R.menu.main, menu);
    }

    @Override
    public boolean onOptionsItemSelected(MenuItem item) {
        switch (item.getItemId()) {
        case R.id.action_location:
            // TODO
            break;
        case R.id.action_marker:
            // TODO
            break;
        case R.id.action_circle:
            // TODO
            break;
        default:
            break;
        }

        return super.onOptionsItemSelected(item);
    }
}
```

9. You may build and run the prep project to make sure it is good.

MapFragment

IOS ANALOGY

MKMapView

The Google Maps API provides MapFragment and MapView classes that you can use to display maps with Google Maps data. MapView displays a map with data from Google Maps services. It has its own lifecycle. MapFragment contains a MapView widget and manages the MapView lifecycle. When possible, use MapFragment to simplify your code.

To use MapFragment to show Google Maps in the GoogleMapApp project, do the following:

1. Add the GoogleMapApp package name to use the same API key you created previously, as shown in Figure 7-27.

   a. Log in to https://console.developers.google.com and select the Google Maps Android project created previously (you don't have to create a new project).

   b. Select **API & auth ➤ Credentials** from the left panel and select the **Edit allowed Android applications** button from an existing key (you don't have to create a new key).

   c. Add a line for the new SHA1;packageName.

   d. Click the **Update** button when done.

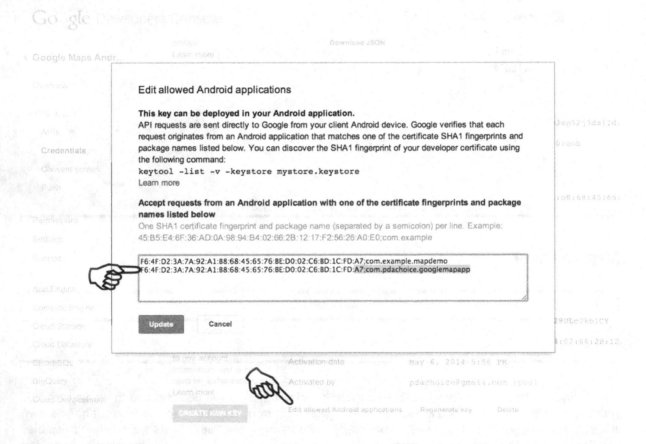

Figure 7-27. Add Android apps

2. Modify $PROJ/AndroidManifest.xml (see Listing 7-54), as follows:

   a. Include the API key for using Google Maps Android API v2.

   b. Add the required platform uses-permission.

   c. Declare <uses-feature> to exclude devices without the required Google Play services APK that is distributed via the Google Play Store. Some devices might not have the required runtime package.

Listing 7-54. GoogleMapApp AndroidManifest.xml

```xml
<?xml version="1.0" encoding="utf-8"?>
<manifest ... >

  <uses-permission android:name="android.permission.INTERNET" />
  <uses-permission android:name="android.permission.ACCESS_NETWORK_STATE" />
  <uses-permission android:name="android.permission.ACCESS_FINE_LOCATION" />
  <uses-permission android:name="android.permission.WRITE_EXTERNAL_STORAGE" />
  <uses-permission android:name="com.google.android.providers.gsf.permission.READ_
GSERVICES" />
  <uses-feature
        android:glEsVersion="0x00020000"
        android:required="true" />
  <uses-sdk
      android:minSdkVersion="7"
      android:targetSdkVersion="19" />
  <application
      ... >
      <meta-data
          android:name="com.google.android.maps.v2.API_KEY"
          android:value="AIzaSyAXxCFcaFgl4sPkF8jH15Yn28ULcOkb1CY" />
      <meta-data
          android:name="com.google.android.gms.version"
          android:value="@integer/google_play_services_version" />
  ...
```

3. Add the google-play-service_lib Android library project to your project setting the same way you did for the MapDemo sample project (see Figure 7-17). From the GoogleMapApp project context menu, select **Properties ...** (shortcut key: command+I), open the project Properties screen, and include the google-play-service_lib Android library project.

4. Add a MapFragment widget to $PROJ/res/layout/screenone_fragment.xml, as shown in Listing 7-55.

   a. Add the namespace xmlns:map="http://schemas.android.com/apk/res-auto" for the Google Map.

   b. Most likely, you want to use SupportMapFragment from the compatibility support library.

Listing 7-55. *MapFragment Widget*

```xml
<?xml version="1.0" encoding="utf-8"?>
<RelativeLayout xmlns:android="http://schemas.android.com/apk/res/android"
    android:layout_width="match_parent"
    android:layout_height="match_parent" >

    <fragment
        xmlns:map="http://schemas.android.com/apk/res-auto"
        android:id="@+id/map"
        android:layout_width="match_parent"
        android:layout_height="match_parent"
        class="com.google.android.gms.maps.SupportMapFragment"
        map:cameraBearing="0"
        map:cameraTargetLat="33.618910"
        map:cameraTargetLng="-117.928947"
        map:cameraTilt="75"
        map:cameraZoom="17"
        map:mapType="normal"
        map:uiCompass="true"
        map:uiRotateGestures="true"
        map:uiScrollGestures="true"
        map:uiTiltGestures="true"
        map:uiZoomControls="true"
        map:uiZoomGestures="true"
        map:useViewLifecycle="false"
        map:zOrderOnTop="false" />
</RelativeLayout>
```

Google MapFragment defines the following common attributes:

- Several cameraXXX attributes describe the map views being modeled as a camera looking down on a flat plane. The rendering of the map is specified by the following properties: cameraBearing, cameraTargetLat, cameraTargetLng, cameraTilt, and cameraZoom.

- mapType allows you to specify the type of map to display. Valid values include *none, normal, hybrid, satellite*, and *terrain*.

- Several uiXXX attributes specify the settings for the user interface of a Google map. uiCompass and uiZoomControls specify whether you want the zoom controls and compass to appear on the map. uiRotateGestures, uiZoomGestures, uiScrollGestures, and uiTiltGestures specify which gestures are enabled/disabled for interaction with the map.

- zOrderOnTop allows you to control whether the map view's surface is placed on top of its window. Note that this will cover all other views that could appear on the map (e.g., the zoom controls and the My Location button).

- useViewLifecycle is only valid with a MapFragment. This attribute specifies whether the lifecycle of the map should be tied to the fragment's view or the fragment itself.

Most of the map attributes can be manipulated in the runtime as well.

Build and run the GoogleMapApp project to see Google Maps in action. In Figure 7-28 a 3D Google map is rendered in the layout file. Without writing a single line of Java code, the map accepts all the gestures, including a two-finger tilt gesture.

Figure 7-28. 3D Google map

GoogleMap

Google Maps is rendered by either a MapFragment or MapView object. To interface with the map programmatically, the key class is the GoogleMap class.

The GoogleMap object handles the following operations automatically:

- Connecting to the Google Maps service.

- Downloading map tiles.

- Displaying tiles on the device screen.

- Displaying various controls, such as pan and zoom.

- Interfacing with the map attributes.

- Responding to pan and zoom gestures by moving the map and zooming in or out.

In addition to these automatic operations, you can control the behavior of maps with API objects and methods. For example, GoogleMap has callback methods that respond to keystrokes and touch gestures on the map. You can also set marker icons on your map and add overlays to it.

Let's demonstrate some of the GoogleMap usages in GoogleMapApp project.

1. Get a reference to the key class, GoogleMap (see Listing 7-56).

    a. Make sure the Google Play Service APK runtime is available and up to date.

    b. Keep a reference to the key class: MapFragment.getMap().

Listing 7-56. *Get GoogleMap Object Reference*

```java
public class ScreenOneFragment extends Fragment {

    private View contentView;
    private GoogleMap googleMap;

    @Override
    public View onCreateView(LayoutInflater inflater, ViewGroup container,
        Bundle savedInstanceState) {
        ...
        // Make sure service is available
        int code = GooglePlayServicesUtil
            .isGooglePlayServicesAvailable(getActivity());
        if (code != ConnectionResult.SUCCESS) {
          Toast.makeText(getActivity(), "Google Play Service Error: " + code,
              Toast.LENGTH_LONG).show();
        }

        // Obtain the googleMap from the MapFragment.getMap().
        Fragment mapFragment = getFragmentManager().findFragmentById(R.id.map);
        googleMap = ((SupportMapFragment) mapFragment).getMap();
        ...
        return contentView;
    }
    ...
}
```

2. Most of the map operations go through the key class, GoogleMap.

    a. Call GoogleMap.setMyLocationEnabled(true) to enable the **My Location** control in the upper-right corner.

    b. In Listing 7-55, the map attributes are initialized in the layout file. These attributes can be manipulated in the runtime using Java API googleMap.getUiSettings().setXXX(...) (see Listing 7-57).

Listing 7-57. *GoogleMap API*

```java
public class ScreenOneFragment extends Fragment {
    ...
    private GoogleMap googleMap;

    @Override
    public View onCreateView(LayoutInflater inflater, ViewGroup container,
```

```
        Bundle savedInstanceState) {
    ...
    // Null check to make sure the map is ready.
    if (googleMap != null) {
        googleMap.setMapType(GoogleMap.MAP_TYPE_NORMAL);
        // enable the My Location button on the top right corner.
        googleMap.setMyLocationEnabled(true);

        // map attributes
        googleMap.getUiSettings().setAllGesturesEnabled(true);
        googleMap.getUiSettings().setCompassEnabled(true);
    }

    return contentView;
  }
  ...
}
```

3. To change the view of the Google map, imagine that you are viewing the map from a camera view. You either move the camera or zoom the camera view, as opposed to moving the physical view in front of you. The changes are encapsulated in the CameraUpdate class. The following method changes the LatLng of the Google map (see Listing 7-58):

    a. Use CameraUpdateFactory to create the CameraUpdate object with the changes that you want to make.

    b. CameraUpdateFactory.newLatLng(latlng) creates a new position while preserving all other CameraPostion properties being used.

Listing 7-58. setLocation Using CameraUpdate

```
public class ScreenOneFragment extends Fragment {
    ...
  private void setLocation(LatLng latlng) {
    CameraUpdate update = CameraUpdateFactory.newLatLng(latlng);
    googleMap.animateCamera(update);
  }
  ...
}
```

4. To indicate a location on the map, create a MarkerOptions object for each pin or marker (see Listing 7-59).

Listing 7-59. MarkerOptions

```java
public class ScreenOneFragment extends Fragment {
  ...
    private void setMarker(LatLng... latlngs) {
      MarkerOptions markerOptions;
      for (int i = 0; i < latlngs.length; i++) {
        markerOptions = new MarkerOptions();
        markerOptions.position(latlngs[i]);
        markerOptions.title("Marker Title").snippet("snippet: some text");
        markerOptions.visible(true).draggable(true);
        markerOptions.icon(BitmapDescriptorFactory
            .fromResource(android.R.drawable.ic_menu_myplaces));
        googleMap.addMarker(markerOptions);
      }
    }
  ...
}
```

IOS ANALOGY

MKAnnotationView/MKPointAnnotation

5. You can also add *circles*, *polygons*, or *polylines* to your map. The following method adds circles (see Listing 7-60):

    a. Create a `CircleOptions` object for each circle shape, and call `addCircle(...)`.

    b. Similarly, use `GoogleMap.addPolygon(PolygonOptions)` or `GoogleMap.addPolyline(PolylineOptions)` to create the polygons or polylines.

Listing 7-60. CircleOptions

```java
public class ScreenOneFragment extends Fragment {
  ...
    private void setCircle(LatLng... latlngs) {
      CircleOptions circleOptions;
      for (int i = 0; i < latlngs.length; i++) {
        circleOptions = new CircleOptions().center(latlngs[i]);
        circleOptions.radius(300); // meters
        circleOptions.fillColor(Color.argb(192, 255, 192, 192));
        circleOptions.strokeColor(Color.RED).strokeWidth(5);
        circleOptions.visible(true).zIndex(0);
        googleMap.addCircle(circleOptions);
      }
    }
  ...
}
```

6. To visualize how the code in Listing 7-60 works, invoke it from the options menu (see Listing 7-61).

Listing 7-61. Options Menu Handler

```java
public class ScreenOneFragment extends Fragment {

  static final LatLng MyPosition = new LatLng(33.6716998, -117.7998752);
  static final LatLng Vancouver = new LatLng(49.261226, -123.113927);
  static final LatLng Newport = new LatLng(33.649679, -117.719968);
  static final float RADIUS = 100;

  ...
  @Override
  public boolean onOptionsItemSelected(MenuItem item) {
    switch (item.getItemId()) {
    case R.id.action_location:
      setLocation(MyPosition);
      break;
    case R.id.action_marker:
      setMarker(MyPosition, Newport, Vancouver);

      break;
    case R.id.action_circle:
      setCircle(MyPosition, Newport, Vancouver);
      break;
    default:
      break;
    }

    return super.onOptionsItemSelected(item);
  }
  ...
}
```

7. Build and run the GoogleMapApp project and select the options menu to see the code in action (see Figure 7-29).

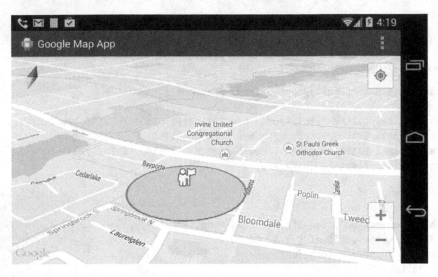

Figure 7-29. Google map circle mark

In real apps, these methods most likely get called based on business rules or on location awareness triggers, geofencing, and so forth.

Note   Everything should work as expected, except the My Location button might not do anything if the Location Access is not enabled in the system Settings app. Be nice to users and let them know why this has happened. We will discuss this in the next chapter.

Location Services

To build *location awareness* into your Android apps, you have two good choices. In my early years, I used the android.location package from the Android SDK, which has been available since API Level 1. Ever since I started using Google Maps in Google Play services, I have used the Google Location Services API. The official Android Developers site recommends using the Google Location Services API. The following excerpt is from https://developer.android.com/guide/topics/location/index.html:

> *The Google Location Services API, part of Google Play Services, provides a more powerful, high-level framework that automates tasks such as location provider choice and power management. Location Services also provides new features such as activity detection that aren't available in the framework API. Developers who are using the framework API, as well as developers who are just now adding location-awareness to their apps, should strongly consider using the Location Services API.*

Both work pretty well in my experience. Location Services and Maps seem to go hand-in-hand in many location-aware apps. To use the Google Maps API, I have already set up a Google Play services library project, which also provides the Google Location Services API. As for now, you probably would only have to use the old Android framework location API for supporting devices on API Level 7 or below, which now only accounts for a very small percentage. If this is your requirement, look up android.location.LocationManager at http://developer.android.com/reference/android/location/package-summary.html. I had great experiences with it.

Let's focus on the recommended choice, the Google Location Services API.

ADT PROJECT PREPARATIONS

We don't need a new prep project for this topic because it makes sense to continue using GoogleMapApp, which already has everything we need to use the Google Location Services API. Map and location awareness–related requirements frequently go hand-in-hand. This existing GoogleMapApp project is also perfect for demonstrating the interactions between the Maps and Location Services APIs.

To use the Google Location Services API alone, you don't need a Google API key. Only the Google Play services library is required.

Connect to LocationClient

IOS ANALOGY

CoreLocation/CLLocationManager

Google Location Services sends the user's current location to your app through a location client, which is an instance of the Location Services LocationClient class. All requests for location information go through this class. For common Location Services tasks, do the following:

1. Select the Google Play services runtime:
    isGooglePlayServicesAvailable(...). In Listing 7-56, you already did this using the Google Maps Android API.

2. Check the Location Access system settings. The method shown in Listing 7-62 does the job.

    Listing 7-62. Check System Settings

    ```
    public class ScreenOneFragment extends Fragment {
        ...
      @Override
      public View onCreate(Bundle savedInstanceState) {
        ...
    ```

```java
        this.checkSystemPreferences();
        ...
    }
    ...
    private void checkSystemPreferences() {
        // Check whether Location Access is enabled in System Settings
        ContentResolver resolver = getActivity().getContentResolver();
        String providers = Secure.getString(resolver,
            Secure.LOCATION_PROVIDERS_ALLOWED);

        // It is nice to let users know what is wrong
        if (providers == null || providers.length() <= 0) {
            AlertDialog.Builder builder = new AlertDialog.Builder(getActivity());
            builder.setTitle("Location Access Not Enabled?");
            builder.setMessage("Go to System Settings?");
            builder.setIcon(android.R.drawable.ic_dialog_alert);
            builder.setPositiveButton("YES", new OnClickListener() {
                @Override
                public void onClick(DialogInterface dialog, int which) {
                    // c. send users to System Settings app
                    Intent intent = new Intent(android.provider.Settings.ACTION_LOCATION_SOURCE_
SETTINGS);
                    startActivity(intent);
                }
            });

            builder.setNegativeButton("NO", null).create().show();
        }
    }
    ...
}
```

3. Create a `LocationClient` instance and use the instance to connect to
    and disconnect from Google Location Services (see Listing 7-63). The
    `LocationClient` constructor takes three arguments:

    a. Context: Such as getActivity()

    b. ConnectionCallbacks: ScreenOneFragment implements
        ConnectionCallbacks

    c. OnConnectionFailedListener: ScreenOneFragment implements
        OnConnectionFailedListener

Listing 7-63. LocationClient

```java
public class ScreenOneFragment extends Fragment implements
    ConnectionCallbacks, OnConnectionFailedListener {
...
private LocationClient locationClient;
```

```
@Override
public void onCreate(Bundle savedInstanceState) {
  super.onCreate(savedInstanceState);
  locationClient = new LocationClient(getActivity(), this, this);
  locationClient.connect();
}

@Override
public void onStop() {
  super.onStop();
  locationClient.disconnect();
}

@Override
public void onConnected(Bundle connectionHint) {
  Toast.makeText(getActivity(), "onConnected", Toast.LENGTH_SHORT).show();
}

@Override
public void onDisconnected() {
  Toast.makeText(getActivity(), "onDisconnected", Toast.LENGTH_SHORT).show();
}

@Override
public void onConnectionFailed(ConnectionResult arg0) {
  Toast.makeText(getActivity(), "onConnectionFailed: ",
      Toast.LENGTH_SHORT).show();
}
...
}
```

4. Build and run the GoogleMapApp project to make sure the code is working.
    You should see a toast showing an **onConnected** status (see Figure 7-30).

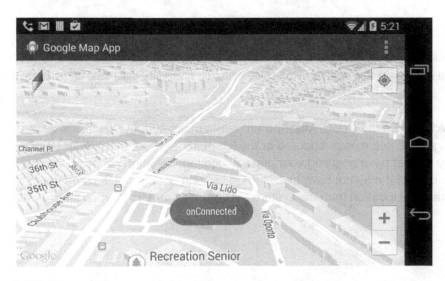

Figure 7-30. LocationClient connected

Keep in mind that most location service operations can only be performed after LocationClient is connected to Google Location Service. You either check the LocationClient connection status, or perform those APIs in the onConnected(...) callback. You will see more of the same considerations in the next section.

GetLastLocation

To get the last known location, simply call LocationClient.getLastLocation() to retrieve the last known location *after* LocationClient is connected to Location Services. Continue with GoogleMapApp. Listing 7-64 gets the current location as soon as LocationClient is connected to Location Services.

Listing 7-64. getLastLocation

```
public class ScreenOneFragment extends ... {
  ...
  @Override
  public void onConnected(Bundle connectionHint) {
    Toast.makeText(getActivity(), "onConnected", Toast.LENGTH_SHORT).show();
    getLastLocation();
  }

  private void getLastLocation() {
    Location currentLocation = locationClient.getLastLocation();
    if (currentLocation != null) { // It can be null
      double lat = currentLocation.getLatitude();
      double lng = currentLocation.getLongitude();
      setLocation(new LatLng(lat, lng));
    }
  }
  ...
}
```

> **Note**   The last known location can be null for many reasons, such as a device still initializing GPS and unable to acquire a location yet. Check null to avoid a null pointer. (In Java, you cannot send messages to null.)

5. Build and run the GoogleMapApp project to make sure the code is working. You should see a map rendered at the location near you. If not, your device may not yet have acquired your current location. Location access could be disabled or it may not have been turned on long enough. Make sure you enable the location from the system Settings app and try it again later.

Geocoder

You can use the Geocoder class to do both geocoding and reverse geocoding:

- Geocoder.getFromLocation(...) performs reverse geocoding.

- Geocoder.getFromLocationName(...) gets the latitude and longitude from an address or location name.

To visualize how the API works, let's continue with GoogleMapApp.

1. Add the method shown in Listing 7-65 to get the first address from a given latitude and longitude using the Geocoder class. The geocoding operations invoke remote service. Use AsyncTask to perform network operations in the background.

    Listing 7-65. Geocoding

    ```java
    public class ScreenOneFragment extends ... {
      ...
      private void geocoding(LatLng loc) {
        AsyncTask<LatLng, Void, List<Address>>task = new AsyncTask<LatLng,
          Void, List<Address>>() {

          @Override
          protected void onPostExecute(List<Address> addresses) {
            String addr;
            if (addresses != null && addresses.size() > 0) {
              addr = addresses.get(0).toString(); // the first address
            } else {
              addr = "No address found";
            }
            Toast.makeText(getActivity(),addr,Toast.LENGTH_SHORT).show();
          }

          @Override
          protected List<Address> doInBackground(LatLng... locs) {
            Geocoder coder = new Geocoder(getActivity(),
                Locale.getDefault());
            LatLng loc = locs[0];
            List<Address> addresses = null;
            try {
              // get one address
              addresses = coder.getFromLocation(loc.latitude,loc.longitude, 1);
            } catch (IOException e) {
              e.printStackTrace();
            } catch (IllegalArgumentException e) {
              e.printStackTrace();
            }
            return addresses;
          }
        };
        task.execute(loc);
      }
      ...
    ```

> **Note**   The Geocoder class has been in the Android SDK since API Level 1. You don't need the Google Play services SDK or a Google API key.

2. To visualize how it works, update the setLocation(...), as shown in Listing 7-66.

Listing 7-66. *Perform Geocoding*

```
public class ScreenOneFragment extends Fragment {
  ...
  private void setLocation(LatLng latlng) {
    CameraUpdate update = CameraUpdateFactory.newLatLng(latlng);
    googleMap.animateCamera(update);
    this.geocoding(latlng);
  }
  ...
```

3. Build and run the GoogleMapApp project and select **Set Location** from the options menu, which triggers the geocoding code (see Figure 7-31).

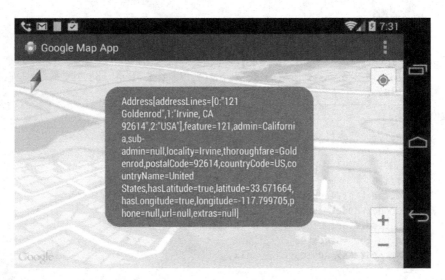

Figure 7-31. Geocoder

You probably don't want to display the raw Address.toString() in the real app. The Java Address class has rich, convenient getters to get specific address attributes, such as getLatitude().

RequestLocationUpdates

You can request location update notifications to track locations or show navigations. To demonstrate location updates usage, continue the GoogleMapApp project with the following code:

1. To request location updates, create a `LocationRequest` object that specifies how the listener receives the location updates (see Listing 7-67), as follows:

   a. **setPriority**: Sets the priority of the request when you have two different requests with different parameters.

   b. **setInterval**: Sets the desired interval for active location updates in milliseconds.

   c. **setSmallestDisplacement**: Sets the minimum displacement between location updates in meters. The updates will be suppressed if the displacement is too small.

   d. **setNumUpdates**: Sets the number of location updates, such as a one-time update only.

   e. **setFastestInterval**: Explicitly sets the fastest interval for location updates in milliseconds when there are multiple coactive requests.

Listing 7-67. Create LocationUpdate Object

```
public class ScreenOneFragment extends ... {
  ...
  private void requestLocationUpdates() {
    // create LocationRequest object to specify how to receive updates
    LocationRequest request = LocationRequest.create();
    request.setPriority(LocationRequest.PRIORITY_HIGH_ACCURACY);
    // request.setFastestInterval(1000);
    // request.setNumUpdates(1);
    request.setInterval(3000); // 3 secs
    request.setSmallestDisplacement(RADIUS / 10);
  }
  ...
}
```

2. Use the `locationClient` object to request location updates with a listener, the `ScreenOneFragment`, and the `LocationRequest` object (see Listing 7-68).

   a. Call `locationClient.requestLocationUpdates(...)` with the preceding request object and a listener.

   b. ScreenOneFragment implements the `LocationListener` interface.

   c. Simply call the `setLocation` method (see Listing 7-66) to set the map location with the updated location, so that you can see the location updates.

Listing 7-68. requestLocationUpdates

```
public class ScreenOneFragment extends Fragment implements LocationListener {
  ...
  private void requestLocationUpdates() {
    ...
    locationClient.requestLocationUpdates(request, this);
  }

  @Override
  public void onLocationChanged(Location loc) {
    Toast.makeText(getActivity(), "onLocationChanged",
        Toast.LENGTH_SHORT).show();
    if (loc != null) {
      setLocation(new LatLng(loc.getLatitude(), loc.getLongitude()));
    }
  }
  ...
```

3. The Location Services API can only be called after the location client
    is connected. I simply call this method as soon as the app receives the
    onConnected(...) callback (see Listing 7-69). To stop location updates, call
    removeLocationUpdates(...) when it is not needed. The app can continue to
    receive location updates and consume the CPU and battery, even when it is
    in the background.

Listing 7-69. requestLocationUpdates onConnected

```
public class ScreenOneFragment extends Fragment implements LocationListener {
  ...
  private LocationClient locationClient;

  @Override
  public void onConnected(Bundle connectionHint) {
    ...
    requestLocationUpdates();
    ...
  }

  @Override
  public void onStop() {
    super.onStop();
    locationClient.removeLocationUpdates(this);
    locationClient.disconnect();
  }
  ...
}
```

You may build and run the app. Location Services works better outdoors. When the app is in the
foreground, it should continue to receive updates and update the map location on the screen.

addGeofences

Geofencing combines awareness of the user's current location with awareness of nearby features, defined as the user's proximity to locations that may be of interest. To mark a location of interest, you specify its latitude and longitude. To adjust the proximity for the location, you add a radius. The latitude, longitude, and radius define a *geofence*. You can have multiple active geofences at one time.

Use an addGeofences method to detect when the user enters or exits a geofence. For each geofence, you can ask Location Services to send you entrance events or exit events, or both. You can also limit the duration of a geofence by specifying an expiration duration in milliseconds. After the geofence expires, Location Services automatically removes it.

Continuing with GoogleMapApp, let's create a monitorGeofences() method that creates geofences and sends intent notifications to the app itself for geofence entrance and exit events.

1. Use Geofence.Builder to create Geofence objects that specify how to monitor the geofence (see Listing 7-70):

   a. setRequestId: Sets the ID of the request when you have two different requests with different parameters.

   b. setTransitionTypes: Sets the desired interval for active location updates in milliseconds.

   c. setCircularRegion: Sets the minimum displacement between location updates in meters. The updates will be suppressed if the displacement is too small.

   d. setExpirationDuration: Sets the number of location updates, such as a one-time update only.

Listing 7-70. Create Geofence Objects

```
public class ScreenOneFragment extends Fragment implements ... {

  static final float RADIUS = 100; // in meters
  ...
  private void monitorGeofences(LatLng... locations) {
    List<Geofence> fences = new ArrayList<Geofence>();
    Geofence.Builder builder = new Geofence.Builder();
    for (int i = 0; i < locations.length; i++) {
      // use Geofence.Builder to create Geofence object
      Geofence fence = builder
          .setRequestId("RequestId:" + i)
          .setTransitionTypes(Geofence.GEOFENCE_TRANSITION_ENTER
              | Geofence.GEOFENCE_TRANSITION_EXIT)
          .setCircularRegion(locations[i].latitude, locations[i].longitude,
            RADIUS).setExpirationDuration(Geofence.NEVER_EXPIRE).build();
      fences.add(fence);
    }
  }
  ...
}
```

2. Use `LocationClient.addGeofences(...)` with geofences and a listener to request a geofence update (see Listing 7-71).

    a. Create a `PendingIntent` instance that specifies an application component to receive geofence intents. In general, it makes sense to use a service component if you want to get updates when the app is not in the foreground. We will implement `MonitorGeofenceService` next. Ignore the compilation error for now.

    b. Designate a listener for an `addGeofences(...)` result. It is not for receiving the geofence events, which are delivered as intents to an application component.

Listing 7-71. addGeofences

```java
public class ScreenOneFragment extends Fragment implements ... {

private PendingIntent pendingIntent;
  ...
  private void monitorGeofences(LatLng... locations) {
    ...
    Intent intent = new Intent(getActivity(), MonitorGeofenceService.class);
    pendingIntent = PendingIntent.getService(getActivity(), 0, intent, 0);

    locationClient.addGeofences(fences, pendingIntent,
        new OnAddGeofencesResultListener() {
          public void onAddGeofencesResult(int statusCode,
                          String[] geofenceRequestIds) {
            if (LocationStatusCodes.SUCCESS == statusCode) {
              Toast.makeText(getActivity(),
                  Arrays.deepToString(geofenceRequestIds),
                  Toast.LENGTH_SHORT).show();
            } else {
              // If adding the geofences failed
            }
          }
        });
  }
  ...
```

3. Create the `MonitorGeofenceService` Android service component (see the "IntentService" section on how to create aHelloService in Chapter 5) to handle the geofence intent (see Listing 7-72).

    a. Always check `hasError`. You cannot assume the intent is only from Location Services.

    b. Get the **transition type** from the intent.

c. Get the **triggering geofences** from the intent.

d. To visualize the geofence events, post a notification to the Android notification bar using NotificationManager.

Listing 7-72. MonitorGeofenceService

```java
public class MonitorGeofenceService extends IntentService {

    public MonitorGeofenceService(String name) {
        super(name);
    }

    @Override
    protected void onHandleIntent(Intent intent) {
        // check for errors
        if (LocationClient.hasError(intent) == false) {
            // Get the type of transition (enter or exit, -1 for invalid)
            int transitionType = LocationClient.getGeofenceTransition(intent);
            String title = null, toastText = null;
            if (transitionType >=0) {
                List<Geofence> fences = LocationClient.getTriggeringGeofences(intent);
                toastText = Arrays.deepToString(fences.toArray());
                title = (transitionType == Geofence.GEOFENCE_TRANSITION_ENTER) ?
                    "Enter" : "Exit";

                addToNotificationTray(transitionType, title, toastText);
            }
        }
    }

    private void addToNotificationTray(int type,String title,String text) {
        Context context = getApplication();
        NotificationCompat.Builder builder =
            new NotificationCompat.Builder(context)
            .setSmallIcon(android.R.drawable.ic_dialog_map)
            .setContentTitle("Geofence").setContentText(title)
            .setContentInfo(text).setAutoCancel(true);

        NotificationManager manager = (NotificationManager) context
            .getSystemService(Context.NOTIFICATION_SERVICE);

        // use type to update the notification later on.
        manager.notify(type, builder.build());
    }
}
```

4. Declare the service component in AndroidManifest.xml (see Listing 7-73).

Listing 7-73. Declare Service Component in the Manifest File

```
<manifest ... >
    ...
    <application  ... >
        ...
        <service android:name="com.pdachoice.googlemapapp.MonitorGeofenceService" />
        ...
    </application>
</manifest>
```

5. As usual, the Google Location Services API can only be called after a location client is connected (see Listing 7-74).

    a. Call the monitorGeofences() method as soon as the app receives the onConnected callback.

    b. To stop monitoring the geofences, use LocationClient. removeGeofences(...). You need to supply an OnRemoveGeofencesResultListener.

Listing 7-74. Start and Stop Geofence

```
public class ScreenOneFragment extends Fragment implements ... {

    static final LatLng MyPosition = new LatLng(33.6716998, -117.7998752);
    static final LatLng Newport = new LatLng(33.618910, -117.928947);
    static final LatLng Vancouver = new LatLng(49.261226, -123.113927);

    ...
    @Override
    public void onConnected(Bundle connectionHint) {
        ...
        monitorGeofences(MyPosition, Newport);
        ...
    }

    @Override
    public void onStop() {
        ...
        locationClient.removeGeofences(pendingIntent,
            new OnRemoveGeofencesResultListener() {

            @Override
            public void onRemoveGeofencesByRequestIdsResult(int arg0, String[] arg1) {
                // no-op
            }

            @Override
            public void onRemoveGeofencesByPendingIntentResult(int arg0,
                PendingIntent arg1) {
```

```
        // no-op
    }
 });
 ...
 }
 ...
 }
```

6. Build and run the GoogleMapApp project. Change the latitude and longitude
    to your location. For safety reasons, do not drive while testing the app. A
    nice walk in your neighborhood should do it. When you enter or leave your
    defined geofences, the app uses `NotificationManager` to post a notification
    on the top-left corner on the notification bar (see Figure 7-32).

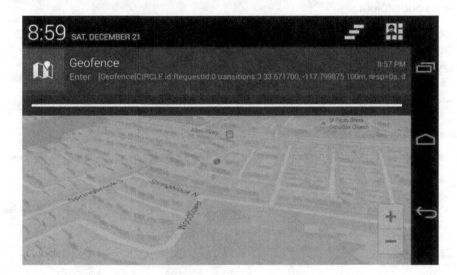

Figure 7-32. Geofence notification

As I am writing now, a simple fitness app popped into my head. Show a Google map with your
current location. Ask the user to provide simple radius input to monitor the geofence with the radius
proximity. By monitoring the existence of the geofence, the app will give users a nice greeting when
they start and complete a jogging exercise. On every location update, the app can also calculate
total distance and number of calories spent, track the time and speed, and record paths and so
forth. All these features can be done using the Google Location Services API!

Mobile Analytics

If you already track user behaviors in your iOS apps, there is no reason you can't do the same in
your Android app. I use *Google Mobile Analytics* for both my iOS apps and Android apps. It doesn't
require your own backend infrastructure support and it already comes with analytics views that you
can easily aggregate or separate for your purpose.

Let's add the Google Mobile Analytics code to the MvcTemplate project so that the feature can be inherited by other apps, because it is very valuable to know how your target users interact with your apps.

> ### ADT PROJECT PREPARATIONS
>
> Let's modify the MvcTemplate project, without creating a new prep project, to demonstrate the Google Mobile Analytics API usage. The Google Analytics code will be automatically inherited from any projects started from it.

Google Mobile Analytics

To use Google Analytics for Android or iOS mobile apps, you first need to set up a Google Analytics account to track your project.

1. If you already have a Google Analytics account, skip this step and go to step 2. Otherwise, sign up for a Google Analytics account at www.google.com/ analytics/ (see Figure 7-33).

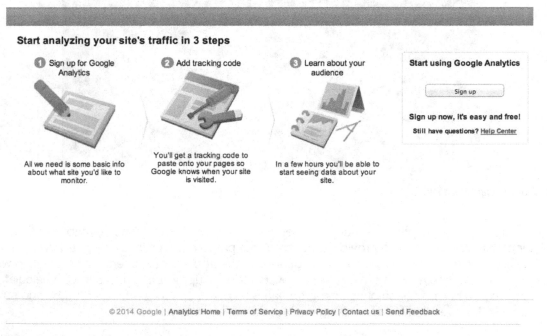

Figure 7-33. Signing up for Google Analytics

2. Click the **Access Google Analytics** button, select the **Mobile App** toggle, and enter the required fields in the **Setting up your account** form (see Figure 7-34).

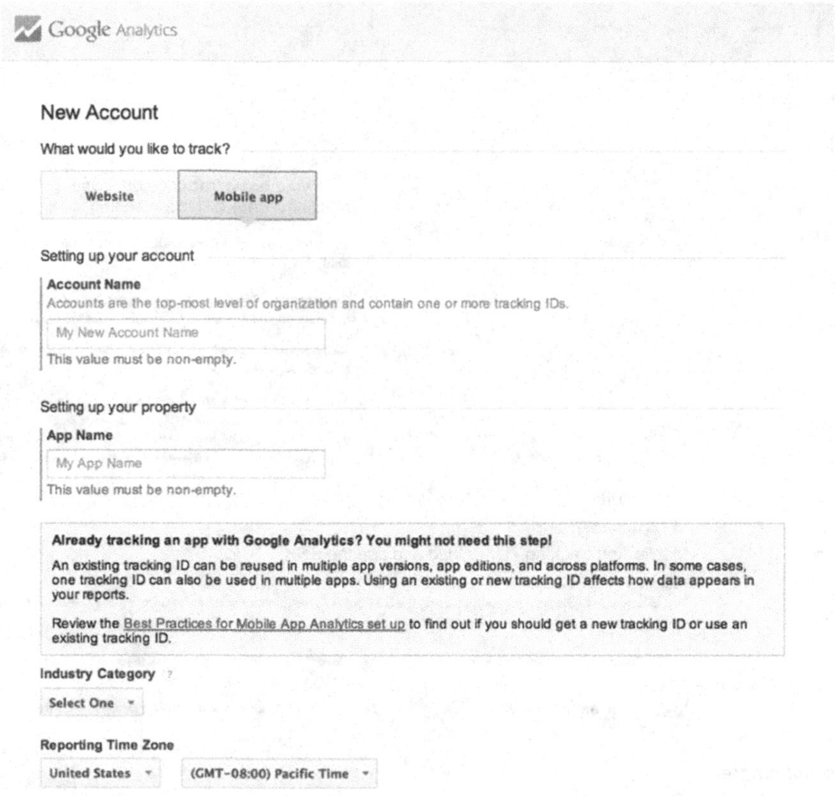

Figure 7-34. Setting up your account

Note   I entered **MyAccount** as the Account Name, and **MyApp** as the App Name. You can enter anything for now. It can be modified to be more meaningful later.

---

3. Click the **Get Tracking ID** button and accept the **Terms of Service Agreement**. You should see the screen in Figure 7-35, which shows that the account and the app's property have been created.

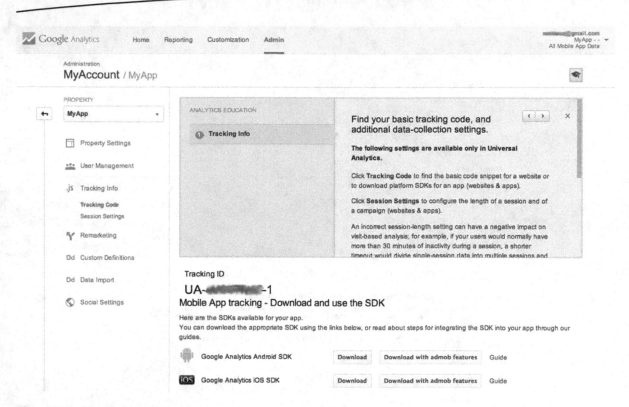

Figure 7-35. GA account created

4. If you already have a Google Analytics account or if you want to continue creating another **Property** for a new tracking ID, do the following:

    a. Sign in at www.google.com/analytics/ and go to the **Admin** tab.

    b. Click the **PROPERTY** dropdown menu and select **Create new property**, as shown in Figure 7-36.

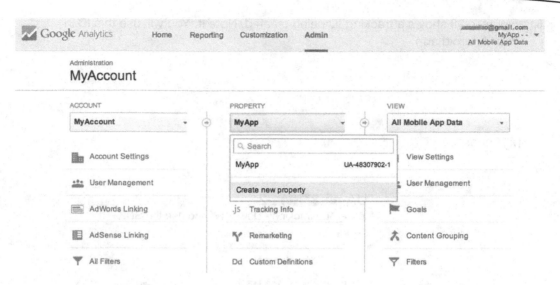

Figure 7-36. Create new property

5. Select the **Mobile app** toggle and enter an App Name, such as *MvcTemplate* (see Figure 7-37). Click **Get Tracking ID** to complete the step.

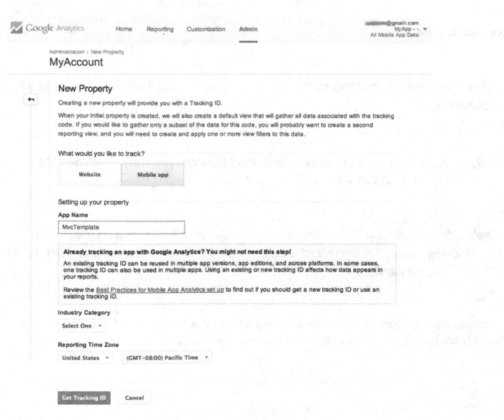

Figure 7-37. New Property

6. Figure 7-38 shows a tracking ID being created. Note it. You will use this ID in your Android app.

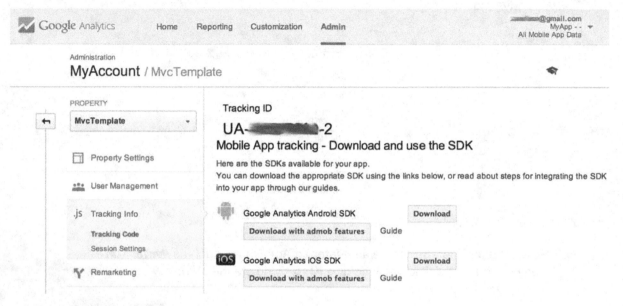

Figure 7-38. *Tracking ID*

> **Note**   You want to protect your tracking ID. You don't want to collect dirty data from hackers in your analytics reports.

7. Figure 7-38 also shows two Download buttons; you may download the Google Analytics Android SDK right now.

> **Note**   You can also download the Google Analytics SDK from https://developers.google.com/analytics/devguides/collection/android/resources. It is a ZIP file that contains a Java library JAR file: libGoogleAnalyticsServices.jar

You should have a Google Analytics tracking ID and the latest Google Analytics Services library, libGoogleAnalyticsServices.jar, ready for your analytical code.

Using the Google Analytics SDK

The following overview of Google Analytics SDK is excerpted from the Google Developers Google Analytics page at `https://developers.google.com/analytics/devguides/collection/`. Please visit this web page for more information.

> *Developers can ... use the Google Analytics reports to measure: the number of active users are using their applications; from where in the world the application is being used; adoption and usage of specific features; crashes and exceptions; in-app purchases and transactions; and many other useful metrics...*

We will only demonstrate the basic usages that are simple but meaningful. They can be done using a single convenient class called `EasyTracker`.

Note   EasyTracker is a subclass of Tracker, designed to ease the burden of adding tracking code to your application.

When you need more advanced tracking features, you will know where to get more information. As a matter of fact, everything in this chapter is covered at `https://developers.google.com/analytics/devguides/collection/android/`.

Let's embed the `EasyTracker` code to in the MvcTemplate project.

1. Drag and drop the `libGoogleAnalyticsServices.jar` onto the `MvcTemplate/libs/` folder in the Eclipse workbench. This adds `libGoogleAnalyticsServices.jar` to the MvcTemplate project build path (see Figure 7-39).

Figure 7-39. Add libGoogleAnalyticsServices.jar library file to the project build path

> **Note** If you have a fairly old version of Eclipse, you might want to double-check whether the JAR file is added to the project build path. From the Project context menu, go to **Properties** (command+i) ➤ **Java Build Path** ➤ **Libraries** (see Figure 7-40). I remembered I needed to manually do **Add JARs...** when using an older version of Eclipse.

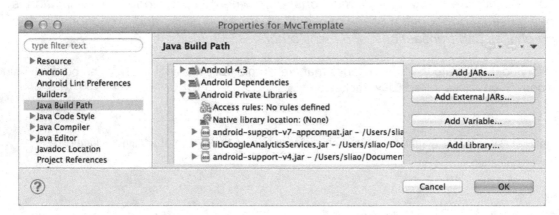

Figure 7-40. Java build path

2. The Google Analytics SDK uploads analytics data to the Google server. You need to declare the uses-permission shown in Listing 7-75 in your manifest file.

Listing 7-75. uses-permission in Manifest File

```xml
<manifest xmlns:android="http://schemas.android.com/apk/res/android"
    package="com.pdachoice.renameme"
    android:versionCode="1"
    android:versionName="1.0" >

    <uses-permission android:name="android.permission.INTERNET" />
    <uses-permission android:name="android.permission.ACCESS_NETWORK_STATE" />
    ...
```

3. To track the start and stop of the MvcTemplate app, add the code in Listing 7-76 to the appropriate activity lifecycle callbacks.

Listing 7-76. Activity Start and Stop

```java
public class MainActivity extends ActionBarActivity {
    ...
    @Override
    public void onStart() {
        super.onStart();
        EasyTracker.getInstance(this).activityStart(this);  // Add this method.
    }
```

```
    @Override
    public void onStop() {
      super.onStop();
      EasyTracker.getInstance(this).activityStop(this);  // Add this method.
    }
    ...
```

4. To measure screen views, add the **Screen** tracking code in each
    Fragment.onResume(...). For example, the code in Listing 7-77 tracks the
    ScreenOneFragment screen visits. You should do the same thing for all three
    fragments in the MvcTemplate project.

Listing 7-77. Track Screen Views

```
public class ScreenOneFragment extends Fragment implements OnClickListener {
    ...
    @Override
    public void onResume() {
        super.onResume();

        EasyTracker tracker = EasyTracker.getInstance(getActivity());
        tracker.set(Fields.SCREEN_NAME, this.getClass().getSimpleName());
        tracker.send(MapBuilder.createAppView().build());
    }
    ...
```

Note   Screen view data is primarily used in the Google Analytics standard Screens report and Engagement
Flow report.

---

5. To measure or collect data about a user's interaction with interactive
    components like button presses, add the **Event** tracking code anywhere
    your code is triggered. For example, Listing 7-78 tracks device orientation in
    landscape mode.

Listing 7-78. Track Events

```
public class MainActivity extends ActionBarActivity {
    ...
    @Override
    public void onConfigurationChanged(Configuration newConfig) {
        super.onConfigurationChanged(newConfig);

        ...
        if (newConfig.orientation == Configuration.ORIENTATION_LANDSCAPE) {
          EasyTracker easyTracker = EasyTracker.getInstance(this);
```

```
        easyTracker.send(MapBuilder
          .createEvent("config_changed",      // Event category (required)
                       "device_orientation",  // Event action (required)
                       "landscape",           // Event label
                       null)                  // Event value
          .build());
      } else if (newConfig.orientation == Configuration.ORIENTATION_PORTRAIT) {
      // Toast.makeText(this, "portrait", Toast.LENGTH_SHORT).show();
      }
      ...
    }
    ...
```

6. Create a file called analytics.xml. It is an Android resource file that must
    be in the MvcTemplate/res/values directory (see Listing 7-79). When using
    EasyTracker, global configuration settings are managed using the resources
    defined in XML. You must enter your own **Tracking ID** in the **ga_trackingId** field.

Listing 7-79. EasyTracker Configuration File

```xml
<?xml version="1.0" encoding="utf-8" ?>

<resources>
  <!--Replace placeholder ID with your tracking ID-->
  <string name="ga_trackingId">UA-xxxxxxxx-x</string>

  <!--Enable automatic activity tracking-->
  <bool name="ga_autoActivityTracking">false</bool>

  <!--Enable automatic exception tracking-->
  <bool name="ga_reportUncaughtExceptions">true</bool>
</resources>
```

Table 7-1 lists the names of the EasyTracker XML attributes that you can use to configure Google
Analytics behavior.

Table 7-1. EasyTracker XML Attributes

Parameter	Type	Parameter	Type
ga_trackingId	string	ga_sampleFrequency	string
ga_appName	string	ga_autoActivityTracking	boolean
ga_appVersion	string	ga_anonymizeIp	boolean
ga_logLevel **(V3 only)**	string	ga_reportUncaughtExceptions	boolean
ga_debug **(V2 only)**	boolean	ga_sessionTimeout	integer
ga_dispatchPeriod	integer		

> **Note** For more information, see the online reference at https://developers.google.com/analytics/devguides/collection/android/parameters#parameters.

Track each screen view and landscape orientation event. Writing mobile code to send *screen view* or *event* hits are easy. It takes more creative thinking about how to organize and analyze the analytical data for your business requirements in Google Analytics reports. Log in to your Google Analytics account to see screen views and events data. You might not know everything about the Google Analytics reports yet, but you will get a fairly good idea about the free analytical and tracking reports and screens available from Google. Figure 7-41 shows the application overview of an app, which you don't need to create the reporting page.

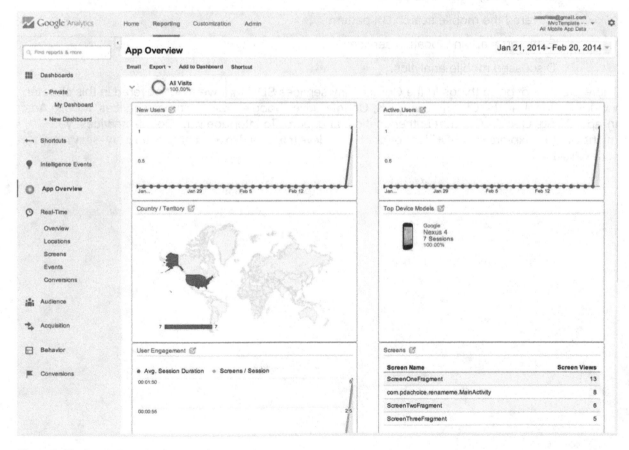

Figure 7-41. Google Analytics app overview

> **Note**   Real-time tracking might not work right away for newly created accounts. You may need to wait anywhere from a couple of hours to a day before you can see the real-time tracking data.

Summary

This chapter highlighted some common mobile use cases, which you might have already implemented in your iOS apps. By no mean does it cover all the mobile use cases. My goal was to show the common techniques using intents to integrate existing code and to incorporate the Google Play services SDK in Android apps. We did the following:

- Created a hybrid app with WebView to display interactive web pages.
- Integrated system apps using intents.
- Covered the mobile search UX pattern.
- Explored map and location services.
- Discussed mobile analytics.

There are a lot of good things in the Google Play services SDK that were not covered in this chapter, including Google+, the Chromecast SDK, Google Drive, Google Wallet, Games services, Mobile Ads, In-app Billing, Google Account authentication, and more. To interface with Google services, you might want to explore this SDK further at `http://developer.android.com/google/play-services/index.html`.

Chapter 8

Pulling It All Together

Recap with a Case Study

Thus far in this book, you have covered many discrete iOS-to-Android mapping topics and created more than 20 ADT projects. Those mapping topics were purposely implemented in individual ADT projects with very few classes. In Chapter 3, you learned the top-down development approach to break the whole app into iOS-like MVC-oriented fragments. In Chapter 4, you learned how to port individual smaller components from counterpart iOS app components, piece by piece. However, all those topics are designed to be self-contained without dependencies so they can serve as independent instructions. In the real programming world, it is the combination of features and use cases that makes your app useful and entertaining. For sure you will need more than one mapping guideline to complete a meaningful app. In this chapter, you are going to port an existing iOS app from start to finish using the mapping topics from Chapters 3 and 4. Nothing is new really: you are still going to repeat the same top-down development approach as you have been, and implement one piece at a time.

Perhaps there is one thing that I have not yet mentioned explicitly in the book yet: which piece should go first, and then what goes next. For any app—including the iOS apps that you are porting from, you must go through the same thinking process. If you remember how you created the iOS apps that you are porting from, that will be a great start because it will make your porting tasks to Android more efficient. Otherwise, you will use the same thinking process that you normally use: decide the dependencies among the pieces and try to reduce the dependencies along the way. After all, there is really no absolutely right or wrong way. This is off our porting topic, but I think you will begin to understand my thinking process in this final exercise.

Again, to show and learn by example, your goal is to port a RentalROI iOS app to the Android platform. Figure 8-1 shows the running iOS app.

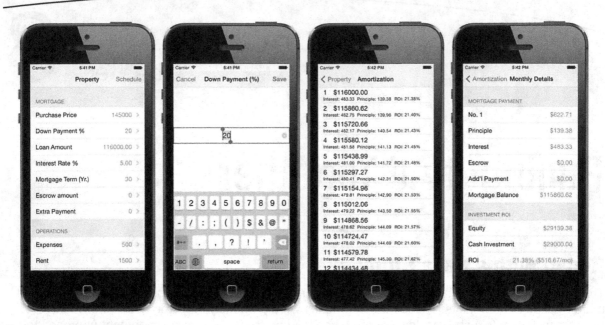

Figure 8-1. *iOS Rental ROI screens*

Figure 8-2 presents the four screens on the Xcode storyboard.

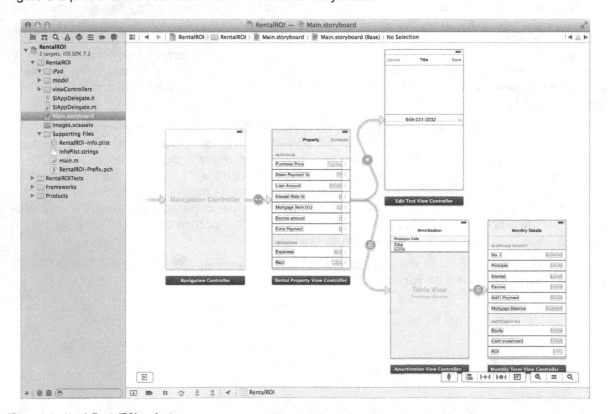

Figure 8-2. *XcodeRentalROI project*

This app performs the following tasks:

- Every time a user enters new rental property parameters, user input is saved using NSUserDefaults

- The amortization schedule is calculated on the remote server. The iOS client simply calls the remote service to get the amortization schedules and stores the data locally.

- If a saved amortization schedule exists, use it instead of making a remote service call.

You are going to port this iOS app to Android and preserve the design decision already made.

> **Note** This is just for exercise purposes. It would be better to calculate the amortization schedules locally without using the remote service, and then you would not need to persist the result.

If you want to see the Objective-C implementations in your Xcode, you can download the Xcode project from http://pdachoice.com/z/service/image/00/RentalROI.zip.

Structure Your App

Your first step is to implement the iOS-like storyboard as instructed in Chapter 3. You want to create a runnable Android app with all the content views connected using the appropriate screen navigation pattern. Recall that you are not really aiming to have a full-featured storyboard because you only need to focus on "connections" instead of telling stories. You are better off ignoring the details of each content view in the first step.

ADT PROJECT PREPARATIONS

Use the MvcTemplate project to create a new ADT project. It will be almost exactly the same as the template project, except you want to rename the Java classes and layout files. A while ago, I actually used the same names from iOS counterparts. Now, I kind of feel this is too iOS-ish and I have started naming the MyCustomViewController as MyCustomViewFragment. There are benefits of having the same name, but as long as you can closely identify the counterpart iOS class, that should be good enough.

1. Copy the MvcTemplate ADT project and paste it to a new project (⌘c, ⌘v) named RentailROI.

2. Rename the Android application package. From the newly created RentalROI project context menu, select **Android Tools ➤ Rename Application Package**. Enter a new package name: **com.pdachoice.RentalROI**.

3. Rename theRentalROI/src/com.pdachoice.renameme Java package. From the package context menu, select **Refactor ➤ Rename...** (Alt+⌘r) and do the following:

    a. Enter a new name: **com.pdachoice.RentalROI**.

    b. Select **Update references**.

4. Rename the ScreenOneFragment:

    a. Rename the Java class as **RentalPropertyViewFragment.java**. From the file context menu, select **Refactor ➤ Rename…** (Alt+⌘r).

    b. Rename the layout file as **rentalpropertyview_fragment.xml** (Alt+⌘r).

5. Rename the ScreenTwoFragment:

    a. Rename the Java class as **AmortizationViewFragment.java**.

    b. Rename the layout file as **amortizationview_fragment.xml**.

6. Rename the ScreenThreeFragment:

    a. Rename the Java class as **MonthlyTermViewFragment.java**.

    b. Rename the layout file as **monthlytermview_fragment.xml**.

7. Modify **res/values/strings.xml** (see Listing 8-1). Update the app name and add some text. You don't need to worry if you miss any text. You can always add or delete it later. I simply look at the iOS app and focus on the intermediate objective; focus on screen navigation for now.

Listing 8-1. *strings.xml Text*

```
<?xml version="1.0" encoding="utf-8"?>
<resources>

    <string name="app_name">Rental ROI</string>
    <string name="label_schedule">Schedule</string>
    <string name="label_property">Property</string>
    <string name="label_amortization">Amortization</string>
    <string name="label_monthlydetails">Monthly Details</string>
    <string name="button_next">Next</string>

    <!-- RentalPropertyView -->
    <string name="morgtage">MORTGAGE</string>
    <string name="operations">OPERATIONS</string>
    <string name="purchasePrice">Purchase Price</string>
    <string name="downPayment">Down Payment %</string>
    <string name="loanAmount">Loan Amount</string>
    <string name="interestRate">Interest Rate %</string>
    <string name="mortgageTerm">Mortgage Term (Yr.)</string>
    <string name="escrowAmount">Escrow Amount</string>
    <string name="extraPayment">Extra Payment</string>
    <string name="expenses">Expenses</string>
    <string name="rent">Rent</string>

    <!-- EditTextView -->
    <string name="save">Save</string>
    <integer name="editTextSize">15</integer>
```

```xml
<!-- Monthly Details -->
<string name="MortgagePayment">MORTGAGE PAYMENT</string>
<string name="no">No.</string>
<string name="principle">Principle</string>
<string name="interest">Interest</string>
<string name="escrow">Escrow</string>
<string name="addlPayment">Add\'l Payment</string>
<string name="mortgageBalance">Mortgage Balance</string>
<string name="investmentRoi">INVESTMENT ROI</string>
<string name="equity">Equity</string>
<string name="cashInvest">Cash Investment</string>
<string name="roi">ROI</string>

</resources>
```

8. Modify **res/menu/main.xml as shown in Listing 8-2**. You need one action item for the "Schedule" UIBarButtonItem.

Listing 8-2. RentalROI Options Menu Layout

```xml
<menu xmlns:android="http://schemas.android.com/apk/res/android"
    xmlns:app="http://schemas.android.com/apk/res-auto" >

    <item
        android:id="@+id/actionSchedule"
        android:title="@string/label_schedule"
        app:showAsAction="always"/>
</menu>
```

9. Fix some errors caused by the new names of the string resources and the menu item id. Update the TextView android:text="..." in amortizationview_fragment.xml (see Listing 8-3).

Listing 8-3. res/layout/amortizationview_fragment.xml Draft

```xml
<?xml version="1.0" encoding="utf-8"?>
<RelativeLayout xmlns:android="http://schemas.android.com/apk/res/android"
    android:layout_width="match_parent"
    android:layout_height="match_parent" >

    <TextView
        android:id="@+id/textViewLabel"
        ...
        android:text="@string/label_amortization"
        ...
```

10. Update the TextView android:text="..." in monthlytermview_fragment.xml (see Listing 8-4).

Listing 8-4. res/layout/monthlytermview_fragment.xml Draft

```
<?xml version="1.0" encoding="utf-8"?>
<RelativeLayout xmlns:android="http://schemas.android.com/apk/res/android"
    android:layout_width="match_parent"
    android:layout_height="match_parent" >

    <TextView
        android:id="@+id/textViewLabel"
        ...
        android:text="@string/label_monthlydetails"
        ...
```

11. Update the TextView android:text="..." in RentalPropertyView_fragment.xml (see Listing 8-5).

Listing 8-5. res/layout/rentalpropertyview_fragment.xml Draft

```
<?xml version="1.0" encoding="utf-8"?>
<RelativeLayout xmlns:android="http://schemas.android.com/apk/res/android"
    android:layout_width="match_parent"
    android:layout_height="match_parent" >

    <TextView
        android:id="@+id/textViewLabel"
        ...
        android:text="@string/label_property"
        ...
```

12. Build and run the prep project to make sure it is good. It should behave the same as the old-time MvcTemplate project with three screens. You will create the fourth screen later.

Choose a Screen Navigation Pattern

When choosing appropriate navigation pattern(s), you will naturally get a very good idea by playing with the iOS. For your own apps, you can examine the storyboard file (see Figure 8-2) and focus on those container view controllers that are normally responsible for screen navigations. Sometimes you may need more than one pattern, such as a navigation stack plus navigation tabs. In this RentalROI app, you clearly can see the iOS storyboard is simply using one UINavigationController (see the "Navigation Stack" section in Chapter 3) for the all the screen navigations. It also uses UITableViewController, which is not a container view controller. It is used for a popular mobile UX pattern, the master list detail drilldown UX pattern. It actually uses the navigation stack screen navigation pattern. You can choose to defer it to the next step.

The RentalROI prep project already inherits the navigation stack from the MvcTemplate project, but it only has three fragments. You still need one more and to make sure all the screens are connected. Your end goal in this step is to break the app into the iOS-like MVC-structured pieces and have all view controllers connected. You should ignore the details of each content view; in other words, a simplified draft runnable storyboard. You still need one more fragment for EditTextView content view, so do the following:

1. Create edittextview_fragment.xml. You can just do copy-paste-rename from monthlytermview_fragment.xml and hard-code the android:text for now. For the immediate goal, just make sure you have the right file name that maps to the iOS counterpart, as shown in Listing 8-6.

Listing 8-6. res/layout/edittextview_fragment.xml Draft

```xml
<?xml version="1.0" encoding="utf-8"?>
<RelativeLayout xmlns:android="http://schemas.android.com/apk/res/android"
    android:layout_width="match_parent"
    android:layout_height="match_parent" >

    <TextView
        android:id="@+id/textViewLabel"
        android:layout_width="wrap_content"
        android:layout_height="wrap_content"
        android:layout_alignParentTop="true"
        android:layout_centerHorizontal="true"
        android:layout_marginTop="@dimen/label_marginTop"
        android:text="Edit Text view"
        android:textSize="@dimen/label_textsize" />

</RelativeLayout>
```

2. Create EditTextViewFragment.java You can just do copy-paste-rename from the MonthyTermViewFragment.java. Make sure it pairs with the edittextview_fragment.xml content view (see Listing 8-7).

Listing 8-7. EditTextViewFragment.java Draft

```java
public class EditTextViewFragment extends Fragment {
  private View contentView;

  @Override
  public View onCreateView(LayoutInflater inflater, ViewGroup container,
      Bundle savedInstanceState) {

    contentView = inflater.inflate(R.layout.edittextview_fragment, container, false);
    return contentView;
  }
  ...
```

3. There are two *segues* in the iOS RentalPropertyViewController that make
    screen transitions. One from the "Schedule" UIBarButtonItem and the other
    from UITableViewCell. Modify the RentalPropertyViewFragment.java to
    make screen transitions (see Listing 8-8).

    a. You need to enable the fragment options menu, inflate the menu
        resource, and handle the action item selected callback to go to the
        AmortizationViewFragment (see the "Options Menu" section in Chapter 4).

    b. To go to the EditTextViewFragment, use the existing Next button temporarily
        for your current purpose. It will be replaced by the ListView item selected
        trigger later.

Listing 8-8. RentalPropertyViewFragment.java

```java
public class RentalPropertyViewFragment extends Fragment implements OnClickListener {

    private final static String tag =
            RentalPropertyViewFragment.class.getSimpleName();

    private View contentView;
    private View nextButton;

    @Override
    public View onCreateView(LayoutInflater inflater, ViewGroup container,
        Bundle savedInstanceState) {
      ...
      setHasOptionsMenu(true);
      ...
    }


    ...

    @Override
    public void onClick(View v) {
      ((MainActivity)getActivity()).pushViewController(new EditTextViewFragment(), true);
    }

    @Override
    public void onCreateOptionsMenu(Menu menu, MenuInflater inflater) {
      super.onCreateOptionsMenu(menu, inflater);
      inflater.inflate(R.menu.main, menu);
    }

    @Override
    public boolean onOptionsItemSelected(MenuItem item) {
      Log.d(tag, "onOptionsItemSelected: " + item.getItemId());
      ((MainActivity)getActivity()).pushViewController(new AmortizationViewFragment(),
true);
      return true;
    }

}
```

4. To update the screen title for each screen, do the following in all four fragments:

```
@Override
  public void onResume() {
      super.onResume();
      getActivity().setTitle(getText(R.string.label_property));
//      getActivity().setTitle(getText(R.string.label_amortization));
//      getActivity().setTitle(getText(R.string.label_monthlydetails));
//      getActivity().setTitle("TODO");
   ...
}
```

> **Note** For the EditTextViewFragment, the title depends on the editing fields. Simply provide any string for now.

5. Build and run the ADT project to make sure you have achieved the first-step goal: structure the app into MVC with a simple runnable storyboard. Right now, each content view only contains labels for identification purpose. This is good enough. Figure 8-3 shows an example.

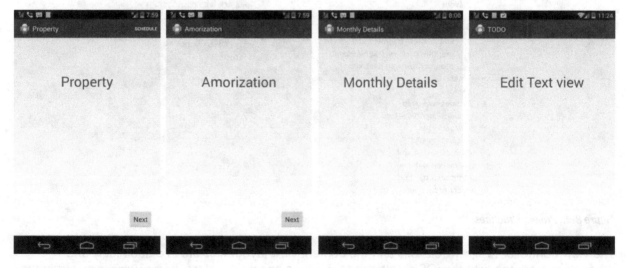

Figure 8-3. AndroidRentalROI draft

Implement Piece by Piece

Let's take a look at the "pieces" you have now in both iOS and ADT. Figure 8-4 shows the project structures of both projects side by side.

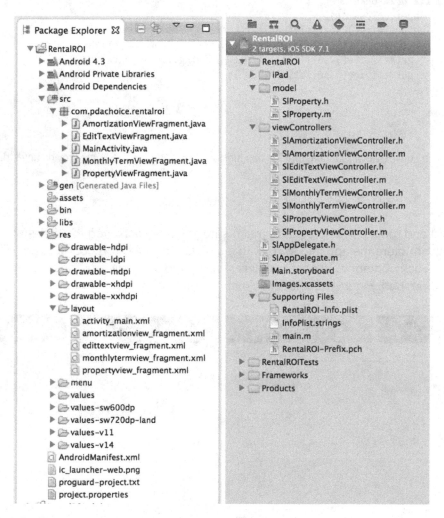

Figure 8-4. Project structures

The view controller `Fragment` classes and the content view layout files are in place nicely and mapped one-to-one with the iOS counterparts. There is one model class, `RentalProperty`, not in the ADT project yet. Let's get the model classes in place to complete the class level mapping between iOS and Android.

To convert the model classes from this iOS app, create the counterpart Java class, `src/com.pdachoice.RentalROI/RentalProperty.java`. Use the Create New Class wizard (see Chapter 2) to create the class skeleton. You don't need anything in it, as shown in Listing 8-9.

Listing 8-9. RentalProperty.java Skeleton

```
package com.pdachoice.RentalROI.model;

public class RentalProperty {
    // TODO: copy content of RentalProperty.h below

    // TODO: copy content of RentalProperty.m below

}
```

Now, you have all the matching classes in your Android ADT project. You will be translating Objective-C classes to Java, one class at a time.

Objective-C to Java Class Porting Steps

You already broke the app into MVC-structured classes that map to a counterpart in iOS. Your next step is to break each class into more pieces, porting iOS methods to Android. For your convenience, you may use Table 8-1 as a step-by-step guide. You will find that the information in the table is common sense after one or more exercises, but I think it makes the translation efforts more systematic and efficient.

Table 8-1. Class Porting Steps

Step	Instructions
1.	For each class, copy the contents of the counterpart Objective-C class (both .h and .m files) to Java.
2.	Delete the trivial Objective-C-only stuff, such as #import <...>, @interface, @implementation, @end, and so forth.
3.	Replace all occurrences on trivial syntax mappings. You may run down the symbols listed in Table 8-2.
4.	Translate the method declarations to Java; focus on method signature syntax only. Defer translating the method bodies by commenting out the Objective-C code in the method body. Do not delete them because they are perfect comments.
5.	Translate initialization code: constructors, or those lifecycle callback methods in Fragment.

Steps 1–3 are simple things. Step 4 may sound easy but it is the key to breaking the class into smaller and mappable pieces. Later, when you need to use any of these methods, you translate the implementation body from the commented Objective-C code.

We will repeatedly use Table 8-1's class porting steps, one class at a time, starting with the model class.

Model Class: RentalProperty

A great deal of the translation effort involves converting the general language programming rules (see the "Language Syntax Comparison in an Absolute Nutshell" table in Chapter 2) and replacing the common data types defined in different languages or SDK. Table 8-2 lists some common types or syntax in both languages. As a matter of fact, it is actually doable to write a script to replace the Objective-C source code with the valid Java syntax defined in Table 8-1. I don't have that script; I simply use the Eclipse editor to run a search and replace by token or regex. This helps me to refresh/preserve my Java language skills.

Table 8-2. Replaceable Objective-C to Java Syntax or Symbols

	Objective-C	Java
Object reference	*	N/A (delete them)
Self	self.	this.
String class	NSString	String
String literal	@"xxx"	"xxx"
Array	NSArray	ArrayList, or JSONArray if string serialization is required
Hash table	NSDictionary	HashMap, or JSONObject if string serialization is required
Boolean	BOOL, YES/NO	boolean, true/false
Integer	NSInteger, NSUInteger	Integer
Null (undefined) value	nil	null
Object	id or NSObject	Object
Method declaration	-(void), -(NSString*), etc.	private void, private String, etc.
Static declaration	+(void), +(NSString*), etc.	private static void, private String, etc.
Constant define	#define var	public static final var
More...		

Table 8-1 only shows the common syntactical mappings. In practice, use the Eclipse editor's Find/Replace feature to make your life easier. You can search and replace language-specific syntax and symbols. Programming language statements or expressions always embed certain patterns and are searchable as well. Take the advantage of these patterns to do global changes or use selected-lines scope. Read your own code and build your own smart search criteria. For example, if you are populating a screen with many UILabels, your Objective-C code would look something like myUILabel.text = [NSString stringWithFormat: @"xxx"] repeatedly. You can use the Find/Replace dialog with the settings shown in Figure 8-5 to replace all the patterns.

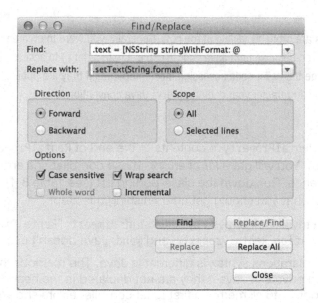

Figure 8-5. Eclipse editor Find/Replace

Follow the Table 8-1 class porting steps to port the RentalProperty class to Java.

1. Copy the `RentalProperty.h` file contents into `RentalProperty.java`. Listing 8-10 depicts what you should get after this step.

   a. Delete the Objective-C language-specific stuff, such as any `#import <...>`, `@interface`, `@end`, and so forth. Java doesn't need them at all.

   b. `@property` can be translated into Java fields. Replace all occurrences of `"@property (nonatomic)"` to `"public"`.

   c. Comment out all the method declarations. They show you that they are public methods. These method signatures repeat in the `.m` file. We will get to them when translating the `.m` file.

Listing 8-10. RentalProperty.java

```java
package com.pdachoice.RentalROI.model;

public class RentalProperty {

    public double purchasePrice;
    public double loanAmt;
    public double interestRate;
    public int numOfTerms;
    public double escrow;
    public double extra;
    public double expenses;
    public double rent;

}
```

> **Note**   Java developers are probably yelling at me now. Generally, you want to create private Java fields with public accessors. However, because both Java and Objective-C use a dot (.) to access public class properties, you won't need to change the caller code accessing these properties if they are public. Let's get the main topics working first. You can refactor your code for proper Java convention later.

2. Copy the iOS RentalProperty.m contents to the end of RentalProperty.java file to start with. You will get a *lot* of errors. These compilations errors are your free guidance. Run down the class-porting list (see Table 8-1). Listing 8-11 is what you should get after finishing this step.

    a. Delete the trivial Objective-C-specific stuff: #import "RentalProperty.h", @implementation RentalProperty, and @end. Java doesn't use them.

    b. Method declarations syntax is different in Java. The methods in .m are considered private in Java if they are not declared in the header file. Add private modifier to *all* methods first to let compiler errors show/suggest making one public method.

    c. Translate the constructor: public RentalProperty() { ... }.

    d. File scope variables are close to the Java private class variables declared with a static keyword.

Listing 8-11. RentalProperty.java with Method Stubs

```java
public class RentalProperty {
  ...

// from RentalProperty.m below
  private static final String KEY_AMO_SAVED = "KEY_AMO_SAVED";
  private static final String KEY_PROPERTY = "KEY_PROPERTY";
  private static RentalProperty _sharedInstance = null;

  private RentalProperty() {
    super();
    this.interestRate = 5.0f;
    this.numOfTerms = 30;
  }

  public static RentalProperty sharedInstance() {
    if (_sharedInstance == null) {
      _sharedInstance = new RentalProperty();
    }
    return _sharedInstance;
  }
```

```java
    public String getAmortizationPersistentKey() {
//     String amortizationPersistentKey = String.format("%.2f-%.2f-%d-%.2f",
//         this.loanAmt, this.interestRate, this.numOfTerms, this.extra);
//     return amortizationPersistentKey;
    return null;
  }

  private ArrayList getSavedAmortization() {
    // NSUserDefaults userDefaults = [NSUserDefaults standardUserDefaults];
    // String savedKey =[userDefaults stringForKey: KEY_AMO_SAVED];
    // String amortizationPersistentKey = [this getAmortizationPersistentKey];
    // if (savedKey.length > 0 && [savedKey
    // isEqualToString:amortizationPersistentKey]) {
    // return [userDefaults arrayForKey:savedKey];
    // } else {
    // return null;
    // }
    return null;
  }

  private void saveAmortization(ArrayList jsonOjb) {
    // // only save one, remove prev first
    // NSUserDefaults userDefaults = [NSUserDefaults standardUserDefaults];
    // String amortizationPersistentKey = [this getAmortizationPersistentKey];
    // [userDefaults setObject:amortizationPersistentKey forKey:KEY_AMO_SAVED];
    // [userDefaults setObject:jsonOjb forKey:amortiz ationPersistentKey];
    // [userDefaults synchronize];
  }

  private boolean load() {
    // NSUserDefaults userDefaults = [NSUserDefaults standardUserDefaults];
    // NSDictionary jo = [userDefaults objectForKey:KEY_PROPERTY];
    // if (jo == null) {
    // return false;
    // }
    //
    // int i = 10;
    //
    // this.purchasePrice = [[jo objectForKey:"purchasePrice"] doubleValue];
    // this.loanAmt = [[jo objectForKey:"loanAmt"] doubleValue];
    // this.interestRate = [[jo objectForKey:"interestRate"] doubleValue];
    // this.numOfTerms = [[jo objectForKey:"numOfTerms"] intValue];
    // this.escrow = [[jo objectForKey:"escrow"] doubleValue];
    // this.extra = [[jo objectForKey:"extra"] doubleValue];
    // this.expenses = [[jo objectForKey:"expenses"] doubleValue];
    // this.rent = [[jo objectForKey:"rent"] doubleValue];
    return true;
  }
```

```
    private void save() {
        // NSDictionary jo = @{"purchasePrice" : [NSNumber
        // numberWithDouble:this.purchasePrice],
        // "loanAmt" : [NSNumber numberWithDouble:this.loanAmt],
        // "interestRate" : [NSNumber numberWithDouble:this.interestRate],
        // "numOfTerms" : [NSNumber numberWithDouble:this.numOfTerms],
        // "escrow" : [NSNumber numberWithDouble:this.escrow],
        // "extra" : [NSNumber numberWithDouble:this.extra],
        // "expenses" : [NSNumber numberWithDouble:this.expenses],
        // "rent" : [NSNumber numberWithDouble:this.rent]
        // };
        //
        // NSUserDefaults userDefaults = [NSUserDefaults standardUserDefaults];
        // [userDefaults setObject:jo forKey:KEY_PROPERTY];
        // [userDefaults synchronize];
    }
}
```

> **Note**   In Eclipse, the autoimport shortcut is Shift+command+o. (I wish Xcode could do autoimport, too).

You have all the method stubs in place with precise comments, plus a constructor. You have achieved the immediate goal.

> **Note**   You really cannot get any better method comments, because these comments are actually code that proved to be working already. ☺

EditTextView Fragment

IOS ANALOGY

The iOS counterpart is EditTextViewController.

Let's move on to the first view controller, `EditTextViewFragment`.

> **Note**   I would've chosen RentalPropertyFragment first if it didn't need EditTextViewFragment. The dependencies can be easily seen in the @import statements.

In the iOS app, this counterpart iOS view controller only has a TextField that presents the text for editing from the presenting view controller. It also displays the name of the text on the UINavigationBar title. Upon the user saving or canceling the edit operations, the modified text is returned to the presenting view controller.

Your immediate goal is to translate the iOS EditTextViewController to EditTextViewFragment.java so that your Android code will do the same. The following are repeated steps to provide more detail for each content view and fragment code (for example, the CommonWidgets project in Chapter 4 and many others).

1. To detail the content view, use Chapter 4's CommonWidgets as your porting guidelines (see the "User Interface" section in Chapter 4). This edittextview_fragment.xml content view contains only one EditText where the user can enter text. This layout is very simple but clean (see Listing 8-12).

    Listing 8-12. edittextview_fragment.xml

    ```xml
    <?xml version="1.0" encoding="utf-8"?>
    <RelativeLayout xmlns:android="http://schemas.android.com/apk/res/android"
        android:layout_width="match_parent"
        android:layout_height="match_parent" >

        <EditText
            android:id="@+id/tfEditText"
            android:layout_width="wrap_content"
            android:layout_height="wrap_content"
            android:layout_centerVertical="true"
            android:layout_centerHorizontal="true"
            android:gravity="center"
            android:ems="18"
            android:inputType="number" >

            <requestFocus />
        </EditText>

    </RelativeLayout>
    ```

2. Port the counterpart EditTextViewController.h into EditTextViewFragment.java (see Listing 8-13).

    a. Copy the .h file content into the Java class file.

    b. Delete all the Objective-C-specific stuff, such as #import<...>, and so forth.

    c. Translate all the iOS @property including IBOutlets to public Java fields.

    d. Initialize IBOutlets references to the appropriate UI widgets. You need to manually do a findViewById(...) to get the reference from the container view object (see the "Common UI Widgets" section in Chapter 4).

    e. It contains a @protocol that defines the delegate's obligation. You can port the iOS pattern for communicating between the presenting controller and the presented controller to Android. The in-file @protocol maps to a Java inner interface nicely.

Listing 8-13. *Translate EditTextViewController.h*

```
public class EditTextViewFragment extends Fragment {
  // from .h
  // @interface EditTextViewController : UIViewController <EditTextDelegate>
  public EditText tfEditText;

  public EditTextViewControllerDelegate delegate;
  public int tag;
  public String header;
  public String text;

  // inner interface
  interface EditTextViewControllerDelegate {
    public void textEditControllerDidFinishEditText(EditTextViewFragment controller, String text);
    public void textEditControllerDidCancel(EditTextViewFragment controller);
  }

  private View contentView;
  ...
  @Override
  public View onCreateView(LayoutInflater inflater, ViewGroup container,
      Bundle savedInstanceState) {
    contentView = inflater.inflate(R.layout.edittextview_fragment, container, false);
    setHasOptionsMenu(true); // enable Option Menu.

    tfEditText = (EditText)contentView.findViewById(R.id.tfEditText);

    return contentView;
  }
  ...

  // TODO: from EditTextViewController.m
}
```

3. Port the counterpart `EditTextViewController.m` into
    `EditTextViewFragment.java`, as shown in Listing 8-14.

    a. Copy the file content into the Java file and follow the class porting steps
        (see Table 8-1).

    b. Android automatically shifts up the `EditText` above the keyboard. You
        can safely delete those iOS shifting keyboard implementation: the
        `keyboardAppeared(...)` method and `NSNotificationCenter` code.

    c. Translate the initialization code in `viewDidLoad()` to the appropriate fragment
        lifecycle callbacks. To set UI widget attributes, you need to do it when you
        have the object reference, such as `onCreateView(...)`. To set the title,
        you set the activity title in `onResume(...)`. Since the iOS lifecycles are not
        one-to-one mapping to fragment lifecycles, sometimes you need to break it
        up into different fragment callback methods.

Listing 8-14. Translate EditTextViewController.m

```java
public class EditTextViewFragment extends Fragment {

  ...
  @Override
  public View onCreateView(LayoutInflater inflater, ViewGroup container,
                           Bundle savedInstanceState) {
    contentView = inflater.inflate(R.layout.edittextview_fragment, container, false);
    setHasOptionsMenu(true); // enable Option Menu.

    tfEditText = (EditText)contentView.findViewById(R.id.tfEditText);

    // this.tfEditText.getText = this.src.text;
    this.tfEditText.setText(this.text);

    return contentView;
  }

  @Override
  public void onResume() {
    super.onResume();
    viewDidAppear(true);
    getActivity().setTitle(header);
    ...
  }


  ...
  // from EditTextViewController.m
  private void viewDidLoad() {
    // this.tfEditText.getText = this.src.text;
    // this.navBar.topItem.title = this.header;
  }

  private void viewDidAppear(boolean animated) {
  // [super viewDidAppear:animated];
  // this.tfEditText.becomeFirstResponder();
  }

  private void didReceiveMemoryWarning() {
  //   [super didReceiveMemoryWarning];
    // Dispose of any resources that can be recreated.
  }

  public void doCancel(Object sender) {
    ((MainActivity)getActivity()).popViewController();
    if(delegate != null) {
      this.delegate.textEditControllerDidCancel(this);
    }
  }
```

```
            public void doSave(Object sender) {
              String returnText = this.tfEditText.getText().toString();
              if(delegate != null) {
                this.delegate.textEditControllerDidFinishEditText(this, returnText);
              }
            }

          }
```

> **Note**   Unlike Objective-C, sending a method to a null object is not allowed in Java. You want to check the null value to avoid NullpointerException.

4. EditTextViewFragment needs a Save action item (see the "Options Menu" section in Chapter 4). Don't mimic the iOS Cancel button because Android simply uses the system Back key. Create res/menu/edittextview_menu.xml as shown in Listing 8-15.

Listing 8-15. edittextview_menu.xml

```xml
<menu xmlns:android="http://schemas.android.com/apk/res/android"
    xmlns:app="http://schemas.android.com/apk/res-auto" >

    <item
        android:id="@+id/actionSave"
        android:title="@string/save"
        app:showAsAction="always"/>
</menu>
```

5. Override the options menu callback methods (see Listing 8-16).

Listing 8-16. EditTextViewFragment Menu

```java
public class EditTextViewFragment extends Fragment {
  ...
  @Override
  public void onCreateOptionsMenu(Menu menu, MenuInflater inflater) {
    super.onCreateOptionsMenu(menu, inflater);
    inflater.inflate(R.menu.edittextview_menu, menu);
  }

  @Override
  public boolean onOptionsItemSelected(MenuItem item) {
    doSave(null);
    return true;
  }
  ...
```

This is all for the first view controller, EditTextViewFragment.

RentalPropertyView

Let's move on to the next view controller: RentalRropertyViewFragment. The purpose of the RentalProperty view screen is to collect user input. The counterpart iOS RentalPropertyViewController is a UITableViewController with static table view cells. UITableViewController naturally maps to Android ListFragment (see the "ListFragment" section in Chapter 3). Since it is using a static cell in iOS, you can also create a static TextView for each label (see the "TextView" section in Chapter 4) and EditText for each input field (see the "EditText" section in Chapter 4). This choice is definitely legitimate and easier, without losing the intended purpose. You can simply edit using these EditTexts. You do not even need the EditTextViewFragment. But it is just too simple for learning purposes.

The first approach appears very clean in my opinion, and I like it better personally, but it may look iOS-ish on an Android platform in some people's eyes. Without getting into the UX discussion, let's do the iOS-ish choice so I can demonstrate how to strictly port iOS code to Android.

Back to porting RentalPropertyViewFragment, your immediate goal is to detail the same L&F in the layout file as shown in Figure 8-6, and port the counterpart iOS class methods to the Java fragment.

Figure 8-6. Property view scene

You will use the Table 8-1 class porting steps repeatedly: copy and paste the Objective-C code from the counterpart RentalPropertyViewController to start with.

6. Copy the Objective-C code in the .h file into RentalPropertyViewFragment.java and use the errors to guide your translation tasks. The end result should be like Listing 8-17.

    a. Delete unwanted stuff, such as #import <...>, @interface, and @end.

    b. The iOS class is extended from UITableViewController. You use ListFragment in Android.

    c. You can safely remove all those IBOutlets because they are for the static cells. They are to be replaced by list items in the ListView.

    d. The RentalPropertyViewController conforms to the EditTextViewControllerDelegate protocol as seen in the .h file. In Java, you do the same by implementing the Java interface.

    e. Ignore the method declarations in header files because the method declaration and the implementation body are combined in Java.

    f. I normally comment out what is not needed instead of deleting it in the beginning; this is for convenience because I might find I need it later.

Listing 8-17. Translate from RentalPropertyViewController.h

```
public class RentalPropertyViewFragment extends ListFragment implements
    OnClickListener, EditTextViewControllerDelegate {

  ...
//  #import <UIKit/UIKit.h>
//
//  @interface RentalPropertyViewController : UITableViewController
//
//  @property (weak, nonatomic) IBOutlet UILabel *lbPurchasePrice;
//  @property (weak, nonatomic) IBOutlet UILabel *lbDownPayment;
//  @property (weak, nonatomic) IBOutlet UILabel *lbLoanAmt;
//  @property (weak, nonatomic) IBOutlet UILabel *lbInterestRate;
//  @property (weak, nonatomic) IBOutlet UILabel *lbNumOfTerms;
//  @property (weak, nonatomic) IBOutlet UILabel *lbEscrow;
//  @property (weak, nonatomic) IBOutlet UILabel *lbExtra;
//  @property (weak, nonatomic) IBOutlet UILabel *lbExpenses;
//  @property (weak, nonatomic) IBOutlet UILabel *lbRent;
//
//  - (IBAction)doAmortization:(id)sender;
//  @end
```

7. Copy the RentalPropertyViewController.m code into
   RentalPropertyViewFragment.java and use the errors to guide your
   translation task. The following are the same steps (see Table 8-1) you used
   previously. The end result should be like Listing 8-18.

   a. Delete unwanted stuff, such as #import <...>, @interface, and @end,
      and so forth.

   b. Translate @property to Java fields with public accessors.

   c. Convert all the method declarations in Java syntax.

   d. Defer the method body translation by commenting out all the method body
      implementations (do not delete them).

   e. For the methods that implement the protocol, you need to make them
      public. If you make them private, the Java compiler will suggest you make
      them public.

Listing 8-18. Translate from RentalPropertyViewController.m (After Translation)

```java
public class RentalPropertyViewFragment extends Fragment
implements OnClickListener, EditTextViewControllerDelegate {

    ...
    // RentalPropertyViewController.m
    static final String URL_service_tmpl =
"http://www.pdachoice.com/ras/service/amortization?loan=%.2f&rate=%.2f&terms=%d&extra=%.2f";

//@interface RentalPropertyViewController () <EditTextViewControllerDelegate> {
//   RentalProperty* _property;
//}
//@end

    private RentalProperty _property;

    private void viewDidLoad() {
       ...
    }

    private void didSelectRowAtIndexPath(int indexPath) {
       ...
    }
    private void prepareForSegue(/*UIStoryboardSegue segue Object sender*/) {
       ...
    }

    public void textEditControllerDidFinishEditText(EditTextViewFragment controller, String
text) {
       ...
    }
```

```java
    public void textEditControllerDidCancel(EditTextViewFragment controller) {
      ...
    }

    public void doAmortization(Object sender) {
      ...
    }
  }
```

> **Note**   It is all about the same idea: move the code from the iOS counterpart; translation will be done in a top-down fashion. In other words, get the Java classes in place first, and then get the Java method stubs in place with precise comments written in the tested Objective-C code. Defer the method body translation until you need to use them by using the provided mapping guidelines.

8. RentalPropertyViewFragment extends from ListFragment. Follow the guidelines in the "Master List with Details Drilldown" section in Chapter 3 (see Listing 8-19).

    a. Extends super class from ListFragment as shown in Listing 8-15. There is no need to inflate your own layout file because the layout is inflated from the super class (see the "Master List with Details Drilldown" section in Chapter 3). Remove the onCreateView(...).

    b. You don't need the nextButton originally copied from the MvcTemplate project.

    c. You still need the options menu. Move the code to onCreate(...).

    d. You can delete the rentalpropertyview_fragment.xml layout file.

Listing 8-19. RentalPropertyViewFragment Extends ListFragment

```java
public class RentalPropertyViewFragment extends ListFragment implements
OnClickListener, EditTextViewControllerDelegate {

  private final static String tag = RentalPropertyViewFragment.class.getSimpleName();

  @Override
  public void onCreate(Bundle savedInstanceState) {
    super.onCreate(savedInstanceState);
    setHasOptionsMenu(true); // enable Options Menu.
  }

// private View contentView;
// private View nextButton;
// @Override
```

```
//  public View onCreateView(LayoutInflater inflater, ViewGroup container,
//      Bundle savedInstanceState) {
//    contentView = inflater.inflate(R.layout.RentalPropertyView_fragment,
//        container, false);
//
//    setHasOptionsMenu(true);
//
//    nextButton = contentView.findViewById(R.id.buttonNext);
//    nextButton.setOnClickListener(this); // Delegate button OnClick events
//    return contentView;
//  }
  ...
```

9. Create a list adapter to supply list items for the ListView (see the "Adapter"
    section in Chapter 3), as shown in Listing 8-20.

> **Tip**   Use BaseAdapter to create an anonymous class. In the Eclipse editor, use Ctrl+<space> to create all
> the method stubs.

Listing 8-20. RentalPropertyViewFragment Extends ListFragment

```java
public class RentalPropertyViewFragment extends ListFragment implements
OnClickListener, EditTextViewControllerDelegate {

  ...
  private BaseAdapter mAdapter;
  @Override
  public void onCreate(Bundle savedInstanceState) {
    super.onCreate(savedInstanceState);
    setHasOptionsMenu(true); // enable Option Menu.

    mAdapter = new BaseAdapter() {

      @Override
      public View getView(int position, View convertView, ViewGroup parent) {
        // TODO Auto-generated method stub
        return null;
      }

      @Override
      public long getItemId(int position) {
        // TODO Auto-generated method stub
        return 0;
      }
```

```
        @Override
        public Object getItem(int position) {
          // TODO Auto-generated method stub
          return null;
        }

        @Override
        public int getCount() {
          // TODO Auto-generated method stub
          return 0;
        }
      };
      this.setListAdapter(mAdapter);
  }
  ...
```

10. Create the iOS-like right-detail table view cell, `rightdetail_listitem.xml`,
    as shown in Listing 8-21. Do not create the iOS caret, which is purely iOS-ish.

Listing 8-21. rightdetail_listitem.xml

```xml
<?xml version="1.0" encoding="utf-8"?>
<RelativeLayout xmlns:android="http://schemas.android.com/apk/res/android"
    android:layout_width="wrap_content"
    android:layout_height="wrap_content"
    android:padding="12dp"
    android:background="#cccccc">

    <TextView
        android:id="@+id/textLabel"
        android:layout_width="wrap_content"
        android:layout_height="wrap_content"
        android:layout_alignParentLeft="true"
        android:layout_centerVertical="true"
        android:text="A Label"
        android:textAlignment="textStart"
        android:textAppearance="?android:attr/textAppearanceLarge" />

    <TextView
        android:id="@+id/detailTextLabel"
        android:layout_width="wrap_content"
        android:layout_height="wrap_content"
        android:layout_toLeftOf="@+id/textLabel "
        android:layout_alignParentRight="true"
        android:layout_centerVertical="true"
        android:text="A Value"
        android:textAlignment="textEnd"
        android:textAppearance="?android:attr/textAppearanceMedium"
        android:gravity="right" />

</RelativeLayout>
```

11. Provide BaseAdapter.getCount(), and getItemId(...), and getItem(...)
implementations, as shown in Listing 8-22.

Listing 8-22. BaseAdapter.getCount()

```java
public class RentalPropertyViewFragment extends ListFragment implements
OnClickListener, EditTextViewControllerDelegate {

    ...
    mAdapter = new BaseAdapter() {
    ...
      @Override
      public int getCount() {
        return 11; // 2 section headers + 9 fields
      }

      @Override
      public long getItemId(int pos) {
        return pos; // not used
      }

      @Override
      public Object getItem(int pos) {
        TextView textLabel = (TextView) getView(pos, null, null)
            .findViewById(R.id.textLabel);
        if(textLabel == null) {
          return null;
        } else {
          TextView detailTextLabel = (TextView) getView(pos, null,
          null).findViewById(R.id.detailTextLabel);

          NameValuePair nvp = new BasicNameValuePair(textLabel.getText()
              .toString(), detailTextLabel.getText().toString());
          return nvp;
        }
      }
    ...

    };
}
...
```

12. You need two types of list item layouts. You need to provide implementations
for the following optional methods (as shown in Listing 8-23):

   a. Override getItemViewType(...). You won't need to provide this if only one
       list item layout is needed.

   b. Override getViewTypeCount(). You will not need to override it if only one list
       item layout is needed.

IOS ANALOGY

Override UITableViewDataSource numberOfSectionsInTableView:. The API design and usage might be different (Android is more flexible but you would need two methods). It serves a similar purpose.

Listing 8-23. BaseAdapter.getItem(pos)

```
public class RentalPropertyViewFragment extends ListFragment
                         implements OnClickListener, EditTextViewControllerDelegate {

    ...
    mAdapter = new BaseAdapter() {
      ...
      @Override
      public int getViewTypeCount() {
        return 2;
      }

      @Override
      public int getItemViewType(int pos) {
        if(pos == 0 || pos == 8) {
          return 0;
        } else {
          return 1;
        }
      }
      ...
    };
  }
  ...
```

13. Provide `BaseAdapter.getView()` implementation as shown in Listing 8-24. In this iOS app, you use a static cell with `IBOutlet` and assign the values in `viewDidLoad()`. In Android, you bind the value with a list item layout, just as you normally do in `cellForRowAtIndexPath:` for `UITableViewController` with dynamic cells.

Note   There is no section header in Android ListView. You can use a different list item layout for section headers. The simple_list_item_1 layout from the Android SDK is just perfect for the iOS-like section header.

Listing 8-24. BaseAdapter.getView()

```java
@Override
public View getView(int pos, View view, ViewGroup parent) {

    if (view == null) { // check null first before recycled object.
        LayoutInflater inflater = getActivity().getLayoutInflater();
        if (pos == 0 || pos == 8) {
            // header list item
            view = inflater.inflate(android.R.layout.simple_list_item_1, null);
        } else {
            // right detail list item
            view = inflater.inflate(R.layout.rightdetail_listitem, null);
        }
    }

    if (pos == 0 || pos == 8) {
        // header list item
        view.setBackgroundColor(Color.argb(32, 0, 128, 128));
        TextView text1 = (TextView) view.findViewById(android.R.id.text1);

        if (pos == 0) {
            text1.setText(getResources().getString(R.string.morgtage));
        } else {
            text1.setText(getResources().getString(R.string.operations));
        }
    } else {
        // right detail list item
        view.setBackgroundColor(Color.argb(0, 0, 0, 0));
        TextView textLabel = (TextView) view.findViewById(R.id.textLabel);
        TextView detailTextLabel = (TextView) view.findViewById(R.id.detailTextLabel);

        switch (pos) {
        case 1:
            textLabel.setText(R.string.purchasePrice);
            detailTextLabel.setText(String.format("%.0f", _property.purchasePrice));
            break;
        case 2:
            textLabel.setText(R.string.downPayment);
            double down = (1 - _property.loanAmt / _property.purchasePrice) * 100.0f;
            if (_property.purchasePrice > 0) {
                detailTextLabel.setText(String.format("%.0f", down));

                if (_property.loanAmt == 0 && down > 0) {
                    _property.loanAmt = _property.purchasePrice * (1 - down / 100.0f);
                }
            } else {
                detailTextLabel.setText("0");
            }
            break;
```

```java
    case 3:
      textLabel.setText(R.string.loanAmount);
      detailTextLabel.setText(String.format("%.2f", _property.loanAmt));
      break;
    case 4:
      textLabel.setText(R.string.interestRate);
      detailTextLabel.setText(String.format("%.2f", _property.interestRate));
      break;
    case 5:
      textLabel.setText(R.string.mortgageTerm);
      detailTextLabel.setText(String.format("%d", _property.numOfTerms));
      break;
    case 6:
      textLabel.setText(R.string.escrowAmount);
      detailTextLabel.setText(String.format("%.0f", _property.escrow));
      break;
    case 7:
      textLabel.setText(R.string.extraPayment);
      detailTextLabel.setText(String.format("%.0f", _property.extra));
      break;
    case 9:
      textLabel.setText(R.string.expenses);
      detailTextLabel.setText(String.format("%.0f", _property.expenses));
      break;
    case 10:
      textLabel.setText(R.string.rent);
      detailTextLabel.setText(String.format("%.0f", _property.rent));
      break;

    default:
      break;
    }
  }

  return view;
}
```

14. You don't have a button and no need to implement OnClickListener(...). Instead, you override onListItemClicked(...) for presenting the EditTextViewFragment (see Listing 8-25).

15. Generally, iOS apps use performSegueWithIdentifier and prepareForSegue to present the destination view controller and to pass data to the destination view controller directly. You can combine the two methods and translate the navigation code in an Android action-handling method, such as onListItemClick as shown in Listing 8-25.

Listing 8-25. onListItemClicked(...)

```java
public class RentalPropertyViewFragment extends ListFragment implements
EditTextViewControllerDelegate {

  ...
  // callback method when list item is selected.
  @Override
  public void onListItemClick(ListView l, View v, int position, long id) {
    // position 0 and 8 are headers
    if(position ==0 || position == 8) {
      return;
    }

    EditTextViewFragment toFrag = new EditTextViewFragment();

    NameValuePair data = (NameValuePair) mAdapter.getItem(position);

    toFrag.tag = position;
    toFrag.text = data.getValue();
    toFrag.header = data.getName();

    toFrag.delegate = this;

    ((MainActivity) getActivity()).pushViewController(toFrag, true);
  }
  ...
```

> **Note**   The iOS-like direct communication between fragments works fine when activity/fragment is not restarted. If the activity restarts, the fragment states/Java fields get destroyed, and the preceding code would not work. For the iOS-to-Android porting guidelines, our MvcTemplate project already declares handling the device configuration changes to prevent restarting the activity for the purpose of mimicking the iOS app behavior. Although you don't need to do anything for this, I just wanted to point it out. See Listing 3-20 and the "Device Orientation" section in Chapter 3 for more information.

16. Translate the class initialization code. For example, `viewDidLoad()` is a very important lifecycle method in `UIViewController` that normally takes care of view controller initialization tasks. You already moved the static `TableView` cell code to `BaseAdapter.getView()`. For the rest, you can simply call the ported Java version `viewDidLoad()` from `onCreate(...)`, as shown in Listing 8-26.

Listing 8-26. onCreate(...) vs. viewDidLoad()

```
public class RentalPropertyViewFragment extends ListFragment implements
EditTextViewControllerDelegate {

    ...
    @Override
    public void onCreate(Bundle savedInstanceState) {
      super.onCreate(savedInstanceState);
      viewDidLoad();
      setHasOptionsMenu(true); // enable Option Menu.
      ...

    }

    private void viewDidLoad() {
      // [super viewDidLoad);
      _property = RentalProperty.sharedInstance();
      _property.load();
    }
    ...
```

17. Earlier, I made all methods visibility private, including RentalProperty.load().
     As soon as it is used, you get an error immediately. Right-click the error: the
     compiler suggests that you change it to public. Go ahead and accept this
     suggestion, as shown in Figure 8-7.

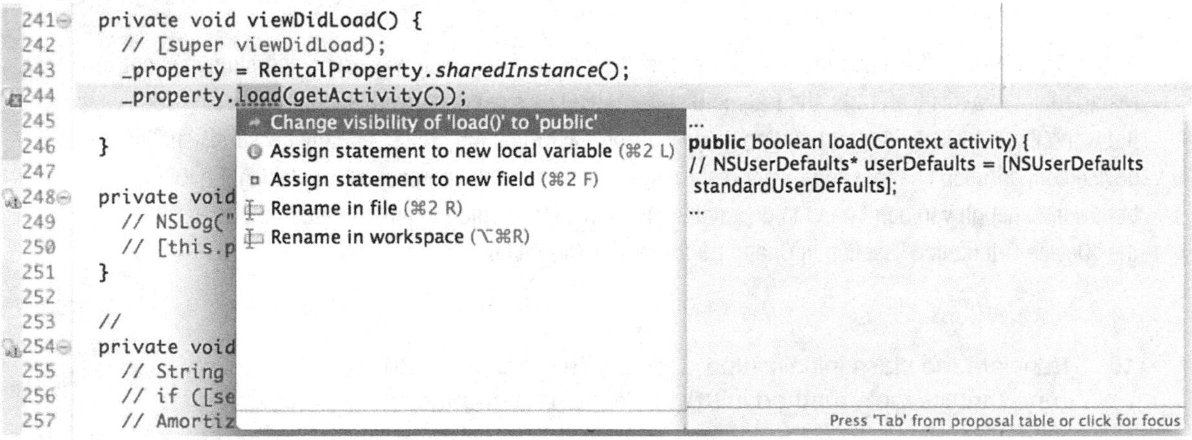

Figure 8-7. Change visibility

18. Let's complete the EditTextViewControllerDelegate callback protocol
     translations (see Listing 8-27).

     a.   The Java interface implementation method needs to be public.

     b.   We are using a list view adapter to supply the list items with data. To update
          the list view item, update the adapter data source and refresh the adapter.

> **IOS ANALOGY**
>
> [tableView reloadData]

Listing 8-27. getTargetFragment()

```java
public class RentalPropertyViewFragment ... implements EditTextViewControllerDelegate {

  ...
  public void textEditControllerDidCancel(EditTextViewFragment controller) {
    // [self dismissViewControllerAnimated:YES completion:nil];
    ((MainActivity)getActivity()).popViewController();
  }

  public void textEditControllerDidFinishEditText(EditTextViewFragment controller,
  String text) {
    ((MainActivity)getActivity()).popViewController();
    int tag = controller.tag;
    switch (tag) {
      case 1:
        _property.purchasePrice = Double.parseDouble(text);  // [text doubleValue];

        String percent = ((NameValuePair)mAdapter.getItem(2)).getValue();
        double down = Double.parseDouble(percent);
        if (_property.purchasePrice > 0 && _property.loanAmt == 0 && down > 0) {
          _property.loanAmt = _property.purchasePrice * (1 - down / 100.0f);
        } else {
//          down = 1.0f - (_property.loanAmt / _property.purchasePrice);
        }

        break;
      case 2:
        float percentage = Float.parseFloat(text) / 100.0f; // [text floatValue] / 100.0;
        _property.loanAmt = _property.purchasePrice * (1 - percentage);

        break;
      case 3:
        _property.loanAmt = Double.parseDouble(text); //  [text doubleValue];

        break;
      case 4:
        _property.interestRate = Double.parseDouble(text); // [text doubleValue];

        break;
      case 5:
        _property.numOfTerms = Integer.parseInt(text); // [text intValue];
        break;
```

```
                case 6:
                    _property.escrow = Double.parseDouble(text);

                    break;
                case 7:
                    _property.extra = Double.parseDouble(text);

                    break;
                case 9:
                    _property.expenses = Double.parseDouble(text);

                    break;
                case 10:
                    _property.rent = Double.parseDouble(text);

                    break;

                default:
                    break;
            }
        mAdapter.notifyDataSetChanged();
        _property.save();
    }
    ...
```

19. Build and run the code to see how your Android app works now. You should have data communicating between the presenting and presented fragments. When the list item is clicked, it presents the EditTextViewFragment with the name and the value of the selected field for editing. After editing is done, the modified text is sent into the presenting RentalPropertyViewFragment via callback and the new text is updated on the list view, as shown in Figure 8-8.

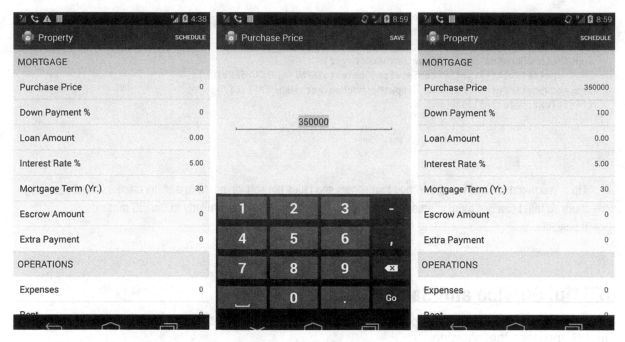

Figure 8-8. Fragment communication

The soft keyboard does not behave the same as the iOS app yet. Examine the commented Objective-C code; the iOS code manually sends becomeFirstResponder to UITextField to bring up the soft keyboard. You can also easily see that Android doesn't dismiss the keyboard either. Listing 8-28 looks very different from iOS, but essentially it serves the same purpose.

Listing 8-28. Soft Keyboard

```
public class RentalPropertyViewFragment  ... {

  ...
  @Override
  public void onResume() {
    super.onResume();
    viewDidAppear(true);
    ...
  }
  ...
  @Override
  public void onPause() {
    super.onPause();
    InputMethodManager imm = (InputMethodManager)
        getActivity().getSystemService(Context.INPUT_METHOD_SERVICE);
    imm.hideSoftInputFromWindow(tfEditText.getWindowToken(), InputMethodManager.HIDE_NOT_ALWAYS);
  }

  ...
```

```java
private void viewDidAppear(boolean animated) {
    // [super viewDidAppear:animated];
    // this.tfEditText.becomeFirstResponder();
    InputMethodManager imm = (InputMethodManager)
            getActivity().getSystemService(Context.INPUT_METHOD_SERVICE);
    imm.showSoftInput(tfEditText, InputMethodManager.SHOW_IMPLICIT);
    tfEditText.selectAll();
}
...
```

> **Tip**   You might want to move the code that shows and hides the soft keyboard to a utility class. I collect
> them so that I can use them in other projects. I also name these methods similarly to the iOS methods,
> if possible.

RESTful Service and Saving Data

Back to the RentalPropertyViewController, when the "Schedule" UIBarButtonItem is selected,
the iOS app does the following:

1. Checks if the amortization schedule is already saved locally.

2. If there is no schedule found in local storage, calls a remote RESTful service
    to get the schedules and save it in local storage.

3. Renders the schedules in a UITableViewController.

The preceding iOS code was previously copied into your Android doAmortization() method.
Your mission is to translate this method to Java code, as shown in Listing 8-29.

Listing 8-29. doAmortization(...)

```java
private static final String KEY_DATA = "data";
private static final String KEY_RC = "rc";
private static final String KEY_ERROR = "error";

public void doAmortization(Object sender) {
//  NSArray* savedAmortization = [_property getSavedAmortization];
//
//  if (savedAmortization != nil) {
//      [self performSegueWithIdentifier:@"toAmortization" sender:savedAmortization];
//  } else {
//      NSString* url = [NSString stringWithFormat: URL_service_tmpl,
//                      _property.loanAmt,
//                      _property.interestRate,
//                      _property.numOfTerms,
//                      _property.extra];
//
```

```
//     [UIApplication sharedApplication].networkActivityIndicatorVisible = YES;
//     NSMutableURLRequest *request = [NSMutableURLRequest
                               requestWithURL:[NSURL URLWithString: url]];
//     [NSURLConnection sendAsynchronousRequest:request queue:[NSOperationQueue currentQueue]
//                     completionHandler:^(NSURLResponse *response, NSData *data,
                                   NSError *error) {
//                         id jsonObject = nil;
//                         [UIApplication sharedApplication].networkActivityIndicatorVisible = NO;
//
//                         if(error == nil) {
//                             jsonObject = [NSJSONSerialization
//                                             JSONObjectWithData:data
//                                             options:NSJSONReadingAllowFragments
//                                             error:&error];
//
//                             NSLog(@"jsonObject: %@", jsonObject);
//                             [_property saveAmortization:jsonObject];
//                             [self performSegueWithIdentifier:@"toAmortization"
                               sender:jsonObject];
//                         } else {
//                             [[[UIAlertView alloc] initWithTitle: error.domain message:
                               error.localizedDescription delegate:nil
                               cancelButtonTitle:@"Close" otherButtonTitles: nil] show];
//                         }
//                     }];
// }
}
```

Saving Data

In `RentalPropertyViewFragment.doAmortization(...)`, the code for saving data, `[_property saveAmortization:jsonObject]` in Listing 8-29), is delegated to the `RentalProperty.java` model class. It is time to translate the iOS "save data" code to Android because there is a caller now. Recall that in topics on saving data (see the "Save Data" section in Chapter 4) there are several choices with mapping guidelines. Let's take a look at your current `RentalProperty.java` in Listing 8-12, and the Objective-C counterpart to decide which option to choose.

The Objective-C code uses `NSUserDefaults` to save `jsonObj`. By following the instructions in "JSON and Saving JSON Document" section in Chapter 4, do the following in `RentalProperty.java` (see Listing 8-30).

1. `NSUserDefaults` should be translated to the Android SharedPreferences framework (see the "SharedPreferences^" section in Chapter 4).

    a. Copy the `SharedPreferences` usage methods (see Listing 4-65 in the SaveData project) into `RentalProperty.java`.

Note   By copying and pasting the SharedPreferences usage methods, you know you are using them a second time. Chances are that you will use them again. You might want to create a PortUtil.java class to collect these methods.

b. The compiler errors tell you that a Context object is needed to call the getSharedPreferences(...) method. This method is declared in the Context class. Let's pass an activity instance to these methods.

Listing 8-30. Shared Preferences Usage

```java
public class RentalProperty {

    ...
    ///////// SharedPreferences usage ////////////////////
    private static final String PREFS_NAME = "MyPrefs";
    private static final int MODE = Context.MODE_PRIVATE; // MODE_WORLD_WRITEABLE

    public void saveSharedPref(String key, String data, Context activity) {
        // get a handle to SharedPreferences object from Context, i.e., Activity
        SharedPreferences sharedPrefs = activity.getSharedPreferences(PREFS_NAME, MODE);
        // We need an Editor object to make preference changes.
        SharedPreferences.Editor editor = sharedPrefs.edit();
        // changes are cached in Editor first.
        editor.putString(key, data);
        // Commit all the changes from Editor all at once.
        editor.commit();
    }

    public String retrieveSharedPref(String key, Context activity) {
        // get a handle to SharedPreferences object from Context.
        SharedPreferences sharedPrefs = activity.getSharedPreferences(PREFS_NAME, MODE);
        // use appropriate API to get the value by key.
        String data = sharedPrefs.getString(key, "");
        return data;
    }

    public void deleteSharedPref(String key, Context activity) {
        SharedPreferences sharedPrefs = activity.getSharedPreferences(PREFS_NAME, MODE);

        SharedPreferences.Editor editor = sharedPrefs.edit();
        editor.remove(key);
        editor.commit();
    }
}
```

2. Translate the Objective-C code in getSavedAmortization(...) and getAmortizationPersistentKey(...), as shown in Listing 8-31.

a. Change the method visibility from private to public. You clearly know there is a caller now.

b. Add a Context method argument.

c. Previously, we choose ArrayList for NSArray (see Table 8-2). Now, it is clear that you need string serialization and should change the return type to JSONArray.

Listing 8-31. *getSavedAmortization(...)*

```
public String getAmortizationPersistentKey() {
    String amortizationPersistentKey = String.format("%.2f-%.2f-%d-%.2f",
        this.loanAmt, this.interestRate, this.numOfTerms, this.extra);
    return amortizationPersistentKey;
}

public JSONArray getSavedAmortization(Context activity) {
//  NSUserDefaults* userDefaults = [NSUserDefaults standardUserDefaults];
//  NSString* savedKey =[userDefaults stringForKey: KEY_AMO_SAVED];
//  NSString* amortizationPersistentKey = [self getAmortizationPersistentKey];
//  if (savedKey.length > 0 && [savedKey isEqualToString:amortizationPersistentKey]) {
//      return [userDefaults arrayForKey:savedKey];
//  } else {
//      return nil;
//  }

    String savedKey = retrieveSharedPref(KEY_AMO_SAVED, activity);
    String amortizationPersistentKey = this.getAmortizationPersistentKey();
    if(savedKey.length() > 0 && savedKey.equals(amortizationPersistentKey)) {
        String jsonArrayString = retrieveSharedPref(savedKey, activity);
        try {
            return new JSONArray(jsonArrayString);
        } catch (JSONException e) {
            return null;
        }
    } else {
        return null;
    }
}
```

3. Translate the commented Objective-C code in saveAmortization(...) to Java (as shown in Listing 8-32).

   a. Change the method visibility from private to public.

   b. Add a Context method argument.

   c. Previously, we choose ArrayList for NSArray (see Table 8-1). We need string serialization now. Let's also change the argument type to JSONArray.

   d. JSONObject cannot be directly saved into SharedPreferences. Let's change the method argument type to String.

Listing 8-32. *saveAmortization (...)*

```
public void saveAmortization(String data, Context activity) {
//  // only save one, remove prev first
//  NSUserDefaults* userDefaults = [NSUserDefaults standardUserDefaults];
//  NSString* amortizationPersistentKey = [self getAmortizationPersistentKey];
//  [userDefaults setObject:amortizationPersistentKey forKey:KEY_AMO_SAVED];
//  [userDefaults setObject:jsonOjb forKey:amortizationPersistentKey];
//  [userDefaults synchronize];
```

```
            String amortizationPersistentKey = this.getAmortizationPersistentKey();
            saveSharedPref(KEY_AMO_SAVED, amortizationPersistentKey, activity);
            saveSharedPref(amortizationPersistentKey, data, activity);
    }
```

4. Translate the commented Objective-C code in load() to Java, as shown in Listing 8-33.

   a. Change the method visibility from private to public.

   b. Add a Context method argument.

Listing 8-33. load (...)

```java
    public boolean load(Context activity) {
//  NSUserDefaults* userDefaults = [NSUserDefaults standardUserDefaults];
//  NSDictionary* jo = [userDefaults objectForKey:KEY_PROPERTY];
//  if (jo == nil) {
//      return NO;
//  }
//
//  self.purchasePrice = [[jo objectForKey:@"purchasePrice"] doubleValue];
//  self.loanAmt = [[jo objectForKey:@"loanAmt"] doubleValue];
//  self.interestRate = [[jo objectForKey:@"interestRate"] doubleValue];
//  self.numOfTerms = [[jo objectForKey:@"numOfTerms"] intValue];
//  self.escrow = [[jo objectForKey:@"escrow"] doubleValue];
//  self.extra = [[jo objectForKey:@"extra"] doubleValue];
//  self.expenses = [[jo objectForKey:@"expenses"] doubleValue];
//  self.rent = [[jo objectForKey:@"rent"] doubleValue];
//  return YES;

        String jostr = retrieveSharedPref(KEY_PROPERTY, activity);
        if(jostr == null) {
          return false;
        }

        try {
          JSONObject jo = new JSONObject(jostr);
          this.purchasePrice = jo.getDouble("purchasePrice");
          this.loanAmt = jo.getDouble("loanAmt");
          this.interestRate = jo.getDouble("interestRate");
          this.numOfTerms = jo.getInt("numOfTerms");
          this.escrow = jo.getDouble("escrow");
          this.extra = jo.getDouble("extra");
          this.expenses = jo.getDouble("expenses");
          this.rent = jo.getDouble("rent");
          return true;
        } catch (JSONException e) {
          e.printStackTrace();
          return false;
        }
    }
```

5. Translate the commented Objective-C code in save(), as shown in Listing 8-34.

    a. Change the method visibility from `private` to public.

    b. Add a Context method argument.

Listing 8-34. save (...)

```
  public void save(Context activity) {
// NSDictionary* jo = @{@"purchasePrice" : [NSNumber numberWithDouble:self.
purchasePrice],
//                      @"loanAmt" : [NSNumber numberWithDouble:self.loanAmt],
//                      @"interestRate" : [NSNumber numberWithDouble:self.interestRate],
//                      @"numOfTerms" : [NSNumber numberWithDouble:self.numOfTerms],
//                      @"escrow" : [NSNumber numberWithDouble:self.escrow],
//                      @"extra" : [NSNumber numberWithDouble:self.extra],
//                      @"expenses" : [NSNumber numberWithDouble:self.expenses],
//                      @"rent" : [NSNumber numberWithDouble:self.rent]
//                      };
//
// NSUserDefaults* userDefaults = [NSUserDefaults standardUserDefaults];
// [userDefaults setObject:jo forKey:KEY_PROPERTY];
// [userDefaults synchronize];
    JSONObject jo = new JSONObject();

    try {
      jo.put("purchasePrice", purchasePrice);
      jo.put("loanAmt", loanAmt);
      jo.put("interestRate", interestRate);
      jo.put("numOfTerms", numOfTerms);
      jo.put("escrow", escrow);
      jo.put("extra", extra);
      jo.put("expenses", expenses);
      jo.put("rent", rent);
    } catch (JSONException e) {
      e.printStackTrace();
    }

    this.saveSharedPref(KEY_PROPERTY, jo.toString(), activity);
  }
```

6. Because you changed the method signatures by adding a Context parameter, you shall see new compilation errors in RentalPropertyViewFragment.java. Simply pass getActivity() to call these methods (see Listing 8-35).

Listing 8-35. save (...)

```
public class RentalPropertyViewFragment ... {
  ...
  private void viewDidLoad() {
    ...
    _property.load(getActivity());
    ...
  }
```

```
...
public void textEditControllerDidFinishEditText(EditTextViewFragment controller,
String text) {
  ...
  _property.save(getActivity());
}
...
```

You have ported the "save data" code from the iOS RentalROI app to the Android app.

Use RESTful Service

Continue the RentalPropertyViewFragment.doAmortization(...) (see Listing 8-29) translation. The Objective-C code uses NSURLConnection to send an HTTP GET message to call a remote RESTful service.

Use the instructions in the "HttpURLConnection: HTTP GET" section in Chapter 4 to port the RESTful service code. Do the following to finish the doAmortization() translation (see Listing 8-36).

1. As you did with the RestClient app in Chapter 4, copy the httpGet() method in the RestClient project (see Listing 4-88) into RentalPropertyViewFragment.java.

2. To better match the iOS NSURLConnection sendAsynchronousRequest: usage, change the return type of the Java httpGet() method to a JSONObject that can contain an HTTP response code and error, as well as the httpBody data.

Note   By copying and pasting the httpGet() method, you know you are using it a second time. Chances are that you will use it again. You might want to create a PortUtil.java class to collect these reusable methods.

Listing 8-36. httpGet utility Method

```
// GET data from url
private JSONObject httpGet(String myurl) {
  InputStream in = null;
  HttpURLConnection conn = null;

  JSONObject jo = new JSONObject();
  try {
    URL url = new URL(myurl);
    // create an HttpURLConnection by openConnection
    conn = (HttpURLConnection) url.openConnection();
    conn.setRequestMethod("GET");
    conn.setRequestProperty("accept", "application/json");

    int rc = conn.getResponseCode(); // HTTP status code
    String rm = conn.getResponseMessage(); // HTTP response message.
    Log.d("d", String.format("HTTP GET: %d %s", rc, rm));
```

```
        // read message body from connection InputStream
        in = conn.getInputStream(); // get inputStream to read data.
        String httpBody = readStream(in);
        in.close();

        jo.put(KEY_RC, rc);
        jo.put(KEY_DATA, httpBody);

    } catch (Exception e) {
        e.printStackTrace();
        try {
            jo.putOpt(KEY_ERROR, e);
        } catch (JSONException e1) {
            e1.printStackTrace();
        }
    } finally {
        conn.disconnect();
    }

    return jo;
}

// a simple util method that converts InputStream to a String.
String readStream(InputStream stream) {
    java.util.Scanner s = new java.util.Scanner(stream).useDelimiter("\\A");
    return s.hasNext() ? s.next() : "";
}
```

3. Use the preceding utility methods to complete translating Objective-C code
    in the RentalPropertyViewFragment.doAmortization() method, as shown in
    Listing 8-37.

    Listing 8-37. doAmortization (...)

```
    public void doAmortization(Object sender) {
    //  NSArray* savedAmortization = [_property getSavedAmortization];
    //
    //  if (savedAmortization != nil) {
    //      [self performSegueWithIdentifier:@"toAmortization" sender:savedAmortization];
    //  } else {
    //      NSString* url = [NSString stringWithFormat: URL_service_tmpl,
    //                     _property.loanAmt,
    //                     _property.interestRate,
    //                     _property.numOfTerms,
    //                     _property.extra];
    //
    //      [UIApplication sharedApplication].networkActivityIndicatorVisible = YES;
    //      NSMutableURLRequest *request = [NSMutableURLRequest requestWithURL:[NSURL
            URLWithString: url]];
    //      [NSURLConnection sendAsynchronousRequest:request queue:
            [NSOperationQueue currentQueue]
```

```objc
//                              completionHandler:^(NSURLResponse *response, NSData *data,
//                          NSError *error) {
//                              id jsonObject = nil;
//                              [UIApplication sharedApplication].
//                               networkActivityIndicatorVisible = NO;
//
//                              if(error == nil) {
//                                  jsonObject = [NSJSONSerialization
//                                               JSONObjectWithData:data
//                                               options:NSJSONReadingAllowFragments
//                                               error:&error];
//
//                                  NSLog(@"jsonObject: %@", jsonObject);
//                                  [_property saveAmortization:jsonObject];
//                                  [self performSegueWithIdentifier:@"toAmortization"
//                                  sender:jsonObject];
//                              } else {
//                                  [[[UIAlertView alloc] initWithTitle: error.
//                                  domain message: error.localizedDescription
//                                  delegate:nil cancelButtonTitle:@"Close"
//                                  otherButtonTitles: nil] show];
//                              }
//                          }];
//  }

    JSONArray savedAmortization = _property.getSavedAmortization(getActivity());
    if (savedAmortization != null) {
      AmortizationViewFragment toFrag = new AmortizationViewFragment();
      toFrag.monthlyTerms = savedAmortization; // will be fixed soon
      ((MainActivity) getActivity()).pushViewController(toFrag, true);
    } else {

      String url = String.format(URL_service_tmpl, _property.loanAmt,
          _property.interestRate, _property.numOfTerms, _property.extra);

      getActivity().setProgressBarIndeterminate(true);
      getActivity().setProgressBarVisibility(true);

      AsyncTask<String, Float, JSONObject> task = new AsyncTask<String, Float,
      JSONObject>() {
        @Override
        protected JSONObject doInBackground(String... parms) {
          Log.d("AsyncTask", ">>>doInBackground");
          String getUrl = parms[0];
          JSONObject jo = httpGet(getUrl);
          Log.d("KEY_DATA", jo.optString(KEY_DATA));
          return jo;
        }

        @Override
        protected void onPostExecute(JSONObject jo) {
          getActivity().setProgressBarVisibility(false);
          Exception error = (Exception)jo.opt(KEY_ERROR);
```

```
        if(error == null) {
          AmortizationViewFragment toFrag = new AmortizationViewFragment();
          String data = jo.optString(KEY_DATA);
          _property.saveAmortization(data, getActivity());

          try {
            toFrag.monthlyTerms = new JSONArray(data);
            ((MainActivity) getActivity()).pushViewController(toFrag, true);
          } catch (JSONException e) {
            e.printStackTrace();
          }
        } else {
          Toast.makeText(getActivity(), error.getMessage(), Toast.LENGTH_LONG).show();
        }
      }
    };
    task.execute(url);
  }
}
```

4. To use `Activity.setProgressBarIndeterminate(...)`, the feature (see "Hybrid App" in Chapter 7) needs to be enabled before `Activity.setContentView(...)` in `MainActivity`, as shown in Listing 8-38.

Listing 8-38. Enable Activity ProgressBar

```
public class MainActivity extends ActionBarActivity {

  @Override
  protected void onCreate(Bundle savedInstanceState) {
    super.onCreate(savedInstanceState);
    requestWindowFeature(Window.FEATURE_PROGRESS);

    // setup the content view.
    setContentView(R.layout.activity_main);

    // b: Adding the first fragment to the navigation stack.
    pushViewController(new RentalPropertyViewFragment(), false);
  }
  ...
}
```

5. When the "Schedule" option action is selected, call the preceding `doAmortization(...)` to get the amortization schedule, as shown in Listing 8-39.

Listing 8-39. doAmortization (...)

```java
public class RentalPropertyViewFragment ... {

    ...
    @Override
    public boolean onOptionsItemSelected(MenuItem item) {
        Log.d(tag, "onOptionsItemSelected: " + item.getItemId());
        doAmortization(null);
        // ((MainActivity)getActivity()).pushViewController(new AmortizationViewFragment(), true);
        return true;
    }
    ...
```

Although you have completely translated RentalPropertyViewFragment.java and
RentalProperty.java from their iOS counterparts, there are two compilation errors because we
haven't translated AmortizationViewFragment yet. While in the process of porting the iOS class to
Android, these compilation errors give you very strong suggestions on what you should do next: the
AmortizationViewFragment.java.

AmortizationView Fragment

Move on to the next view controller, AmortizationViewController. In the iOSRentalROI app,
AmortizationViewController receives an amortization schedule and presents the schedule in a table
view. This is exactly the master list UX pattern described in the "Master List with Details Drilldown"
section in Chapter 3. There is nothing new here: you use ListFragment and create an adapter, a.k.a.,
data source in iOS and provide the details of all UI elements.

Follow the class porting steps (see Table 8-1) to port the iOS AmortizationViewController to
AmortizationViewFragment.java.

1. Copy the content of the counterpart header file into
    AmortizationViewFragment.java to start with. Listing 8-40 shows the end
    result of this step.

    a. Delete all the Objective-C-specific stuff, such as #import<...>.

    b. Objective-C @property gets mapped to a Java field, such as monthlyTerms.

    c. The counterpart iOS class inherits from UITableViewController. That is a
        strong hint that you should use ListFragment. You also need an adapter to
        bind the list item view with data (see the "Adapter" section in Chapter 3).

    d. You don't want to override onCreateView(...) to return a view from your
        custom layout file. You can delete the amortizationview_fragment.xml file
        because it is not needed.

    e. You don't need the Button and the OnClickListener implementation.
        Delete them.

Listing 8-40. Translate AmortizationViewFragment.h

```java
public class AmortizationViewFragment extends ListFragment {

// @interface AmortizationViewController : UITableViewController
// @property (nonatomic, strong) NSArray* monthlyTerms;
// @end

  public JSONArray monthlyTerms;
  private BaseAdapter mAdapter;

  @Override
  public void onCreate(Bundle savedInstanceState) {
    super.onCreate(savedInstanceState);

//    setHasOptionsMenu(false); // enable Option Menu.

    mAdapter = new BaseAdapter() {

      @Override
      public View getView(int pos, View view, ViewGroup parent) {
        return null;
      }

      @Override
      public int getCount() {
        return 0;
      }

      @Override
      public long getItemId(int pos) {
        return pos; // not used
      }

      @Override
      public Object getItem(int pos) {
        return null;
      }

    };
    this.setListAdapter(mAdapter);
  }

  @Override
  public void onListItemClick(ListView l, View v, int position, long id) {
    // TODO Auto-generated method stub
    super.onListItemClick(l, v, position, id);
  }

  ...
```

2. Copy the contents of the AmortizationViewController.m into
   AmortizationViewFragment.java to start the translation steps. Listing 8-41
   shows the end results:

   a. Follow the Table 8-1 class porting steps.

   b. This is one of those simple cases. You can delete those methods from the
      Xcode template that do nothing. You only have the UITableViewController
      related methods and the prepareForSegue method left.

Listing 8-41. AmortizationViewController.m

```
public class AmortizationViewFragment extends ListFragment {
    ...
// #pragma mark - Table view data source

// - (NSInteger)tableView:(UITableView *)tableView numberOfRowsInSection:(NSInteger)section {
//     return [self.monthlyTerms count];
// }
//
// - (UITableViewCell *)tableView:(UITableView *)tableView cellForRowAtIndexPath:(NSInde
//         xPath *)indexPath {
//     static NSString *CellIdentifier = @"Cell";
//     UITableViewCell *cell = [tableView dequeueReusableCellWithIdentifier:CellIdentifier
//                         forIndexPath:indexPath];
//
//     // Configure the cell...
//     NSDictionary* monthlyTerm = [self.monthlyTerms objectAtIndex:indexPath.row];
//     int pmtNo = [[monthlyTerm objectForKey:@"pmtNo"] intValue];
//     double balance0 = [[monthlyTerm objectForKey:@"balance0"] doubleValue];
//     cell.textLabel.text = [NSString stringWithFormat: @"%d\t$%.2f", pmtNo, balance0];
//     double interest = [[monthlyTerm objectForKey:@"interest"] doubleValue];
//     double principal = [[monthlyTerm objectForKey:@"principal"] doubleValue];
//     cell.detailTextLabel.text = [NSString stringWithFormat:@"Interest: %.2f\
//                         tPrinciple: %.2f", interest, principal];
//
//     return cell;
// }
//
// -(void) tableView:(UITableView *)tableView didSelectRowAtIndexPath:(NSIndexPath *)indexPath
// {
//     NSDictionary* monthlyTerm = [self.monthlyTerms objectAtIndex:indexPath.row];
//     [self performSegueWithIdentifier:@"toMonthlyTerm" sender:monthlyTerm];
// }

// #pragma mark - Navigation
//
// // In a story board-based application, you will often want to do a little preparation
//         before navigation
// - (void)prepareForSegue:(UIStoryboardSegue *)segue sender:(id)sender {
//     MonthlyTermViewController* destVc = segue.destinationViewController;
//     destVc.monthlyTerm = sender;
// }
}
```

3. Create the list item layout file, res/layout/monthlyterm_listitem.xml, as shown in Listing 8-42, using the iOS storyboard prototype cell as your mockup (see Figure 8-9).

Listing 8-42. monthlyterm_listitem.xml

```xml
<?xml version="1.0" encoding="utf-8"?>
<RelativeLayout xmlns:android="http://schemas.android.com/apk/res/android"
    android:layout_width="match_parent"
    android:layout_height="wrap_content"
    android:padding="@dimen/borderPadding" >

    <TextView
        android:id="@+id/textLabel"
        android:layout_width="match_parent"
        android:layout_height="wrap_content"
        android:layout_alignParentTop="true"
        android:layout_centerVertical="true"
        android:layout_marginBottom="@dimen/borderPadding"
        android:paddingLeft="@dimen/paddingItem"
        android:textAlignment="textStart"
        android:textAppearance="?android:attr/textAppearanceMedium" />

    <TextView
        android:id="@+id/detailTextLabel"
        android:layout_width="match_parent"
        android:layout_height="wrap_content"
        android:layout_below="@id/textLabel"
        android:paddingLeft="@dimen/paddingItem"
        android:textAlignment="textStart"
        android:textAppearance="?android:attr/textAppearanceSmall" />

</RelativeLayout>
```

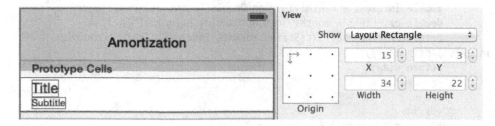

Figure 8-9. iOS UITableViewCell prototype cell

4. Use the iOS UITableViewController Data Source implementation as your guide to complete the Android ListFragment adapter implementation, as shown in Listing 8-43.

Listing 8-43. Monthly Terms Adapter Impl

```java
public class AmortizationViewFragment extends ListFragment {
  ...
  @Override
  public void onCreate(Bundle savedInstanceState) {
    ...
    mAdapter = new BaseAdapter() {

      @Override
      public View getView(int pos, View view, ViewGroup parent) {
//      UITableViewCell *cell = [tableView dequeueReusableCellWithIdentifier:
//                                 CellIdentifier forIndexPath:indexPath];
//      // Configure the cell...
//      NSDictionary* monthlyTerm = [self.monthlyTerms objectAtIndex:indexPath.row];
//      int pmtNo = [[monthlyTerm objectForKey:@"pmtNo"] intValue];
//      double balance0 = [[monthlyTerm objectForKey:@"balance0"] doubleValue];
//      cell.textLabel.text = [NSString stringWithFormat: @"%d\t$%.2f", pmtNo, balance0];
//      double interest = [[monthlyTerm objectForKey:@"interest"] doubleValue];
//      double principal = [[monthlyTerm objectForKey:@"principal"] doubleValue];
//      cell.detailTextLabel.text = [NSString stringWithFormat:@"Interest:
//                                 %.2f\tPrinciple: %.2f", interest, principal];

        if (view == null) { // check null first before recycled object.
          view = getActivity().getLayoutInflater().inflate(R.layout.monthlyterm_listitem, null);
        }
        TextView textLabel = (TextView) view.findViewById(R.id.textLabel);
        TextView detailTextLabel = (TextView) view.findViewById(R.id.detailTextLabel);

        JSONObject monthlyTerm = (JSONObject) monthlyTerms.opt(pos);

        int pmtNo = monthlyTerm.optInt("pmtNo");
        double balance0 = monthlyTerm.optDouble("balance0");
        textLabel.setText(String.format("%d\t$%.2f", pmtNo, balance0));

        double interest = monthlyTerm.optDouble("interest");
        double principal = monthlyTerm.optDouble("principal");
        detailTextLabel.setText(String.format("Interest: %.2f\tPrinciple: %.2f",
interest, principal));
        return view;
      }

      @Override
      public int getCount() {
//return [self.monthlyTerms count];
        return monthlyTerms.length();
      }

      @Override
      public Object getItem(int pos) {
        JSONObject monthlyTerm = (JSONObject) monthlyTerms.opt(pos);
        return monthlyTerm;
      }
```

```
      @Override
      public long getItemId(int pos) {
        return pos;
      }
    };
    ...
  }
...
```

5. Translate the iOS segue code in the onListItemClick(...) action handling
    code, as shown in Listing 8-44.

Listing 8-44. Presenting MonthlyTermViewFragment

```
public class AmortizationViewFragment extends ListFragment {
  ...
//
//  -(void) tableView:(UITableView *)tableView didSelectRowAtIndexPath:(NSIndexPath *)indexPath {
//      NSDictionary* monthlyTerm = [self.monthlyTerms objectAtIndex:indexPath.row];
//      [self performSegueWithIdentifier:@"toMonthlyTerm" sender:monthlyTerm];
//  }

//  #pragma mark - Navigation
//
//  // In a story board-based application, you will often want to do a little preparation
before navigation
//  - (void)prepareForSegue:(UIStoryboardSegue *)segue sender:(id)sender {
//      MonthlyTermViewController* destVc = segue.destinationViewController;
//      destVc.monthlyTerm = sender;
//  }

  public void onListItemClick(ListView l, View v, int position, long id) {
    MonthlyTermViewFragment toFrag = new MonthlyTermViewFragment();

    JSONObject jo = (JSONObject) mAdapter.getItem(position);
    toFrag.monthlyTerm = jo;

    ((MainActivity) getActivity()).pushViewController(toFrag, true);
  }
  ...
}
```

You have translated all the Objective-C code to AmortizationViewFragment.java from the
counterpart AmortizationViewController. There is a compilation error that tells you that the
monthlyTerm Java field is missing in MonthlyTermViewFragment.java. To visualize what you have
done, you may comment the error out temporarily to build and run the app. You should see the
Amortization screen, as shown in Figure 8-10.

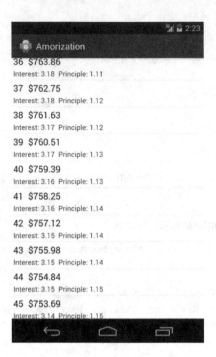

Figure 8-10. Amortization schedules

MonthlyTermView Fragment

Move on to the last class, `MonthlyTermViewController`. In the iOS RentalROI app, the `MonthlyTermViewController` displays the monthly term data on the content view. Your Android `MonthlyTermViewFragment` shall do the same.

Follow the same class porting steps (see Table 8-1) to port `MonthlyTermViewController` to `MonthlyTermViewFragment.java`.

1. The monthly term is displayed in a `UITableView` using static cells. Previously, we choose to use `ListFragment` and a custom adapter to show these static items in list view in `RentalPropertyViewFragment.java` for demonstrating how to implement communication between fragments. To demonstrate a legitimate alternative option, let's map the iOS static `UITableViewCell` to a static `TextView` in res/layout/monthlytermview_fragment.xml (see Listings 8-45 and 8-46). It is more straightforward, too.

   Listing 8-45. dimens.xml

   ```
   <resources>
       ...
       <!-- Monthly Details -->
       <dimen name="heightHeader">44dp</dimen>
       <dimen name="heightItem">40dp</dimen>
       ...
   </resources>
   ```

Listing 8-46. *monthlytermview_fragment.xml*

```xml
<?xml version="1.0" encoding="utf-8"?>
<ScrollView xmlns:android="http://schemas.android.com/apk/res/android"
    android:layout_width="match_parent"
    android:layout_height="wrap_content" >

  <RelativeLayout
    android:layout_width="match_parent"
    android:layout_height="wrap_content" >

    <TextView
        android:id="@+id/tvHeader1"
        android:layout_width="wrap_content"
        android:layout_height="@dimen/heightHeader"
        android:layout_alignParentLeft="true"
        android:layout_alignParentRight="true"
        android:layout_alignParentTop="true"
        android:paddingLeft="@dimen/paddingItem"
        android:gravity="center_vertical"
        android:background="#20008080"
        android:text="@string/MortgagePayment"
        android:textAppearance="?android:attr/textAppearanceSmall" />

    <TextView
        android:id="@+id/lbPaymentNo"
        android:layout_width="wrap_content"
        android:layout_height="@dimen/heightItem"
        android:layout_below="@+id/tvHeader1"
        android:layout_marginLeft="@dimen/paddingItem"
        android:gravity="center_vertical"
        android:text="@string/no"
        android:textAppearance="?android:attr/textAppearanceMedium" />

    <TextView
        android:id="@+id/lbTotalPayment"
        android:layout_width="wrap_content"
        android:layout_height="@dimen/heightItem"
        android:layout_below="@+id/tvHeader1"
        android:layout_alignParentRight="true"
        android:layout_marginRight="@dimen/paddingItem"
        android:gravity="center_vertical"
        android:textAppearance="?android:attr/textAppearanceMedium" />

    <View
        android:id="@+id/line1"
        android:layout_width="wrap_content"
        android:layout_height="1dp"
        android:layout_marginLeft="@dimen/paddingItem"
        android:layout_marginRight="@dimen/paddingItem"
        android:layout_below="@+id/lbTotalPayment"
        android:background="@android:color/darker_gray" />
```

```xml
<TextView
    android:layout_width="wrap_content"
    android:layout_height="@dimen/heightItem"
    android:layout_below="@+id/line1"
    android:layout_marginLeft="@dimen/paddingItem"
    android:gravity="center_vertical"
    android:text="@string/principle"
    android:textAppearance="?android:attr/textAppearanceMedium" />

<TextView
    android:id="@+id/lbPrinciplePayment"
    android:layout_width="wrap_content"
    android:layout_height="@dimen/heightItem"
    android:layout_below="@+id/line1"
    android:layout_alignParentRight="true"
    android:layout_marginRight="@dimen/paddingItem"
    android:gravity="center_vertical"
    android:textAppearance="?android:attr/textAppearanceMedium" />

<View
    android:id="@+id/line2"
    android:layout_width="wrap_content"
    android:layout_height="1dp"
    android:layout_marginLeft="@dimen/paddingItem"
    android:layout_marginRight="@dimen/paddingItem"
    android:layout_below="@+id/lbPrinciplePayment"
    android:background="@android:color/darker_gray" />

<TextView
    android:layout_width="wrap_content"
    android:layout_height="@dimen/heightItem"
    android:layout_below="@+id/line2"

    android:layout_marginLeft="@dimen/paddingItem"
    android:gravity="center_vertical"
    android:text="@string/interest"
    android:textAppearance="?android:attr/textAppearanceMedium" />

<TextView
    android:id="@+id/lbInterestPayment"
    android:layout_width="wrap_content"
    android:layout_height="@dimen/heightItem"
    android:layout_below="@+id/line2"
    android:layout_alignParentRight="true"
    android:layout_marginRight="@dimen/paddingItem"
    android:gravity="center_vertical"
    android:textAppearance="?android:attr/textAppearanceMedium" />

<View
    android:id="@+id/line3"
    android:layout_width="wrap_content"
    android:layout_height="1dp"
```

```
        android:layout_marginLeft="@dimen/paddingItem"
        android:layout_marginRight="@dimen/paddingItem"
        android:layout_below="@+id/lbInterestPayment"
        android:background="@android:color/darker_gray" />

<TextView
        android:layout_width="wrap_content"
        android:layout_height="@dimen/heightItem"
        android:layout_below="@+id/line3"

        android:layout_marginLeft="@dimen/paddingItem"
        android:gravity="center_vertical"
        android:text="@string/escrow"
        android:textAppearance="?android:attr/textAppearanceMedium" />

<TextView
        android:id="@+id/lbEscrowPayment"
        android:layout_width="wrap_content"
        android:layout_height="@dimen/heightItem"
        android:layout_below="@+id/line3"
        android:layout_alignParentRight="true"
        android:layout_marginRight="@dimen/paddingItem"
        android:gravity="center_vertical"
        android:textAppearance="?android:attr/textAppearanceMedium" />

<View
        android:id="@+id/line4"
        android:layout_width="wrap_content"
        android:layout_height="1dp"
        android:layout_marginLeft="@dimen/paddingItem"
        android:layout_marginRight="@dimen/paddingItem"
        android:layout_below="@+id/lbEscrowPayment"
        android:background="@android:color/darker_gray" />

<TextView
        android:layout_width="wrap_content"
        android:layout_height="@dimen/heightItem"
        android:layout_below="@+id/line4"

        android:layout_marginLeft="@dimen/paddingItem"
        android:gravity="center_vertical"
        android:text="@string/addlPayment"
        android:textAppearance="?android:attr/textAppearanceMedium" />

<TextView
        android:id="@+id/lbAddlPayment"
        android:layout_width="wrap_content"
        android:layout_height="@dimen/heightItem"
        android:layout_below="@+id/line4"
        android:layout_alignParentRight="true"
        android:layout_marginRight="@dimen/paddingItem"
        android:gravity="center_vertical"
        android:textAppearance="?android:attr/textAppearanceMedium" />
```

```xml
<View
    android:id="@+id/line5"
    android:layout_width="wrap_content"
    android:layout_height="1dp"
    android:layout_marginLeft="@dimen/paddingItem"
    android:layout_marginRight="@dimen/paddingItem"
    android:layout_below="@+id/lbAddlPayment"
    android:background="@android:color/darker_gray" />

<TextView
    android:layout_width="wrap_content"
    android:layout_height="@dimen/heightItem"
    android:layout_below="@+id/line5"

    android:layout_marginLeft="@dimen/paddingItem"
    android:gravity="center_vertical"
    android:text="@string/mortgageBalance"
    android:textAppearance="?android:attr/textAppearanceMedium" />

<TextView
    android:id="@+id/lbMorgageDebt"
    android:layout_width="wrap_content"
    android:layout_height="@dimen/heightItem"
    android:layout_below="@+id/line5"
    android:layout_alignParentRight="true"
    android:layout_marginRight="@dimen/paddingItem"
    android:gravity="center_vertical"
    android:textAppearance="?android:attr/textAppearanceMedium" />

<TextView
    android:id="@+id/tvHeader2"
    android:layout_width="wrap_content"
    android:layout_height="@dimen/heightHeader"
    android:layout_alignParentLeft="true"
    android:layout_alignParentRight="true"
    android:layout_below="@+id/lbMorgageDebt"
    android:paddingLeft="@dimen/paddingItem"
    android:background="#20008080"
    android:gravity="center_vertical"
    android:text="@string/MortgagePayment"
    android:textAppearance="?android:attr/textAppearanceSmall" />

<TextView
    android:layout_width="wrap_content"
    android:layout_height="@dimen/heightItem"
    android:layout_below="@+id/tvHeader2"
    android:layout_marginLeft="@dimen/paddingItem"
    android:gravity="center_vertical"
    android:text="@string/equity"
    android:textAppearance="?android:attr/textAppearanceMedium" />
```

```xml
<TextView
    android:id="@+id/lbEquityInvestment"
    android:layout_width="wrap_content"
    android:layout_height="@dimen/heightItem"
    android:layout_below="@+id/tvHeader2"
    android:layout_alignParentRight="true"
    android:layout_marginRight="@dimen/paddingItem"
    android:gravity="center_vertical"
    android:textAppearance="?android:attr/textAppearanceMedium" />

<View
    android:id="@+id/line6"
    android:layout_width="wrap_content"
    android:layout_height="1dp"
    android:layout_marginLeft="@dimen/paddingItem"
    android:layout_marginRight="@dimen/paddingItem"
    android:layout_below="@+id/lbEquityInvestment"
    android:background="@android:color/darker_gray" />

<TextView
    android:layout_width="wrap_content"
    android:layout_height="@dimen/heightItem"
    android:layout_below="@+id/line6"
    android:layout_marginLeft="@dimen/paddingItem"
    android:gravity="center_vertical"
    android:text="@string/cashInvest"
    android:textAppearance="?android:attr/textAppearanceMedium" />

<TextView
    android:id="@+id/lbCashInvested"
    android:layout_width="wrap_content"
    android:layout_height="@dimen/heightItem"
    android:layout_below="@+id/line6"
    android:layout_alignParentRight="true"
    android:layout_marginRight="@dimen/paddingItem"
    android:gravity="center_vertical"
    android:textAppearance="?android:attr/textAppearanceMedium" />

<View
    android:id="@+id/line7"
    android:layout_width="wrap_content"
    android:layout_height="1dp"
    android:layout_marginLeft="@dimen/paddingItem"
    android:layout_marginRight="@dimen/paddingItem"
    android:layout_below="@+id/lbCashInvested"
    android:background="@android:color/darker_gray" />

<TextView
    android:layout_width="wrap_content"
    android:layout_height="@dimen/heightItem"
    android:layout_below="@+id/line7"
    android:layout_marginLeft="@dimen/paddingItem"
```

```
            android:gravity="center_vertical"
            android:text="@string/roi"
            android:textAppearance="?android:attr/textAppearanceMedium" />

    <TextView
            android:id="@+id/lbRoi"
            android:layout_width="wrap_content"
            android:layout_height="@dimen/heightItem"
            android:layout_below="@+id/line7"
            android:layout_alignParentRight="true"
            android:layout_marginRight="@dimen/paddingItem"
            android:gravity="center_vertical"
            android:textAppearance="?android:attr/textAppearanceMedium" />

    </RelativeLayout>
</ScrollView>
```

2. Copy the content of the counterpart header file into `MonthlyTermViewFragment.java` to start with. The end result should be like Listing 8-47.

    a. Delete all the Objective-C-specific stuff, such as #import<...>.

    b. @property should be translated to Java fields and the IBOutlet object reference should be initialized using findViewById(...).

Listing 8-47. *Copy and Translate MonthlyTermViewController.h*

```
public class MonthlyTermViewFragment extends Fragment {
//   @property (nonatomic, strong) NSDictionary* monthlyTerm;
//
//   @property (weak, nonatomic) IBOutlet TextView lbPaymentNo;
//   @property (weak, nonatomic) IBOutlet TextView lbTotalPayment;
//   @property (weak, nonatomic) IBOutlet TextView lbPrinciplePayment;
//   @property (weak, nonatomic) IBOutlet TextView lbInterestPayment;
//   @property (weak, nonatomic) IBOutlet TextView lbEscrowPayment;
//   @property (weak, nonatomic) IBOutlet TextView lbAddlPayment;
//   @property (weak, nonatomic) IBOutlet TextView lbMorgageDebt;
//   @property (weak, nonatomic) IBOutlet TextView lbEquityInvestment;
//   @property (weak, nonatomic) IBOutlet TextView lbCashInvested;
//   @property (weak, nonatomic) IBOutlet TextView lbRoi;

    JSONObject monthlyTerm;

    TextView lbPaymentNo;
    TextView lbTotalPayment;
    TextView lbPrinciplePayment;
    TextView lbInterestPayment;
    TextView lbEscrowPayment;
    TextView lbAddlPayment;
    TextView lbMorgageDebt;
    TextView lbEquityInvestment;
```

```java
  TextView lbCashInvested;
  TextView lbRoi;

  private View contentView;

  @Override
  public View onCreateView(LayoutInflater inflater, ViewGroup container,
    Bundle savedInstanceState) {
   contentView = inflater.inflate(R.layout.monthlytermview_fragment, container, false);

    lbPaymentNo = (TextView)contentView.findViewById(R.id.lbPaymentNo);
    lbTotalPayment = (TextView)contentView.findViewById(R.id.lbTotalPayment);
    lbPrinciplePayment = (TextView)contentView.findViewById(R.id.lbPrinciplePayment);
    lbInterestPayment = (TextView)contentView.findViewById(R.id.lbInterestPayment);
    lbEscrowPayment = (TextView)contentView.findViewById(R.id.lbEscrowPayment);
    lbAddlPayment = (TextView)contentView.findViewById(R.id.lbAddlPayment);
    lbMorgageDebt = (TextView)contentView.findViewById(R.id.lbMorgageDebt);
    lbEquityInvestment = (TextView)contentView.findViewById(R.id.lbEquityInvestment);
    lbCashInvested = (TextView)contentView.findViewById(R.id.lbCashInvested);
    lbRoi = (TextView)contentView.findViewById(R.id.lbRoi);

    return contentView;
  }
  ...
```

3. Copy the contents of the MonthlyTermViewController.m into
    MonthlyTermViewFragment.java. The translation result should be like
    Listing 8-48.

    a. Follow the Table 8-1 class porting steps. Only the viewDidLoad() method
        needs to be translated.

    b. Call viewDidLoad() from onCreateView(...) after those Java fields are
        initialized.

Listing 8-48. Copy and Translate MonthlyTermViewController.m

```java
public class MonthlyTermViewFragment extends Fragment {

  ...
  @Override
  public View onCreateView(LayoutInflater inflater, ViewGroup container,
    Bundle savedInstanceState) {

    ...
    viewDidLoad();
    return contentView;
  }
  ...
```

```
    // copy from iOS counterpart impl file
    private void viewDidLoad() {
//  double principle = [[self.monthlyTerm objectForKey: @"principal" ] doubleValue];
//  ...
//  double totalPmt = principle + interest + escrow + extra;
//  ...
//  RentalProperty* property = [RentalProperty sharedInstance];
//  double invested = property.purchasePrice - property.loanAmt + property.extra *
paymentPeriod;
//  double net = property.rent - escrow - interest - property.expenses;
//  double roi = net * 12 / invested;
//
//  self.lbTotalPayment.text = [NSString stringWithFormat: @"$%.2f", totalPmt];
//  ...

    double principle = this.monthlyTerm.optDouble("principal");
    double interest = this.monthlyTerm.optDouble("interest");
    double escrow = this.monthlyTerm.optDouble("escrow");
    double extra = this.monthlyTerm.optDouble("extra");
    double balance = this.monthlyTerm.optDouble("balance0") - principle;
    int paymentPeriod = this.monthlyTerm.optInt("pmtNo");
    double totalPmt = principle + interest + escrow + extra;

    RentalProperty property = RentalProperty.sharedInstance();
    double invested = property.purchasePrice - property.loanAmt + property.extra *
paymentPeriod;
    double net = property.rent - escrow - interest - property.expenses;
    double roi = net * 12 / invested;

    this.lbTotalPayment.setText(String.format("$%.2f", totalPmt));
    this.lbPaymentNo.setText(String.format("No. %d", paymentPeriod));
    this.lbPrinciplePayment.setText(String.format("$%.2f", principle));
    this.lbInterestPayment.setText(String.format("$%.2f", interest));
    this.lbEscrowPayment.setText(String.format("$%.2f", escrow));
    this.lbAddlPayment.setText(String.format("$%.2f", extra));
    this.lbMorgageDebt.setText(String.format("$%.2f", balance));
    this.lbEquityInvestment.setText(String.format("$%.2f", property.purchasePrice -
balance));
    this.lbCashInvested.setText(String.format("$%.2f", invested));
    this.lbRoi.setText(String.format("%.2f%% ($%.2f/mo)", roi * 100, net));
    }
}
```

4. This is all about the last class translation. Build and run the AndroidRentalROI app to make sure it behaves the same as the iOS app. I normally put the iOS and Android apps side by side for testing. Even for testing activities, it takes less time to test iOS and Android apps in parallel. Figure 8-11 shows the Android version running on my Nexus 4 device.

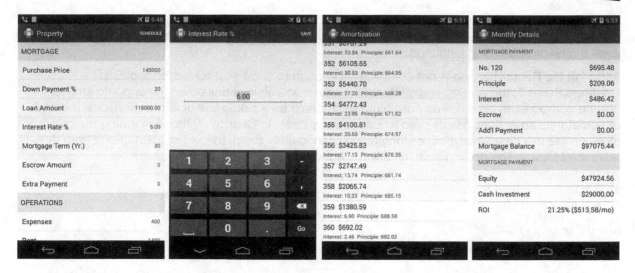

Figure 8-11. AndroidRentalROI

Summary

This chapter intended to show how to port the whole app, end to end, by applying the individual mapping topics introduced in Chapters 3 and 4, such as master list details drilldown, navigation patterns, basic UI widgets, saving data, using remote services, and view animation.

You started by using the MvcTemplate project to jumpstart the project creation. Your Android apps immediately inherited three fragments with a navigation stack in place. Using the RentalROI app as an example, you broke down the app into iOS-like MVC-structured classes by analyzing the screen navigation and implementing the simplified Android storyboard. The result was a set of connected fragments that map to counterpart iOS view controller classes. This was essentially the key step. Not only for porting purposes, it is always good to apply this MVC design pattern to break dependencies.

You continued to drill down each class, one by one. You copied the contents of the counterpart iOS class to the corresponding Android class to preserve the iOS methods and properties in the Android Java class. This way, the business logics were preserved. Furthermore, these methods could be translated from the counterpart iOS methods. The content of the methods were generally expressions. Translating expressions are generally straightforward. Using a global find-and-replace makes this type of translation quick and fun. When you encounter platform-specific SDK or topics, use this book's table of contents to find the instructions to guide you through porting efforts.

The class porting steps shown in Table 8-1 and the searchable syntax or symbols shown in Table 8-2 are provided for beginners. When you get used to the porting method, you will start seeing more searchable patterns. Being good at regex (regular expressions) definitely helps, but I try not to use it most of the time. A lot of times, I prefer using Find and Replace one click at a time, rather than Replace All, so that I can spot the code being replaced. Learning is the main objective in your early

Android journey. Replacing all through a sophisticated regex pattern substitution might take away precious learning opportunities. Reading, typing, and debugging the code seems the best way to learn a new programming language.

Although the RentalROI app is not complicated enough to show you advanced topics in Chapters 6 and 7, the porting steps remain the same: you always drill down the app into smaller porting components (as small as possible), which could be a single line of expression, or a method, or sometimes an entire class or even a common use case. In Chapter 7, those mapping topics are more on the use case level. Still, as long as you can identify them, follow the instructions from those advanced topics. The porting strategy always works for me.

Part 4

Final: The Beginning of Disparity

We have been focusing on common mobile topics using counterpart iOS analogies, but there are disparate areas that I tried not to get into for learning objectives. The mapping guidelines and instructions work perfectly for their intended purposes. However, you don't want to create iOS-ish Android apps—and most importantly, you don't want to stop right here.

Some of the topics introduced in this book actually could be too iOS-ish from the perspective of UI or design approaches. As you become more advanced in Android programming, you will want to keep an open eye for Android-specific things. To avoid misleading you in the long run, let me single out the following topics.

Provide an Android Mobile UX for Your Android Users

As you plan or design your app for Android, keep in mind that different platforms may have different rules and conventions. This is particularly true for UI design guidelines. Android apps should not look like iOS apps. On the official Android Developers site, there is a page called "Pure Android" at `http://developer.android.com/design/patterns/pure-android.html`.

Without getting into the user experience (UX) details, allow me to excerpt some bulleted points from the web page, just to get my points across:

- Don't use bottom tab bars
- Don't use labeled Back buttons on action bars
- Don't use right-pointing carets on list line items

I could not agree more because this pretty much summarizes the UI design mistakes I often made by blindly porting the iOS UI to Android. I find this short document very useful for when I need to switch my UI-thinking mode.

Handle Runtime Changes

By default, Android activities restart when a device configuration changes, such as device orientation. Two things happen:

- The activity/fragment restarts and goes through the regular lifecycles—destroyed and re-created, and so forth.

- The bundle system restarts and loads the appropriate application resources.

This is a unique Android behavior that is different from iOS apps. In this book, we disable this default restart behavior primarily for porting purposes. However, you may encounter situations where you can take advantage of letting the system restart the activity that causes reloading of appropriate alternative application resources. This is a unique but important topic, but I do not go into detail. On the official Android Developers site, there is a page called "Handling Runtime Changes" at `http://developer.android.com/guide/topics/resources/runtime-changes.html`.

By reading this topic, you will learn when you can take advantage of restarting the bundled system. I also found it is well written especially where it describes the Android runtime system. If you want to have a better understanding of the Android system, then do not miss reading this topic.

Communicate with Other Fragments

To communicate between fragment view controllers, we chose to send and receive parameters directly between the presenting fragment and the presented fragment. Pure Android developers are probably screaming at me right now. There is a good article that specifically addresses the proper solution with sample code on the official Android Developers site at `http://developer.android.com/training/basics/fragments/communicating.html`.

Based on this web page, all the communication between two fragments should go through their parent activity. In practice, I am not against either way, but you do want to pay attention to the performance overhead when you send serialized data via bundle for communication between fragments directly.

There are no chapters (other than the Appendix) in Part IV of the book. You have gotten this far: you will be the author continuing with your own next chapters.

The Official Android Developers Site

IOS ANALOGY

iOS Dev Center at `https://developer.apple.com/devcenter/ios/index.action`.

Just like the iOS Dev Center, the official Android Developers site (`http://developer.android.com/index.html`) is the only place you need to go to get the Android SDK API syntax, rules, and definitions.

This site is also where you get the ADT tools, product updates, and official announcements. A lot of training materials and valuable guidelines can be found there as well.

For your convenience, this book includes some tables excerpted from the Android Developers site. They are referenced by topics that appear in Chapters 5 and 6. I find these tables helpful for understanding the topics. You can merely glance through them, however. You don't need to memorize them.

Table A-1 lists the XML attributes defined for the *Android service component* (see the "Services" section in Chapter 5).

Table A-1. Service Component XML Attributes

Attribute	Description
android:description	Descriptive text for the associated data.
android:enabled	Specify whether the service is enabled or not (that is, it can be instantiated by the system).
android:exported	Flag indicating whether the given application component is available to other applications.
android:icon	A drawable resource providing a graphical representation of its associated item.
android:isolatedProcess	If set to true, this service will run under a special process that is isolated from the rest of the system.
android:label	A user-legible name for the given item.
android:logo	A drawable resource providing an extended graphical logo for its associated item.
android:name	Required name of the class implementing the service, deriving from the service.
android:permission	Specify a permission that a client is required to have in order to use the associated object.
android:process	Specify a specific process that the associated code is to run in.
android:singleUser	If set to true, a single instance of this component will run for all users.
android:stopWithTask	If set to true, this service with be automatically stopped when the user removes a task rooted in an activity owned by the application.

> **Note**   For more information about these attributes, see the online reference at the Android Developers site at http://developer.android.com/guide/topics/manifest/service-element.html.

Table A-2 lists the XML attributes defined for *broadcast receivers* (see the "Broadcast Receivers" section in Chapter 5).

Table A-2. Broadcast Receiver Attributes

Attribute	Description
android:description	Descriptive text for the associated data.
android:enabled	Specify whether the service is enabled or not (that is, it can be instantiated by the system).
android:exported	Flag indicating whether the given application component is available to other applications.
android:icon	A drawable resource providing a graphical representation of its associated item.
android:label	A user-legible name for the given item.
android:logo	A drawable resource providing an extended graphical logo for its associated item.
android:name	Required name of the class implementing the service, deriving from the service.
android:permission	Specify a permission that a client is required to have in order to use the associated object.
android:process	Specify a specific process that the associated code is to run in.
android:singleUser	If set to true, a single instance of this component will run for all users.

> **Note**   For more information about these attributes, see the online reference at the Android Developers site at http://developer.android.com/guide/topics/manifest/receiver-element.html.

Table A-3 lists the XML attributes defined for *content providers* (see the "Content Providers" section in Chapter 5).

Table A-3. Content Provider Attributes

Attribute	Description
android:authorities	Specify the authorities under which this content provider can be found.
android:description	Descriptive text for the associated data.
android:enabled	Specify whether this provider is enabled or not (that is, can be instantiated by the system).
android:exported	Flag indicating whether the given application component is available to other applications.
android:grantUriPermissions	If true, the Context.grantUriPermission or corresponding Intent flags can be used to allow others to access specific URIs in the content provider, even if they do not have an explicit read or write permission.
android:icon	A drawable resource providing a graphical representation of its associated item.
android:initOrder	Specify the order in which content providers hosted by a process are instantiated when that process is created.
android:label	A user-legible name for the given item.
android:logo	A drawable resource providing an extended graphical logo for its associated item.
android:multiprocess	Specify whether a component is allowed to have multiple instances of it running in different processes.
android:name	Required name of the class implementing the provider, deriving from ContentProvider.
android:permission	Specify a permission that a client is required to have in order to use the associated object.
android:process	Specify a specific process that the associated code is to run in.
android:readPermission	A specific permission name for read-only access to a content provider.
android:singleUser	If set to true, a single instance of this component will run for all users.
android:syncable	Flag indicating whether this content provider would like to participate in data synchronization.
android:writePermission	A specific permission name for write access to a content provider.

Note   For more information about these attributes, see the online reference at the Android Developers site at http://developer.android.com/guide/topics/manifest/provider-element.html.

Table A-4 lists the types of the Android *configuration qualifiers* and qualifier values (see the "Configuration Qualifiers" section in Chapter 6).

Table A-4. Configuration Qualifiers

Configuration	Qualifier Values	Description

MCC and MNC	Examples:
	`mcc310`
	`mcc310-mnc004`
	`mcc208-mnc00`
	etc.
		The mobile country code (MCC), optionally followed by mobile network code (MNC) from the SIM card in the device. For example, `mcc310` is US on any carrier, `mcc310-mnc004` is US on Verizon, and `mcc208-mnc00` is France on Orange.
		
		If the device uses a radio connection (GSM phone), the MCC and MNC values come from the SIM card.
		
		You can also use the MCC alone (for example, to include country-specific legal resources in your application). If you need to specify based on the language only, then use the *language and region* qualifier instead (discussed next). If you decide to use the MCC and MNC qualifier, you should do so with care and test that it works as expected.
		
		Also see the configuration fields `mcc` and `mnc`, which indicate the current mobile country code and mobile network code, respectively.

Language and region	Examples:
	`en`
	`fr`
	`en-rUS`
	`fr-rFR`
	`fr-rCA`
	etc.
		The language is defined by a two-letter ISO 639-1 language code, optionally followed by a two-letter ISO 3166-1-alpha-2 region code (preceded by lowercase "r").
		
		The codes are *not* case-sensitive; the r prefix is used to distinguish the region portion. You cannot specify a region alone.
		
		This can change during the life of your application if the user changes his or her language in the system settings. See Handling Runtime Changes for information about how this can affect your application during runtime.
		
		See Localization for a complete guide to localizing your application for other languages.
		
		Also see the locale configuration field, which indicates the current locale.

Layout direction	`ldrtl` `ldltr`	The layout direction of your application. `ldrtl` means "layout-direction-right-to-left." `ldltr` means "layout-direction-left-to-right" and is the default implicit value. This can apply to any resource such as layouts, drawables, or values. For example, if you want to provide some specific layout for the Arabic language and some generic layout for any other "right-to-left" language (like Persian or Hebrew) then you would have: `res/layout/main.xml` (Default layout) `layout-ar/main.xml` (Specific layout for Arabic) `layout-ldrtl/main.xml` (Any "right-to-left" language, except for Arabic, because the "ar" language qualifier has a higher precedence.) To enable right-to-left layout features for your app, you must set `supports Rtl` to "true" and set `targetSdkVersion` to 17 or higher. *Added in API level 17.*

(continued)

Table A-4. (*continued*)

Configuration	Qualifier Values	Description
smallestWidth	sw<N>dp Examples: sw320dp sw600dp sw720dp etc.	The fundamental size of a screen, as indicated by the shortest dimension of the available screen area. Specifically, the device's smallestWidth is the shortest of the screen's available height and width (you may also think of it as the "smallest possible width" for the screen). You can use this qualifier to ensure that, regardless of the screen's current orientation, your application has at least <N> dps of width available for its UI. For example, if your layout requires that its smallest dimension of screen area be at least 600dp at all times, then you can use this qualifier to create the layout resources, res/layout-sw600dp/. The system will use these resources only when the smallest dimension of available screen is at least 600dp, regardless of whether the 600dp side is the user-perceived height or width. The smallestWidth is a fixed screen size characteristic of the device; *the device's smallestWidth does not change when the screen's orientation changes.* The smallestWidth of a device takes into account screen decorations and system UI. For example, if the device has some persistent UI elements on the screen that account for space along the axis of the smallestWidth, the system declares the smallestWidth to be smaller than the actual screen size, because those are screen pixels not available for your UI. Thus, the value you use should be the actual smallest dimension *required by your layout* (usually, this value is the "smallest width" that your layout supports, regardless of the screen's current orientation). Some values you might use here for common screen sizes: 320 for devices with screen configurations such as: 240×320 ldpi (QVGA handset) 320×480 mdpi (handset) 480×800 hdpi (high density handset) 480 for screens such as 480×800 mdpi (tablet/handset) 600 for screens such as 600×1024 mdpi (7" tablet) 720 for screens such as 720×1280 mdpi (10" tablet) When your application provides multiple resource directories with different values for the smallestWidth qualifier, the system uses the one closest to (without exceeding) the device's smallestWidth. *Added in API level 13.* Also see the android:requiresSmallestWidthDp attribute, which declares the minimum smallestWidth with which your application is compatible, and the smallestScreenWidthDp configuration field, which holds the device's smallestWidth value. For more information about designing for different screens and using this qualifier, see the Supporting Multiple Screens developer guide.

(continued)

Table A-4. (*continued*)

Configuration	Qualifier Values	Description
Available width	w<N>dp Examples: w720dp w1024dp etc.	Specifies a minimum available screen width, in dp units at which the resource should be used—defined by the <N> value. This configuration value will change when the orientation changes between landscape and portrait to match the current actual width. When your application provides multiple resource directories with different values for this configuration, the system uses the one closest to (without exceeding) the device's current screen width. The value here takes into account screen decorations, so if the device has some persistent UI elements on the left or right edge of the display, it uses a value for the width that is smaller than the real screen size, accounting for these UI elements and reducing the application's available space. *Added in API level 13.* Also see the screenWidthDp configuration field, which holds the current screen width. For more information about designing for different screens and using this qualifier, see the Supporting Multiple Screens developer guide.
Available height	h<N>dp Examples: h720dp h1024dp etc.	Specifies a minimum available screen height, in "dp" units at which the resource should be used—defined by the <N> value. This configuration value will change when the orientation changes between landscape and portrait to match the current actual height. When your application provides multiple resource directories with different values for this configuration, the system uses the one closest to (without exceeding) the device's current screen height. The value here takes into account screen decorations, so if the device has some persistent UI elements on the top or bottom edge of the display, it uses a value for the height that is smaller than the real screen size, accounting for these UI elements and reducing the application's available space. Screen decorations that are not fixed (such as a phone status bar that can be hidden when full screen) are *not* accounted for here, nor are window decorations like the title bar or action bar, so applications must be prepared to deal with a somewhat smaller space than they specify. *Added in API level 13.* Also see the screenHeightDp configuration field, which holds the current screen width. For more information about designing for different screens and using this qualifier, see the Supporting Multiple Screens developer guide.

(*continued*)

Table A-4. (*continued*)

Configuration	Qualifier Values	Description
Screen size	small normal large xlarge	small: Screens that are of similar size to a low-density QVGA screen. The minimum layout size for a small screen is approximately 320×426 dp units. Examples are QVGA low density and VGA high density. normal: Screens that are of similar size to a medium-density HVGA screen. The minimum layout size for a normal screen is approximately 320×470 dp units. Examples of such screens a WQVGA low density, HVGA medium density, WVGA high density. large: Screens that are of similar size to a medium-density VGA screen. The minimum layout size for a large screen is approximately 480×640 dp units. Examples are VGA and WVGA medium density screens. xlarge: Screens that are considerably larger than the traditional medium-density HVGA screen. The minimum layout size for an xlarge screen is approximately 720×960 dp units. In most cases, devices with extra large screens would be too large to carry in a pocket and would most likely be tablet-style devices. *Added in API level 9.* Using a size qualifier does not imply that the resources are *only* for screens of that size. If you do not provide alternative resources with qualifiers that better match the current device configuration, the system may use whichever resources are the best match. If all your resources use a size qualifier that is *larger* than the current screen, the system will **not** use them and your application will crash at runtime (for example, if all layout resources are tagged with the xlarge qualifier, but the device is a normal-size screen). *Added in API level 4.* See Supporting Multiple Screens for more information. Also see the screenLayout configuration field, which indicates whether the screen is small, normal, or large.
Screen aspect	long notlong	long: Long screens, such as WQVGA, WVGA, FWVGA. notlong: Not long screens, such as QVGA, HVGA, and VGA. *Added in API level 4.* This is based purely on the aspect ratio of the screen (a "long" screen is wider). This is not related to the screen orientation. Also see the screenLayout configuration field, which indicates whether the screen is long.

(continued)

Table A-4. (*continued*)

Configuration	Qualifier Values	Description
Screen orientation	port land	port: Device is in portrait orientation (vertical). land: Device is in landscape orientation (horizontal). This can change during the life of your application if the user rotates the screen. See Handling Runtime Changes for information about how this affects your application during runtime. Also see the orientation configuration field, which indicates the current device orientation.
UI mode	car desk television appliance	car: Device is displaying in a car dock. desk: Device is displaying in a desk dock. television: Device is displaying on a television, providing a "ten foot" experience where its UI is on a large screen that the user is far away from, primarily oriented around DPAD or other non-pointer interaction. appliance: Device is serving as an appliance, with no display. *Added in API level 8, television added in API 13.* For information about how your app can respond when the device is inserted into or removed from a dock, read Determining and Monitoring the Docking State and Type. This can change during the life of your application if the user places the device in a dock. You can enable or disable some of these modes using UiModeManager. See Handling Runtime Changes for information about how this affects your application during runtime.
Night mode	night notnight	night: Night time. notnight: Day time. *Added in API level 8.* This can change during the life of your application if night mode is left in auto mode (default), in which case the mode changes based on the time of day. You can enable or disable this mode using UiModeManager. See Handling Runtime Changes for information about how this affects your application during runtime.

(*continued*)

Table A-4. (*continued*)

Configuration	Qualifier Values	Description
Screen pixel density (dpi)	ldpi mdpi hdpi xhdpi nodpi tvdpi	ldpi: Low-density screens; approximately 120dpi. mdpi: Medium-density (on traditional HVGA) screens; approximately 160dpi. hdpi: High-density screens; approximately 240dpi. xhdpi: Extra high-density screens; approximately 320dpi. *Added in API Level 8.* nodpi: This can be used for bitmap resources that you do not want to be scaled to match the device density. tvdpi: Screens somewhere between mdpi and hdpi; approximately 213dpi. This is not considered a "primary" density group. It is mostly intended for televisions and most apps shouldn't need it—providing mdpi and hdpi resources is sufficient for most apps and the system will scale them as appropriate. This qualifier was introduced with API level 13. There is a 3:4:6:8 scaling ratio between the four primary densities (ignoring the tvdpi density). So, a 9×9 bitmap in ldpi is 12×12 in mdpi, 18×18 in hdpi and 24×24 in xhdpi. If you decide that your image resources don't look good enough on a television or other certain devices and want to try tvdpi resources, the scaling factor is 1.33*mdpi. For example, a 100px × 100px image for mdpi screens should be 133px × 133px for tvdpi. Using a density qualifier does not imply that the resources are *only* for screens of that density. If you do not provide alternative resources with qualifiers that better match the current device configuration, the system may use whichever resources are the best match. See Supporting Multiple Screens for more information about how to handle different screen densities and how Android might scale your bitmaps to fit the current density.
Touchscreen type	notouch finger	notouch: Device does not have a touchscreen. finger: Device has a touchscreen that is intended to be used through direction interaction of the user's finger. Also see the touchscreen configuration field, which indicates the type of touchscreen on the device.

(*continued*)

Table A-4. (*continued*)

Configuration	Qualifier Values	Description
Keyboard availability	keysexposed keyshidden keyssoft	keysexposed: Device has a keyboard available. If the device has a software keyboard enabled (which is likely), this may be used even when the hardware keyboard is *not* exposed to the user, even if the device has no hardware keyboard. If no software keyboard is provided or it's disabled, then this is only used when a hardware keyboard is exposed. keyshidden: Device has a hardware keyboard available but it is hidden *and* the device does *not* have a software keyboard enabled. keyssoft: Device has a software keyboard enabled, whether it's visible or not. If you provide keysexposed resources, but not keyssoft resources, the system uses the keysexposed resources regardless of whether a keyboard is visible, as long as the system has a software keyboard enabled. This can change during the life of your application if the user opens a hardware keyboard. See Handling Runtime Changes for information about how this affects your application during runtime. Also see the configuration fields hardKeyboardHidden and keyboardHidden, which indicate the visibility of a hardware keyboard and the visibility of any kind of keyboard (including software), respectively.
Primary text input method	nokeys qwerty 12key	nokeys: Device has no hardware keys for text input. qwerty: Device has a hardware qwerty keyboard, whether it's visible to the user or not. 12key: Device has a hardware 12-key keyboard, whether it's visible to the user or not. Also see the keyboard configuration field, which indicates the primary text input method available.
Navigation key availability	navexposed navhidden	navexposed: Navigation keys are available to the user. navhidden: Navigation keys are not available (such as behind a closed lid). This can change during the life of your application if the user reveals the navigation keys. See Handling Runtime Changes for information about how this affects your application during runtime. Also see the navigationHidden configuration field, which indicates whether navigation keys are hidden.

(*continued*)

Table A-4. (*continued*)

Configuration	Qualifier Values	Description
Primary non-touch navigation method	nonav dpad trackball wheel	nonav: Device has no navigation facility other than using the touchscreen. dpad: Device has a directional-pad (d-pad) for navigation. trackball: Device has a trackball for navigation. wheel: Device has a directional wheel(s) for navigation (uncommon). Also see the navigation configuration field, which indicates the type of navigation method available.
Platform version (API level)	Examples: v3 v4 v7 etc.	The API level supported by the device. For example, v1 for API level 1 (devices with Android 1.0 or higher) and v4 for API level 4 (devices with Android 1.6 or higher). See the Android API levels document for more information about these values.

Note   For more information about these qualifiers, see the online reference at the Android Developers site at http://developer.android.com/guide/topics/resources/providing-resources.html#AlternativeResources.

Index

V

W, X, Y, Z

Get the eBook for only $10!

Now you can take the weightless companion with you anywhere, anytime. Your purchase of this book entitles you to 3 electronic versions for only $10.

This Apress title will prove so indispensible that you'll want to carry it with you everywhere, which is why we are offering the eBook in 3 formats for only $10 if you have already purchased the print book.

Convenient and fully searchable, the PDF version enables you to easily find and copy code—or perform examples by quickly toggling between instructions and applications. The MOBI format is ideal for your Kindle, while the ePUB can be utilized on a variety of mobile devices.

Go to www.apress.com/promo/tendollars to purchase your companion eBook.